The Coherence of EU Reg

Regional Policy and Development Series

Series Editor: Ron Martin, Department of Geography, University of Cambridge

Throughout the industrialised world, widespread economic restructuring, rapid technological change, the reconfiguration of State intervention, and increasing globalisation are giving greater prominence to the nature and performance of individual regional and local economies within nations. The old patterns and processes of regional development that characterised the post-war period are being fundamentally redrawn, creating new problems of uneven development and new theoretical and policy challenges. Whatever interpretation of this contemporary transformation is adopted, regions and localities are back on the academic and political agenda. *Regional Policy and Development* is an international series which aims to provide authoritative analyses of this new regional political economy. It seeks to combine fresh theoretical insights with detailed empirical enquiry and constructive policy debate to produce a comprehensive set of conceptual, practical and topical studies in this field. The series is not intended as a collection of synthetic reviews, but rather as original contributions to understanding the processes, problems and policies of regional and local economic development in today's changing world.

The Coherence of EU Regional Policy

Contrasting Perspectives on the Structural Funds

Edited by John Bachtler and Ivan Turok

Regional Policy and Development Series 17

Jessica Kingsley Publishers
London and Philadelphia

Regional Studies Association
London

First published in the United Kingdom in 1997 by
Jessica Kingsley Publishers Ltd
116 Pentonville Road
London N1 9JB, England
and
1900 Frost Road, Suite 101
Bristol, PA 19007, U S A

with

the Regional Studies Association
Registered Charity 252269

Figure 3.2 reprinted by kind permission of SagePublications Ltd from M. Dunford (1994) 'Winners and losers: The new map of economic inequality in the European Union.' *European Urban and Regional Studies 1*, 2, 95–114

Library of Congress Cataloging in Publication Data
A CIP catalogue record for this book is available from the Library of Congress

British Library Cataloguing in Publication Data
The coherence of EU regional policy: contrasting perspectives on the structural funds. – (Regional policy and development; 17)
1. European Regional Development Fund 2. Regional planning – European Union countries – Finance 3. European Union countries – Economic policy
I. Bachtler, John II. Turok, Ivan

ISBN 1 85302 396 5

Printed and Bound in Great Britain by
Athenaeum Press, Gateshead, Tyne and Wear

Contents

List of Figures

List of Tables

Preface

Widespread concern about the economic and political coherence of Europe has led to substantial increases in the political priority and expenditure of the regional policy of the European Union. For many regions the Structural Funds now represent a significant source of finance for social and economic regeneration. The Funds appear to be promoting a broader, more collective approach to regional development than has often been the case hitherto. Yet the use of the Funds poses formidable challenges for regional and national authorities, especially the requirements for integrated strategic regional planning, a partnership approach between the European Commission, national and local government and among regional actors, and the integration of economic development, environmental and social objectives.

These crucial issues were addressed by participants in a debate at the European conference *Regional Futures: Past and Present, East and West* organised by the Regional Studies Association in Gothenburg, Sweden, in May 1995. The debate demonstrated considerable diversity of experience in different countries and regions and contrasting perspectives on the impact and effectiveness of the Structural Funds. In particular, it highlighted important issues regarding the coherence of EU structural intervention and Member State policies, the institutional tensions between European, national and local bodies, and the impact of new partnerships on local development.

In the latter part of 1995 and early 1996 we invited contributors to the RSA debate, and other researchers and practitioners in the field of EU regional policy, to prepare chapters which would bring together a rich selection of practical experience of the Structural Funds. The aim has been to present a wide-ranging assessment of the design and implementation of regional development strategies under the Structural Funds with a variety of contrasting perspectives from EU, national, regional and local levels and reflecting both academic and policy viewpoints. This book brings together more than 20 contributions from throughout the UK and other parts of

Europe and is intended to make a timely contribution to the debate over the future of EU regional policy in the context of decisions made at the Inter-Governmental Conference and the longer term review of EU regional policy scheduled for the end of the decade.

We would like to thank all of the authors for their contributions, and particularly the tolerance of those who submitted early. We are grateful to our colleagues in the European Policies Research Centre and the Centre for Housing Research and Urban Studies for their advice and, specifically, to Moira Lowe, Rosemarie Rey, Jean Rodger and Louise Cullen for their administrative and secretarial support. Most of all, we owe a big debt to John MacQuarrie and Mary-Louise Rooney for their commitment, good humour and sheer hard work in making the production of this book possible.

John Bachtler and Ivan Turok

PART ONE

Overview of Regional Problems and Policies

CHAPTER 1

Introduction

Ivan Turok and John Bachtler

The structural and cohesion policies of the European Union (EU) are important for the economic and social integration of Europe. They are among the most significant areas of EU action in many respects. They have a direct impact on the lives of millions of citizens and may help to make the concept of Europe more relevant and meaningful to ordinary people. Annual expenditure on the Structural and Cohesion Funds has risen substantially in recent years and will reach 30 billion ecu by 1999. This will amount to 36 per cent of the Community budget, second only to agriculture. As the only major sphere of EU policy with explicit geographical targeting of resources, they are the main mechanism for tackling the large regional and social disparities within Europe by funding investment in long-term development projects. They also play an important political role in helping to compensate less developed parts of the Union for the adverse effects of exposure to competition from more advanced economies and giving something back to Member States which are net contributors to the EU budget. In several countries the value of EU subventions in this field now exceeds national expenditure on regional assistance.

The local 'reach' and locus of the Funds is highly significant. These are not standardised programmes administered by a remote and centralised bureaucracy. Under the principles of policy integration and partnership working, the preparation and implementation of development programmes often involves a more decentralised and collective approach to regional policy than has been practiced by national governments hitherto. There is expected to be 'horizontal' interaction between many regional and local authorities, social partners such as trade unions and business and voluntary and environmental groups as well as engagement with 'vertical' partners in national government departments and sections of the European Commission.

At their most effective, the regional partnerships emerging in some places are pioneering new, more creative and robust forms of governance based on trust and dialogue rather than central control and direction. Through training courses, job creation schemes, road improvements, environmental clean-up and small business support, regional programmes offer tangible benefits to many of the 180 million people living in officially designated areas.

The structural policies also impinge upon national systems of public administration, since implementation is complex and subject to intricate rules and procedures. Every three to six years, national governments and the Commission negotiate a financial envelope and map of eligible areas. Authorities within the Member States are then required to prepare regional development plans for each area designated under Objectives 1, 2, 5b and 6. These are subjected to independent scrutiny and then negotiated line-by-line with the Commission prior to revision. The mutually-agreed programmes set out a detailed strategy and resource allocation for the period. They contain a wide range of measures within the fields of business development, human resources, physical infrastructure, environmental improvement, rural development, urban regeneration and community economic development which are intended to be complementary and integrated. The budgets combine a mixture of EU funding – European Regional Development Fund (ERDF), European Social Fund (ESF), European Agriculture Guidance and Guarantee Fund: Guidance Section (EAGGF), Financial Instrument for Fisheries Guidance (FIFG) and European Investment Bank (EIB) loans. They also include national, regional and local government support and private sector contributions.

Once approved, the programmes are implemented and resources allocated through negotiation and interaction between the local partners or a more arms-length process of competitive bidding in countries. The combination of a three to six-year strategic time horizon with the scope to alter patterns of resource allocation in between as a reaction to the concerns expressed by organisations working at the sharp end of delivery could prove innovative and effective. It may provide a novel mechanism for regional planning which allows for much-needed flexibility and local initiative to pursue opportunities in response to accelerating change in the wider economy. The implementation process is overseen by specialist programme 'monitoring' and 'management' committees which meet regularly, in some cases supported by full-time independent executives and part-time advisory committees. Monitoring of financial and physical outputs is required through the lifetime of the programmes, complemented by interim and final evaluations of their efficiency and effectiveness.

In practice, the structural policy objectives, target areas, instruments and administrative procedures of the EU often diverge from national policies towards regional development, which generates suspicion, friction and even conflict between governments and the Commission. While some countries are able to administer the Funds through existing institutions and policy frameworks, others have had to establish new organisational arrangements for managing their programmes. For several countries the learning-curve has been long, steep and difficult to climb. Government departments have had to gain familiarity with new terminology and development concepts (such as 'additionality' and 'subsidiarity'), and management and monitoring processes that can seem cumbersome and bureaucratic at times. There is a built-in tension between Commission concerns that the resources translate into additional, tangible activities on the ground and government interest in substituting EU funds for domestic expenditure at a time of increasing financial constraint. The regionalised approach to economic development has been a source of particular difficulty in countries where regional government does not exist. Government responses have often aggravated local authority concerns about excessive central interference.

The operation of the structural and cohesion policies has not been easy for the European Commission either. The three main funds are administered by different Directorates-General (DG), each with their own political and administrative priorities. At least five other DGs have an interest or responsibility in structural and cohesion policy and the Finance DG demands close financial auditing with considerable paperwork. Perspectives and approaches often vary within directorates, complicated by the different professional backgrounds, competencies and cultures of Commission officials. The Commission does not have a good reputation for timely decisions or efficiency and is often criticised by local partners, particularly outside the four cohesion countries (Ireland, Spain, Portugal and Greece) where the funds make a major contribution to development resources. In general, the credit for high-profile projects seems to go to local or national bodies, and the Commission's role in promoting good programme management or innovative policy thinking tends to get obscured by criticisms of its excessive bureaucracy, slowness or interference in local decisions.

With the current EU budgetary planning period scheduled to end in 1999, the structural policies are due for major review and reform. The internal political and administrative pressures that have accumulated over the last eight years require this anyway. In addition, the EU has to take some momentous decisions soon with far-reaching implications for regional policy. First, the steps towards monetary union and the Maastricht 'convergence criteria' are forcing most EU countries to undertake or accelerate fundamental structural changes, involving restrictions on public expenditure, deregulation, privatisation and economic liberalisation. The ultimate spatial consequences are uncertain, but the distribution of gains and losses is likely to be uneven in the short and medium term. Second, negotiations for EU enlargement are about to start, heralding the accession of at least four new countries (Poland, Hungary, Czech Republic and Slovenia). Their levels of income per capita are much lower than most existing Member States so the EU will face the considerable regional and social challenges arising from a simultaneous deepening and widening of Europe with a budget that may be little more than at present.

The main purpose of this book is to bring together some of the rich and diverse practical experience of the Structural Funds in different European regions and countries. It also aims to provide different perspectives on the policies and their implementation from the point of view of academics, independent evaluators and policy-makers. The structural policies are difficult to research because of their technical complexity, political intricacy and variable operation in different places. Previous studies have tended to be limited in geographical scope and lacking in detailed insights into the process. This book aims to provide a more comprehensive and in-depth understanding based on contemporary analyses and evaluations by people who have often had close personal involvement in studying, administering or advising the policy process. The chapters are all original contributions and many stem from substantial research and policy experience.

Given the wide scope of the Structural Funds, it has been necessary to prioritise somewhat and be selective in the book's coverage. The prime concern is with the structural policies rather than the cohesion issues that emerged with the accession of Spain, Portugal and Greece to the EU in the 1980s. The focus is on economic restructuring and development programmes, particularly in regions affected by the decline of traditional industries (Objective 2). There is less analysis of 'structurally-backward' regions (Objective 1) or agricultural and rural areas (Objective 5), although several chapters include some discussion of these issues and indeed Chapters 9 and 11 focus on Objective 1 programmes in the Scottish Highlands and Islands and Northern Ireland.

The book is structured in four parts. Part One provides an overview of the structural policies, their evolution and changing regional economic trends within the EU. Michie and Fitzgerald explore the basic rationale for the Structural Funds in the long-standing regional disparities within Europe and the prospect of further divergence as a result of market integration and monetary union. Social solidarity and cohesion have always featured in the European project, often as counterweights to the business agenda of global competitiveness and free trade. The enlargement of Europe over the last decade has complicated structural policy by widening regional inequalities and adding new types of problem regions.

Armstrong and de Kervenoael then consider the patterns and processes of contemporary regional economic change in the EU. They examine the theoretical arguments and empirical evidence for regional convergence and divergence, concluding that neither process has dominated since the early 1980s. Nevertheless, individual regions have seen their relative positions deteriorate and the probability of turbulent economic change for at least the next decade means there continues to be an important role for the structural policies to play.

Part Two of the book considers a wide range of EU-funded regional development programmes and initiatives in the UK. Martin discusses the effects on local institutional arrangements and policies. He suggests that the Structural Funds have had a more visible impact on local authority practices than on the economy of eligible areas. They have encouraged more local networking and partnership activity, and a renewed interest in regionalism and strategic planning. Although there are positive aspects in such developments, there are many limitations too that follow from their opportunistic, funding-driven nature and the tight control exercised by central government.

In Chapter 5 Turok examines an important new feature of the regional programmes in Britain – the insertion of a theme concerned with regenerating the most deprived localities, sometimes called community economic development. It is an interesting innovation and likely to become more significant in the future but has given rise to a host of difficulties in implementation. These are partly a result of local and national institutional obstacles as well as unhelpful rules and inflexible procedures governing the Structural Funds. The experience in Western Scotland provides some pointers to the way forward.

Parts of London benefited from the Funds for the first time in the mid-1990s, indicating another shift towards supporting small areas within metropolitan regions. North discusses the institutional and economic challenges involved in developing a regeneration strategy for an area of this kind with essentially arbitrary boundaries. Trying to match the development opportunities in more prosperous parts of the area with the poverty elsewhere has been technically difficult, particularly to protect jobs for unemployed local residents. Planning and decision-making procedures for the Funds have also proved cumbersome and incapable of producing a strategic, co-ordinated outcome, partly because of interference from gatekeepers and the randomness of competitive bidding.

Nearly ten per cent of the Structural Funds are devoted to Community Initiatives targeted at specific themes and areas with particular problems. Dabinett focuses on those concerned with tackling the decline of industries such as shipbuilding, steel and coal mining. In principle they are an efficient way of responding to emerging crises and supporting local initiatives. They have also encouraged useful collaboration and networking among local authorities. However, there have been many practical difficulties in trying to add another structure and modest funding stream to a fragmented and overcrowded development environment that lacks overall strategy and co-ordination.

The English regions have a distinctive experience of the Structural Funds, and Bentley and Shutt's chapter looks at how the West Midlands and Yorkshire and Humberside have negotiated and implemented Objective 2 programmes. Existing development strategies were largely ignored as central government outposts in these regions took charge of the process. Arbitrary geographical boundaries and institutional proliferation have created further difficulties in integrating EU regional plans and expenditure with existing arrangements.

The Structural Funds are particularly significant in Objective 1 regions following an EU decision to concentrate some 70 per cent of the resources over the period 1994–1999 there. Bryden examines the ambitious policies of the Highlands and Islands programme. He argues that inadequate strategic analysis during plan preparation and resistance to partnership working have impeded effective implementation to date. There have also been difficulties in targeting resources towards the poorest areas, integrating large *ad hoc* projects to form coherent local development programmes, and ensuring a high degree of additionality in the use of the Funds.

Similar problems have arisen in the Northern Ireland Objective 1 programmes, as shown in Chapter 11 by McEldowney. They argue that there was a lack of novelty or integration among the wide-ranging EU-funded measures in the 1989–1993 programme of industrial development. Detailed evaluation found an uneven outcome, with some positive and tangible achievements, but considerable scope for improvement. They advocate a more focused approach to programme design in future if European support is to make a bigger difference to local policies and practices.

Environmental issues have featured more prominently in EU objectives and regulations in recent years. Goodstadt and Clement consider how and why this has happened, before focusing on efforts to promote mutually-supportive economic development and environmental measures in Clydeside. Efforts to integrate these objectives date back several decades, with an emphasis on the improvement of vacant and derelict urban land. Although much has been achieved with EU support, difficulties have been experienced with the relatively short timescale of the Structural Fund programmes, moves towards quantitative, commercially-oriented appraisal and evaluation procedures, and securing co-funding from less committed local partners.

Comparative research is important in drawing more general conclusions about the structural policies. Roberts and Hart provide a helpful review of seven diverse programmes drawn from Objective 1, 2 and 5b regions. They found that the preparation of regional strategies was hampered by inexperience, arbitrary boundaries and lack of guidance from the Commission. Subsequent negotiations over the Single Programming Documents (SPDs) tended to exclude local and regional partners. Implementation has raised concerns about the exclusiveness of some committees and the complexity of administrative procedures. Despite these drawbacks, they conclude that European programmes have injected a useful degree of longer-term, strategic thinking into local and regional development practices in the UK.

Part Three of the book examines the design and implementation of regional development strategies elsewhere in Europe. Bachtler and Taylor start the section with a wide-ranging overview of the formal strategies adopted in the 88 Objective 2 areas of the EU, that is those affected by industrial decline and unemployment. Several similarities in objectives and approach, alongside important differences, indicate that a variety of influences have been at work, including the general preferences of the Commission, national priorities and regional and local factors such as the nature of inherited problems and policies. Despite the rich detail and impressive diversity, many of the strategies fail to convince the reader that they stem from systematic analysis of their local economic situation and reflect the collective commitment of the various local partners.

Schrumpf discusses the impact of EU structural policies on Germany. They have had a profound influence on the national approach to regional policy as well as the institutional arrangements. The Funds have been particularly important in eastern Germany, but also in old industrial areas of western Germany. Evaluation suggests that they have had a tangible impact on economic progress, but this is hard to quantify and probably modest in scale. National economic developments and sectoral policies continue to dominate local economic trends, prompting Schrumpf to suggest that the focus on small and medium enterprises may be misguided.

The Netherlands had a very different approach to regional policy from the EU when the country first gained access to the Structural Funds. Bekker and Kleyn show how the systems have converged over time and how the Dutch have learned useful lessons about the need for integration, unified budgets, and clear objectives, targets and timescales in regional development policy. Some difficulties in reconciling the approaches remain and the Dutch would prefer a more decentralised and flexible system of programme design and management, and a broader, more qualitative approach to area designation and programme evaluation.

The Austrian approach had more in common with EU regional policy, including the partnership principle and emphasis on endogenous development. However, there were important differences too: a more informal, organic approach to policy making and evaluation and a more flexible method of designating problem regions to allow for growth centres to be included. These differences have created anomalies in the formulation and operation of programmes, excessive fragmentation and an unwarranted administrative burden, prompting some questioning of the EU approach.

Finland and Sweden are the newest members of the EU and an entirely new regional designation, Objective 6, was introduced to meet their special circumstances. Johansson describes the intricate changes in public administration that these countries had to make to accommodate the Commission's requirements before they could access the Structural Funds. Different approaches were adopted (centralised in Finland, decentralised in Sweden), reflecting the different history of regional policy and state procedures. While the new systems appear to have had some benefits, there have been significant teething problems too.

The final part of the book includes chapters reviewing the lessons emerging from the operation of the Structural Funds and considering the future challenges. They are written mainly by senior policy-makers from the Member States, whose perspective necessarily differs from academics and consultants and stems partly from a concern about the relationship with national policies and procedures and the impact and cost-effectiveness of the Funds.

Kearney writes as an ex-Commission official who has been closely involved in supervising the monitoring and evaluation of EU regional programmes in several countries. He provides insights into the Commission's policy thinking and practical difficulties experienced in managing the process with a small core staff and tight timescale. It has been a rapid learning process for all concerned, with acknowledged weaknesses and limitations. He argues that the increasing emphasis given to evaluation should help to improve procedures in future, although the political, economic and technical challenges faced are considerable.

Relationships between the UK government and the Commission have sometimes been strained. As a former senior official in the Department of Trade and Industry, Wells provides a forthright account of the evolution of the structural policies and the part played by the UK government on issues such as evaluation and the environment. He expresses several reservations about the management and operation of the Funds and the role of the Commission in that process, criticising its use of Community Initiatives, the lack of objectivity in area designation, the slow and complicated procedures, unwarranted downgrading of support for infrastructure and neglect of private sector involvement.

Lagrange is generally more positive about the Structural Funds, which have become an integral part of regional development policy in France. There is more similarity between French and EU procedures than in many countries, which has made things easier. Differences have included the EU's greater emphasis on partnership, longer time horizons for funding and more systematic requirements for evaluation, all of which are regarded as virtues. Lagrange concludes by expressing some concerns about the bureaucratic procedures, delay and inconsistent decision-making within the Commission.

The reunification of Germany provides an interesting indication of the major economic challenges facing the entry of Central and Eastern European countries to the EU and the implications for the structural policies. Drerup, a senior official in the German Federal Ministry for Economics, explains that the country has benefited from very substantial EU resources, but the procedures to access them have given rise to several concerns of undue interference by the Commission and confusion over regional development objectives. For example, in negotiating Objective 1 support for eastern Germany, the Commission insisted on a much broader development programme than the federal government thought desirable or feasible in practical terms.

Finally, in Chapter 22 we address the agenda for reforming EU regional policy. The chapter summarises the key issues emerging from the contributions in the book and reflects on the achievements of the Structural Funds to date. We discuss the wide range of challenges facing the reform of the Structural Funds with regard to the objectives, focus and structure of policy and programming procedures, and the implications of monetary union and EU enlargement. We conclude with a review of the current state of reform discussions and some of the options and scenarios confronting EU and Member State regional policymakers.

CHAPTER 2

The Evolution of the Structural Funds

Rona Michie and Rona Fitzgerald

Introduction

The purpose of the Structural Funds is to promote economic and social cohesion within the European Union – that is to reduce regional disparities within and between the Member States. Successive enlargements and the integration process itself have raised the priority of this objective. The development of the Structural Funds must be considered in the context of the expanding scope of European Community policy making and constitution building, and the changing dynamics of the relationship between the European institutions and the Member States. The notion of 'Europe of the Regions' has been widely promoted and debated. The trend towards regionalism complements other trends such as globalisation, cultural homogenisation, the emergence of the fledgling democracies in Central and Eastern Europe and the accelerated pace of the integration process in Europe.

The aim of this chapter is to outline the arguments used to support regional policy at European Union level, to trace the evolution and expansion of the Structural Funds and to identify the challenges posed to this policy area from the integration process itself, from the changing international economic environment and from the future enlargement of the European Union. It begins by looking at the rationale for structural intervention at European level, moves on to trace the development and expansion of the Structural Funds in tandem with the integration process and concludes with the issues and factors that present future challenges for the operation of regional policy in the European Union.

Rationale

As the scope of European Regional Policy has increased and the proportion of the European Union budget available for the Structural Funds has expanded, economists, political scientists and sociologists have offered a number of theoretical perspectives on the rationale for the Funds (Swann 1992; Tsoukalis 1991; Molle 1994). Central to the rationale is the argument that regional socio-economic disparities across the Union are unacceptably wide and that the Union has a responsibility to reduce these differences.

In its simplest terms, the problem is expressed as the core-periphery nature of the Union with a core of wealthy states and a less developed periphery. A glance at the map of Gross Domestic Product per capita illustrates the core-periphery nature of the Community's regional imbalances, ranging from 190 per cent of the EU15 average (Hamburg, Germany) to 42 per cent (Alentejo, Portugal) (Eurostat data for 1993 in purchasing power parties). Without a strong regional policy to reduce such differences, centralising forces will, arguably, dominate (Swann 1992, p.284). Further, many aspects of the integration process encourage the concentration of industrial activity in the centre of the Community, while the periphery may be bypassed. Successive enlargements exacerbated the disparities among the regions of the European Community, manifesting themselves as a North-South divide, with Ireland considered as part of the south.

> The spatial characteristics of the Community's regional imbalance conformed to the core-periphery concept used by economists and social scientists to analyse the inequalities between or among regions. The result was that the Community built its structural policy largely on the assumption of a poor periphery (Scotland, Ireland, Portugal, central and southern Spain, Corsica, southern Italy, Greece and eastern Germany) and a rich core (southern England, north eastern France, the low countries, north western Germany, and northern Italy). (Dinan 1994, p.404)

Clearly, the core-periphery pattern is a crude representation of the complexities of regional socio-economic change across the EU (see Chapter 3). However, the existence of major differences between different parts of the Union is the premise for EU policy intervention. Also, at international level, the Member States of the European Community take part in the integration process because they expect welfare gains from it, but there are also costs and these costs are not distributed evenly among the participating states. The argument is that the Union is best placed to tackle the negative impact of integration and to allocate resources for a 'fairer' distribution of the benefits of integration (Armstrong 1994; Dinan 1994; Swann 1992; Molle 1994; Tsoukalis 1992).

The issue of solidarity is also cited – if there was not a clear commitment to redress regional imbalances, the weaker economies might feel less inclined to participate in the further integration of the European Community/Union. The issue of solidarity was emphasised by Jacques Delors when he became President of the European Commission in 1985 as a crucial factor for the future development of the Union. In a speech to the European Parliament he cautioned members that enlargement negotiations with Greece, Spain and Portugal had:

> revealed a tension in Europe which is, let's face it, a tension between north and south. It stems not only from financial problems but from a lack of understanding, from a clash of culture, which seems to be promoting certain countries to turn their backs on the solidarity pact that should be one of the cornerstones of the Community, solidarity being conceived not in terms of assistance, but rather as an expression of the common-weal, contributing to the vigour of the European entity. (Commission of the European Communities, Bulletin EC 3/4 – 1985, p.6, 1985)

The Commission under Delors continued to view this solidarity as crucial. It also viewed the commitment to redistribution as essential to get agreement on the Single Market programme and, ultimately, political and monetary union. The acceleration of European Community integration in 1985 through the Single Market programme, the entrance of Greece, Portugal and Spain into the Community and the consequent tremendous increase in EC inter-regional imbalances, combined with an increasing demand for co-ordination of regional policy, led to a further, more wide-ranging, reform of the Community's regional policy in 1988.

EU Regional Policy 1970–1986

The European Commission's involvement in regional development can be traced back to 1957 when the Treaty of Rome required the Community to ensure 'harmonious' development by reducing regional differences and the backwardness of less-favoured regions. However, it was not until the mid-1970s that specific policy measures and budgets allocated to regional development were introduced, specifically with the establishment of the European Regional Development Fund in 1975. Since then regional policy has attracted an increasing share of Community resources. By the time the

Maastricht Treaty on European Union was concluded in 1991, economic and social cohesion had been elevated to become one of the EU's fundamental principles.

The Community's main instruments of regional development are the Structural Funds (the European Regional Development Fund, the European Social Fund, the European Agricultural Guidance and Guarantee Fund: Guidance Section and the Financial Instrument for Fisheries Guidance). The European Regional Development Fund (ERDF) was created with the objective of correcting 'the principal regional imbalances within the Community resulting in particular from agricultural preponderance, industrial change and structural under-employment' and its main purpose was to 'finance investments in industrial, handicraft, or services activities, thereby creating new jobs or protecting those already existing' (Commission of the European Communities 1975).

In the first instance the ERDF was regarded as a compensation mechanism *(juste retour)* for countries that contributed an above-average amount to the EC budget. At this stage the limited ERDF resources were allocated on a quota basis and implemented through Regional Development Programmes, exclusively in support of the regional policies of Member States, and to areas designated by Member States.

In an attempt to raise the profile of Community regional policy at the end of the 1970s, the Commission proposed to take a systematic approach to analysing regional problems and the development of regional policy. This included the evaluation of the regional impacts of other important areas of common policy and the co-ordination of regional policies in Member States. The outcome was the creation of a 'non-quota' section of the ERDF, making five per cent of the expenditure quota-free and independent of designated areas. How the funds were to be used was to be decided by a unanimous Council of Ministers decision. For the first time, funding was allocated to Common Programmes/Initiatives rather than individual applications for support by individual Member States.

The next revision of Community regional policy culminated in new guidelines in 1984. The objectives of the ERDF were redefined to emphasise the development and structural adjustment of lagging regions and the conversion of declining industrial regions. The need to make Community regional policy more effective was recognised and, consequently, the Commission proposed to extend the quota-free part considerably, tie investment to regional development plans and develop a common procedure for designating areas eligible for Community regional policy assistance. This met resistance from Member States and the compromise was a prolongation of the quota system, but within flexible minimum and maximum limits. In absolute terms, the ERDF budget had increased almost tenfold during the 1975–1985 period (from 258 million ecu (mecu) in 1975 to 2290 mecu in 1985) and the ERDF's share of the EU budget increased from 4.8 to 7.5 per cent.

The 1988 Reform of the Structural Funds

The accession of Spain, Greece and Portugal to the Community brought a substantial widening of regional disparities within the Community and led to a doubling of the population of the least-favoured regions. In addition, the process of market liberalisation which had begun with the Single Market White Paper was expected to increase risks of regional imbalance. Indeed, several Commission reports warned of the dangers of not sharing the 'reward' of the Single European Market, of the 'serious risks' of aggravated regional imbalance in the course of market liberalisation and the need for adequate accompanying measures to speed adjustment in the structurally weak regions and countries. The increased regional imbalances were perceived as a threat to the realisation of the Single Market; the rationale behind the 1988 reform of the Community's regional policy was to improve the effectiveness of the Structural Funds and, therefore, economic and social cohesion in the Community.

The reform of the Structural Funds was completed at the end of 1988 with a redefinition of the 'tasks of the Structural Funds and their effectiveness' and with the 'co-ordination of their activities between themselves and with the operation of the European Investment Bank and the other financial instruments' (Commission of the European Communities 1988a; 1988b). On this basis, common criteria for designating problem regions, the scope and forms of assistance, guidelines and reporting requirements were developed.

The reform also introduced a number of principles for the implementation of EU regional policy:

- the submission of plans by the Member States under priority objectives
- the implementation of partnership between competent authorities at national, regional and local levels
- the additionality of Community measures
- the compatibility of structural policy with other Community policies (e.g. competition policy, environment policy)

- the concentration of resources, with particular emphasis on the least-prosperous regions
- the co-ordination and combination of different Community instruments.

The programme approach involved a shift from individual project support to programme financing with plans covering, initially, a period of three or five years. Each Member State had to submit regional development plans, linked to the priorities and objectives of the Funds, outlining their intentions as to the use of Community resources to the Commission for approval. The plans were negotiated with the Commission to construct Community Support Frameworks (CSFs), which outlined the aid priorities for the Community in relation to what was proposed by the Member State. The CSFs outlined the priorities to which subsequent implementation measures, in the form of Operational Programmes (OPs) or other instruments, related.

Both planning and implementation were to be undertaken within a partnership between competent authorities at different administrative levels. Partnership was defined as 'close consultations between the Commission, the Member States concerned and the competent authorities designated by the latter at national, regional or local level, with each party acting as a partner in pursuit of a common goal' (Commission of the European Communities 1988a, Article 4). National authorities were given delegated discretion to appoint members of the partnership.

The issue of additionality was a fundamental principle underpinning the reform of the Structural Funds and ensuring their effectiveness. In principle, it meant that national government expenditure should match EU expenditure and that EU funds should not be used as a substitute for funds from national sources. Compatibility implied that the proposed plans and measures be coherent overall with both EU and national policies and, in particular, environmental and competition policies. Concentration of resources implied concentration of available financial resources: on the least prosperous regions, on a small number of priorities and on a small number of sectors. This was mainly undertaken through designation procedures for different types of assisted areas and by focusing on a small number of priorities and sectors during the planning process. Finally, financial co-ordination was to be achieved through co-financing and integration between EU financial instruments and also integration with national incentives.

In terms of budgets, the reform involved a doubling of the Structural Fund budgets (from 6.3 billion ecu (becu) in 1987 to 14.1 becu in 1993) and a doubling of the budget allocated to underdeveloped regions. The intention was to allocate up to 80 per cent of the ERDF budget (4.5 becu in 1989) to Objective 1 regions, although this was not quite achieved (see below).

The 1988 reform assigned a number of specific objectives to the Structural Funds, to which they would be either jointly or separately assigned, as follows:

- Objective 1: Development of structurally-backward regions (ERDF, ESF, EAGGF)
- Objective 2: Converting regions in industrial decline (ERDF, ESF)
- Objective 3: Combating long-term employment (ESF)
- Objective 4: Increasing youth employment (ESF)
- Objective 5(a): Adjustment of agricultural structures (EAGGF)
- Objective 5(b): Development of rural areas (EAGGF, ERDF, ESF).

Eligibility criteria and connections between funding instruments and objectives are as shown in Table 2.1.

The 1993 Reform of the Structural Funds

The origin of the second Structural Fund reform dates to the European Council meeting in Maastricht in December 1991. The perception of many Member States that the Community should move towards closer economic and political union was accompanied by a recognition that measures to achieve economic convergence would be endangered without associated action to improve economic and social cohesion. The Maastricht Treaty on European Union upgraded the importance of EC regional policy, with the Treaty establishing economic and social cohesion as one of the pillars of the Community structure, and agreement being reached to set up a new 'Cohesion Fund' for the poorer Member States. Reflecting these developments, the Structural Fund budget was increased from approximately 43.8 becu over the 1988–1993 period to over 141 becu for 1994–1999 (at 1992 prices).

The amendments made to the operation of the Structural Funds during the second reform were fairly minimal. The main changes concerned eligibility criteria, programming periods and administrative procedures. The Objective 1 regions for 1994–1999 were set out in the 1994 Structural Fund Regulations, while areas eligible under Objectives 2 and 5b were chosen on the basis of proposals submitted by Member States (rather than unilaterally by the Commission, as previously). The Regulations continued to be based on the same principles contained in the 1988 Regulation, that

Table 2.1 Objectives, allocated Structural Funds and eligibility criteria

Objective	*Support available from*	*Eligibility criteria*
Objective 1	ERDF, ESF, EAGGF	Regions at NUTS level II[1] with GDP per head less than 75 per cent of the Community average or regions included as special cases.
Objective 2	ERDF, ESF	Regions at NUTS level III with: • higher than average unemployment the last three years • industrial employment as percentage of employment above Community averagethe last 15 years • an observable fall in industrial employment relative to reference year or substantial job losses in specific industries
Objective 3	ESF	Not regionally restricted.
Objective 4	ESF	Not regionally restricted.
Objective 5a	EAGGF,	Not regionally restricted.
Objective 5b	EAGGF, ESF, ERDF	Regions with: • high share of agriculture employment in total employment • low level of agricultural income • low level of socio-economic development • other factors like de-population, peripherality, size of holdings.

Source: CEC 1993

1 The Nomenclature of Territorial Units for Statistics (NUTS) was established to provide a single uniform breakdown for the production of regional statistics. The nomenclature sub-divides each Member State into a number of NUTS I regions, each of which in turn is sub-divided into NUTS II regions, which are themselves sub-divided into NUTS III regions. In total there are 71 NUTS I regions, 183 NUTS II regions and 1044 NUTS III regions.

is planning, partnership, additionality, compatibility, concentration and co-ordination.

In addition to the changes which would affect the existing three Funds, a new Structural Fund was established, the Financial Instrument for Fisheries Guidance (FIFG), to support diversification of the fisheries sector. Changes were also made to Objectives 3 and 4, widening Objective 3 to include the occupational integration of young people, and introducing a new Objective 4 focusing on adaptation of the workforce to industrial change.

Coverage in the EU12

Objective 1 regions cover over a quarter of the EU12 population (26.6%) and include the entire territories of Greece, Ireland and Portugal, together with most of Spain, much of Italy and all of the east German *Länder*. In addition, Objective 1 includes parts of more prosperous Member States, notably Hainaut in Belgium and Flevoland in the Netherlands. The basic eligibility criterion for Objective 1 is that per capita GDP at NUTS II should be less than 75 per cent of the EU average. However, this requirement has been applied with considerable flexibility and there are a number of Objective 1 regions which do not fulfil this criterion.

Objective 2 regions cover around one-sixth of the EU12 population (16.8%) and include parts of all the Member States except Greece, Ireland and Portugal. Objective 2 designation is based on the NUTS III region and the criteria are primarily concerned with levels of unemployment resulting from industrial decline. Unlike the other three spatially-restricted objectives which were designated for the period 1994–1999, Objective 2 areas were initially designated only until the end of 1996.

Objective 5b covers under one-tenth of the EU12 population (8.2%) and again includes parts of all the Member States except for the three Objective 1 countries. The primary criterion for Objective 5b designation is a low level of socio-economic development as measured by GDP per capita. In addition, designation depends on one of the following: a high level of agricultural employment, a low level of agricultural income or demographic disadvantage.

Budgetary Allocations

It was agreed before the 1988 reform to double the Structural Funds from 6.3 becu in 1987 to 14.1 becu in 1993 (totalling approximately 43.8 becu over the 1988–1994 programming period), concentrating aid on the poorest, most structurally underdeveloped (Objective 1) regions.

The commitment appropriations for the Structural Funds (including the FIFG) in the EU12 for the 1994–1999 period are 141,471 becu (rising from just over 20 becu in 1994 to 27.4 becu in 1997). Some 68 per cent of the appropriations have been allocated to the Objective 1 regions (see Table 2.2). It is intended that the additional Structural Fund assistance, together with the Cohesion Fund, will permit a doubling of commitments in real terms for the four Cohesion Member States (Greece, Ireland, Portugal and Spain) between 1992 and 1999.

Table 2.2 Community appropriations for the Structural Funds for 1994–1999 (mecu at 1992 prices)

	Structural Funds	*Objective 1*
1994	20,135	13,220
1995	21,480	14,300
1996	22,740	15,330
1997	24,026	16,396
1998	25,690	17,820
1999	27,400	19,280
Total	**141,471**	**96,346**

Source: CEC 1993

As provided for in the revised Regulations, the Commission made indicative allocations by Member State for each of the Objectives (see Table 2.3). Much of the criticism of the Commission's handling of budget designations following the 1988 reform of the Funds centred on the alleged lack of transparency and objectivity in the financial allocations to Member States and regions under the different objectives. Article 12 of the Framework Regulation makes clear the Commission's approach for making allocations under Objective 1–4 and 5b: 'taking account of national prosperity, population of the regions, and the relative severity of structural problems, including the level of unemployment and, for appropriate objectives, the needs of rural development' (Commission of the European Communities 1993b, p.56). Spain, Germany and Italy benefit most in terms of straightforward funding allocations, followed by Greece and Portugal.

At the Edinburgh European Council in 1992 it was agreed that a Cohesion Fund, provided for in the Maastricht Treaty, would be set up with an allocation of 15.15 becu over a seven-year period (1993–1999). The Fund was intended for the four EC Member States whose GDP per capita was less than 90 per cent of the Community average, that is Greece, Portugal, Ireland and Spain. The Fund provides financial support for projects in two specific areas: environmental protection, to ensure that the four Member States in question are better equipped to comply with EU environmental policies; and transport infrastructure, considered vital for the completion of the trans-European networks and the Single Market.

Improvements in these two areas would have a very significant effect on regional competitiveness and so were central to the notion of cohesion. Assistance is provided for up to 85 per cent of the total cost of projects.

Table 2.3 Indicative funding allocations 1994–1999 (1994–1996 for Objective 2 regions) (mecu at 1994 prices)

	Objective:-						
Member State	*1*	*2*	*3 & 4**	*5A EAGGF*	*5A FIFG*	*5B*	*Total*
Belgium	730	160	465	170	21.6	77	1623.6
Denmark	–	56	301	127	135.5	54	673.5
France	2190	1765	3203	1742	170.7	2238	11,308.7
Germany	13,640	733	1942	1068	65.8	1227	18,675.8
Greece	13,980	–	–	–	–	–	13,980
Ireland	5620	–	–	–	–	–	5620
Italy	14,860	684	1715	680	118.6	901	18,958.6
Luxembourg	–	7	23	39	1.0	6	76
Netherlands	150	300	1079	118	41.2	150	1838.2
Portugal	13,980	–	–	–	–	–	13,980
Spain	26,300	1130	1843	326	105.6	664	30,368.6
UK	2360	2142	3377	361	78.3	817	9135.3
Total†	**93,810**	**6977**	**13,948**	**4631**	**738.8**	**6134**	**126,238.8**

* Excluding amounts made available to Objective 1 regions. † EU12

Source: European Commission

Projects receiving support from the Structural Funds are not eligible for support from the Cohesion Fund. The approximate ratio of spending has been set at 60:40 in favour of transport.

Community Initiatives

The Community Initiatives (CIs) are separate spending programmes co-financed by the Structural Funds. Unlike the Community Support Frameworks, they are based on guidelines drawn up by the Commission. During the 1988–1993 programming period, the number of Community Initiatives increased enormously, together accounting for almost nine per cent of the Structural Fund budget. While acknowledging that the Community Initiatives were an area of Community regional policy which had been criticised by the Member States, the Commission maintained that they are an important instrument with a genuine Community dimension, enabling measures to be undertaken which extend beyond national borders. They also provide a means of experimenting with innovative measures and they permit the Community to respond, at relatively short notice, to unforeseen regional development needs that emerge in the course of a programming period.

The conclusions of the Edinburgh Council gave the following guidance for future Community Initiatives: '(they) should primarily promote cross-frontier, transnational and inter-regional co-operation and aid to the outermost regions, in accordance with the principle of subsidiarity' (Commission of the European Communities 1993a, p.11). A fundamental review of Community Initiatives was undertaken in June 1993 with the launch of a Green Paper consultative document with the aim of encouraging 'a wider debate about the priorities which need to be tackled by Community Initiatives during the coming period...based on lessons which can be drawn from the experience in the first phase' (Commission of the European Communities 1993a, p.4).

Following this review, a new set of thirteen Community Initiatives was launched in mid-1994: INTERREG II (inter-regional co-operation); RECHAR II (coal dependent regions); RESIDER II (steel dependent regions); RETEX (textile dependent regions); KONVER (defence-industry dependent regions); URBAN (urban areas); SME (small and medium size firms in disadvantaged regions); PESCA (fisheries dependent regions); LEADER II (rural areas); ADAPT (adaptation of the workforce to industrial change); EMPLOYMENT (employment and training measures for disadvantaged groups); REGIS (ultra-peripheral regions); and an Initiative for the Portuguese textile industry. An additional Initiative has since been launched in the Republic of Ireland/Northern Ireland (the Peace Initiative).

Accession of New Member States in 1995

The accession of Sweden, Austria and Finland to the EU had little overall impact on the EU's regional policies. Past reforms of the Funds were often in response to the accession of poorer Member States. However, the new members' GDPs are not substantially different from the Community average and the current Structural Fund framework was therefore considered to be adequate to cope with an EU comprising fifteen Member States. The main adjustments required included the allocation of funding to the new entrants (5884 mecu for the 1995–1999 period) and dealing with areas which did not fit the traditional Objective 1, 2 and 5b categories but which were considered to be sufficiently disadvantaged to require attention.

Although these countries are relatively prosperous in relation to other members of the EU, they do have areas of low income and high unemployment and, particularly in Sweden and Finland, regional policy has a strategic dimension since there is a very low population density in many of the remote northern regions. From the point of view of the accessants, integration into the Structural Fund programmes was one of the most important points to be covered by the Membership Treaties. In the Treaty of Accession additional funds were provided to account for allocations for the new members within the existing programme period up to 1999 (see Table 2.4). As the existing Objectives 1, 2 and 5b had limited applicability in the acceding countries (in particular, the Nordic countries), the Membership Treaty established a new Objective 6 within the Structural Funds with the aim 'to promote the development and structural adjustment of regions with an extremely low population density' (less than eight inhabitants per square kilometre) (see also Chapter 17 for further details).

Table 2.4 Structural Fund allocations to the New Member States 1995–1999 (mecu at 1995 prices)

Member State	*Objective 1*	*Objectives 2 & 5b*	*Objective 6*	*Total*
Austria	184	1439	–	1623
Finland	–	1193	511	1704
Sweden	–	1190	230	1420
Total	**184**	**4591**	**1109**	**5884**

Source: European Commission

The total of 5884 mecu (at 1995 prices) represents an additional expenditure of 4.5 per cent compared to an expansion of 7.4 per cent in the Community's population. In addition to the Objective 6 areas, a region in eastern Austria (Burgenland) with 269,000 inhabitants (3.5% of the population) was added to the list of the EU's Objective 1 regions.

Conclusion: Challenges for Regional Policy

Several key political, economic and social factors will affect the future operation of regional policy in the European Union. These include the integration process itself, notably the commitment to political and monetary union, changes in the international economic environment and enlargement of the Union.

The European Union is engaged in constitution building with a view to expanding its policy capacity, particularly with a view to strengthening the Single European Market with a single European currency. Through the Maastricht Treaty on European Union, the Member States set out a series of steps towards a common currency. The implications of EMU for disadvantaged regions cannot be predicted, although some economists believe that disparities will widen rather than contract. One of the key issues will be how the Union responds to increased pressure for intervention. The Member States have agreed a ceiling for the Union's budget so the question will be about resource reallocation rather than resource generation. This is always a complex political process with both economic and political implications.

The institutional framework in the Union is considered inadequate to accommodate political and monetary integration. The particular focus for concern is the weak role of the European Parliament and the so-called democratic deficit. While the European Parliament has assumed an increased role in the policy process of the EU in recent years, it does not have the power to check the executive as legislatures do in liberal democratic nation states. Furthermore, the Council of Ministers enacts laws without direct reference to the parliaments of the states in which the law has force. The integration process itself and the continuing enlargement of the Union also raises questions about the functioning of the Commission as a political and administrative body.

There is awareness of the need for reform, indeed the rhetoric of the Union has included this issue for some time. However, there is not widespread agreement as to what configuration this reform should take and there are differing emphases between Member States and between elites and electorates. At the centre of this dilemma are questions relating to national sovereignty, the relationship between the Member States and the European institutions and the capacity of the present institutional framework to be both efficient and representative. The result is that there is uncertainty about the future of regional policy, both in terms of the volume of funding for the Structural Funds and the priority of future policy objectives.

The changing international economic environment also has implications for regional policy. Increasing competitiveness, globalisation, the emphasis on innovation and the shift towards a more service-orientated society with an enhanced role for 'learning' are all factors contributing to the difficulties of regions that are peripheral, disadvantaged or 'lagging' behind. The case for intervention has been made, but the political will and the capacity for the Union to sustain a high level of structural intervention are dependent on a number of factors such as enlargement, the need to compete internationally and the requirement to be innovative and efficient.

The issue of enlargement, whether to the south or the east, presents further challenges for regional policy. The position of the Central and Eastern European countries (CEECs) is indicative of the scale of economic difficulties. Gross Domestic Product per capita in the CEECs is about 30 per cent of EU average. The main challenge facing these countries is to continue the move towards a market-driven economy and to put in place the legal and administrative framework necessary for membership of the European Union.

The Commissioner for Regional Affairs has been keen to underline the commitment of the Member States to the existing disadvantaged regions and to avoid a situation where these states become hostile to the enlargement because they feel they will lose out in terms of the Structural Funds. She suggests that transitional provisions are necessary to regulate the application of individual policies concerning enlargement towards the East because the operation of the Funds needs to be reformed and existing policy goals need to be pursued more rigorously (Wulf-Mathies, October 1995). The Commissioner also underlines the fact that the administrative apparatus of the CEEC states would not be capable of managing the complex processes of the Structural Funds for a number of years, therefore a gradual incorporation into Community structures would also be in the interest of these countries.

The nature of co-operation and integration within the Community differs from traditional inter-state co-operation because its founders aspired to create a new political entity, a United States of Europe. The Structural Funds were seen as instruments to tackle the disparities that exist between the Member States. The objectives of regional policy are both economic and political. Regional policy will become increasingly problematic as well as important in the context of further integration and enlargement. The demonstrable impact of regional policy will be crucial and the demand will be for efficiency, effectiveness and transparency in the manner in which Structural Funds are applied and accounted for. In an increasingly complex economic and political milieu, the issue of coherence will be critical.

CHAPTER 3

Regional Economic Change in the European Union

Harvey Armstrong and Ronan de Kervenoael

Introduction

The European Union (EU) is, above all else, a vehicle for delivering economic integration. History will judge the EU as a success or failure largely in terms of its effects on the economic welfare of its citizens. Regional economic restructuring is the key to economic success in the EU. The more attenuated the response within each region, the longer and more painful will the process be before the benefits of integration can be achieved.

Unfortunately, the EU is still a long way from having a fully integrated set of regional economies. In terms of GDP per capita, as noted in the previous chapter, the EU's regional problems are revealed as having a crude 'core-periphery' pattern, as Figure 3.1 shows. Recent accessions to the EU have, if anything, brought this core-periphery pattern even more sharply into focus. East Germany has proved, as Figure 3.1 reveals, to be one of the most disadvantaged regions in the EU and ranks alongside the highly disadvantaged southern Mediterranean and western Atlantic peripheral regions in the scale of its problems. Even the three most recent (1995) accessions – Sweden, Austria and Finland – have simply accentuated the core-periphery pattern since Austria's most disadvantaged areas (e.g. Burgenland) are in the east while those for Sweden and Finland are in the sub-arctic north.

The core-periphery pattern of EU regional disparities is a long-standing one and is no accident of history. Economic integration is an on-going and global process. It is a process which pre-dates the formation of the EEC. The integration process is driven by transport improvements which gradually over time have broken down the barriers to trade. It is also pushed along by technological improvements which reduce transport costs in the production

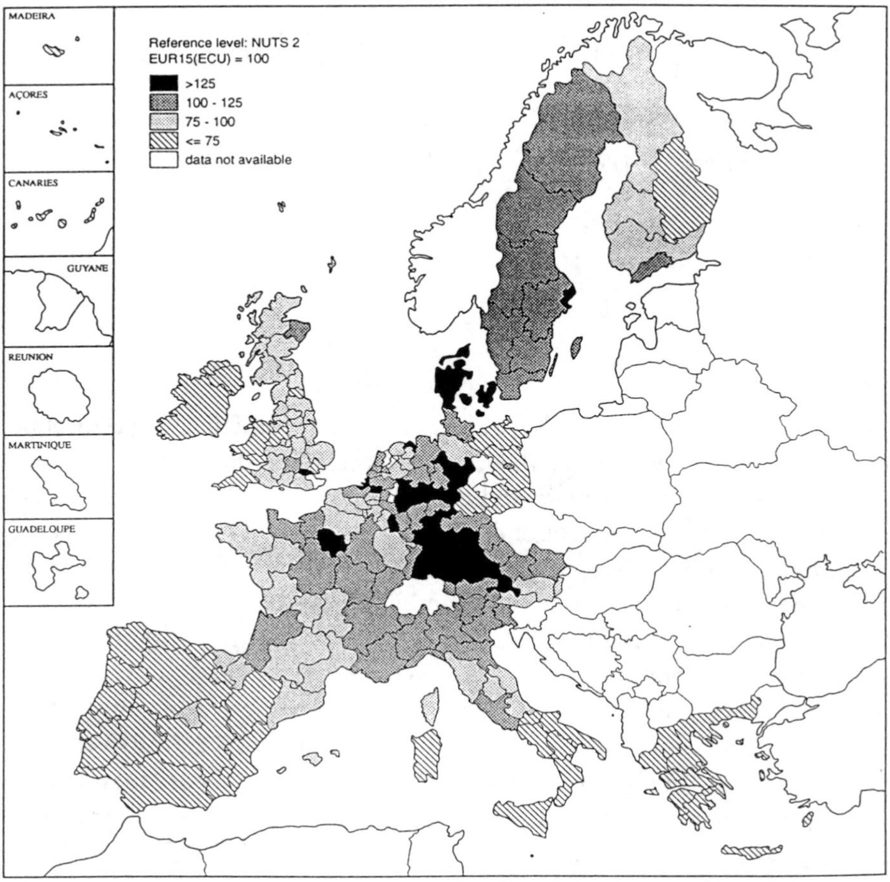

Source: Eurostat 1996

Figure 3.1 Regional GDP per capita: EUR15 Regions, 1993

process and by the gradual liberalisation of capital markets and world trade under initiatives such as bilateral agreements to reduce tariffs and multilateral agreements such as the General Agreement on Trade and Tariff (GATT). The existing core-periphery pattern of EU regional disparities reflects the impact of this gradual process of integration stretching over a prolonged period of European trade and factor mobility. The geographically more central regions of Europe have had many advantages in this steadily-integrating system; advantages reinforced by the presence in the geographical core of most of the great financial and administrative cities of Europe.

Although international comparisons are difficult to make, there is strong evidence to suggest that EU regional economic disparities are considerably wider than the nearest equivalent entity – the USA – since 'regional income disparities in the EU are 2.5 times those in the USA. They are four times those in Australia which, although it has a much smaller population, achieves its more balanced development across a larger territory' (Commissioner Wulf-Mathies, speech to the Regional Policy Commission of the European Commission, Brussels, 29 November 1995).

With an inheritance from the past of such large regional disparities, it is not surprising that an issue of paramount importance is whether integration within the EU is leading to a narrowing of regional disparities or not: the 'convergence versus divergence' debate. The nature of the process of regional economic change forms the subject matter of this chapter. The next section examines the theoretical basis of the process. The following section discusses the empirical evidence for the period since 1950, and the final section considers a number of important convergence processes in more detail.

Theoretical Perspectives on the Growth Process

The neo-classical convergence processes

In traditional neo-classical growth theory under free market conditions, growth leads to convergence in regional per capita income values as the poorer regions catch up with those initially richer. In the more modern versions of this theory (see Barro and Sala-i-Martin 1992; Mankiw 1995), the picture painted is a little more complex, but still an optimistic convergence one:

- regional per capita incomes still converge, but not to a single ('steady state') value
- major shocks to the system, such as the 1970s oil crises, may lead to a temporary widening of disparities where they hit some regions

harder than others (Barro 1991). Eventually, however, the convergence processes come back on stream.

In the neo-classical model with open regional economies, three main convergence processes are at work:

1. Savings and capital accumulation: regions with an initial head start and higher per capita income levels will find, over time, as savings are ploughed back into new investment, that diminishing returns set in. Regions initially behind now find that they have more attractive and profitable investment opportunities which allow them to grow faster and hence converge on their more prosperous rivals.
2. Factor mobility: in an open regional economy context capital will tend to flow (seeking higher returns) to those regions which are initially behind in the growth process. Labour migration in the opposite direction will also occur. Together, these flows will help to narrow regional disparities.
3. Technology transfer: in an open regional setting technology transfer from the more advanced regions to those lagging behind should occur quickly, boosting per capita incomes in the poorer and initially technologically backward regions.

Despite a number of problems (see Crafts 1992 and Mankiw 1995 for surveys), the neo-classical model does identify a number of realistic convergence processes. Supporters of the neo-classical view of regional disparities point to the experience of per capita income disparities within the USA which have narrowed almost continuously since 1880 (Barro and Sala-i-Martin 1991), and to widespread evidence of convergence in many parts of the world. In concentrating on convergence forces operating in a market environment, the theory is also in tune with the kind of world which EU economic integration is attempting to achieve.

The various processes of the neo-classical model are not the only forces which can lead to convergence. Regional policy itself, if successfully prosecuted, can act as an important mechanism bringing about convergence. So too can government fiscal transfers (by either state or federal governments) brought about by taxing richer regions heavily and then making expenditures in poorer regions. The power of federal-level transfers should not be underestimated. The twentieth century has seen the steady growth of spending and tax powers of central and federal governments at the expense of regional and local governments.

It should be noted that these fiscal transfers, and other measures such as the introduction of minimum wage policies (which invariably favour poorer regions), education, health and other welfare programmes, and international trade and tariff policies designed to protect industries in disadvantaged regions (e.g. textiles), are discretionary policy measures and are therefore very different from the automatic free market processes of the neo-classical model.

The possibility of cumulative growth (divergence)

Set against the neo-classical view that growth is essentially convergent over time are a whole series of theories which highlight the possibility that growth may lead to divergence. In extreme cases the growth process may lead to explosively divergent growth with the initially richer regions rapidly outpacing their poorer neighbours. In other cases the process is a 'damped' one with clear limits on the extent and pace to which divergence occurs over time but with no real tendency for regions to converge on one another.

TRADITIONAL DIVERGENT GROWTH MODELS

Many of the earliest models of regional growth, which concentrated on the demand for a region's goods and services, have tended to predict divergent growth. Regions are open economies highly reliant on exports to other regions within the same country or further afield. As a result, export-base theories of regional growth have a long provenance (e.g. North 1955). Export-led growth does not necessarily result in divergence, but a number of versions of the export base approach do tend to imply that a process of cumulative causation may occur. An initial boost to export demand can trigger local multiplier effects which stimulate the region further. A growing region can then enjoy the many different benefits which firms get from being in a dynamic environment (agglomeration and localisation economies). These advantages, in turn, help to make the export sector even more competitive. Moreover, as the initially-favoured region expands it will draw towards itself from other regions the migrants and capital investment flows necessary to sustain further expansion. A virtuous growth circle is therefore set up.

Other types of export-led models also tend to predict divergent growth. Such is the case with the growth pole model of Perroux (1970) with its stress on key industries which tend to attract linked firms towards them. Much of the current popularity of measures designed to attract large foreign direct investment (FDI) manufacturing plants from Japan, and to encourage local input suppliers to the new plants, evokes a strong echo of the growth pole model. Again, however, it should be noted that the early theories do not predict that divergent growth will always be the case. Much of the polarisation hypothesis work of Myrdal (1957) and Hirschman (1958), for example, stresses adverse forces which tend to result in the dual economies so typical of many Third World countries – clearly cases of divergent regional growth. These models, however, also acknowledge the presence of beneficial effects such as the neo-classical processes discussed earlier, which tend to reduce regional disparities. The resulting pattern is, therefore, the outcome of a balance of divergence and convergence forces. In some cases, particularly within countries at an early stage in the development process, the result is divergent growth and a dual economy. Later on, as development proceeds, the convergence forces come to predominate (Williamson 1965).

Growth theories rooted in export continue to have strong adherents. In particular, in Kaldorian models of growth (Dixon and Thirlwall 1975) exports are the engine of a region's growth and the principal constraint on its growth rate is a balance of payments one. In these models growth can become divergent in nature as a result of a variety of processes which ensure that an initial spurt of growth can trigger additional productivity gains for a region's firms, thus strengthening their head start in export markets.

MODERN DIVERGENT GROWTH THEORIES

One of the most interesting recent developments has been the emergence of new growth theory. Variants of this approach suggest that the growth process may well be divergent. This new approach is particularly interesting because it is based firmly in the neo-classical tradition and yet still gives divergent growth (see Romer 1986; Crafts 1992).

New growth theory seeks to introduce a more realistic role for technological change than is the case in the standard neo-classical model. In new growth theory a key role is given to the ability of a region to acquire technical knowledge and human capital, although these are not quite the same thing since 'knowledge refers to society's understanding about how the world works (and) human capital refers to the resources expended transmitting this understanding to the labour force' (Mankiw 1995, p.298). Regions with an initial head start in the growth process can encourage knowledge generation and can embark on a highly favourable and cumulative growth process. Human capital, research and knowledge acquisition are the driving forces behind this growth process.

While new growth theory essentially builds upon traditional neo-classical foundations, other recent approaches adopt a more radical approach to divergent growth. In post-Fordist scenarios a contrast is drawn between convergence forces which prevailed in the hey-day of the 'Fordist golden age' of the 1950s and 1960s and the subsequent crisis of Fordism which set in during the 1970s and which, it is argued, has continued ever since, resulting in divergence forces prevailing. In the 1950s and 1960s advances in productions systems were reinforced by social and institutional changes (e.g. Keynesian macroeconomic demand management; new types of wage determination; income redistribution policies – including regional policies) which ensured that aggregate demand was sufficient to sustain rapid growth (Dunford 1994). By the late 1970s this golden age, characterised by rapid regional convergence, had given way to a 'double-sided crisis' (Lipietz 1992) in which declining productivity growth and lower profitability of investment (on the supply side) combined with aggregate demand stagnation, exacerbated by monetarist policies, effectively brought to an end the convergence process. The result was that 'at this point, two of the mechanisms which had underpinned convergence ceased to operate: an earlier wave of productive investments in less developed areas came to an end; while the rise in unemployment in developed areas closed off the opportunities for emigration' (Dunford 1993, p.742).

Closely associated with the post-Fordist view of the growth process has been the debate on new industrial districts (Malecki 1995). Although the concepts expressed in this debate do not necessarily imply that regional growth will be divergent (since new industrial districts could potentially emerge in all regions eventually), the literature does suggest that districts with a head start are likely to continue to flourish and that the growth process involved is a divergence one.

Proponents of new industrial districts have argued that most firms (and particularly the larger multi-national businesses) are now operating in a radically changed world. Faced with the emergence of global markets and rapid technological change, companies have been forced to adopt more flexible methods of organisation, more flexible methods of utilising their labour forces and skill acquisition and much more flexible sets of interrelationships involving networking with other businesses.

One of the outcomes of these far-reaching changes in the organisation of production 'has been the rise of new industrial cities, spatially distinct areas of economic activity where a specialised set of trade-oriented industries has taken root and flourished, setting off employment-growth and population-growth trajectories which are the envy of many other places' (Park and Markusen 1995, p.81). This is clearly a divergence growth story when it is expressed in this manner, although it should be noted that the 'winners' are not necessarily the new Silicon Valleys of the world. Some of the new industrial districts highlighted in the research literature were formerly declining industrial areas. This is the case, for example, with the widely-quoted case of Emilia-Romagna in Italy (see Pyke, Becattini and Segenberger 1990). Moreover, lagging regions also have opportunities to adopt successful ways since, in regions such as Emilia-Romagna and Tuscany, the creation of agglomerations of firms with personal and family networking can be greatly enhanced by 'offensive' restructuring strategies (Dunford 1994, p.111). These include the active participation of regional and local governments (Leonardi and Nanetti 1990). Therefore, whether or not the emergence of new industrial districts leads to divergent or convergent growth at a pan-European level is an open question. It may, for example, be the case that divergent growth will occur at first but that, given time, the lessons learned in the new industrial districts will spread to other regions and the networks of banks, chambers of commerce, local authorities and the like will eventually reach out across much wider parts of the EU. In these circumstances the whole process may eventually be associated with convergence in the growth process.

Empirical Evidence of Regional Convergence in the EU

With so many alternative theories of the regional growth process available, it is not surprising that attention has been switched to the empirical evidence among regions within the EU. This research is greatly hampered by the lack of good harmonised statistics for a full set of EU regions for extended periods of time. As a result, the research to date has tended to concentrate on GDP per capita (for which EU regional data exist in discontinuous form back to 1950) and neglect other indicators of regional disadvantage.

Whether or not EU regions are experiencing convergent or divergent growth remains an issue of considerable controversy. Part of the reason for this appears to be the result of researchers using different data sets and different time periods. It is quite possible, for example, to observe convergence in regional disparities during one time period and divergence during another, particularly as regional disparities are known to usually widen during economic recessions as the downturn bears more heavily on the weaker regions. Recent research, however, has begun to suggest that a number of conclusions can be tentatively drawn (see Armstrong and Vickerman 1995 for a collection of recent studies). A number of these which merit particular attention and further research are as follows:

(a) *Convergence tendencies appear to have predominated in the period prior to 1975 in the EU.* Most studies suggest that EU regional GDP per capita disparities have narrowed over time (at least since 1950) in the EU. Barro and

Sala-i-Martin (1991), for example, in a widely-quoted study for 73 EU regions in seven core Member States, found that regional GDP per capita values had narrowed continuously over the period since 1950. While the underlying rate of convergence appears to have varied from decade to decade, that part resulting from convergence within each Member State (as distinct from convergence between the different Member States) was remarkably steady at two per cent per annum. At this rate of convergence, regional GDP per capita disparities are halved every 35 years.

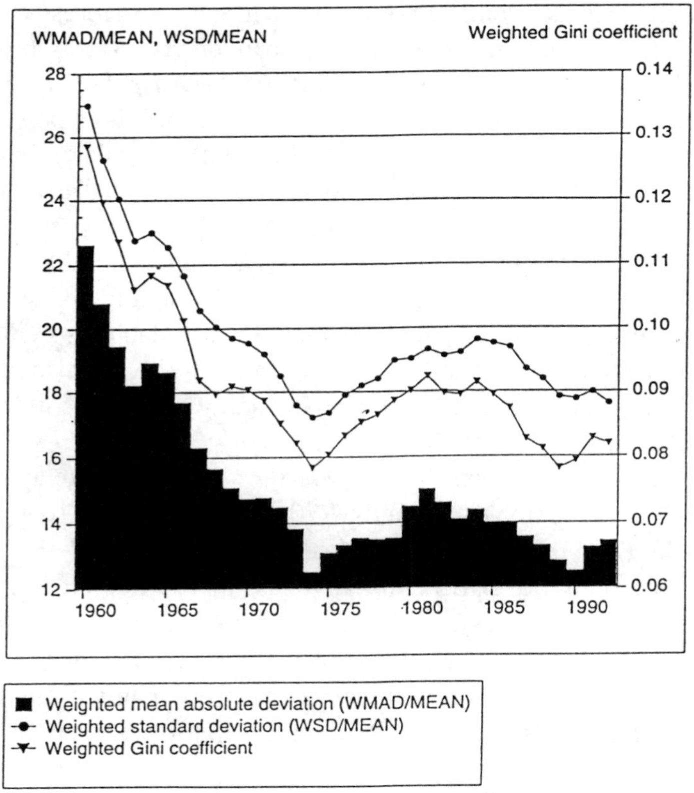

Note: GDP data are in current market prices and expressed at purchasing power parties using Eurostat's PPS system.

Source: Dunford (1994), figure 2.

Figure 3.2 Disparities in GDP per capita among the 12 pre-1995 Member States of the European Union, 1960–1992.

While results such as these remain controversial, a surprising large number of studies have tended to confirm the broadly convergent nature of the growth and integration process within the EU up until the mid-1970s. Boltho (1990) has found broad evidence for convergence both within individual EU Member States and across a wide set of regions in all twelve (pre-1995) EU Member States. Similarly, Dunford (1994) has used national GDP per capita data for the EU (in the absence of a continuous time series of regional-level data) to show that there was strong convergence up until around 1975, in marked contrast to the situation since then (Figure 3.2).

These results are widely supported by other studies, although many of these question the estimates of the speed at which convergence occurred in these earlier periods and also point to the patchy nature of the process with some poorer regions catching up more quickly than others (Armstrong 1995a; Cardoso 1993; Dewhurst and Mutis-Gaitan 1995; Neven and Gouyette 1995).

The evidence for historical convergence within the EU is powerful but not yet overwhelming. Severe data problems remain, particularly for the data sets for the early decades of the 1950s and 1960s. Equally, there is no guarantee that convergence has always been the case in the past in Europe. The evidence from the broad EU level is, however, given additional credibility by the detailed work for regions within individual EU member states (see, for example, the work on the extended Spanish data sets by Mas *et al.* 1995; and Cuadrado-Roura and Garcia-Greciano 1995). It is also borne out by work on the regions in other countries including the USA, Canada, Japan and Australia (Armstrong 1995c).

(b) The rate of regional convergence is very slow. All studies are agreed that even in the decades prior to the mid-1970s the rate at which convergence has taken place among EU regions has been extremely sluggish. Even at two per cent per annum (the Barro and Sala-i-Martin 1991 result), this means that EU regional disparities have been taking a massive 35 years to halve. More recent work suggests that even this two per cent rate may have been optimistic (Armstrong 1995b) with convergence occurring at one per cent per annum in the 1950s, although this then rose to three per cent per annum in the 1960s.

(c) The 1970s mark a turning point. The mid-1970s appear to have marked something of a turning point in the convergence process in the EU. The sustained convergence witnessed in the 1950s and 1960s in the EU gave way quite quickly to a much more confused situation in the late-1970s and 1980s, as Figure 3.2 has already suggested.

The stark contrast between the situation prior to the 1970s and the situation since has excited considerable debate. Some researchers have presented evidence that regional disparities have tended, on balance, to widen since the 1970s. The evidence when national GDP per capita data sets are used (e.g. Figure 3.2) is not conclusive since disparities can be seen to have widened between 1975 and 1985 but then narrowed since. Dunford (1993), however, also finds extensive evidence of divergence for regions within each of the main EU Member States when the period 1977–1989 is examined. When unemployment rates are considered, the evidence for divergence in the period since 1975 is much stronger as Figure 3.3 shows. This is supported by more detailed econometric analysis of regional unemployment rates in both Germany and Britain in the 1980s (Button and Pentecost 1995). Other researchers have found that a mixture of both divergence and convergence processes may have been at work simultaneously in the EU in the 1980s and early 1990s (Cheshire and Carbonaro 1995). By contrast, a second body of opinion has argued that it is convergence which has continued into the 1980s and 1990s, although at a greatly reduced rate of perhaps as low as one-half of one per cent per annum (see, for example, Barro and Sala-i-Martin 1991; Armstrong 1995b).

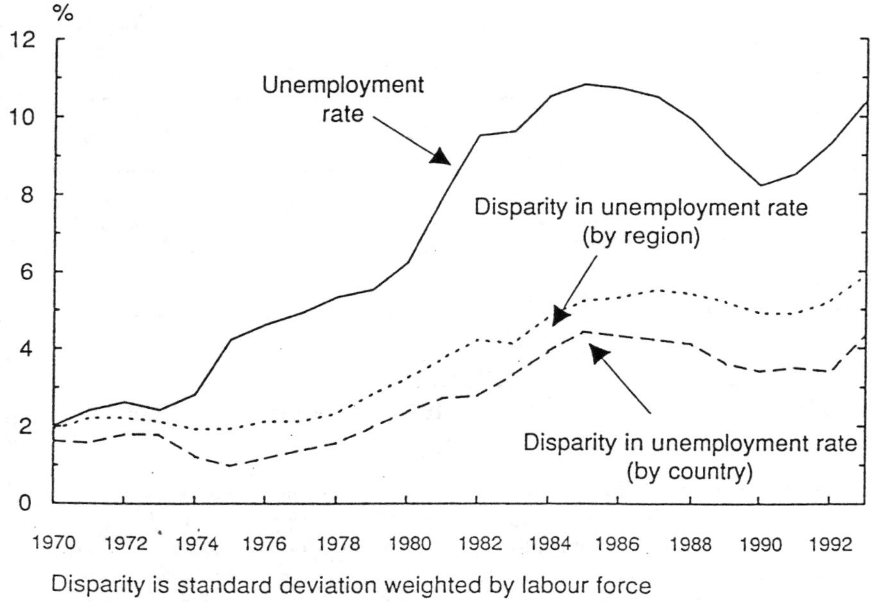

Source: European Commission, *Competitiveness and Cohesion: Trends in the Regions: Fifth Periodic Report on the Social and Economic Situation and Development of the Regions of the Community,* Office for Official Publications, Luxembourg, 1994b, p.46.

Figure 3.3 Trends in unemployment rates in the EU, 1970–1993

What are we to make of this apparently conflicting evidence? Part of the reason for the confusion arises from the tendency of different studies to use different start-dates and different end-dates for their study periods. Great caution must be taken when this is done because regional disparities almost always widen during recessions and narrow again during upturns in the economy. This can be seen in Figure 3.4 which plots a weighted coefficient of variation measure of regional disparities in the EU NUTS II regions for the full period for which data exist (1975–1993). This shows that disparities were at their widest in the early 1980s and again in the early 1990s, both downturn periods for the European economy. Hence, if one considered only the period 1975–1981 one would find divergence to have been the case, yet the period 1985–1989 would suggest convergence was occurring. The results, therefore, are very sensitive to the start and end years chosen for analysis.

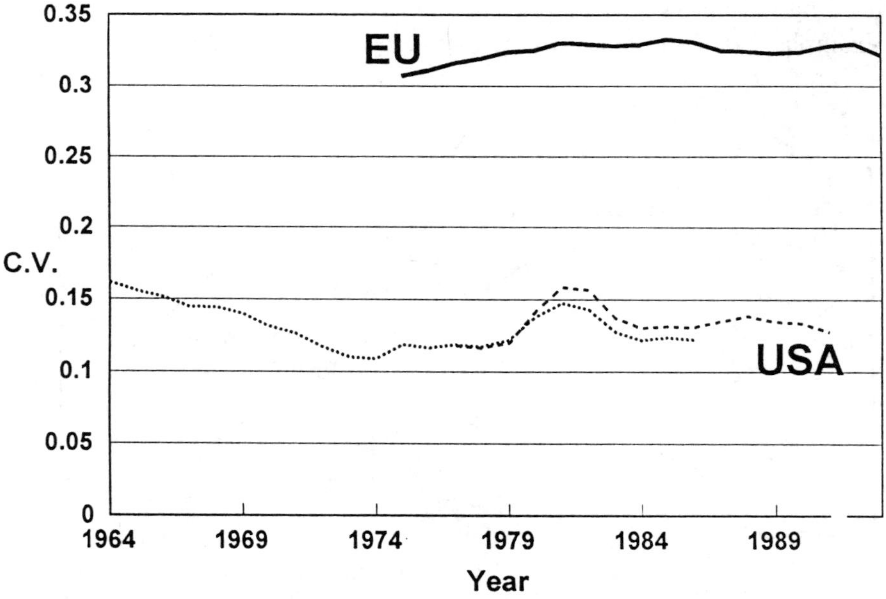

Note: The graphs give population weighted coefficients of variation. In the case of the USA data, disparities measure Gross State Product (GSP) per capita values (at constant prices) for 48 mainland USA states. Washington DC has been excluded. Two separate USA time series exist for GSP data. For the EU, the series utilised Gross Value Added (GVA) per capita data from a data set assembled by Cambridge Econometrics. The data refer to 62 NUTS I regions in the pre-1995 twelve Eu member states (see note 1, Table 2.1).

Source: Armstrong (1995c)

Figure 3.4 Regional disparities in the EU and USA

Despite the differences
and 1990s have been ve
any convergence which
interspersed with period
only small amounts and
the process of converge
EU in the 1980s and earl

Some clues as to why
analysis. In the USA,
inter-state GSP per capi
shows. While the early 1
US regional disparities
to have been very simil
such as this strongly s
parochial European aff

Finally, it should be
the EU have been relati
gence nor strong divergence is revealed, this does not mean that individual regions are trapped in some fixed position in the regional rank order. In fact, there is a lot of evidence that quite a lot of switching around within the regional rankings has occurred. Table 3.1, for example, gives the results of a markov chain analysis of the changing positions of regions within the distribution of per capita GDP values for the twelve-year period 1980–1992 (Armstrong 1995c). Markov chain analysis is an excellent method for searching for this type of position-shifting (Quah 1993). In Table 3.1, 140 NUTS II regions have been divided into five equal sized classes in terms of their GDP per capita values. Regions moving upward or downward by one or more classes in the years between 1980 and 1992 are listed in Table 3.1. The table shows that considerable movement of individual regions has occurred, with both gainers and losers being identified.

Regional disparities within the EU are not, therefore, set in stone, even in the more stable situation which we have seen in the 1980s and 1990s. Individual regions have it within themselves to radically change their individual circumstances.

The Weaknesses of EU Regional Convergence Processes

Ascertaining why convergence forces have been so weak in the EU both in the decades prior to 1970 and, more importantly, in the 1980s and early 1990s, is clearly of vital importance. In this section the reasons for the

42 THE COHERENCE OF EU REG

Table 3.1 'Movers' among 140 EUR 1

1. Regions moving downwards by one or more classes, 1980–92

Muenster (Ger)
Arnsberg (Ger)
Sterea Ellada (Gr)
Asturias (Sp)
Cantabria (Sp)
Picardie (Fr)
Haut-Nor
Nord-
Pa

2 NUTS II regions (1980–92)*

	2. Regions moving upwards by one or more classes, 1980–92
	Limburg (Bg)
	Niederbayern (Ger)
	Oberpfalz (Ger)
	Oberfranken (Ger)
	Unterfranken (Ger)
	Schwaben (Ger)
mandie (Fr)	Giessen (Ger)
Pas-de-Calais (Fr)	Kassel (Ger)
s de la Loire (Fr)	Lüneburg (Ger)
Drenthe (NL)	Aragon (Sp)
Zuid-Holland (NL)	Com. Valenciano (Sp)
North West (UK)	Veneto (It)
	Lazio (It)
	Luxembourg (GD)
	Utrecht (NL)
	Noord-Brabant (NL)
	Yorkshire/Humberside (UK)
	South East (UK)
	South West (UK)
	West Midlands (UK)

* The regions listed above are those which have shifted upwards or downwards (in terms of their GDP per capita values) by one or more classes within the distribution of regions ranked by GDP per capita values between 1980 and 1992. Regions have been grouped into five equal sized classes in terms of their 1980 GDP per capita values. The table utilises markov chain analysis.

Source: Armstrong (1995c)

apparent lack of potency of neo-classical and discretionary convergence processes is considered.

Automatic neo-classical convergence processes

At first glance, the EU appears to be functioning quite well as an integrating market system. As such, one might expect traditional neo-classical convergence forces to be strong. Trade in manufactured goods, for example, and capital mobility among the regions and Member States of the EU have grown rapidly and this part of the process of economic integration is probably functioning as well as can be expected at the present stage in the evolution of the EU.

EU capital markets are also highly integrated now. Individual Member State exchange controls had already been largely abolished prior to 1989. The Single European Market (SEM) legislation introduced between 1989 and 1992 has effectively removed remaining barriers to capital mobility. There is now considerable evidence that the individual Member States of the EU have capital markets which essentially operate as if they were regions within a single country (Armstrong, Balasubramanyam and Salisu 1996). That is, they show extremely close linkages with one another and have developed the ability to enable the rapid transfer of financial resources for investment purposes.

In reality things are not so rosy as this. The SEM legislation introduced between 1989 and 1992 was designed to try to remove non-tariff barriers to trade and the remaining barriers to capital mobility. However, these non-tariff barriers remain severe. Remaining barriers are particularly serious for many types of services (e.g. business and financial services such as banking and insurance) where only limited cross-border trade occurs; for public procurement activity by governments which tends to favour local suppliers; and for some types of manufactured goods where technical, environmental pollution and safety standards pose severe trade barriers. It will be many years before these barriers finally come down, despite the success of the SEM legislation. Indeed, many economists argue that until the EU can achieve a single currency it will be impossible to have genuinely free trade and capital mobility. Much remains to be done before trade and capital mobility can play their full role in helping to eliminate regional disparities within the EU.

In some respects the EU can claim considerable success in devising policies to remove some of the remaining barriers to trade. For example, the EU now has an active policy designed to improve pan-European road and rail transport links and advanced telecommunications systems. The EU already has a very well-developed road and rail network and can claim considerable success in putting in place the key cross-border links designed to enhance the system. Indeed, the EU has played a key role in helping to produce an integrated motorway network and high speed rail system.

Much more serious difficulties for the convergence process emerge when one considers the role of labour migration and technology transfers as mechanisms for reducing regional disparities within the EU, despite the importance attached to these mechanisms by traditional neo-classical models. Labour migration is a source of particular concern, despite the various attempts to ease restrictions on labour mobility in the SEM legislation. The neo-classical process by which poorer regions shed surplus labour is revealed by relatively high net out-migration rates for Ireland, East Germany and parts of Portugal, Northern France and Southern Belgium (Commission of the European Communities 1994g). All of these areas are highly disadvantaged and can therefore be expected to be shedding labour if the neo-classical model is to be believed. The problem, however, is that net out-migration rates for other highly disadvantaged parts of the EU are extremely low.

The enormity of the existing financial, language and other barriers to internal migration within the EU suggests it will be a very long time indeed before labour migration can fulfil the theoretical role as a convergence process mapped out for it in the neo-classical model. Indeed, some would argue that it will never attain this role, pointing to the fact that large-scale out-migration can strip a region of the most productive members of its workforce – the young, highly educated and skilled workers – thus fundamentally weakening its growth prospects. Others note that trade itself can act as a substitute for migration by allowing the weaker regions to concentrate on labour-intensive goods, thus effectively shipping out their labour surplus in the form of low-cost goods rather than as migrants. Nor can we expect to see the growth of large-scale cross-border daily commuting of workers within the EU. All of the available evidence suggests that commuting flows across EU borders remain remarkably low despite clear opportunities for workers (Falleur and Vandeville 1995). The barriers to such flows clearly must remain very powerful ones.

Turning to the final neo-classical convergence process – technology transfer – the evidence too suggests that considerable progress remains necessary. In principle, one would expect technology transfer to be rapid between regions within countries. Within any one Member State or within a highly integrated entity such as the EU, it can be expected that technology transfer will be swift. Many companies operate with plants in various EU Member States, facilitating the inter-plant transfer of technology. In addition, the integrated nature of the EU capital market means that new technology embodied in state-of-the-art plant and machinery will be quickly transmitted via investment flows. In practice, technology transfer is almost certainly very slow and fragmentary in nature. New technological processes are probably transmitted more quickly than new product technology where there is a vested interest in maintaining secrecy, particularly in the early stages of the product life cycle. The limited available evidence suggests that even new process technology may be being transmitted across the EU only very slowly (Van der Linden and Dietzenbacher 1995).

Discretionary EU policy convergence mechanisms

Discretionary convergence mechanisms remain embryonic at EU level. Considerable scope exists to strengthen policies which would help to reduce EU regional disparities. Unfortunately, the Member States have exhibited extreme reluctance to relinquish the kind of powers to the EU which would be necessary if significant convergence policies are to be set up.

The EU can claim a single success in the development of central discretionary policies which significantly cut regional disparities in the EU: the Structural Funds. The vast bulk of Structural Funds' assistance is targeted at the disadvantaged regions of the EU. This makes them quite a powerful instrument for the reduction of disparities, although it should be noted that these funds were of only minor importance prior to 1989. Indeed, although by 1999 they will comprise 35.6 per cent of the full EU budget, the small size of the EU budget (relative to the budgets of Member State governments) means that the fiscal strength of the Structural Funds remains limited. In 1993, for example, the size of the Structural Funds' and Cohesion Fund spending even in the areas eligible for the greatest assistance (Greece, Spain, Portugal and Ireland) was equivalent to only 2.3 per cent of GDP there. Even by 1999 this figure will rise only to 2.9 per cent. The weakness of the Structural Funds as fiscal transfer mechanisms should not, of course, be confused with their more important role of stimulating long-term growth by working on supply-side factors such as infrastructure and business performance.

Set against the success of the Structural Funds is the failure by the EU to develop central discretionary policies which effectively lead to convergence. The EU remains chronically short of the array of policies designed to encourage convergence to be found in truly federal entities such as the USA. In particular, the EU has an extraordinarily weak array of fiscal policy powers. It controls only 2.3 per cent of the total EUR12 tax take (Prud'homme 1994). With so little control of either taxes or spending, the EU simply lacks the financial 'clout' to develop the interpersonal transfers (e.g. pensions, unemployment benefits) or the intergovernmental transfers (e.g. equalisation grants favouring poorer states) so typical of federal countries. The result of this is that the EU has only a very weak regionally-redistributive fiscal system (Costello 1993; European Parliament 1991).

Perhaps the other most significance weakness in the EU's armoury of weapons to attack regional problems lies in the paucity of central employment and social programmes. Social policy almost always works in favour of disadvantaged regions. Policies to stimulate training and retraining and to help groups of workers such as women suffering exclusion from the labour market tend automatically to favour disadvantaged regions where such groups are typically over-represented. Despite the long existence of a European Social Fund, social policies of this type remain very weak within the EU. The embryonic nature of EU social policy remains a barrier to the further reduction of regional disparities.

Conclusion

While the EU can claim some success in raising the living standards of its citizens and in helping to facilitate a slow convergence in regional disparities in the post-war period, much more needs to be done. This chapter has examined the evidence available on the process of regional change within the EU and on the many different, and often conflicting, forces at work. Some of these forces, such as the free market mechanisms of factor mobility and technology transfer and the intervention of the Structural Funds and Member States' own regional policies, have helped to narrow regional disparities.

Other forces at work, including, sadly, a number of the EU's own policies such as the Common Agricultural Policy, have actually exacerbated regional problems. On balance, the evidence suggests that in the period from 1950 to the mid-1970s the EU enjoyed a narrowing of its regional problems. The situation since the mid-1970s has been much more confused with periods of convergence interspersed with periods of divergence. The current situation poses a great threat to future integration such as EMU and also challenges the enormous progress already achieved by the EU. The EU can only survive if all parts of its citizenry feel that they have something to gain.

With so many radical changes such as EMU and further enlargement of the EU likely, it is a particularly difficult moment to speculate on likely future developments for EU regional disparities. There is a division of opinion between those who foresee a gradual re-emergence of convergence forces once the current period of turmoil and rapid reforms is over. Others have pointed out that there may be profound changes occurring in the global economy and the new types of economic relationships emerging may lead to a widening of disparities in the future.

In the medium term the EU is likely to be confronted with an array of conflicting forces, some tending to bring about convergence while others tending to widen disparities. Also, one must not lose sight of the fact that the EU is continuing to press forward with further steps along the integration process. Each step brings with it its own distinctive set of short- and medium-term regional restructuring effects. Each time a set of countries accede, such as Sweden, Finland and Austria in 1995, the industries in each region of the pre-existing EU must adjust and reorganise. Alongside the opportunities for trade and expansion into new markets there are also the challenges of extra competition and the need to restructure company operations.

Each act of integration therefore has its own unique set of regional impacts. In the immediate future there will be a whole series of overlapping sets of impacts: the gradual implementation of the full SEM, economic and monetary union, the implementation of the Uruguay Round GATT accord, and enlargement to Central and Eastern Europe. It is impossible, given the current state of knowledge, to predict whether the combined effect of these changes will result in regional convergence rather than divergence. The balance of probabilities suggests that the EU is in for at least a decade of turbulent change in which the underlying convergence process is likely to be held in abeyance by profound structural changes. There is much work for the Structural Funds and the Member States' own regional policies to do.

PART TWO

Regional Development Strategies in the UK

CHAPTER 4

The Effects of EU Regional Policy on Local Institutional Structures and Policies

Steve Martin

Introduction

EU regional policy is intended to promote greater political, economic and social cohesion in Europe. However, there have been contradictory claims about its impacts and the extent to which it has led to convergence between regions. This second part of the book presents a series of contributions to the debate based on research in the United Kingdom. It examines the impact and influence of the Structural Funds at different spatial scales and through various elements of EU regional policy.

This chapter first begins the debate by exploring the problems involved in assessing the economic impacts of EU regional policy. It argues that they are almost impossible to measure accurately, but that the scale of resources devoted to regional policy within the Union is so small that existing 'compensatory payments' cannot realistically be expected to make more than a marginal contribution to redressing regional imbalances. EU regional policy has, though, led to what might be seen as potentially significant changes in the policies of local and regional agencies and institutions within the UK. This chapter focuses in particular on the impacts on local authorities for two reasons. First, they have a longer history of involvement in bidding for, and using, the Structural Funds than most other local agencies. Second, in most areas, local government continues to play a leading role in co-ordinating regeneration programmes and liaising with national government and the European Commission.

Drawing upon a stratified sample of 53 per cent of local authorities in England, Scotland and Wales and a series of deatailed case studies of a further 40 authorities, this chapter highlights three areas of activity in which local authorities believe they have become significant players – the implementation of EU legislation, networking with local and regional authorities in other parts of Europe and the formation of local and intra-regional partnerships to draw down EU funding to support economic development/regeneration schemes in their areas.

I suggest that there is evidence of increasing local authority involvement in 'European issues' and that, in some areas, the availability of EU assistance has led to changes in local economic policies and styles of policy making. However, local agencies still have relatively little influence over decisions which determine the overall distribution of EU funding. Their attempts to access and use EU funding must therefore be seen in the wider context of national government's strong 'gatekeeper' role and the way in which it has imposed constraints on local authority spending and systematically centralised power in Whitehall and Westminster. Moreover, in many areas, the commitment of agencies to genuine local partnership is either absent or fragile. Most local authorities and other agencies are primarily concerned to maximise their own 'share' of available funding, irrespective of broader considerations about the most effective forms of regeneration for their areas. Thus the local and regional input to bids and strategies for EU funding is provided largely by local government and, to a lesser extent, Training and Enterprise Councils (TECs), Local Enterprise Companies (LECs), colleges and the private sector and there is very little evidence of genuine involvement by the voluntary sector and local communities. Nevertheless, the tentative embracing by some local authorities and other agencies of more strategic, pluralist and participative approaches to regeneration is to be welcomed and may, in the long term, prove to be a significant impact of EU regional policy on local governance.

Economic Impacts of EU Regional Policies

The UK has been a significant beneficiary of EU regional policy. Between 1989 and 1993 it received 6275.7 million ecu (1993 prices) – almost 10 per cent of the total funds allocated through Community Support Frameworks (CSFs) (Commission of the European Communities 1995e). Following the agreement reached at the Edinburgh European Council, the proportion of total EU funding allocated to Objective 1, 2 and 5b areas in the UK between 1994 and 1999 has fallen, but the level of funding increased in absolute terms because of the growth in the Structural Funds as a whole. The extent to which EU regional policy has strengthened the economies of these regions is, however, extremely difficult to assess. As Dunford (1993) points out, there are currently no published studies which assess the overall economic impact of the Structural Funds in the UK. At EU level, recent monitoring of the overall performance of Objective 1, 2 and 5b regions during the period 1986–1993 has shown that some Objective 1 regions exceeded the Community average GDP per capita growth rate and many Objective 2 and 5b regions outperformed the rest of the Community in reducing unemployment (Commission of the European Communities 1994b). However, the effects of regional policy are swamped by broader economic change, even in the case of large Objective 1 regions in southern Europe which have received the bulk of the Structural Funds. As a result, it is impossible to address the counterfactual question of the degree to which Member States' economies would have converged in the absence of the Structural Funds through traditional econometric analysis. There are now numerous studies of the specific impacts of particular measures, sub-programmes and programmes financed under the Structural Funds. However, detailed empirical evaluations of this sort tend to focus on immediate output measures such as the length of road built, hectares of land reclaimed or jobs created, which cannot gauge the extent to which regional policy leads to convergence between regions because it is impossible to determine what part they play in the overall economic regeneration of target areas (McEldowney 1991).

In the UK context, assessment of the impacts of the Structural Funds has been further complicated by the 'additionality problem', which results from the way in which EU funding has apparently substituted for resources lost through reductions in domestic regional policy assistance to disadvantaged areas and cuts in the budgets and borrowing limits of local authorities and other agencies (including TECs/LECs and Urban Development Corporations (Local Authority Associations 1994; McAleavey 1993; Thomas 1992). The opaqueness of the public expenditure process has allowed the UK Treasury to apply the principle of 'global additionality', whereby it is claimed that, in the absence of the European Regional Development Fund (ERDF), overall spending totals would have been lower. This has made it almost impossible for the Commission to determine baseline expenditure levels against which the increases resulting from its assistance may be judged (Pearce and Martin 1996). As a result, some Integrated Development Operations appear to consist of 'various elements of expenditure which would have occurred in any case' (Keating 1993) and cannot, therefore, be claimed to have had any net additional economic impact.

Local Authority Responses to Closer European Integration

Whilst the economic impacts of EU regional policy are difficult to evaluate, there is growing evidence that it is having other, perhaps equally important, impacts in terms of changing approaches to local policy making in the UK. Increasing recognition at local level of the importance of closer European integration has been manifested in three main areas of local authority activity. First, there has been a growing awareness and recognition of EU legislation among UK local authorities. Second, recent years have witnessed a mushrooming in the number and range of contacts between UK local authorities and their counterparts in other Member States and in Central and Eastern Europe. Third, authorities have become increasingly pro-active in seeking to maximise the benefits, particularly the amount of EU regional policy expenditure, accruing to their areas.

Most authorities have taken measures to ensure that they fulfil new statutory responsibilities resulting from the increasing volume of primary and secondary EU legislation which is of direct relevance to them as major employers, property owners and monitoring, enforcing and licensing bodies (Local Government International Bureau 1991). In particular, EU directives and regulations have had significant impacts on service areas such as personnel, trading standards and environmental health. By the mid-1990s many authorities had developed internal systems to ensure that they were aware of, and complying with, new requirements placed upon them by EU laws and there was evidence of increasingly widespread expertise in this area. Thus our survey of 270 local authorities in England, Scotland and Wales showed that, by 1995, 76 per cent were confident of their capacity to respond appropriately to new EU legislation (Martin 1997a). This indicated a considerable improvement on the situation which, according to a similar survey, existed in the early 1990s (Audit Commission 1992).

Many authorities have also sought to inform other local agencies and businesses of the implications of new EU laws. Measures enacted as part of the Single European Market (SEM) programme were seen by many local authorities as being of particular importance. Perceived threats to local economies included new competition from businesses in other EU states and the restructuring of the European economy, which was expected to cut over-capacity in key industrial sectors leading to greater spatial and sectoral concentration of production. Some authorities undertook formal audits of the likely impacts of the SEM measures on local businesses. Examples include Birmingham City Council's analysis of the sectoral strengths and weaknesses of the city's economy and studies of the impacts of the SEM and reform of the Common Agricultural Policy on rural economies commissioned by Shropshire County Council, North Yorkshire County Council and the Borders Regional Council (Martin 1993). Many authorities also staged awareness-raising events designed to assist local businesses to prepare for the advent of the SEM. These included 'Europe weeks', exhibitions, conferences and information leaflets, often produced in association with the Department of Trade and Industry's '1992 programme'. In some areas local authorities provided specific training seminars and consultancy for local firms, alerting them to legislation which could have a particular impact on their businesses. A few (for example, Cleveland County Council) sought to promote trading links between local firms and other Member States by assisting local businesses to attend trade fairs and exhibitions, often in 'twinned' towns and cities.

The second main area of local authority activity has been the pursuit of closer ties with local and regional governments in other Member States and in Central and Eastern Europe. Until relatively recently, most authorities maintained traditional twinning relationships based around cultural and ceremonial links. However, many have realised that collaboration through groupings of authorities may prove more effective in obtaining resources for joint projects, sharing good practice and lobbying national governments and the Commission on matters of shared interest. The Local Government International Bureau estimated that, by 1992, there were more than 20 major local authority networks with an EU focus (Local Government International Bureau 1992). Many of these have since spawned 'offshoots'. By 1995 a third of UK authorities also had access to the services of Brussels offices through which they could, potentially, cultivate contacts with other local and regional authorities and with the Commission (Martin 1997a).

One of the most frequently cited examples of a 'successful' network is the Coalfield Communities Campaign, which is credited with having persuaded the Commission to set up an entirely new programme of compensatory measures (RECHAR) to offset the effects of pit closures (Benington and Harvey 1994). The Eurocities Association has taken on a similar role in highlighting the needs of urban areas and lobbying the Commission for initiatives which address these. A third example of the potential benefits of networking is the success of Kent County Council and its partners in Nord Pas de Calais and West Flanders in persuading the Commission to 'stretch' the criteria for eligibility for theCommunity initiative INTERREG (an institute desined to prepare border areas for the abolition of internal frontiers wthin the EU – adopted in 1990) to include co-operation across maritime borders. Other prominent networks with strong UK participation include the Assembly of European Regions, the Atlantic Arc (part of the Council for Peripheral Maritime Regions), the European association of industrial regions RETI (a network of regions which have traditionally been dependent on heavy, manufacturing industry) and the OUVERTURE network (designed to promote co-operative links between regions and cities and their counterparts in Central and Eastern Europe).

Some local authorities have expressed doubts about the value of networking and, given the political posturing which inevitably surrounds many such initiatives, the benefits are difficult to assess (Hooge and Keating 1994). Many authorities have relied on national local authority associations and bodies to represent their interests, believing that it is inappropriate and ineffective for individual authorities to be engaged in broader European policy debates. A recent example of this approach is the campaign orchestrated at national level by the Local Government International Bureau to try to ensure that the role of sub-national government in EU policy making was included on agenda for the 1996–97 InterGovernmental Conference.

Some networking between authorities has yielded little or no real benefit for the authorities concerned or their areas. A number of county councils have, for example, withdrawn from the Assembly of European Regions complaining that it has not helped them to form links with other authorities which share their specific (often sectorally based) concerns. Equally, however, many British local authorities have gained additional funding from Community Initiatives and Article 10 projects through networks involving partners in other Member States. Some authorities also see their participation in the early 1990s in these small scale initiatives and projects as having paved the way for the much greater prize of securing Objective 2 or 5b status in 1994. Examples include the London boroughs which participated in the Urban Pilot Initiatives and subsequently gained Objective 2 status, Kent County Council's involvement in INTERREG – which was followed by the granting of Objective 2 status to east Kent – and Shropshire County Council's involvement in trans-national, rural-based projects funded under Article 10 – which was followed by the designation of the 'Marches' area along the border with Wales as an Objective 5b region.

Furthermore, whilst most local authorities admit to being primarily motivated by funding opportunities, some (including, among our case studies, the London Boroughs of Islington and Southwark and (the now abolished) Cleveland County Council) have participated in trans-national networks in order to learn from other areas by exchanging views and good practice at a time when they believed that UK policy debates had become sterile and uninformative. Other authorities stress entirely altruistic motives for involvement in links with less affluent areas (particularly central and eastern Europe), whilst some believe that they have been able to use networks to gain political kudos and influence within the Commission. This latter group includes, for example, Birmingham City Council, which believes it was able to gain influence through the leading role it has played in the Eurocities network, (the former) Strathclyde Regional Council through its work on the OUVERTURE, Kent County Council's creation of the Transmanche region (with Nord Pas de Calais) and the formation by Southampton, Bournemouth, Portsmouth and Poole of the 'Transmanche Metropole' (with Caen, Rouen and Le Havre). These authorities claim that, in addition to helping them to gain funding, networks are valuable because they symbolise and help to cultivate a sense of European unity. Networking has also been seen by some leading local politicians as a means of raising their profiles in 'Europe' and gaining access to the 'Euro-elites' which make up the Committee of the Regions and sit on the executives of leading networks.

The third and most important area of activity by UK local authorities has been their attempts to maximise receipts of EU funding. The availability of regional policy assistance has undoubtedly been the main stimulus for local authorities' interest in 'European issues'. Sixty-eight of the authorities surveyed saw Europe 'primarily as a source of funding' and 75 per cent stated that EU assistance was one of their most important sources of funding for economic regeneration. Not surprisingly, this was most evident among authorities in Objective 1, 2 and 5b regions (Scottish regional councils (100%), Scottish district councils (93%), English metropolitan district councils (89%) and Welsh districts (88%)).

The methods by which local authorities seek to access EU regional policy assistance have become increasingly sophisticated. In the late 1970s and early 1980s few authorities actively sought ERDF funding. Reflecting the project-based application process at that time, most bids were submitted on a project-by-project basis and were for resources to alleviate the effects of particular economic set-backs. Local authorities tended to cultivate strong bi-lateral links with the Commission, operating independently of neighbouring authorities and other local agencies, and the bulk of the EU assistance they received was normally devoted to large infrastructure projects. Examples include assistance to Corby District Council and South Glamorgan County Council to alleviate the effects of steel closures, Birmingham's city centre regeneration strategy and harbour and road improvements in the Highlands and Islands region.

The 1988 reform of the Structural Funds led to very significant changes in UK local authorities' approaches to accessing EU assistance (see Chapter

2). A combination of the substantial increase in the amount of available assistance and the designation of large parts of Britain as priority areas under Objectives 2 and 5b meant that a growing number of authorities sought to gain funding. By 1993 the process of lobbying for resources was therefore taken extremely seriously by a very large number of authorities which had not previously been actively involved, notably London boroughs and many English shire district councils.

Local Authority Structures and Strategies

The importance attached to EU regional policy and other 'European issues' by a growing number of UK local authorities is manifested in a number of changes to their internal structures and in new forms of external collaboration.

There have been two particularly significant internal responses to EU regional policy. First, there has been a wave of recent appointments of 'European officers'. Whilst some authorities have had specialist 'European' staff since the mid-1980s, they have, until recently, been in a small minority (Audit Commission 1992). By 1995, however, 73 per cent of authorities had appointed one or more 'European officers', 50 per cent had one or more full-time 'European officers', one in ten had a specialist 'European Unit' and more than half of all full-time 'European officers' were employed on Principal Officer grades or above (Martin 1997a). Not surprisingly, the larger authorities and those located in Objective 1, 2 or 5b regions (Scottish regional councils, English county councils and metropolitan districts in the north of England and Midlands) had the largest numbers of 'European officers' and tended to have appointed them at the most senior grades.

Second, many authorities have begun to develop corporate approaches to drawing down EU regional assistance and responding to other EU policy initiatives. Even in the most active authorities, these issues have, until quite recently, been seen as the preserve of specialist 'European officers' – who have normally been based in Economic Development or Planning Departments. Recently, however, some authorities have developed 'European' strategies and action plans covering all departments. Many have also moved their 'European officers' and 'European Units' to the Chief Executive's Department (John 1994). This has two benefits: it signals a corporate commitment to responding to 'European issues' and it has enabled 'European officers' to take a more corporate view of the opportunities associated with EU funding. We found that, in 1995, 43 per cent of authorities which had specialist 'European officers' had located them in the Chief Executive's

Department, 24 per cent in Economic Development and 12 per cent in Planning Departments. Similar percentages applied to the departmental location of 'European Units'.

The increasingly corporate approach to 'European issues' is also evidenced in the attempts being made by local authorities to involve a wider range of officers from across service departments in the preparation of programmes and projects for which EU funding is sought. By 1995, 35 per cent of authorities had created cross-departmental-officer working groups specialising in 'European issues' and 27 per cent had nominated 'European contacts' in each department (Martin 1997a). Most authorities also report that elected members are becoming better informed about and increasingly involved in 'European issues', although many admit that councillors are principally concerned with finding out 'what's in it' for their areas and remain unaware of the broader implications of closer European integration. Not surprisingly, therefore, increased member involvement is particularly marked in London boroughs (more than 20 of which bid for Objective 2 funding in 1993) and Scottish regional councils (many of which became eligible for Objective 1 (Highlands and Islands) or Objective 5b for the first time in 1994).

Externally, one of the most significant impacts of EU regional policy at the local level has been the way in which the programmatic approach, embodied in CSFs, has encouraged partnership between local authorities and other 'social and economic partners'. In this respect EU regional policy has reinforced the co-operative effect of domestic programmes, notably City Challenge and the Single Regeneration Budget (Chester-Kadwell and Martin 1994). Local authorities have also been forced to place greater reliance on partnership because constraints on mainstream budgets have meant that they can no longer provide sufficient funding of their own to match that obtained by their areas from the Structural Funds (Martin 1997b).

Whilst central government has stressed the need for local public-private partnerships, its allocation of resources through competitive bidding and the process of local government review, have in pratice tended to discourage collaboration across local authority boundaries. By contrast, EU programmes have provided a real incentive for neighbouring authorities to collaborate with each other.

Attempts at 'region building' (through increased intra-regional collaboration) have been signalled by the growing number of Brussels offices which are funded by regional consortia. Examples include the Scotland Europa Office, the Wales European Centre, the offices for the North-East and East Midlands regions and Birmingham City Council's recent decision to give up its own office in favour of a facility which it will share with other West

Midlands authorities. This trend is in marked contrast to the situation in the early and mid-1980s when authorities such as Birmingham City Council, Strathclyde Regional Council and Kent County Council opened offices to gain a competitive edge over their neighbours. There have, though, been problems, notably in Nottinghamshire where the County Council has been represented by the office it co-funds with other county councils in the region while Nottingham City Council has operated through a separate office which it shares with a number of district councils and the TEC. Moreover, sharing a Brussels office, though symbolically important, does not guarantee greater intra-regional collaboration. Indeed, in some cases it owes more to a desire to reduce running costs than to present a unified 'voice' on behalf of the region.

In spite of the inevitable fragmentation caused by the lack of an elected regional government, the explicitly 'regional' or 'sub-regional' focus of CSFs has spawned strategic alliances between authorities – particularly at what might be called the 'lobbying' or 'bidding' stage (Martin 1996). However, as was illustrated by the process of preparing regional strategies for the present round of Structural Fund assistance, the strength, coherence and significance of regional and sub-regional collaboration varies considerably. Moreover, through its regional offices in England and the Welsh and Scottish Offices, central government dominates the planning and implementation process. These offices determine the composition of the regional monitoring committees and have usually provided most of the staff who comprise the secretariat. Also, as in previous rounds, the plans setting out the proposed uses of EU regional policy assistance in each region for 1994–1996/99 round were formally submitted to the Commission by central government not local partners.

However, there is scope for local and regional actors to become involved at a number of stages in the process. Although the framework regulations for 1994–1996 allowed for a dominant role to be played in the UK by national government, they also required that strategies be established through close consultations between the Commission, the Member State concerned and the competent authorities designated by the latter at national, regional or other level (Commission of the European Communities 1993d). This was seen as an attempt by the Commission to secure an enhanced role for local agencies, some of which responded by working more closely together in order to make the best possible case for their regions and their preferred strategies.

A number of witnesses to the recent Commons Trade and Industry Select Committee's enquiry into regional policy considered that these efforts had been largely irrelevant because there was very little evidence of meaningful local input to Single Programming Documents (SPDs). According to this view, central government departments in effect wrote the same economic strategy for each area 'apart from the fact that the name of a particular region was tippexed out and new names written in' (Trade and Industry Select Committee 1995). However, as the Select Committee notes, Commission officials argue that these deficiencies were at least partially remedied during the period of negotiations with central government which followed the submission of regional plans. Many local authorities support the Commission's view, claiming that they were able to exert significant influence through informal discussions with the officials in Brussels. Because there were wide variations between regions in terms of local authorities' willingness to collaborate, the attitudes of other economic and social 'partners' and differences of approach between central government's regional offices (Martin and Pearce 1993), it is possible to use experiences from different areas to support either view.

Relatively strong regional coalitions were, for example, forged in the West Midlands, the north-east of England and in some sub-regions (including east Lancashire and Coventry-Warwickshire). The district councils in east Lancashire and the authorities in the West Midlands in the Objective 2 region believe that by operating together they were able to increase the EU funding they received. The east Lancashire authorities have a history of intense local rivalry. However, prompted by the fear that they would lose Objective 2 status from 1994 onwards because of improvements in employment rates in the sub-region, they worked hard to present a 'united front', operating in part through an alliance known as the East Lancashire Promotional Partnership. They believe that the effectiveness of this sub-regional co-operation enabled them to convince the Commission of the continuing needs of their areas in a way which would not have been possible had each borough attempted to present its own individual case in isolation from the others. Similarly, the authorities within the West Midlands report that they have worked more closely together in recent years following indications from the Commission that presenting a 'regional' case for Objective 2 was likely to be the most successful approach. Naturally, once the total allocation for the region has been decided, each authority then attempts to maximise its own share of this. Until that point in the process, however, Birmingham and the smaller authorities which surround it (especially Coventry City Council and the Black Country authorities) have worked together to produce a more integrated strategy for the area as a whole. They believe that this has contributed to their success in securing the largest Objective 2 programme in the UK for the period 1994–1996.

In contrast, local agencies in the north-west of England and Yorkshire and Humberside found it far more difficult to collaborate and it seems that rather flimsy, informal regional alliances only just held together, largely because of strong indications from Brussels that co-operation was a prerequisite of funding. In the South West region, Devon and Cornwall County Councils claim to have worked closely in preparing a sub-regional strategy and Objective 5b programmes. They have also forged formal links with business and other partners through the newly formed West Country Development Corporation. They admit, however, that it has been more difficult to integrate their plans for the sub-region with strategies for the South West as a whole, a fact which seems to have been acknowledged by central government which has recently established what is, in effect, a 'branch' of the South West Regional Office in Plymouth to handle the special needs of the sub-region.

In spite of the evidence that, in some areas, agencies have collaborated more fully than in the past, this has not necessarily led to improved plans or better implementation. For example, Lloyd (1995) has argued that the strategies produced for Objective 2 regions in the UK simply 'rolled forward' previous plans. In his view they 'were lacking in imagination...framed around a desire to draw down, spend and account for European Structural Funds assistance for particular (predetermined) projects' (p.161). Local authorities claim that this lack of innovation is largely because of the retrospective receipt of EU funding. They argue that because EU funding is not normally approved until after projects have been implemented, they cannot risk applying for assistance for schemes which they are not already committed to proceeding with and which they are confident will meet the relevant eligibility criteria. Given this, and the bureaucratic delays which frequently occur between approval and payment of grant aid, authorities believe that they must inevitably 'play safe'. This is turn encourages the development of a patchwork quilt of *ad hoc*, unco-ordinated, 'funding driven' initiatives. According to many local authorities, progress towards greater integration and strategic decision making would require an easing of the constraints placed on local budgets and powers by national government and more efficient mechanisms for the allocation and distribution of EU funding at regional, national and European levels.

Discussion

In this chapter I have suggested that the availability of EU regional policy assistance has had potentially significant impacts on the activities and perspectives of UK local authorities. It has opened up a range of new opportunities for networking with other local and regional authorities across Europe through which they can 'communicate criticisms of policy and generate ideas for new policy initiatives' (Peterson 1995). It has also provided many authorities with resources for regeneration initiatives and led to new opportunities for bureau enlargement by individual local authority officers and elected members.

There is some evidence then that the availability of EU regional policy assistance is contributing to the emergence of new styles of policy making at the local level. There are signs of a more widespread appreciation of the implications of closer European integration even among local authorities which have not traditionally been active in 'European issues'. Moreover, in some areas, embryonic regeneration partnerships are being forged between neighbouring authorities and with other agencies, and these have begun to re-kindle interest in strategic planning. In this respect, EU regional policy has provided a valuable counterweight to 'the absence of positive strategic planning at regional level' (Roberts 1993) and UK central government's strong 'principled and political opposition to regionalism' (Moore 1992) throughout the last twenty years.

However, this chapter has also highlighted a number of important and persistent problems. Although signs of increased intra-regional collaboration may be welcomed, the commitment to genuine partnership is at best 'patchy'. In theory, EU regional policies could enable local partners to identify and exploit synergies through the integration of multi-funded programmes supported by the Commission, national government and a wide range of local agencies (including local authorities, business, TECs and LECs, English Partnerships and the voluntary sector). In practice, however, many 'partnerships' operate in a purely instrumental fashion, designed to draw down the maximum possible level of external assistance, and few would survive in the absence of this funding. Whilst regional strategies purport to take a long-term view, most are, in practice, geared to securing resources in the short/medium term. They cannot, therefore, be seen as evidence of a radical shift in the style of local governence. Whereas some of the ways in which EU policies have shaped and shifted local priorities (for example the move away from support for hard infrastructure projects (notably road building) to softer initiatives such as investment in human capital and business development) may be welcome, there is clearly a danger that increasing dependence on EU funding can distort local programmes. Thus local authorities and other local agencies, increasingly intent on drawing down the maximum possible levels of EU assistance, have undoubtedly 'bent' their priorities in order to put forward projects which meet EU eligibility criteria but which may not address the strategic needs of their areas.

It is clear that, as their budgets have diminished, local authorities have lost the capacity to implement their own economic strategies except by working with, and ceding power to, other local agencies. This is, of course, precisely what central government intended, but it means that emerging 'partnership' is a product of the weakening of UK local government rather than evidence of a genuine recognition of the interests which local authorities share with other local agencies. Moreover, partnerships are overwhelmingly dominated by local government and private sector élites which are the major beneficiaries of EU programmes. Whilst EU funding has encouraged these existing 'players' to take on new roles, it has done little to enhance the influence of the voluntary or community sectors.

UK national government has been at the forefront of attempts to increase community involvement in regeneration schemes – notably through City Challenge and the Single Regeneration Budget (which in turn has influenced the development of the EU's URBAN Community Initiative launched in 1994 and aimed at making the problems facing inner city areas in many parts of the Union, in innovative ways, through support for economic, social and environment schemes). However, Britain lacks a participative tradition and does not have a strong sense of civic society. As a result, much more pro-active approaches to building local capacity will be required if a wider range of local interest groups are to be genuinely involved in the process of bidding for and using EU funding.

Similarly, in the absence of a regional tier of government in the UK, building coalitions of interest between local authorities has been an extremely time consuming and difficult processand become more problematic because of the introduction of Regional Challenge, which extended the principle of allocating resources through competition to EU funds and therefore gives added impetus to the search 'competitive advantage' over neighbouring authorities.

Furthermore, there is a series of concerns about the weakness of UK sub-national government and the continued dominance of the policy making process by central government. Central government regional offices effectively control monitoring committees and the agencies which were able to participate in the formulation of regional plans for EU funding in 1993 were carefully delineated by central government to include its own client groups. Furthermore, ministers continue to act as the gatekeepers for EU funding by virtue of their seat at the Council of Ministers and through the formulation of SPDs (Anderson 1990). They also continue to play a leading role in the designation of areas which are eligible for Structural Fund assistance (Wishlade 1994), and the Treasury retains tight control over local authority budgets and thus the levels of funding available to match EU assistance. Moreover, there is a continuing concern that the introduction of integrated regional offices in England represents an attempt by Whitehall to seize the vacant regional ground (Morphet 1993) by putting in place arrangements which will eventually enable regional directors to wield substantial powers (similar to those enjoyed by the Scottish and Welsh Office) and to portray themselves as the 'voice' of their regions.

The demise of the Scottish regional councils, Welsh county councils and some English counties is a further cause for concern. In the short term the process of local government review has undoubtedly intensified conflicts between authorities and made collaboration on bids for EU funding more difficult (Martin and Pearce 1994). In the longer term the breaking up of some of the largest authorities is likely to hamper attempts by UK sub-national government to forge links with the Commission and with much larger regions in other member states (Barber and Millns 1993; AMA 1992).

There is growing evidence that strong 'bottom up' networks of local agencies combined with local administrations possessing the power and resources to animate them is an important ingredient in the success of many of Europe's most prosperous regions (Bennett and Krebs 1994; Leonardi 1992; Marin 1990; Grahl and Teague 1990). Some commentators believe that in the long term it will be possible to secure an enhanced role for such networks in the UK through bodies such as the Committee of Regions and by gaining formal recognition of the role which sub-national government plays in the EU's policy making processes. They argue that the emerging institutional patterns and power relations are complex and fluid and that sub-national government will flourish as the sovereignty of the nation state is first 'perforated' and then withers away (Marks 1993). In the context of local economic regeneration, EU regional policies have already led to modest changes in the style of policy making and implementation in some areas which, whilst not unproblematic, may in the long term stimulate institutional innovations and a modest improvement in the competitiveness of UK regions. However, in spite of British local authorities' growing awareness of the opportunities associated with closer European integration and their increasing technical and political competence in exploiting them, really significant changes await the relaxation of central government's tight grip on the scope for local discretion and self-determination and recognition of new forms of constitutional and political expression at the regional level.

Acknowledgement

This chapter draws upon an earlier conference paper written by the author and Graham Pearce. The author acknowledges with gratitude Graham's contribution, and research assistance provided by Tanya Crook. The research on which it is based was funded by the Economic and Social Research Council (Award Number R000234671).

CHAPTER 5

Inserting a Local Dimension into Regional Programmes

The Experience of Western Scotland

Ivan Turok

Introduction

The Structural Funds have traditionally been deployed as instruments of regional policy, with limited concern for disparities within regions. They have also been used to promote economic growth, with less interest in distributional issues, social conditions and the quality of everyday life. The current regional programmes in Britain, and to a lesser extent France, mark an interesting departure in some respects. Unlike previous programmes, or those in other European countries, they seek to target part of their resources towards disadvantaged areas within their regions. Equally important, they imply a broader and more inclusive approach to development than practised in the past. A preliminary indication can be obtained from the terminology used for this 'priority for action': it is called Community Economic Development, Economic and Social Cohesion, or Urban and Community Regeneration. In Britain this priority has been allocated between a tenth and two-fifths of the total funds within each programme (see Table 5.1), so it is clearly important. France is the only other EU country where Structural Funds are explicitly allocated to this objective, and on a more limited scale than in Britain (see Chapter 13).

The new priority could be even more significant for the future. Encouraged by the European Commission, it is being expanded in the 1997–1999 programmes. It could also pave the way for a more radical reshaping of the Structural Funds, based on the themes of spatial concentration, community involvement and socio-economic development. Arguments for this could be put forward on various grounds. For example, enlargement of the EU

Table 5.1 Community economic development in British Objective 1 and 2 regions (1994–1996)

	Value of SF devoted to CED (mecu)	*Share of total SF in CED*	*Proportion of region's population in target areas*	*SF spend per capita in target areas (ecu)*
Eastern Scotland	11.9	9.8%	22%	48
East London	19.5	26.5%	35%	101
East Midlands	15	18.9%	20%	109
Greater Manchester	55.8	17.0%	33%	60
North-East England	33.9	11.0%	25%	52
Plymouth	3.2	11.2%	14%	87
South Wales	61.3	32.6%	46%	78
Strathclyde	40.3	14.1%	24%	72
West Cumbria	3.37	13.5%	20%	70
West Midlands	88.5	23.9%	35%	83
Yorkshire and Humberside	58.8	18.8%	35%	65
Average for Objective 2	**35.6**	**17.9%**	**28%**	**75**
Merseyside	180.5*	44.2%	35%	374
Highlands and Islands	23.5*	15.1%	15%	427
Overall Average	**45.8**	**19.7%**	**28%**	**125**

Note: * over three rather than six years to permit comparisons with Objective 2 regions.

Source: Derived from European Commission (1995); Lloyd *et al.* (1996).

eastwards will strain the already stretched budget, encouraging rationing through a more spatially targeted approach. Increasing polarisation between areas in Britain (Hills 1995) and widening intra-regional disparities throughout Europe (Commission of the European Communities 1994g) could justify stronger local rather than regional programmes. Growing income inequalities and higher unemployment, together with rising crime and other symptoms of 'economic and social exclusion', may also force policy makers to broaden the development agenda and be more receptive to people who actually experience the problems. Conventional measures to promote regional economic growth, involving physical infrastructure, business development and standardised training, do not work well in the most deprived areas. A more imaginative, integrated and participative approach seems essential.

Such lessons are already emerging from experience with the new priority. It has presented the main partners at all levels, local through to European, with major challenges in devising effective policies using established instruments and procedures. These will obviously intensify if the Structural Funds are reoriented as suggested. Promoting economic and social cohesion is far more complicated than building roads and factories or running standard training programmes. There are difficult conceptual and practical issues to be addressed: what is the appropriate scope and definition of this form of development, since it is potentially very wide? What are the key areas of social improvement and how do they relate to economic regeneration? What institutional mechanisms are suitable, how should they be financed and how can innovation be encouraged? How should target areas be identified and how selective should the policy be? Can a 'bottom-up' approach involving community participation be built into a longer term strategic perspective? Indeed, what is the relationship between local initiatives and wider city and regional development strategies, and how can the inevitable tensions and trade-offs be reconciled? Put another way, what are the relative costs and benefits of local targeting for regional development?

This chapter discusses experience in Strathclyde (Western Scotland), which was the first regional programme in Britain to propose such a priority. Better progress has been made here than elsewhere in developing answers to the above questions, reflecting the longer history of urban regeneration, partnership working and tradition of pragmatism. The regional partnership first suggested this priority to the Commission when negotiating the 1994–1996 SPD, calling it Economic and Social Cohesion. This was an opportune time, since the issue of exclusion was a mounting concern and the contribution of local initiatives to development and employment was gaining increased recognition (e.g. Commission of the European Communities 1995a). The Commission was so persuaded of the idea's merits that it ended up encouraging all the other Objective 1 and 2 regions in Britain to include something similar in their plans. The chapter starts by setting the priority in a broader conceptual context.

Community Economic Development and the Structural Funds

The term 'Economic and Social Cohesion' is more of an abstract goal than a description of the measures being promoted through the Structural Funds. The concept of Community Economic Development (CED) is more concrete, although it still contains ambiguities (Boothroyd and Davis 1993). Put simply, it can be defined as the range of activities intended to improve the economic and social welfare of a community, with the emphasis on employment and income as fundamental to the sustainability of physical and social improvements. Beyond this broad statement, CED can perhaps best be specified in terms of four key themes or elements drawn from current thinking and practice.

First, CED is partly intended to counter the historical neglect and inadequacy of mainstream government programmes concerned with infrastructure, the environment, education, training and business development by reorienting them to serve marginalised communities better. A key objective is to attract more jobs and investment towards these areas, partly because the commuting distances of the poor tend to be short and the ability of the unemployed to compete for jobs diminishes the further they are from where they live. Other aims are to help local people to compete for jobs more effectively and to enable them to create their own jobs through business formation. They may involve directing a larger share of the resources of local authorities, further education colleges and government agencies towards areas of need, but it probably also entails refashioning and enhancing their services to meet these needs more effectively. By actively engaging local people in the process, policies and services may be made more relevant and responsive to their requirements. For example, it is increasingly apparent that many households need jobs for women and men (i.e. both partners) if it is to be worth getting back into work, because wages at the bottom of the labour market have fallen, rents and dependency on housing benefit have risen and it is harder to get back onto income support once relinquished. Such 'facts of life' are very familiar to poor people but often overlooked by policy makers, which is why consulting and listening to them is so important. Locally-based arrangements may also become more innovative and cohesive and their impacts more durable by building links between separate, centrally-devised programmes. Partnerships involving the major agencies and the community are potential mechanisms to promote this kind of programme bending, co-ordination and decentralisation of control.

Second, CED means encouraging economic development by investing in a foundation of local social institutions. Community groups and networks of various kinds provide a crucial framework of mutual support, knowledge, confidence and trust for economic progress. This community strength or 'social capital' is 'essential for economic renewal... Social capital can encourage new investment as well as making existing investment go further; it is the glue that bonds the benefits of economic and physical capital into marginalised communities' (Commission on Social Justice 1994, p.308). Social cohesion may make places more attractive to live and invest, encourage creativity and risk, help people setting up businesses to find funds, advice, suppliers and customers, and make it easier for the unemployed to gain assistance and information for job seeking. An absence of it certainly makes things very difficult. In many older inner city areas, communities may have retained some of their past cohesion and organisation, providing a base on which to build. However, isolation and despair seem more common in peripheral housing estates, requiring greater effort at community capacity building alongside the provision of economic infrastructure. Patient investment of this kind could begin to harness the energy and initiative of people towards socio-economic reconstruction and development. Its importance is already well recognised in rural areas such as the Highlands, as the House of Commons' Scottish Affairs Committee recently discovered: 'Highlands and Islands Enterprise told us that their social powers were jealously guarded. The social or community role was seen as vital to economic development; for example, the provision of a village hall provided a community with the means for working together and could lead in turn to pressure on the LEC for assistance on projects' (Scottish Affairs Committee 1995, p.viii).

Third, part of the purpose of CED-type activity is to maximise the job possibilities arising from the third sector or 'social economy', in recognition of the fact that the mainstream economy is unlikely to generate sufficient opportunities to absorb all those seeking work for the foreseeable future (Blakely 1994). Opportunities to gain transferable skills, create local jobs, form businesses and generate incomes may stem from public spending on housing and environmental improvements, leisure, amenity and cultural projects, and other social investments. In future more may arise from supporting the proliferation of local schemes to cater for unmet needs for services of various kinds, including child care, security, home help, information technology, maintenance of open areas and recycling of used products (CEC 1995a). The privatisation and contracting out of public services create greater need and opportunity for local provision. Realising these possibilities requires a more creative approach to project development and financial packaging than normal. Public bodies need to provide more flexible resources to support this kind of activity, and to accept greater risks in the process, recognising the inherent value in local control and ownership. Exploring alternatives also requires greater experimentation.

Fourth, CED involves fostering links between localities and integrating local development measures with city-wide and regional strategies. This may help to counteract the marginalisation of communities and divisive competition that may otherwise develop between them for resources, population and jobs. Such links are also important to share experience and avoid having to continually re-invent ideas pioneered elsewhere. In addition, collaboration is required to secure economies of scale and expertise in service provision. Certain functions may be better provided at city level, such as labour market intelligence, employer liaison, specialised training programmes and investment funds. A strategic perspective for CED is also important to manage the tensions between local and city/regional objectives and to address the complex issues of displacement, spill-over effects, etc that arise from local actions.

The Origins in Strathclyde

The CED priority in Strathclyde emerged against the background of a long tradition of support for this type of activity, albeit without a consistent definition or identity for it. Regeneration agencies had been set up in most large, deprived areas of Glasgow and in some of the surrounding industrial towns within the previous decade. This reflected a growing acceptance among the major city and regional authorities that some resources should be specifically targeted towards disadvantaged communities. The 1991 census revealed that Glasgow had the highest proportion of households without anyone in work of any local authority in Britain. The city's manufacturing jobs fell dramatically from 107,500 in 1978 to 37,000 by 1993, while the net increase in the service sector was only 6500. The population fell from 1.1 million in the 1950s to only 623,000 in 1991. In some inner city and peripheral areas there are vast areas of derelict land and bleak housing estates with serious problems of unemployment, deprivation and drug abuse. City unemployment is officially 14 per cent (19% for men), but this obscures considerable hidden unemployment through people recorded as sick or retired but actually able and keen to work if jobs were available. Official male and female activity rates are much lower in Glasgow than in the rest of Scotland.

Integrated area initiatives operating within partnership structures were seen as an effective method for promoting local regeneration. The Western Scotland SPD asserted: 'The model is successful and could be further developed' (Strathclyde European Partnership 1995, p.54). The partners wanted to extend Structural Funds to these agencies, particularly ERDF. They had received little of it in the past, partly because there was more matched funding available for infrastructure projects elsewhere (e.g. in the new towns); the take-up of mainstream business development and training programmes was low in poor areas; and potential projects here compared unfavourably in terms of conventional economic outputs (e.g. private sector leverage) with investments in more prosperous areas. There was also a suspicion lurking in some quarters that economic development in Glasgow's inner areas and peripheral estates was neglected because of an official mindset that tended to dismiss the city as a poor location for industry and full of unemployable people.

Agreement among the partners to support 'arms-length' agencies arose partly because of the relative maturity of the partnership and its fairly balanced composition. The existence of an independent secretariat for about five years has helped considerably. It is not directed by any single partner, but is financed by and accountable to the partnership as a whole. It has always tried to promote relationships with and between the partners based on openness and trust. Local regeneration initiatives have proved useful vehicles for partners to collaborate on tangible projects. In addition, the originator of the partnership, Strathclyde Regional Council, had pursued an area-based anti-poverty strategy since the late 1970s, with a strong social and community orientation that influenced other regeneration thinking. It had also supported local economic agencies since helping to set up the Govan Initiative in 1986. The Urban Programme (jointly funded by the Scottish Office and local authorities) has been important in providing relatively unconstrained, long-term resources for social and economic projects in deprived areas, particularly those run by voluntary and community groups. In 1993 the Scottish Office proposed a more integrated, area-based approach, concentrating most of the resources onto fewer areas (Scottish Office 1993). Well before this, the Scottish Development Agency and local authorities such as Glasgow District had seen advantages in devolving certain economic development and training functions to dedicated local agencies in order to provide a more responsive service. They and their successors have been supporting small area partnerships for almost 20 years (Keating and Boyle 1986). Key lessons include the need for effective collaboration between organisations, the importance of community involvement and the need for a comprehensive, strategic approach linking different aspects of regeneration (Scottish Office 1993).

Part of the purpose of the CED priority was simply to divert more resources for economic development to agencies in the deprived areas. Most were short of funds (particularly for innovative and integrated initiatives) because support from the main partners was restricted and typically tied to projects with specific, short-term outputs. The CED priority also sought to broaden the scope of established activity. The SPD stated that it wished to encourage more imaginative projects and acknowledged the need for flexibility and patience before benefits were achieved (SEP 1995). It also favoured integrated actions at the local level to ensure they reinforced each other. It suggested there was 'evidence of the clear advantages to local regeneration objectives from a partnership approach – both from cohesion at the strategic planning/development stages and from an integrated approach to implementation' (SEP 1995, p.54). Beyond these general assertions and aspirations there was little discussion of the concept of economic and social cohesion or CED.

Delimiting the CED Priority

CED was one of four priorities for action in the regional programme, which had two overarching objectives: to enhance the competitiveness of the western Scotland economy in order to improve economic growth, job prospects and the quality of life and to improve economic and social cohesion within the region in order to increase economic opportunities for individuals and communities faced with growing social and economic exclusion (SEP 1995, p.21). The strategy sought to tackle the region's problems of continuing industrial and employment decline, out-migration, structural economic weaknesses and the social and physical consequences of industrial decline. It focused on developing the indigenous business sector and involved direct financial and consultancy support for SMEs, improvement of the business environment, development of human skills through training programmes and promotion of tourism. The total value of European funds was 286 million ecu (mecu), 33 per cent of which was devoted to business development, 38 per cent to business infrastructure, 13 per cent to tourism and 14 per cent to CED.

The CED strategy amounted to making funds available for two types of activity or 'measures'. First, there was 27.5 mecu of ERDF for 'business development and sustainability'. The aim was: 'To support the development of the local economies of the areas by the development of existing businesses and the creation of new businesses, particularly those linked to local community initiatives, environmental improvement programmes and commercial developments' (SEP 1995, p.57). The list of eligible projects was wider than this, including business premises, finance and consultancy services, derelict land clearance, vocational training facilities, new transport initiatives and access roads to industrial sites. The emphasis was on hard and soft infrastructure to attract investment and facilitate the start-up and growth of local businesses rather than on more interventionist measures to develop businesses directly. The message was that disadvantaged areas have underutilised physical and human assets that could contribute to regional economic growth, given extra investment. The overall target of the measure was to reduce unemployment in the designated areas by creating 650 jobs in local businesses. It did not indicate by how much unemployment might be reduced nor the likely displacement effects and net regional impact. It could not have been thought through carefully since it implied a public cost of £70,000 per job created locally. At worst this could be interpreted as the cost of diverting jobs into the disadvantaged areas from elsewhere in the region – a rather high opportunity cost.

Second, there was 12.8 mecu of ESF for 'human resource development'. The aim was: 'To provide and enhance pathways to employment by developing a range of spatially targeted training and related actions aimed at residents from disadvantaged areas that integrate with ERDF supported and other socio-economic development schemes in the area' (SEP 1995, p.59). Possible projects included different kinds of vocational and foundation training, recruitment subsidies, employment guidance and counselling, job search support, business start-up training and schemes to promote home-school-employer links. The overall object was to reduce unemployment in the designated areas by developing people's skills, with no quantified target in this case. ESF had been used in the past in disadvantaged areas to support training, counselling and confidence-building. In future it would need to be integrated better with ERDF support and part of a broader economic strategy for the area.

The definition of these measures was rather conventional, perhaps reflecting the tentative status of the priority and the cautious climate of opinion in the public sector at the time. Doubts had arisen about the viability of community enterprise and financial stringency discouraged imaginative thinking and risk-taking. Partnership policies usually progress slowly and incrementally and Strathclyde's has been no exception. The SPD approach was based on creating jobs locally by attracting inward investment and supporting local businesses and helping people to get these and other jobs by enhancing their skills. There was little mention of wider dimensions of CED, such as the role of the social economy in absorbing unemployment, the building of community capacity and the reshaping of mainstream economic and social policies. There was also no discussion of the relationship between the local strategy in each area and city-wide regeneration, or with the broader regional programme. There was a possibility that the priority could end up as a gesture, separate from and marginal to the rest of the programme, which would be 'business as usual'.

During 1995 a formal Advisory Group was set up by the partnership to oversee implementation of the priority, to appraise project bids and make recommendations to the Programme Management Committee. It consisted of 12 individuals appointed for their expertise from the partner organisations, including the local regeneration initiatives. They took a slightly broader view of CED than the SPD, in keeping with the spirit of economic and social cohesion, and set out with the secretariat to encourage a wider range of schemes to come forward. They commissioned a former council official with considerable experience in the field to visit the target areas in order raise awareness of the priority, to encourage new project proposals and to examine the obstacles faced. The group also devised explicit criteria and a scoring system for appraising proposals. These tended to reiterate the objectives of the priority (for project integration, partnership, local involvement, economic viability, local regeneration mechanisms, etc), without being more specific. They were deliberately loose to allow applicants flexibility to present projects in their own terms. However, one of the drawbacks of this style was the limited guidance provided about what measures the partnership considered important, with a danger of misinterpretation and confusion on the part of organisations applying for funds. The open-ended approach could also result in the priority becoming a collection of diverse and discrete projects, probably useful at the local level but showing little overall coherence.

Strathclyde's method of selecting target areas was cleverer than that elsewhere. The first criterion was common enough, based on socio-economic need and using indicators such as unemployment, income, health, crime and qualifications. Second, a degree of inter-agency commitment was required to tackle the area's problems in a co-ordinated way, preferably in the form of a local partnership organisation including the local community and private sector. Third, an agreed economic strategy or business plan was needed that analysed the problems and set out the approach to tackling them, with clear priorities and targets (SEP 1995). So it was not an abstract statistical exercise that simply identified areas of greatest need; it required local political backing and a delivery mechanism/strategy to be in existence. This was partly pragmatic, reflecting the short time-scale of the programme and the need to proceed quickly with committing the funds (it had two years to do three years' work because of late approval of the plan by the Commission). It did not offer localities resources to build capacity or to develop their strategies and projects, unlike some of the regional programmes in England. For example, Merseyside had a six-year programme and could afford more time for planning and development. It also needed this more since it did not inherit the same institutional structures.

A detailed account of the procedure that was followed and the justification for including or excluding specific areas has not been produced. It seems to have started with basic lists of the most deprived areas identified in recent statistical analyses undertaken by the Scottish Office and Strathclyde Region

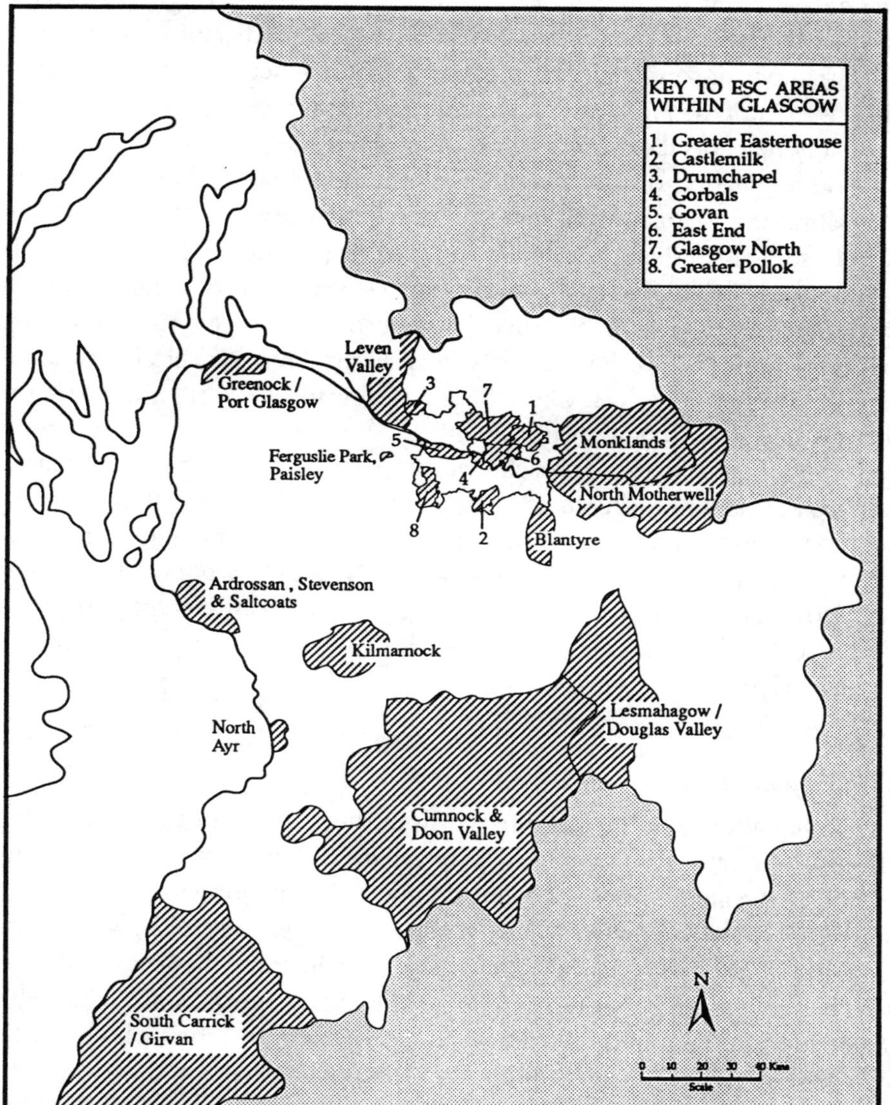

Source: Based on 1994–96 SPD

Figure 5.1 Economic and social cohesion areas within Western Scotland

followed by selection of those that met the second and third criteria, even if only in fairly rudimentary terms. This resulted in 16 areas being included at the outset, eight in Glasgow and eight outwith the city (Figure 5.1). Four more were included the following year after local partnership organisations were set up in areas that already met the criterion of need. Several other areas that were not included subsequently applied for recognition. This will probably be considered for the next programme.

The population of the 20 areas is about a quarter of the regional total, indicating that the approach is less selective than appears at first sight. It is also less selective than in several other regions (column 3, Table 5.1, p.68), so the level of resources available per capita is very limited (column 4, Table 5.1). The target areas in Strathclyde are also quite large, with an average population of 27,700. This is partly to ensure viability for certain economic development services. However, there is considerable variation between areas: some cover whole districts while others cover single housing estates, reflecting the pragmatic approach that was pursued. No distinction was made between areas with different development needs and potential. Some areas are so large in terms of population and physical area that the resources cannot be expected to have much impact (Glasgow North has a population of over 69,000). In Merseyside there are 38 target areas with an average population of 12,700 and a level of Structural Funds five times higher per person than in Strathclyde.

Local Champions

Implementation of CED has differed from the other priorities in requiring projects to demonstrate some local consultation or bottom-up involvement, although the amount has not been specified. The intention was that most of the resources would go to the local regeneration agencies, which would have established arrangements for community participation and acted as drivers for change. Most are registered as limited liability companies with charitable status to avoid tax. They are controlled by boards of directors who typically comprise individuals representing the main public agencies, the local community and private sector. There are tensions between their responsibilities to their parent bodies and their legal obligations as company directors, which has sometimes worked to the detriment of the local agencies. There are undoubted advantages in the individuals formally representing their parent bodies, in terms of the link into mainstream policies and resources and the legitimacy derived from having representatives of the community and private sector on board. However, their depth of commitment to the companies has been questioned occasionally, since their principal loyalties and responsibilities lie elsewhere. Several agencies have experienced financial and political difficulties at some time because their directors were less supportive or diligent than they should have been.

The levels of community representation on the company boards range from a small proportion to 50 per cent. In most cases this is not regarded as a sufficient or particularly effective means of local accountability. Tensions have sometimes arisen between the go-ahead style of some agencies and the requirements of their community representatives for greater consultation and control. Some have established other mechanisms for local people to be involved, for example through consultative forums, informal liaison with community groups or simple everyday feedback from clients. The agencies have different approaches, stemming partly from their different origins and objectives. Some have arisen from community-based Urban Programme schemes while others perceive themselves as having a narrower economic remit. Some have grown very quickly by developing ideas for new projects and applying energetically to a range of public bodies to sponsor them. Consequently, they differ greatly in size – from half a dozen staff at one extreme to over a hundred staff and an annual budget of £5m at the other. The Govan Initiative is the largest and longest-established.

The strengths of this approach include the relative autonomy and local presence of the local agencies. At their best they act as vigorous advocates or champions for their areas, pressing for increased support from public and private organisations based elsewhere. They are in closer contact with local conditions than higher authorities and so are better placed to understand and respond to local needs and opportunities. This is particularly important in the peripheral estates because of the city-centre orientation of the main partners. The local agencies have pressed for a range of facilities to be provided close-by. In addition, closer contact with realities on the ground has sometimes stimulated innovative thinking and acted as a useful corrective to far-fetched proposals introduced from elsewhere. The agencies operate outside the scope of normal public sector procedures, which can be bureaucratic and fragmented, so decision making should be quicker. Issues can also be treated in a more holistic and integrated way because the agencies are smaller, less compartmental and free from many statutory responsibilities. Their independent status enables them to tap into different financial sources and assemble funding packages in creative ways, although such cocktails have proved difficult to administer.

The weaknesses include the inequity resulting from the fragmentation and uneven institutional capacity that has developed between target areas.

Table 5.2 shows the wide variation in the allocation of Structural Funds under the CED priority that has resulted. The figures are not complete but limited to the 1996 round of ESF projects (about a third of the ultimate total) and all the ERDF projects approved at the time of writing (early 1996). ERDF support is particularly uneven: areas outside Glasgow have received only one-sixth of the funds committed to areas within the city. The variable take-up of ESF and ERDF reflects many factors, including different local priorities, knowledge and competence in dealing with the two funds and unequal access to match funding. Castlemilk has a go-ahead, well-managed agency, presumably with better access to co-financing because of its status as a Scottish Office-led Partnership area. Govan does not feature very prominently because its experience and track record have enabled it to submit several of its projects under other priorities. This is rare among the local initiatives.

Table 5.2 Value of Structural Funds approved to target areas in Strathclyde

	Value of ESF in 1996 (£000)	*Value of ERDF in 1994–1996 (£000)*	*Number of projects approved*
Castlemilk	399.7	1536.5	10
Gorbals	61	1449.7	4
Greater Easterhouse	67.6	911.3	4
North Motherwell	293.1	330.6	6
East End	219.5	365	9
Cumnock and Doon Valley	286.6	–	3
Govan	16.6	213.1	3
North Ayrshire/3 Towns	248	–	4
Greenock/Port Glasgow	159.4	64.8	6
Lesmahagow/Douglas Valley	31.8	189.5	5
Drumchapel	230.4	–	6
Leven Valley	109.3	101.1	4
Pollok	162.6	–	1
Glasgow North	119	–	4
Blantyre	–	72	1
Monklands	66.3	–	2
Ferguslie Park	19.1	–	1
North Ayr	15.8	–	2
Kilmarnock	–	–	–
South Carrick/Girvan	–	–	–
Several/unspecified	1910	623.2	17

Source: Author's compilation

Another weakness of this approach is the competition between agencies in different areas for resources and jobs, which undermines collaboration and means wasted effort on duplicating services and failing to share experience. Local agencies may be inclined to a parochial perspective and try to provide everything themselves, disregarding city-wide programmes offering greater economies of scale and expertise. Support for local agencies may be used by the major partners as a gesture for the failure of their mainstream policies in these areas. Tensions also develop between local agencies eager to see development of any kind in their areas and the strategic planning policies of city and regional authorities. Monitoring and evaluation tend to be neglected in favour of an action orientation. In short, there are some question marks surrounding the local agencies' accountability, capacity to operate strategically and ability to manage development schemes. This is partly understandable considering the hazardous economic and political circumstances in which they operate and is compounded by the capricious support from the main public bodies.

Some of the limitations of the local agency approach are overcome by several city-wide schemes, such as the Wise Group and Glasgow Works (both are combined work experience and training programmes) and the Glasgow Regeneration Fund (an investment fund). They afford economies of scale, reduce fragmentation of effort and control duplication between areas. Many of their projects are actually organised and delivered at the local level, allowing community consultation and involvement to ensure their relevance and acceptability. Such initiatives feature in the several/unspecified category in the bottom row of Table 5.2.

Obstacles

The CED resources are allocated via a process of competitive bidding. Agencies apply for funds once they have devised a project proposal and secured match funding for it from other public bodies. This has become more difficult as a result of financial cutbacks. Sponsors have also sought to spread the cost and risk by financing a smaller share of any single project. The period 1995–6 was particularly tough because of impending local government reorganisation. The Urban Programme has always been hard to match with European funds because of uncoordinated procedures. The further education colleges have provided notional match funding rather than cash, so cash flow is a problem with their support. The Local Enterprise Companies (LECs) have been nervous about the risks involved in backing novel initiatives, particularly in fields considered beyond their main remit.

Table 5.3 shows that the local authorities have been the biggest co-funders of ESF projects run by local regeneration agencies, followed by the colleges. The LECs have been relatively poor supporters of these projects, despite their larger discretionary resources. Early on some of them applied for funds to support their own standard programmes, such as Training for Work. Their bids were rejected on the grounds that they were 'top-down' and showed no local involvement in their design. The LECs have been better supporters of ERDF projects and have also provided core funding for some of the local agencies.

Table 5.3 Sources of matched funding for 1996 ESF projects

Source of matched funding:	*Projects run by local regeneration agencies (£000)*	*Projects run by other organisations (£000)*
Local authorities	439.7	1584.5
Colleges	246.9	1673.6
Local Enterprise Companies	179.4	985.5
Local regeneration agencies	102.7	87
Other public sector	92.3	27.6
Total	**1061**	**4358.2**

Source: Author's compilation

Another key point to emerge from Table 5.3 is the relative unimportance of local agencies in running ESF projects compared with other bodies. This contradicts the original objectives of the CED priority. In fact, organisations such as the colleges, LECs and, to a lesser extent, local authorities are far more inclined to co-fund their own schemes than those of other agencies, causing some concern about whether they have been adapted to local conditions. Table 5.4 shows that local agencies secured less than a fifth of the total ESF resources in 1996, with nearly half of all the projects. The colleges were the biggest beneficiaries, followed by the LECs and local authorities getting a similar amount to the local agencies. Non-local organisations have far more substantial resources of their own to use as match. This suggests there are 'gatekeeping' tendencies at work, potentially operating to the disadvantage of local bodies. Some centralisation may be desirable, as noted above, since there are important economies of scale and established expertise available among many non-local organisations. However, the unequal balance between local and non-local bodies seems to be an issue for further consideration.

Table 5.4 Recipients of ERDF and 1996 ESF resources

	Value of 1996 ESF approvals (£000) (and no. of projects)		*Value of ERDF approvals (£000) (and no. of projects)*	
Local regeneration agencies	864	(30)	3275.4	(13)
Local authorities	832.6	(7)	1827.5	(7)
Local Enterprise Companies	866.5	(4)	175	(3)
Colleges	1305.6	(17)	64.8	(1)
Third sector/voluntary	547.2	(8)	514	(2)
Total	**4415.9**	**(66)**	**5856.7**	**(26)**

Source: Author's compilation

Table 5.4 shows that ERDF resources have been allocated more closely in line with the intention. Here the secretariat and advisory group have been promoting locally-based initiatives more vigorously, and they have secured more than half the funds. These figures are dominated by a few very large projects which received over half a million pounds each. They involved the conversion of empty buildings into training facilities and workspaces with child care and other services on site. Such items are in short supply in low income areas and empty buildings (usually resulting from school closures) offer rare opportunities for new community facilities. They can also accommodate different public organisations and services in a single location, which can help to break down institutional barriers between them. Most of the projects funded to date have been oriented towards skills development, personal services and workshops for business start-ups. Few resources have been devoted to projects with the potential for significant job creation, such as infrastructure to attract investment.

There have been many procedural obstacles to using the Structural Funds as intended. For example, the separation of ESF and ERDF limits project integration, which is supposed to be a key feature of CED activity. The two funds have very different time-scales and financial systems, so administrative issues obstruct integration. Table 5.2 (p.80) shows the different geographical destinations of ESF and ERDF, demonstrating a clear lack of integration. The ESF split between Objectives 2 and 3 also causes confusion and fragmentation. In theory, Objective 3 ESF is closer to CED-type training because it is concerned with disadvantaged groups, but it is operated on a sectoral rather than a geographical basis and is not managed by the Strathclyde secretariat. In addition, the strict annual cycle of ESF coupled with delays in approval lead to a volatile stop-go delivery pattern as many training courses cannot afford to start until the go-ahead is obtained. This disrupts momentum and smooth programming. Courses are often squeezed into the second half of the year, trainees are recruited at short notice and the crucial process of preparing them before and afterwards is dislocated. The arbitrary rule to finish courses by 31 December is unhelpful, especially as January is a bad month to start job hunting. Many local agencies are discouraged from applying for ESF at all because of the cash flow burden from delays in approval and late payment. Uncertainties of any kind tend to discourage innovation, again contrary to the spirit of CED actions. Problems also arise with ERDF, particularly for large physical schemes which require substantial funding up front. Few agencies can undertake more than one at a time because of this. The secretariat have worked hard to accelerate the approval process but other sources of delay persist. Local agencies are fragile financially, so especially vulnerable to these problems. The larger partners are favoured by the current arrangements, as shown by Table 5.3 and Table 5.4, contrary to intentions.

In addition, it has taken time for the CED priority to get known and understood, because of its novelty. Consequently, the budget was under-committed at the time of writing and innovative and experimental projects were only just starting to come forward. It was a learning process for all concerned. For many local organisations effective CED activity could only be built on direct experience and experimentation, which takes time and patience. They were seeking more continuity, predictability and flexibility from European funding in future.

Conclusion

Strathclyde is beginning to grapple with the challenge of introducing local development into a regional programme. It has started to devise practical responses to the difficult questions of what measures are appropriate to promote socio-economic development and how target areas should be selected and suitable delivery mechanisms identified. Relevant projects are starting to come forward and progress is being made to commit the earmarked resources. It is a learning process for many of those involved and takes time to recondition the partners to understand, accept and contribute positively to the new approach. There is clearly scope for improvement, in terms of the scale, range and geographical distribution of development efforts, and greater commitment appears necessary at all levels to enhance and accelerate this work.

At local level the model of local regeneration agencies would benefit from further consideration of aspects such as their arrangements for accountability and community involvement and their planning and development capabilities. At city and regional levels increased financial and technical support are required to enable many local agencies to operate in a way that goes beyond the delivery of programmes designed elsewhere. Greater co-ordination and collaboration between agencies should also be encouraged, based on a broader view of what they are trying to achieve and involving more cross-fertilisation of information and experience and joint projects in areas such as labour market intelligence, employer liaison and specialised training. In addition, the priority would benefit from a stronger definition and guidelines and more pro-active efforts to encourage and assist suitable projects to come forward. Resources could be set aside for capacity building, training and project facilitation in areas where local agencies are weak or non-existent. More transparent procedures for selecting areas and approving proposals will be necessary as the stakes are raised and greater resources are forthcoming. Without increased clarity and direction there is a danger of project proliferation in a strategic vacuum.

Taken together, this suggests that a closer relationship involving an interactive process of dialogue between the regional partnership and local agencies would be useful. It would be based on negotiating mutually-acceptable strategies and offering positive support. This is different from the arms-length, competitive bidding process that prevails at present, organised around discrete projects. It is important that there is better strategic guidance from the main partners, based on a broad view of what they are trying to achieve and set within the wider regional context. Local regeneration plans could then be formulated to reflect diverse local needs and priorities in a considered manner. Once such strategies and plans are agreed, detailed decision making about specific projects and their operation would ideally be decentralised to each area in order to maximise the speed of response, local flexibility and the potential for seamless, people-centred programmes to be operated.

At national and European levels much more flexibility is needed in the rules and administrative systems governing the Structural Funds, particularly ESF, to encourage genuine integration and innovation in local development. Combating social and economic exclusion is new territory requiring imaginative approaches which are bound to be undermined by cumbersome and rigid procedures. Continuity and long-term support are also important, given the depth and scale of the problems confronted. In addition, careful consideration needs to be given to the balance between local and regional programmes, since they are interdependent in many ways and one is insufficient without the other. The wholesale replacement of regional by local programmes should be avoided. Finally, with stronger geographical targeting, the whole process of area selection and the full costs and consequences of resource concentration warrant further research since they are largely unknown yet critical to the success of this approach.

Acknowledgements

This chapter draws on the ideas and evidence from a larger study of the new CED priority across Britain led by Peter Lloyd and undertaken with Richard Meegan, Sophy Krajewska and Graham Haughton for the European Commission (Lloyd *et al.* 1996). Considerable thanks are due to Laurie Russell, Lorraine Irvine and Sally-Anne Lowe from the Strathclyde European Parliament secretariat for providing extensive information and advice, and to members of the Economic and Social Cohesion Advisory Group for sharing their experience. Thanks are also due to Margaret Dunn for drawing the map and Judith Anderson for help with data compilation. The usual disclaimers apply.

CHAPTER 6

EU Conversion Programmes for Capital Cities

The Case of London

David North

Introduction

One of the most interesting, but also contentious, aspects of the spatial distribution of the UK's share of the Structural Funds for the 1994–1999 period, as well as the 1993 changes to the UK Government's map of regional aid, has been the decision to give assistance, for the first time, to part of London. This marks a recognition of the fact that the consequences of de-industrialisation are not concentrated solely in the former industrial regions of northern England, Scotland and Wales but have also become increasingly evident within those areas which formed the production base of the capital city. It is also an indication that the increasingly uneven pattern of economic change at the intra-regional as well as the inter-regional scale, which has been demonstrated in recent national level research (e.g. Townsend 1993; Champion and Green 1992) as well as research on particular regions such as the South East (e.g. Allen 1992), is beginning to be taken on board by politicians and policy makers at both national and European levels.

Various revisions to the Structural Fund regulations in 1993 meant that it became easier for part of a capital city like London, situated within the core region of the national economy, to become eligible for Objective 2 status. In particular, the more flexible interpretation of the designation criteria in terms of unemployment rates and the period over which industrial job losses have occurred, together with greater involvement of Member States in the selection of eligible areas, have meant that it is possible to assist areas of industrial decline which lie outside the worst affected regions (Wishlade 1994). Within the EU there has been an increase in the number of relatively small areas which have obtained Objective 2 status for the 1994–1999 period, many of which qualify as 'urban communities suffering from industrial decline' (Gore 1995). London has not been the only leading city to obtain Objective 2 funding as a similar status has been given to areas which are facing structural problems within (West) Berlin and Madrid as well. Thus Structural Fund assistance for these 'capital cities' marks a new departure for the EU, which will require particularly close monitoring and evaluation to identify the effects (both intended and unintended) of giving assistance to what are relatively small parts of large and diverse metropolitan economies.

This chapter focuses upon that part of London which has been given Objective 2 status: East London and the Lee Valley (ELLV). After a summary of the various processes which led to the designation of this area, the chapter concentrates first on some of the challenges and opportunities involved in developing an economic regeneration strategy for a small part of a large metropolitan economy and, second, on the influence of different interests and levels of government on the plan formulation and delivery process. It needs to be emphasised that this chapter was written at a time when agreement has only just been reached on the detailed allocation of the Objective 2 funds for the 1994–1996 period. It is too early, therefore, to carry out a systematic evaluation of the regeneration strategy for the ELLV.

The De-Industrialisation of London

De-industrialisation is not a new phenomenon for London as the capital has been experiencing manufacturing employment decline for the last three decades, despite having a relatively favourable industrial mix (Fothergill and Gudgin 1979). Over the 1981–1991 period, London's manufacturing employment was reduced by almost half from 684,000 to 359,000 – the rate of employment loss being more than double that of the nation as a whole and in spite of London's slight structural advantage (Graham and Spence 1995). Until the 1980s most of London's manufacturing decline had been concentrated in the inner areas. However, over the last 15 years the rate of industrial decline has accelerated in outer London as 'the fourth wave sectors' (e.g. electrical engineering, electronic consumer goods, aerospace) which brought prosperity to the outer suburbs during the post-war period have suffered a succession of factory closures as part of corporate rationalisation and relocation strategies.

The full impact of the collapse of London's industrial areas during the 1980s was cushioned to some extent by the boom in service sector employment, particularly the 30 per cent employment growth over the 1981–1991 period of financial and business services associated with London's leading role as an international finance centre. However, it was only when employment in many service sectors was hit by the 1990s recession that unemployment rates started to soar in some outer London boroughs and politicians and policy makers became concerned about the structural difficulties facing the former industrial areas in particular. In the outer London borough of Enfield, for example, the number of unemployed increased by 159 per cent between 1990–1993 with the unemployment rate reaching 17 per cent. This prompted Enfield Borough Council, which had previously turned its back on economic development policy, to take a more active interest in economic regeneration and, in conjunction with neighbouring authorities, to press for Government help in tackling the problems facing the area.

Regional Assistance for London

In its revision of regional aid policy in 1993 the UK Government gave serious consideration to giving Assisted Area status to parts of London which had suffered the brunt of de-industrialisation and were experiencing above average levels of unemployment. The London boroughs had both collectively and individually lobbied for regional aid for many years, but this time the UK Government seemed to be more prepared to listen to their case. In August 1993 the Department of Trade and Industry (DTI) gave two parts of London the status of Intermediate Area (IA), initially for a period of three years: the Park Royal industrial area in west London, and part of the upper Lee Valley in north east London, both of which had been amongst London's foremost manufacturing areas for most of this century. Although the decision could be justified on the basis of the above-national-average unemployment rates which these areas were experiencing, the influence of political considerations should not be overlooked – a factor which Martin (1993) has recognised in relation to the shift towards assisting areas which have formed the basis of the Conservative's political success. As an IA, the London boroughs qualified for DTI regional aid – principally under Regional Selective Assistance.

Obtaining IA status laid the necessary foundation for bidding for Structural Funds for the Lee Valley. During the second half of 1993 the application for Structural Funds was put together, in competition with applications for Park Royal and parts of the East Thames Corridor/Gateway. The eventual outcome of the negotiations between the UK Government and the European Commission was to give Objective 2 status to a segment of north-east London centred on the Lee Valley but including a substantial part of the east end of London as well. Whereas the UK Government's original proposal was for an area of approximately equal width along the length of the Lee Valley, the Commission extended the area at the southern end to achieve a greater focus on the main concentrations of population and the areas of greatest deprivation and social need. The designated ELLV Objective 2 area had a resident population of 550,000 people in 1991 (i.e. about 7 per cent of London's population), extending from just north of the area covered by the London Docklands Development Corporation in Newham and Tower Hamlets to the outer edge of London, abutting the M25 motorway, in Enfield.

The Government's case centred on an unemployment rate of 22 per cent in 1993, which was more than double the UK and the EU averages, and a 23 per cent decline in industrial jobs (some 26,000 jobs) over the 1984–1991 period, with a more than 50 per cent decline in many of the engineering sectors which had been the mainstay of the area's manufacturing base.

As with other Objective 2 areas, eligibility is for two periods of three years starting in 1994 in order to allow for adjustments to be made in the designations because of changing economic conditions. As others have noted, this is inevitably giving rise to considerable uncertainty which is hampering the strategy formulation process (Bachtler and Michie 1994). The total Structural Fund allocation for the 1994–1996 period for the ELLV is £57m (74 mecu), of which £42m is in the form of ERDF and £15m of ESF. The matching public sector funding is to be provided in various forms, although the Government's decision to direct a quarter of London's Single Regeneration Budget's allocation towards ELLV will be the principal source.

In line with the EU's regulation relating to complementarity and partnerships, a coalition of different stakeholders has come together in the form of the Lee Valley Partnership to produce the programme of economic regeneration for ELLV. This is largely consistent with the partnership approach which the UK Government now sees as the most important foundation of its strategy towards urban areas – as evidenced by the City Challenge Initiative and the Single Regeneration Budget (Bailey 1995). The key partners comprise the six local authorities (the boroughs of Enfield, Hackney, Haringey, Newham, Tower Hamlets and Waltham Forest), three Training and Enterprise Councils, three City Challenge Companies, the Lee Valley Regional Park Authority, the private sector in the form of business leadership teams, the higher and further education sector and the voluntary sector. This broad (and arguably unwieldy) partnership is being led and co-ordinated by the new Government Office for London (GoL), one of ten Integrated Regional Offices in England created in April 1994 to co-ordinate the policies of four major Government spending departments at the regional level. GoL

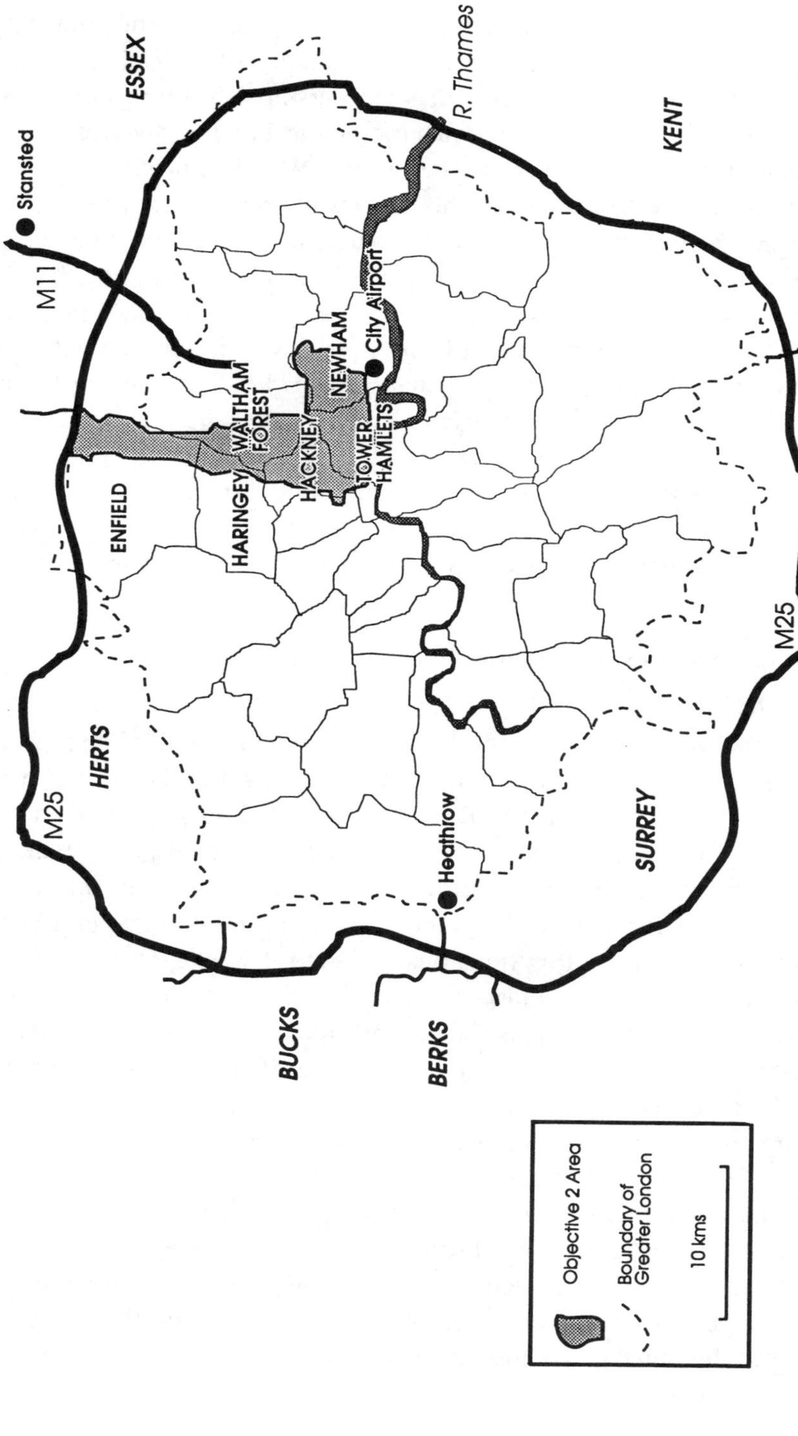

Figure 6.1 East London and Lee Valley Objective 2 area

in fact interprets its role as bringing together the right collection of organisations to deliver change in the area and to administer the various UK Government and European funds available to the partners, the prime responsibility for the formulation and the implementation of a regeneration strategy being that of the London Lee Valley Partnership. Given the vacuum which has existed in strategic policy making at the London level over the last decade, it remains to be seen whether this varied assortment of different interests can put their own parochial interests to one side in order to develop a commitment to the production of a coherent and feasible strategy capable of reversing the decline of ELLV as a whole. It might be argued that, in the case of the ELLV (and possibly other UK Objective 2 areas), 'partnership' has become a kind of marriage of convenience which has been put together for the purpose of acquiring Structural Funds rather than one which is based upon a shared vision for the regeneration of a sub-region.

Having outlined the processes which have led up to the ELLV receiving Objective 2 status under European regional policy, the following section now considers some of the challenges and dilemmas that the conversion of a declining industrial area within a major metropolitan economy involves.

The Regeneration Strategy for the ELLV: Some Key Issues

Achieving functional coherence

An immediate problem in considering the future of the ELLV area is that it no longer forms such a coherent, functional area within London as perhaps it once did. Historically, the River Lee provided an important means of transport from the London docks to the factories which grew up along its banks, and distinct industrial districts developed specialising in particular trades such as furniture-making and with strong trading linkages between businesses. However, this functional coherence weakened once the river ceased to be used as a transport artery and the traditional manufacturing industries went into decline. Today, there appears to be little connection or common interest between the inner city parts of the area on the one hand and the outer suburbs on the other.

Arguably, one of the advantages of the ELLV Objective 2 area is that unlike, for example, the Government's former urban programme areas, it is not exclusively an 'inner city' area but brings together both inner and outer urban areas at the sub-regional scale. At least in principle, therefore, there is the potential of using the economic regeneration opportunities which exist in the outer areas to tackle the problems experienced by the communities living in the inner areas. The east end of London has long been one of the poorest parts of the capital with unemployment rates on a par with those experienced in the peripheral regions (the unemployment rate in the boroughs of Hackney and Tower Hamlets reaching 26% in 1993). A substantial proportion of the people living within these areas have been excluded from the labour market because of either inappropriate skills or a lack of them altogether, this being particularly acute amongst the non-white population who comprise more than a third of the population in these areas. Whilst these inner areas have received assistance under various guises of urban policy since the mid-1970s, this has failed to compensate for the cuts in main programme spending which have taken place (Robson 1994). Thus, in the case of the inner city part of the ELLV area, the allocation of Objective 2 funds is being made to one of the most deprived urban areas not only within London but also within the UK as a whole. In fact, the ELLV inner boroughs were all amongst the worst of the 366 English districts which were ranked on the DoE's deprivation index in 1991 (Department of Environment 1995): Newham (rank 1), Hackney (rank 3), Tower Hamlets (rank 7) and Haringey (rank 10).

In contrast, the experience of economic decline in the outer part of the ELLV is, as outlined above, more recent, with unemployment only reaching politically sensitive levels over the last five years. Although there is also an increasing problem of economic exclusion in these areas, it is not on the same scale as that found in the inner city areas. The legacy of the manufacturing era is a relatively skilled workforce together with large areas of vacant and derelict land on the edge of London and close to the national motorway network. Central to the conversion plan, therefore, is how best to use these assets to bring about the economic regeneration of the ELLV as a whole.

The designation of the Objective 2 area so as to include both inner and outer parts of north-east London, therefore, brings together local economies and communities with very different experiences of economic decline over different time-scales. For the first time it presents an opportunity to tackle the problems of inner and outer urban areas jointly, working at a sub-regional scale. The challenge facing policy makers is how best to use the economic regeneration potential which exists in one part to tackle the problems of economic and social exclusion that exist in the other. In other words, a strong linkage needs to be forged between initiatives designed to trigger economic regeneration (e.g. via inward investment) and initiatives designed to reintegrate marginalised communities (e.g. via education, training and investment in public transport).

The need for a regional perspective

Whilst all regional and local economies within advanced economies can be expected to have a high degree of openness to national and global level economic processes, this is likely to be especially the case for an area like ELLV which is a relatively small segment of a much larger metropolitan economy. The boundaries of the ELLV designated area are essentially arbitrary and there is clearly going to be a large degree of economic interaction with other parts of the London and South-East economy. This could present both opportunities and problems for the regeneration of the ELLV area. On the one hand, the high degree of openness could make it easier to tap into some of the economic dynamism and growth which is occurring in other parts of the region. On the other, there is always the danger of those benefits which do result from EU assistance leaking out to other parts of the metropolitan economy.

There are, at least, two key opportunities which could stem from being part of a much wider metropolitan economy. First, the job opportunities for residents of the ELLV area are much greater than those which are available within the area itself since London is certainly the largest and probably the most highly differentiated labour market within the UK. In principle, therefore, it should be possible to improve educational attainment and skills training for local residents to help them compete more effectively for the jobs within other parts of London, and particularly within Central London. However, it has to be recognised that this is difficult to achieve as the inability of residents in inner east London to gain access to the new jobs created in central London and the Docklands over the last decade has shown (House of Commons 1989; Brownill 1990). Thus whilst they may be physically close to the locations of job growth, the unemployed of inner east London are economically very distant. The challenge facing policy makers is, therefore, how best to improve the skills, attitudes and job awareness of ELLV residents so that they can take advantage of the employment opportunities which exist in adjacent areas.

Second, it could be argued that the regional context for the ELLV Objective 2 area is considerably more favourable than that of other Objective 2 areas within the UK. Despite the problems being experienced by particular local economies, the South-East regional economy as a whole remains one of the strongest and most buoyant within the UK, responsible for over 40 per cent of the GNP and with a GDP per head which is 19 per cent above the national average (SERPLAN 1990; 1993). Moreover, whilst the South-East has about a third of the UK's population, it has a 55 per cent share of employment in R&D and a 52 per cent share of employment in the finance sector (Minns and Tomaney 1995). On the face of it, therefore, the ELLV is well positioned to benefit from the growth dynamic which is at work within the South-East region. The conversion of the ELLV clearly depends upon the ability of policy makers and investors to tap into the growth dynamic which is occurring within the region as a whole. Thus, arguably, the regional context is more conducive to various innovative- and growth-orientated forms of economic regeneration than is the case with other assisted locations in the UK.

Although the location of the ELLV within the city/regional economy does open up a number of possibilities which may not be available in other Objective 2 areas, it also presents problems as well. The first is that it is not the only part of London which is desperately seeking new investment. A key regional planning priority is to achieve a better balance between the east and the west of the region, mainly by trying to optimise the potential that exists for development (in terms of the availability of both land and labour reserves and skills) in the area which flanks the Thames to the east of London (generally termed the East Thames Corridor/Gateway) (Department of Environment 1994). Thus the ELLV is not the only priority area for economic regeneration within London and it will have to compete strenuously with other parts of the capital for inward investment.

A second problem is that of trying to ensure that the inhabitants of the ELLV themselves benefit from any new investment that occurs. As pointed out previously, most of the large sites which are available for industrial and commercial development are located in the upper Lee Valley, towards the outer edge of the Objective 2 area. In the same way that the unemployed of the area have largely been by-passed by the employment generation which has occurred in adjacent areas, so there is also a danger that they will lose out in competing for jobs in any new developments within the designated area itself. It would be a missed opportunity if these new jobs went to those already in work in outer London or the outer metropolitan area rather than leading to a reduction in the numbers of unemployed within the ELLV area itself. However, past trends suggest that this is a distinct possibility. Clearly, major improvements are needed not just in terms of equipping the unemployed with appropriate skills, attitudes, and information but also in terms of improved public transport services linking the employment areas in the upper Lee with the main housing areas in the lower Lee if there is to be any chance of optimising these 'trickle down' benefits.

Identifying the competitive advantages

The challenge being faced by policy makers in ELLV is to discover a new economic role for this part of London which will initiate a period of sustained investment and job creation. This involves identifying what are likely to be the future competitive advantages of the area and how they relate to its previous strengths. Key questions in deciding how best to use the opportunity provided by the Structural Funds include whether or not the decline of manufacturing will continue or whether there are signs of resilience, what is the potential of various forms of service employment and how much emphasis should be placed on the attraction of inward investment as opposed to trying to release the growth potential of businesses that are already in the area.

Despite the backdrop of manufacturing decline, the original ELLV conversion plan submitted by GoL to the European Commission in 1994 emphasised the resilience of manufacturing within the area and considered that it was still possible to build upon the strengths existing in certain manufacturing sectors. Although it is true that a greater proportion of employment remains in manufacturing compared with London as a whole (16.6% in ELLV in 1993 compared to 9.1% in Greater London), and there are still a large number of small and medium sized enterprises (SMEs) which are engaged in various types of production activity, it is questionable as to whether this sub-region can resist the continued downward trend in manufacturing employment which is forecast for London as a whole; for example, the London Planning Advisory Committee forecast that only 7.3 per cent of London's jobs will still be in manufacturing by the year 2006 (London Planning Advisory Committee 1993a).

Given the scale of the problems facing the ELLV, as well as the short time span for which Objective 2 status is guaranteed, it is not entirely surprising that considerable emphasis has been placed on the need to attract inward investment in manufacturing. However, it is important to be realistic about the chances of doing so as recent experience in London is not promising. With the important exception of foreign firms in the finance and business services sector which have established in central London, very few major inward investment projects have been attracted to London in recent years. The trend for most of the large manufacturing investments from the Far East and Europe to be attracted to UK Development Areas is, arguably, set to continue because of their lower production costs combined with generous incentive packages and, in the case of regions like Northern Ireland, the political pressures involved (Gudgin 1995). It needs to be questioned, therefore, whether the ELLV can compete effectively for major inward investments in manufacturing. A more effective use of resources is likely to be a strong and effective company retention policy which helps existing businesses to grow and become more competitive as well as trying to ensure that the more expansionist and dynamic businesses stay within the sub-region rather than move away from London as has been the trend in the past.

Whilst there may continue to be a residual base of manufacturing in the area, the bulk of any new jobs can be expected to come from service activities. The future of London, like many other major world cities, will be as a centre of information generation and exchange and consumption rather than as a centre for goods production (Hall 1989). Here, at least, ELLV would appear to have a major advantage, being part of a city with a wide range of international business, financial and cultural activities. However, recent trends are not altogether encouraging. Over the period 1984–1991, the main growth in service employment in the ELLV was banking and finance, achieving a growth of 60 per cent, and this was largely the result of an overspill from the rapid growth of jobs in this sector in the City of London during the 1980s. When this is omitted, the growth in service employment was a more modest 15 per cent – with employment in some sectors actually declining. Certainly the growth in service employment which has occurred over the period has not been sufficient to compensate for the decline in manufacturing employment. These trends, therefore, show that it would be wrong to assume that service activities will expand to fill the vacuum left by manufacturing.

There appears to be a reluctance in the original GoL conversion plan for the ELLV to identify those service sectors for which the ELLV area may offer competitive advantages. One such sector is, arguably, the distribution sector, which is expected to account for an increasing proportion of London's industrial employment – rising from 30 per cent in 1991 to 46 per cent by 2006 (London Planning Advisory Committee 1993b). The outer part of the ELLV area would seem to be well placed to attract distribution activities, given its strategic location in relation to the London market and links with the rest of the UK and Europe through the motorway system. The planned development of the East End as 'London's European Gateway', centred on a Channel Tunnel Rail Link Interchange at Stratford, is also likely to prove a stimulus to distribution activities. It is certainly true that in the past there has been a reluctance on the part of planners and economic development officers to encourage the development of warehousing and distribution facilities, compared with other types of commercial and industrial activity, for reasons to do with their lower employment densities, the lower quality employment provided and their higher traffic generation capacities. However, 'distribution', in its more generic sense, can involve a whole range of interrelated activities – such as light assembly operations, bespoke design services, repair and maintenance services, and various computerised services – which provide a range of skilled as well as semi-skilled and unskilled employment. One possible future for the ELLV, therefore, might lie with a series of high-quality distribution or logistics parks which contain a range of affiliated activities.

A rather different type of activity which also has considerable potential, given the rich cultural and ethnic diversity of the ELLV, is a broad range of arts, music, entertainments and media industries. This is being recognised in the plans for the economic regeneration of the area and has been linked to support for small businesses, particularly ethnic businesses. The considerable challenge facing this approach is to find appropriate ways of unleashing the indigenous talent within these inner city communities through programmes of business skills training and the provision of collective support services. Again, the proximity of these communities to the large entertainment and tourism market of the capital does provide unrivalled opportunities for this kind of development.

Having identified some of the key issues involved in the development of a regeneration strategy for ELLV, the next section makes some observations about the various stages which are involved in converting the plan for the ELLV into action on the ground.

The Implementation Process: from Priorities to Projects

For the 1994–1999 round of Structural Fund spending the European Commission made a number of changes to the process, aimed at achieving some simplification of the planning and decision making procedures, obtaining greater transparency in the funding allocation process and also at tightening up on the monitoring and evaluation of the programme. However, from the perspective of the various partners involved in the ELLV area, the process is proving to be complex, often uncertain in its outcome, and to be making huge and costly demands on staff time and resources. There are a number of reasons for this including the UK Government's centralist approach to allocating and controlling European funds, the relative inexperience in London of the Structural Funds process and the difficulties of operationalising the various partnerships formed to bid for the funds.

In making some more specific observations on the process, this section focuses, first, on the drawing up of the Single Programming Document

(SPD), second, on the selection of projects to receive funding under the agreed SPD and, third, on the monitoring process.

The Single Programming Document

The SPD for ELLV was submitted by GoL to the Commission in April 1994. This identified five priorities (Table 6.1) for the regeneration of the ELLV, together with thirteen more specific measures for achieving these priorities. Following the European Commission's standard procedures, an independent appraisal of the SPD was made during the summer of 1994 and formed the basis of negotiations during the autumn of 1994 between the Commission and GoL (together with the partners) on the revisions which were needed to the SPD. These negotiations resulted in a revised set of five priorities (Table 6.1) and sixteen measures, an agreed programme of funding and specified the desired output targets.

Table 6.1 The conversion programme priorities for the ELLV Objective 2 area

Priorities in original SPD	*Priorities in revised SPD*
1. Improvement of the Physical Infrastructure for Business	1. Business Development Support
2. Transport and Communications	2. Actions for Knowledge-Based Industries and Advanced Technological Development
3. Business Development Support	3. Targeted Inward Investment
4. Developing Human Resources	4. Action to develop Cultural Industries and Advanced Producer Services
5. Environment and Image	5. Targeted assistance to create Access to Employment for Communities

SPD = Single Programme Document
Source: SPD 1994, SPD 1995

A comparison of the priorities identified in the original SPD with those in the revised version shows that some major changes occurred as a result of the negotiations between the Commission and the various ELLV partners. It is clear that the ELLV partners (and GoL in particular) and the Commission have had their own separate agendas and that whereas the original SPD reflected the priorities of the former, the agreed SPD comes much closer to the Commission's preferred priorities and, significantly, has certain similarities with the priorities agreed for other Objective 2 areas within the UK. At the centre of the Commission's changes has been the aim of achieving a clearer focus on economic development, so that all the priorities relate clearly to it rather than, for example, to physical regeneration or transport improvements *per se*.

The main shift has been from an emphasis on 'hard infrastructure' in the original SPD to one on 'soft infrastructure' in the revised version. Whereas the ELLV partners wanted to place a lot of emphasis on investing in improvements to the physical infrastructure of the area, particularly on land reclamation in the upper Lee Valley, together with improving the transport infrastructure, the Commission wanted to see more emphasis placed on upgrading the technological capacity and knowledge base of the area and upon supporting those new industries (such as cultural industries and advanced producer services) which were most likely to address the entrepreneurial potential of those living in the lower Lee Valley. The latter also reflects the Commission's concern to ensure that the needs of the most disadvantaged within the ELLV are being addressed. Moreover, given the principle of achieving additionality in the use of Structural Funds, there was some concern that European monies would end up substituting for existing UK public sector funds, especially in the field of transport investment (notably road infrastructure improvements).

One of the main concerns of the Commission in revising the SPD has been to achieve greater integration between different priorities than appeared to be the case in the original document. For example, rather than having a separate priority concerned with human resources (i.e. skills training), the Commission's view has been that the policy measures concerned with training should be included under several priorities, resulting in a spread of the European Social Fund monies between different priorities rather than all being concentrated under a separate priority. Similarly, the expenditure of ERDF on transport projects, such as improvements to transport interchanges, has been included under the new priority concerned with 'targeted assistance to create and access employment to communities' and alongside training and community business initiatives in aiming to improve the employment prospects for the more disadvantaged within the community. However, whilst the revised plans may reflect a clearer focus and integration than those originally submitted by GoL, this does not of course guarantee real integration at the project selection stage.

The project bidding and selection process

With final agreement being reached on the revised SPD in December 1994, the next six months were taken up with the preparation and submission of bids to GoL by the different partners, negotiation over the bids and decisions on the projects to receive funding. The following observations are made on the basis of a preliminary analysis of the 227 bids which were submitted and those which were successful in the first round. Unfortunately, this analysis is not complete as, at the time of writing, decisions on some of the bids had had to be deferred because of some uncertainty as to whether they met the Commission's criteria; for example, agreement still has to be reached between GoL and the Commission on those business support projects which involved revenue expenditure which seeks to enhance the new Business Link developments in the ELLV area.

One of the problems of combining the essentially top-down process of arriving at the SPD with the more bottom-up process of making bids is that there is unlikely to be a perfect match between the allocation of ERDF and ESF funds to the different priorities and the pattern of bids which are received. This disparity becomes more marked when there is also variability in the quality of the bids between different priorities. Thus, for example, only 60 per cent of the funds allocated to Priority 4 ('action to develop cultural industries and advanced producer services') were used, even though the measure relating to cultural industries was over-subscribed by 250 per cent; although 27 bids were received under this measure, only three reached the minimum quality threshold set to receive funding. Similarly, whereas 33 bids were received relating to Priority 2 ('actions for knowledge-based industries and advanced technological development'), only eight did sufficiently well on the scoring system used by GoL to receive support, resulting in an underspend for this priority in the distribution of first round funds.

Table 6.2 compares the distribution of the bids which were received for ERDF funding between the five priorities of the SPD with the distribution of those which were successful. Just over a third of the bids were successful (or just under a third if the deferred bids are excluded). Whilst the average size of the ERDF bids was around £350,000, there was considerable variation in the size of the bids submitted – ranging from several bids for less than £10,000 for community and environmental projects at one extreme to a bid for nearly £6m for the first phase of the Lee Valley Science Park at the other. Variation on this scale makes it difficult for those responsible for the decisions to achieve their targets in terms of the allocation of funds between different priorities, different parts of ELLV and the different interests involved in the partnership. The chances of being successful are greater under those priorities which favour larger organisations and large-scale investments than under those which attract much smaller bids from small organisations. For example, although 40 per cent of the total number of bids related to

Table 6.2 Distribution of bids and successful bids for ERDF funding between the five priorities

Priorities in CSF	*Bids*		*Successful bids*	
	Number	*Value (£m)*	*Number*	*Value (£m)*
1. Business Development Support.	41 (18%)	15.6 (20%)	11 (13%)	4.7 (16%)
2. Actions for knowledge-based industries, etc.	33 (15%)	11.5 (15%)	19 (23%)	4.3 (15%)
3. Targeted inward investment.	24 (11%)	25.0 (32%)	10 (12%)	9.3 (32%)
4. Action to develop cultural industries, etc.	39 (17%)	8.2 (11%)	15 (18%)	3.1 (11%)
5. Targeted assistance to create access to employment.	90 (40%)	17.8 (23%)	28 (34%)	7.8 (27%)
Total	**227 (100%)**	**78.1 (100%)**	**83*(100%)**	**29.3 (100%)**

* includes 17 bids on which a final decision has been deferred.
Source: Analysis of GoL bid lists

Priority 5 ('targeted assistance to create and access employment for communities'), they accounted for only 23 per cent of the total value of all the bids (the average bid size being £197,000); the distribution of successful bids shows that not only were just 34 per cent under Priority 5 but also that almost half of the ERDF being spent under this priority has been allocated to two major railway station upgrading schemes, resulting in less money to be divided between the numerous bids from voluntary sector organisations. In comparison, whereas only 11 per cent of the total number of bids related to Priority 3 ('targeted inward investment'), they represented a 32 per cent share of the total value of the ERDF bids (the average bid size being £1.042 m) and this share was maintained in the eventual allocation. These bids are for a range of site and property development projects, together with a marketing strategy for ELLV, being submitted by various development partnerships (including English Partnerships), the local authorities and the Lee Valley Partnership.

Despite the shift of emphasis in the SPD away from ERDF spending on 'hard infrastructure' and towards 'soft infrastructure', the largest slice of the first-round allocation has tended to go on bids relating to site and premises development and on transport infrastructure. In fact, over a third of spending has gone on just two of the fifteen measures (measure 8: 'site development, services, on site access roads and related environmental improvements'; and measure 15: 'development of public transport to improve access to employment'). Including two other measures (measure 3: 'expansion of premises in existing industrial areas to facilitate company growth'; and measure 9: 'development of new premises'), some 56 per cent of the ERDF allocation appears to have been allocated to 'hard infrastructure' type projects. There is some indication from these figures that because of variations in the numbers and sizes of the bids relating to different priorities, together with variations in the quality of the bids coming from the different types of partner organisation, the emphasis has tended to switch back towards the proposals contained in the original SPD and away from the revised proposals on which the agreed SPD has been based.

The effect of this is that a disproportionate amount of the European funding has gone into the upper Lee Valley, since this is where the main 'hard infrastructure' projects are concentrated. The upper Lee boroughs (Enfield, Haringey and Waltham Forest) have received a disproportionately large share of the funding compared with the lower Lee boroughs (Hackney, Newham and Tower Hamlets). The large capital projects concerned with recycling land, providing the physical development required to attract new industry into the area and with improving transport communications up and down the Lee corridor are largely concentrated in this area. The upper Lee boroughs received 40 per cent of the £29m ERDF funding for the first round, whilst having just 28 per cent of the population of the Objective 2 area. In other words, whereas the average ERDF spend over the Objective 2 area is £47 per capita for the first round, it varies from £118 per capita in Haringey and £80 per capita in Enfield to £34 per capita in Tower Hamlets and £32 per capita in Newham. It might be thought that the bias towards the upper Lee in the ERDF allocation is redressed by the ESF allocation, but figures for the first round allocation suggest that this is not the case. Although the lower Lee boroughs have 72 per cent of the population of the Objective 2 area, they received just 64 per cent of the £9.5m of ESF funding for the first round.

Looked at in relation to the population distribution, therefore, there does appear to be a clear shift in the funding towards the upper Lee part of the Objective 2 area, at least in the first round of project selection. The fact that this is apparent in the case of both ERDF- and ESF-funded projects would seem to indicate that any bias is not solely the result of the concentration of the more expensive capital projects in the upper Lee. Other factors have also contributed, including the number of bids coming forward from the different areas and, in particular, how the bids measure up against GoL's scoring system (in order to try to meet the EU's requirements for transparency in the funding allocation process, GoL has devised its own scoring system as a basis for justifying to project bidders how decisions were reached. Each bid is given a point score on a range of criteria which are grouped under the headings of value for money, quality and deliverability, and various measure specific criteria. Account is also taken of the degree to which each project contributes to the overall objectives of the programme. Projects generally had to attain a pre-specified threshold score in order to receive funding, although a judgmental element also influenced the final decision). If a higher proportion of the bids from the inner city boroughs are judged to be below the quality threshold that has been set, this could also affect the geographical distribution of successful bids. In fact, it would be surprising if the adoption of a competitive bidding process did result in an equal allocation of funds throughout the ELLV area, but there are clearly dangers that the process of allocating funds may end up reinforcing existing inequalities throughout the region. Moreover, the eventual distribution of funds makes it even more important that the people living in the most disadvantaged communities of east London benefit from the kinds of projects which are being funded in the upper Lee area. The point of designating ELLV as an Objective 2 area would be seriously undermined if any new jobs created as a result of the higher per capita levels of spending in the upper Lee Valley benefited workers living outside the Objective 2 boundaries rather than those living in the inner city parts of the ELLV.

Monitoring and evaluating the programme

As indicated above, one of the changes made to the 1994–1999 round of Structural Funds has been to place a greater emphasis upon monitoring and evaluation. Development plans are required to set specific quantifiable objectives as a basis for assessing cost-effectiveness and efficiency in the use of Structural Funds. Those obtaining the funds are now expected to measure the achievements of individual projects in relation to the output targets which have been set for the various priorities and measures. It is clearly too early to assess the monitoring procedures being used in the ELLV, although it is possible to comment upon the way in which the outputs of the programme have been arrived at.

As others have noted (for example, Gore 1995; Lloyd *et al.* 1995a), the preoccupation of the UK Government regional offices administering the Structural Fund programme is with the immediate outputs rather than the broader outcomes (or impacts) of the programme. Thus the concern is with the number of businesses assisted, the amount of derelict land reclaimed and the numbers of jobs created or retained rather than with the extent to which the programme has stimulated economic activity within (and even beyond) the designated area and has resulted in a reduction of unemployment amongst the most disadvantaged groups living in the area. To assess these broader outcomes is clearly far more demanding methodologically in terms of its data demands than is the measurement of outputs, much of which can be done by those responsible for project implementation. However, the measurement of the outputs is itself not without its own problems.

Table 6.3 The agreed target outputs for Structural Fund expenditure in ELLV (1994–1996)

Jobs created	8,250
Jobs retained	14,900
No. of people receiving training	9950
Business start-ups/relocations	1,115
Business advised/assisted	13,200
Derelict land improved (hectares)	110
New and improved space (sq.m)	73,000

Source: SPD 1994

Table 6.3 shows the target outputs resulting from the expenditure of £57m in ELLV, as contained in the SPD for ELLV. Through the various land and property developments combined with business assistance and the attraction of inward investment, the aim is to create around seven thousand new jobs and to save around fifteen thousand existing jobs; this amounts to a Structural Fund cost-per-job created/saved of approximately £2500, which of course becomes at least double this when account is taken of matching sources of funding. Having set these overall targets, as well as more specific targets for each priority and measure, the process then becomes one of adding up the targets set for individual projects as a result of the negotiation that takes place between those submitting the bid and GoL. In effect, therefore, there are two kinds of targets: a largely centrally determined one and one resulting from a more atomistic process, there being no necessary coincidence between the two. Thus, for example, the sum of the targets for those projects contributing to the provision of new and improved industrial and commercial space is almost double the original target in the SPD, whereas the sum of the 'jobs retained' targets for individual projects is only a third of that in the SPD. This disjuncture between the two target-setting processes once again demonstrates the problems of combining the largely top-down plan formulation exercise with the essentially bottom-up and fragmented nature of the project-based implementation process.

A second comment on the output setting and achievement process, at least in so far as it is being practised by GoL (and it would seem the UK Government generally), is that a kind of output paranoia has taken over, with many organisations being more concerned with demonstrating that they are well on the way towards reaching their targets because of a fear of some of the funding being withheld than with making decisions which are most likely to have the greatest long-term impact. The extremely short and unrealistic time-scale (especially given the various delays that have occurred) has undoubtedly contributed to these pressures. The growth of an audit culture, more generally within government and public-funded agencies, is in danger of leading to a preoccupation with detailed form-filling and achieving immediate results rather than a concern for more strategic issues and longer term impacts.

Some Final Thoughts

The allocation of EU Structural Funds to a radial segment of London comprising both inner and outer areas provides a unique opportunity to develop a more strategic and integrated approach to economic development at the sub-regional scale. As noted by Bachtler and Michie (1994, p.795), one advantage of the EU's procedures is that 'it has promoted a more broadly based and collective approach to strategic regional thinking and regional development than might otherwise have been the case'. This is certainly true of London where there has been a fragmentation of responsibility for economic development since the demise of the Greater London Council in 1986. Thus the designation of ELLV as an Objective 2 area could signal the beginning of a partnership approach to economic and social regeneration at a sub-regional scale. Although it would be premature to evaluate the ELLV Objective 2 programme, there are some important lessons which need to be drawn from the experience of the 1994–1996 phase of Objective 2 funding.

First, the approach to developing a strategy for the sub-region has tended to be funding and project driven rather than one based on a clear and coherent regeneration strategy which, in turn, is based on a comprehensive assessment of the economic potential of the area. Although the lead partner organisations made a start in 1993 on producing a strategy for the Lee Valley, the focus shifted towards developing projects and bidding for funds once Objective 2 status had been achieved in 1994. It is only now, in 1996, that greater consideration is being given by the partners to the need to move towards a more strategy-led process which identifies the goals, objectives and policy priorities before seeking appropriate sources of funding. A related problem of the strategy being funding led is that it tends to relate to the area contained within the rather arbitrary Objective 2 boundaries rather than relating to the Lee Valley sub-region as a whole. It is also important that those responsible for developing the strategy take a 'helicopter view' of what is happening in order to identify how the sub-region can maximise the advantages and minimise the disadvantages of processes operating at the regional scale.

Second, it is clear that the partnership approach has been one between 'unequals' rather than 'equals'. It has been the local authorities, and the ones in the upper Lee area in particular, which have been the dominant partners in the bidding process during the first round. Moreover, boroughs have tended to be competing with each other to try to maximise individual shares of the resources available rather than putting in joint bids which cut across borough boundaries and relate to the interests of ELLV as a whole. The role of the voluntary sector in the bidding process has been particularly problematic, not only because of its fragmented and disorganised nature but also because voluntary sector agencies frequently lack the experience and expertise in writing bids. Unlike the larger organisations, they are also not in a position to be able to forward fund projects. If the 'partnership approach' is to have any real meaning, therefore, there is clearly a need to develop more regeneration projects which are both ELLV-wide and involve partners from different sectors. Perhaps it would have been unrealistic to expect this to have happened from the outset, given the inexperience of joint working in the area. On the positive side, however, there is now at least some recognition by the partners of the problems involved and some commitment to achieving greater levels of co-operation between them in the next round of Objective 2 funding.

Third, the use of 'the corridor concept' to link areas of economic opportunity and areas of social need is a novel aspect of the way in which this particular Objective 2 area has been designated. However, the ability to be able to use economic regeneration to achieve social regeneration is arguably the greatest challenge facing policy makers within ELLV and will require some innovative thinking. Improvements to functional linkages, including the public transport infrastructure, within the Lee Valley corridor are necessary but not by themselves sufficient to ensure that the most deprived communities benefit. There also needs to be considerable investment in training and skills development if the most disadvantaged residents of ELLV are to benefit from the new jobs being created. At the same time, it also needs to be recognised that the causes of social and economic exclusion are invariably deep-seated and are unlikely to be solved within the six-year period for which Objective 2 status has been given.

Finally, the decision to give Objective 2 status to ELLV does provide an interesting example of current EU thinking on the desirability of targeting relatively small urban areas within much larger metropolitan economies. Yet even within what is a relatively small area there is, arguably, a need for a finer grain of both spatial and sector targeting in order to try to maximise the impact of both the resources available and the leverage from other sources. This also makes sense because of the relatively modest size of the Structural Funds available to ELLV (£19m per year or £35 per year per head of population) and the short time span involved. Already much of the physical regeneration of ELLV is being focused on a selected number of 'development nodes' and some other smaller-scale projects have been focused on the most disadvantaged communities. Arguably, this selective approach also needs to be extended to include 'economic nodes' comprising clusters of related economic activity which can demonstrate economic potential. The main point, however, is that such targeting needs to be based on a clearly defined strategy for the regeneration of the Lee Valley which makes explicit connections with its regional context rather than upon the randomness of the present competitive bidding process.

CHAPTER 7

The EU Community Initiatives and the Management of Industrial Change in the UK

Gordon Dabinett

'The Community's industrial landscape continues to be characterised by a relatively strong presence of traditional sectors, partly restructured but still liable to shed large amounts of jobs in the process of further restructuring. These industries tend to be regionally concentrated. More modern sectors in which it is vital that the Community maintains its competitivity and thus its share in world markets, are also facing the need to adapt in the face of competitive pressures in the increasingly globalised economy.' (Commission of the European Communities 1993a, p.22)

Introduction

The Community Initiatives were originally a feature of the Structural Funds reform in 1988 and subsequently, after a review in 1993, they were continued within the new framework period of 1994–1999 (Commission of the European Communities 1994f). The Initiatives were designed to deal with the spatial consequences of introducing the Single European Market or spatial variations in economic conditions which might inhibit its implementation. For the period 1989–1993 the Community Initiatives were allocated almost ten per cent of the total Structural Funds, some 5.8 billion ecu (becu) (1989 prices). The Initiatives were allocated a similar proportion of the Structural Funds for the period 1994–1999, but the increase in the overall Funds resulted in an increase in the Community Initiatives budget to 13.45 becu (1994 prices). The total expenditure may be regarded as relatively low in relation to the overall scale of problems addressed, but the manner in which these funds have been targeted at specific areas has meant they have often been regarded as more significant.

This chapter looks at one particular group of responses within this aspect of regional policy – those measures which have attempted to address industrial decline: RENAVAL in shipbuilding areas, RESIDER in steel areas, RECHAR for coalmining areas, RETEX in areas of textiles and clothing and KONVER for defence areas. This particular set of Initiatives have been allocated less than 2.5 per cent of the Structural Funds, but the EU places particular value on them in promoting local and partnership responses to managing industrial change on the ground and assisting the achievement of regional integration (Commission of the European Communities 1993a). The chapter continues by briefly outlining the broad context and operating framework of these specific Initiatives and then goes on to examine their implementation in the UK.

The Community Initiatives to Manage Industrial Change

The management of industrial change has been consistently an important element within the Community Initiatives. Whilst a cursory examination of the purposes of all the Initiatives indicates that concern with industrial change has not been restricted to RENAVAL, etc (Commission of the European Communities 1994f), the specific scope and spatial targeting of the industrial change Initiatives has been regarded as crucial to their purpose. The Community Initiatives to manage industrial change have operated within both of the Structural Fund periods, but the operational periods of individual instruments varied (see Table 7.1). RENAVAL and RESIDER were first introduced as Community Programmes prior to 1988, and KONVER, in 1993, was preceded by the PERIFRA Programme in 1991 and 1992. The Initiatives were generally implemented in Objective 1, 2 and 5b areas and, in some cases, in areas outside these designated regions. Whilst the two textiles Initiatives allocated funds largely to Objective 1 areas, the other four Initiatives concentrated primarily on localities outside these lagging regions. Indeed, only 29 per cent of RECHAR, RESIDER and KONVER was allocated to the highest priority Objective 1 regions for 1994–1997, serving to highlight the potential significance of these particular Community Initiatives to regions in the UK.

The eligibility of areas to benefit from the Community Initiatives dominated the debate in each round of allocations, and subsequent bidding for funds by individual areas. In detail, the eligibility criteria varied between Initiatives but the norm established after 1993 was to define areas using the

Table 7.1 EU allocation of Structural Funds and Community Initiatives to the UK regions 1989–1993 and 1994–1999 (mecu)

Measure	*1989–1993*	*1994–1999*	*Total*
Objective 1 areas	497	2267	2764
Objective 2 areas	3052	2060 (94–96)	5112
Objective 5b areas	338	341	679
RENAVAL	87	0	87
RESIDER	5 (88–90)	43 (94–97)	48
RECHAR	175	155 (94–97)	330
RETEX	6 (93)	35 (94–97)	41
KONVER	20 (93)	96 (94–97)	116

Source: Commission of the European Communities, Directorate-General for Regional Policies, Info Technique Fact Sheets; Commission for the European Communities (1994f)

lowest level of spatial aggregation (NUTS III level units, such as UK counties or Travel-To-Work-Areas). These areas were eligible if at least a thousand jobs had been lost in the sector or future job losses had been publicly announced or were at risk as accepted jointly by the Commission and the Member State (Commission of the European Communities 1994f).

The figure of one thousand jobs was not applied universally to earlier Initiatives. For example, RENAVAL I emphasised actual and threatened job losses in shipbuilding but also looked to more general criteria of economic performance, such as a rise in unemployment. It can only be assumed that the Commission felt that whilst introducing clarity and simplicity into the eligibility criteria after 1993, nothing was lost in the scope to make flexible and appropriate responses.

Further evidence of the Commission's view that the Community Initiatives provided an opportunity to respond to change at a local level is provided by the actual measures eligible for ERDF and ESF grant funding. Broadly, they all sought to bring about environmental improvements, renovation of the social and economic infrastructure, promotion of new economic activities – in particular those undertaken by small firms – promotion of tourist activities and provision of training (Commission of the European Communities 1994f). In the shipbuilding, steel and coal areas the Initiatives attempted to deal with the consequences of decline, whereas in the cases of KONVER and RETEX an existing industrial base required conversion to other activities or adjustment to a new commercial environment. Indeed, the Green Paper prepared by the Commission in 1993 argued that 'it is particularly, though not exclusively through Community Initiatives that the cohesion effort of the Community has become better appreciated and understood at a decentralised level...to give the Community reality and a relevance on the ground' (Commission of the European Communities 1993a, p.3).

The EU Community Initiatives in the UK

All five sectors addressed by the Community Initiatives exhibited dramatic and often rapid job losses in the UK during the 1980s (see Table 7.2). In all these sectors change was not a recent feature, with many problems being deeply rooted in the industrial-economic history of the nation. Furthermore, many of the industries were spatially concentrated, leading to clear regional impacts referred to as the north-south divide (Balchin 1990), but also creating severe local impacts where localities were dependent on these industries, such as the colliery villages. As a result, the UK Government and the local authorities in the areas affected were to take full advantage of the Community Initiatives introduced to manage industrial change. However, their introduction was neither easy nor straightforward.

Table 7.2 Employment change in GB coal mining and manufacturing employment (1981–1991)

	1981	*1991*	*1981–1991*	
Sector	*employment (000)*	*employment (000)*	*change*	*% change*
Deep coal mines	272	74	-198	-73
Iron and steel industry	125	48	-77	-62
Shipbuilding and repair	121	47	-74	-61
Textiles and clothing	491	325	-166	-34
Ordnance and aerospace	213	161	-52	-25
All other manufacture	5106	3993	-1113	-22

Note: The sector definition above will not be identical to Community Initiatives definition. For example, military shipbuilding will not be contained in defence sector and, similarly, defence sector includes civil aerospace employment.

Source: NOMIS (figures rounded)

As described earlier, RENAVAL and RESIDER were first introduced as integral elements of EC-led policies to reduce capacity in the shipbuilding and steel industries. Job losses in these two sectors within the UK between 1981 and 1991 were very similar (see Table 7.2) but only one area, the South Yorkshire and Scunthorpe Steel Area, was designated under RESIDER I and allocated 5 million ecu (mecu), whilst six areas benefited from RENAVAL, being allocated a total of some 87 mecu. This performance related to two main factors. First, the initial programmes were predominantly operated through Whitehall and, to a lesser extent, the regional offices of national government departments. Thus particular local needs or situations were not necessarily fully recognised and European funding was a relatively new experience for many agencies at the local level (House of Commons 1995). Second, many closure areas did benefit from European assistance, but primarily under Objective 2 Structural Funds expended through the main Operational Programmes. For example, in South Yorkshire the RESIDER funding was overshadowed by the 126 mecu allocated to the sub-region Integrated Development Operations Programme (IDOP) (Sheffield Business School 1992). However, this situation was to change in subsequent Community Initiatives as, generally, the role of local economic development and involvement of local authorities was to increase (Armstrong and Twomey 1993).

Notably, the Coalfields Communities Campaign (CCC) is often quoted as an exemplar and probably the most influential and widely known of the local sectoral networks that emerged during the 1980s and 1990s (Geddes 1992). CCC was set up by local authorities in the UK which had been severely affected by the job losses in deep coal-mining following the 1984/1985 national miners strike. This collaboration was then to be extended into Europe during 1988 and was formalised in a framework of co-operation, later to be known as EUR-ACOM (European Association of Coal Mining Areas). Its first major task was to lobby the European Commission for a programme of aid for the regeneration of the coalfield areas. Subsequently, formal approval for RECHAR was given by the Commission in December 1989 and, significantly, the position of the UK government, which was initially neutral, swung to a position of support when it was realised that the UK would be the largest beneficiary (Fothergill 1992). However, the final twist in this account of lobbying and policy development was to come in the approval of the RECHAR package for the UK, not granted until February 1992. The funds were only released after the Commission had obtained assurances from the British government that the UK public expenditure system had been changed generally to allow grants from ERDF to be fully additional to the coal-mining areas. This decision led Fothergill (1992) to claim that 'the collective action of coalfield authorities successfully breached the UK government's long-standing restrictions on the additionality of EC grants.' (p.76).

The scope of local authorities to represent local communities, and the specific needs of sectors as they were represented in individual localities, is also illustrated by the textiles and clothing industry. The need to develop alternative policy responses was a fundamental feature of Local Action for Textiles and Clothing (LATC), begun in 1983 as a series of informal meetings to exchange thinking on fashion centres in various UK cities. By 1985 it had grown to become a formal organisation representing more than 20 local authorities. Whilst still pursuing its main purpose of information exchange, LATC also began to play a greater advocacy role. Subsequently, when consultations on RETEX were undertaken by the Commission during 1991–1992, LATC took on an inter-regional co-ordinating role, offering the Commission a consensual agenda for the operation of the programme in the UK. Totterdill (1992) claims that this was an interesting example of local networks which occurred against a background where 'strong representations from other Member States were often made by elected Regional Authorities, with well-resourced access to Brussels.' (p.41). However, the contribution of the local responses in the UK has to be put in the context that the UK gained small benefits from RETEX, since 80 per cent of the allocation went to Objective 1 regions. Totterdill (1992) also argues that, despite the programme being implemented by a national programme committee, European Commission support for the sector and localities in the UK remained highly fragmented.

The scope of networks and collaborative lobbying to influence national and EU policies is further illustrated by the case of KONVER and the issues of defence conversion and the peace dividend (Dabinett 1993). Although the international events of 1989 triggered deep cuts in defence budgets and widespread job losses in the defence industry and military bases, the immediate response tended to be fragmented and muted. Significantly, the defence sector covered areas not traditionally supported by national or European regional policies, such as East Anglia and the South-East. Consequently, the first responses emanated from within the EU with the introduction of the PERIFRA annual programme in 1991 (Arms Conversion Project 1995). This year was to prove to be a watershed, but the diversity and political sensitivities surrounding defence issues meant subsequent inter-local authority and pan-European collaboration occurred piecemeal, often addressing different agenda (Arms Conversion Project 1995; Association of County Councils 1992; European Defence Observatory 1994; Network Demilitarised 1994). Despite this growth in local-based activity and the successful lobbying for KONVER II (with the UK securing 19% of the total allocation), this Initiative has been implemented as a national programme led by the Department of Trade and Industry in Whitehall with the regional offices, local authorities, Training and Enterprise Councils and other agencies perceived as 'bodies to be consulted' (T. Sainsbury MP, Hansard 21 October 1993, p.304).

It is impossible to provide a definite narrative of a complex set of measures such as the Community Initiatives, but clearly the inter-relationships between the local, national and European levels of government were a dominant feature. However, any claim that the Initiatives provided a Whitehall by-pass for local authorities in the UK would be overly simplistic, or at least not a general experience. Similarly, the notion of partnership inherent in EU regional policy and recent approaches to local economic development (Mackintosh 1992) might have existed but consisted of unequal partners and a dynamic set of relationships. Practice in many areas would also suggest that the Community Initiatives were not fully integrated with other forms of EU regional policy in the areas benefiting from such resources. A further feature were the time-scales, where often the programmes were being agreed mid-way through their operational period as a result of protracted negotiations between the UK national government and the Commission. It could be argued that in many areas the funding from the Initiatives was seen as a windfall, the importance of which depended on the extent to which the monies were the main source of public support for regeneration in the locality. The delay in implementation, uncertainty of eligibility and the annual basis of early funding contributed to such an approach.

One criticism of the Community Initiatives is that intervention came too late. Rather than being an integral part of any response to closure, rationalisation and job loss, the measures only addressed the need to ameliorate the worst effects of such change. The enabling European Commission Article did allow areas at risk from job losses to be eligible as well as areas already affected by employment decline, but this was never used in the UK. The fortunes of the particular industries were very often closely entangled with national government policies on public ownership and procurement. Consequently, any early disclosure of job losses might have raised acute political dilemmas. However, the Initiatives probably did allow a more flexible and immediate response than might have occurred within the overall Structural Funds frameworks operating within the UK (House of Commons 1995).

At worst, the development of the five Community Initiatives examined here was no more than a form of competitive infighting as individual areas and stakeholders argued for and negotiated a share of the spoils. At best, a further element was added to the already crowded arena in which players seeking different objectives played out their ambitions and strategies for the areas or communities they represented. The Initiatives may be seen as an extension of the fragmented and opportunistic nature of local economic development in the UK at this time (Audit Commission 1989), where any new source of funding offered an opportunity for local agencies to fill a vacuum in national policies to ameliorate economic, environmental and social problems in their localities. What, then, has been the outcome and relevance of these initiatives when implemented in the areas so adversely affected by the processes of industrial restructuring that occurred in the 1980s?

The Management of Industrial Change

In examining the implementation of the five Community Initiatives designed to assist in the management of industrial change it is possible to reflect on a wide and diverse set of activities by asking three simple questions:

- What areas were assisted?
- What resources were attracted?
- What type of projects received support?

Much of the early stages surrounding the introduction of the Community Initiatives was dedicated to deciding which geographical areas would be eligible to benefit from each programme of support. The review of the Community Initiatives in 1989 had resulted in a much more standard approach to eligibility, but these broad criteria still left a lot of scope for local areas to lobby the EU for inclusion. In all cases, the UK national government played a key part in this process (House of Commons 1995). In addition, despite clear criteria for eligibility in terms of activities and job losses, the lack of reliable or commonly agreed data on employment levels was still an issue in submissions from the UK. The broader issue surrounding eligibility related to the proportion of assistance allocated to areas outside designated Objective 1, 2 or 5b regions. Whilst the early Community Initiatives were allocated entirely to these priority regions, it was acknowledged by the Commission itself in its Green Paper that 'a limited amount of Community Initiatives resources should be able to be spent outside eligible areas' (Commission of the European Communities 1993a). In practice, the first tranche of Community Initiatives funding went primarily to the UK regions containing Objective 2 areas, such as Scotland, Wales, the North and Yorkshire and Humberside. However, one outcome of a programme such as RECHAR was to see the East Midlands receive substantial funds, and KONVER also opened up the South-East and Eastern regions to EU funding in this period. Indeed, the role of the defence factor was acknowledged in the redrawing of the UK assisted areas map in 1994 with areas traditionally regarded as prosperous being included, such as Weymouth and Portland (Ball 1995).

Whilst this raises major questions about the purpose and role of regional policy and the use of various spatial units to represent local needs (Ball 1995), it also poses fundamental dilemmas in relation to spatial responses to industrial change. The areas assisted highlight the underlying purpose of the Initiatives to address regions previously dependent on certain categories of industrial employment. As a result, they primarily address spatial disparities resulting directly from restructuring. Simply, this could be described as money chasing problems rather than the resourcing of clear strategies for regional renewal and development. The former approach plays down the linkages between sectors and firms that can occur over space but can also ignore the ability of such areas to diversify or regenerate, referred to as the adaptive capacity in a study of defence dependency (Commission of the European Communities 1992b). This study also drew attention to the varied impacts that job losses may have, since these will depend on the structural characteristics of the region. At present the allocation of funds on the basis of simple job loss counts gives this relationship little consideration, but does provide support to immediate regeneration efforts.

The issue of relating Community Initiative funding to wider regional strategies, and hence public policy expenditure activities, is highlighted even more critically when answering the question about the level of funding provided by these mechanisms for regeneration. In total, over 620 mecu of Structural Fund allocations were secured by this route. On its own this represents a significant injection of capital, and one which was, in principle, also matched by national expenditure in the UK. Thus the UK involvement in these Initiatives can be seen as particularly successful, if simply regarded as an exercise in recouping resources from Brussels. For example, a major share of RECHAR was allocated to the UK, 47 per cent in 1989–1993 and 39 per cent in 1994–1997, and UK KONVER programmes attracted 15 per cent and 19 per cent of EU funds over similar periods. However, the relatively small contribution that such measures could make to tackling the overall economic, social and environmental problems associated with restructuring in the UK is shown by comparisons with the main Structural Funds allocated over the same periods (see Table 7.1, p.111). Furthermore, it is interesting to note that whilst funds from this European source were increasing over the late 1980s and early 1990s, the UK Government expenditure on regional industrial policy was falling from £690m in 1988/89 to only £287m in 1993/94 (House of Commons 1995).

As Fothergill (1992) comments, 'the most important point to emerge is just how little can be achieved with even quite large sums. Economic regeneration is not a cheap process' (p.72), but continues to add that 'RECHAR by itself was never intended to be a total solution' (p.72). The Initiatives have to be put in the context of wider Structural Funds expenditure and national spending mechanisms – which highlights the institutional mechanisms associated with funding, in particular additionality. The disagreement between the European Commission and UK government on additionality and the role of this in the approval of RECHAR has already been outlined. The issues surrounding this debate have been explained elsewhere (Fothergill 1992; Thomas 1992) and, following reassurances given by the UK government in 1992 and subsequent improved monitoring by the EU in 1993, it was believed that the UK met the additionality requirement. However, the CCC argued that only a partial and temporary solution was found to this complex concept and that it highlighted an increasing experience of local authorities and other agencies unable to pursue or fund projects in the absence of sufficient resources to provide match funding (House of Commons 1995).

Additionality is but one specific element within the more general objective of the EU to seek partnership working in its regional measures. In particular, the Community Initiatives 'are at their most effective...when the measures funded respond to locally generated ideas and translate into additional and tangible action on the ground' (Commission of the European Communities 1993a). Thus the application of this partnership principle to implementation should lead to the direct involvement of local and regional interests, thereby matching a top-down response from the Commission with a bottom-up approach to delivery. It might be assumed that the vehicle within which this is achieved is the programming documents or operational programmes for the Structural Funds. However, it has been suggested that these have failed to provide a suitable mechanism for encouraging regional strategies or long-term local regeneration (House of Commons 1995; Lloyd *et al.* 1995b). Furthermore, the organisations responsible for the implementation of the measures, the Monitoring Committees, have been criticised for following Ministerial guidance rather than the interests of their constituent agencies (House of Commons 1995). Apart from RECHAR, the balance of partnerships – and, hence, control of funding – appeared to be held largely by Whitehall. Whilst the new government offices for the English regions established in 1994 might serve to influence and bend nationally-determined priorities and objectives (Mawson and Spencer 1995b), there is as yet little evidence of this on the ground in the areas affected by job losses and closures.

This apparent central control was easier to exert in the face of increasing organisational fragmentation at the local level as various initiatives and 'next step' agencies were set up, such as Training and Enterprise Councils, Urban Development Corporations, City Challenge and Single Regeneration Budget Companies. However, perhaps ultimately, these mechanisms and procedures of governance would matter little if the areas suffering from the severe consequences of restructuring actually benefited from appropriate and successful projects.

It is an extremely difficult task to establish the success or exact contribution of the Community Initiatives to any economic change in the areas targeted. Many programmes have been fully operational for less than five years and any effects are likely to be hidden by general economic factors and the contribution of other local, national and European measures to regenerate these areas. However, evidence from empirical studies suggests that the conditions for many of those made redundant by restructuring still remains bleak (Hinde 1994; Turner and Gregory 1995) and available statistics show how sub-regions such as South Yorkshire, the north-east of England and South Wales still had levels of unemployment above the European average and GDP per capita below the average in 1993 (Commission of the European Communities 1994b). But what sort of projects have the Initiatives supported?

The broad pattern of Community Initiatives project expenditure was predetermined by the objectives of the Structural Funds and allocation of ERDF and ESF. Thus wider criticism of the Structural Funds, which suggest that measures often offer remarkably similar prescriptions (Lloyd *et al.* 1995b), might be applied to the Community Initiatives. There has also been debate about the extent to which regional aid should support 'hard infrastructure', such as physical projects, or fund the development of a 'soft infrastructure' based on training, common support services, business and technology agency interactions and other forms of networking (House of Commons 1995). However, variations occurred between individual Community Initiative programmes in the UK as a result of locality and sector differences (see Table 7.3). For example, a high proportion of the RECHAR I programme was ERDF aided, but with some variation between areas: 91 per cent of expenditure in South Wales was to be aided by ERDF, 83 per cent in the largest areas of Yorkshire and the East Midlands and 80 per cent in the North-West. This level of support reflects the need for capital investment projects in these areas. Indeed, 37 per cent of RECHAR I was allocated to environmental improvements and building factory units and 19 per cent allocated to improving the social infrastructure in response to the severe physical problems faced by the coalfield areas. All programmes after 1988 were to include ESF funding. This amounted to 34 per cent of the RETEX programme in 1993 and 35 per cent of KONVER I. A more detailed examination of projects included in these programmes indicates a wider acceptance of the need to promote non-physical schemes. Thus only six per cent of total project costs of RETEX 1993 was allocated to the conversion of mills and only 16 per cent of KONVER I was to be spent on the conversion of military bases. The largest categories of project expenditure for both these programmes were SME support and assistance for training and retraining.

Table 7.3 Examples of Community Initiatives projects

Project category	*Community Initiative*		*(% of project costs)*	
	RESIDER I	*RECHAR*	*RETEX 1993*	*KONVER 1993*
Infrastructure	14	65	6	16
Business development	76	15	38	31
Human resources	0	18	36	37
Institutional capacity	10	2	19	16
All	100	100	100	100

Note: *Infrastructure* = Conversion of military sites, textile mills, environmental works, social infrastructure, tourism, etc.
Business development = Support for SMEs, innovation, common services, investment, know-how and technical assistance, etc.
Human resources = Education, training and retraining.
Institutional capacity = Feasibility studies, exchanges, groups and networks, conversion and promotion agencies.

Source: Commission of the European Communities, Directorate-General for Regional Policies, Info Technique Fact Sheets

Therefore, whilst there is evidence of well-tried and tested capital investment projects like land reclamation and factory construction, there were also examples of more innovative and networking approaches – such as fashion centres (Totterdill 1992) and defence conversion projects (Arms Conversion Project 1995). These later types of scheme highlight the predominance of initiatives aimed at SMEs (see Table 7.3). Some concern has been expressed at this priority since the industrial sectors subject to restructuring were, and are still, dominated by the behaviour of large, and often multi-national, companies. Whilst this case is less clear-cut in the textiles and clothing sector, the role of large companies, global trading, investment patterns and international sourcing do seem to be important issues effectively ignored or, at best, not fully engaged with. It could be argued that restructuring of such sectors cannot be managed effectively without some mechanism to involve these larger firms and wider processes.

Conclusions

Whilst the Community Initiatives examined here illustrate that the EU recognised the need for local and regional strategies to manage industrial change, their contribution to anything other than the amelioration of the immediate impacts of decline is hard to discern. A view from many of the coalfields, shipbuilding, steel and textiles towns and defence communities would suggest that the measures have done little to offset the collapse of these sectors, as unemployment remains high, some industries suffer further cuts and regeneration projects fail to create sufficient new job opportunities for those made redundant. The Initiatives, by themselves, have been unable to redress the spatial imbalances resulting from industrial restructuring, although in some areas regeneration has begun. However, as observed above, this is a harsh criticism of a mechanism which by its nature could only have limited impacts. Indeed, those communities affected by de-industrialisation and further rounds of restructuring rely as much, if not more, on wider national and European frameworks of assistance. Thus criticisms concerning the lack of a regional strategy and the absence of integration with other economic development measures should also be directed at those generally responsible for regional policy (House of Commons 1995). In a review of the local responses made to defence cuts in the UK it was clear that the vacuum left by the absence or the inadequacy of any national policy was the main spur to locally-based interventions (Dabinett 1993).

Indeed, the experience of the Community Initiatives in the UK throws up a number of contradictions. On the one hand, the substantial share of funds attracted to the UK could be seen as a success but, on the other hand, the debates still surrounding the extent of additionality suggests that the needs of individual areas may not have been fully recognised and regeneration not adequately funded. Similarly, the significance attached to the local authority networks indicates the emergence of new and innovative patterns of institutional arrangements in the UK. But these developments can also be seen as a reflection of the failure of national government to represent the areas affected by decline in a satisfactory way and the absence of a regional level of government to address this deficit.

However, it is the nature of much of the local activity which emerged within the remit of the Community Initiatives which provides grounds for more optimism. First, there is some evidence that local and innovative approaches have been developed, albeit within a predominantly fragmented and competitive policy environment for local economic development. This is particularly so in specific localities which were dominated by the industries suffering decline. Second, as Geddes (1992) comments, the development of collaboration and networking among local authorities was a particularly significant development. This chapter has illustrated various examples of such collaboration, often pursuing a variety of aims. Despite this variation, they were a crucial element in securing funds for individual areas and providing a vehicle for political expression and debate about the nature of policies towards these localities.

CHAPTER 8

European Regional Policy in English Regions

The West Midlands and Yorkshire and Humberside

Gill Bentley and John Shutt

Introduction

The European Structural Funds have become extremely important for the United Kingdom's declining and laggard industrial regions. As described in detail earlier in this book European Commission has a system of programming regional expenditures which assumes the existence of regional strategies and coherent regional administrations. In the United Kingdom the Single Programming Documents (SPDs) for the current Objective 1 and 2 areas were finalised by December 1994, at the time when the UK Government was establishing its new system of English Integrated Regional Offices – now known as Government Offices for the Regions (GORs) (Mawson and Spencer 1995a). The GORs are outposts of national government in the regions, rather than regional governments as found in many of the Member States.

The introduction of the SPD process raises questions about regional policy formulation and planning in the late 1990s, particularly in the absence of regional government. Questions also arise about spending priorities and the reduced institutional capacity for project delivery in the light of SPD priorities and the current conditions in UK economic development agencies. The aim of this chapter is to compare and contrast the approaches to negotiating and implementing the Objective 2 SPDs in the English regions, focusing on the West Midlands and Yorkshire and Humberside. The comparison is used to draw out some of the strategic regional issues of practical and theoretical significance. A growing literature is debating the emerging pattern of governance in relation to regional economic growth. At the same time, practitioners have to grapple with real issues of policy administration and the problems of uneven development. The chapter shows that despite differences between the areas in the problems being experienced, and in the degree of Europeanisation of local institutional structures, the operation of the Structural Funds has turned out to be markedly similar and centralised. It concludes that further detailed evaluation and public debate are required if improvements are to made to the European regional policy process in England in the late 1990s.

The 1995 Mid-Term Position – the West Midlands and Yorkshire and Humberside

The SPD process

The SPDs for 1994–1996 in Objective 2 regions in Britain were initially drafted by the Department of Trade and Industry (DTI) and Department of the Environment (DoE). Following the establishment of the new English Integrated Regional Offices in early 1994, the processing was pursued by these offices. Eleven Objective 2 plans were submitted by the Government in March/April 1994, followed by a protracted period of appraisal and negotiation to ensure the SPDs met EU regulations and requirements (Ramsden 1994; Lloyd *et al.* 1995a). Key to the appraisals were the principles of concentration, programming, synergy and additionality (Commission of the European Communities 1993d; Commission of the European Communities 1994a). The latter proved problematic, there being difficulties in the UK in demonstrating this requirement, but the SPDs were approved in December 1994.

One might expect the Structural Fund process to be different in each region because of important differences in local institutional structures and arrangements. The two regions are interesting because the degree of Europeanisation is different (John 1994): the West Midlands is arguably more 'embedded' in Europe whereas Yorkshire and Humberside is more on the 'periphery'. In the SPD process this made little difference because of the strong role played by central government through the regional offices. As a result, the European connections of cities and localities and European project networking were rarely reflected in the documents. Despite regional differences in problems, local priorities and institutions, the outcomes of the SPD process were markedly similar; the SPDs are inward looking and UK oriented rather than looking towards a new integrated Europe and the implications for English regions in the 21st century.

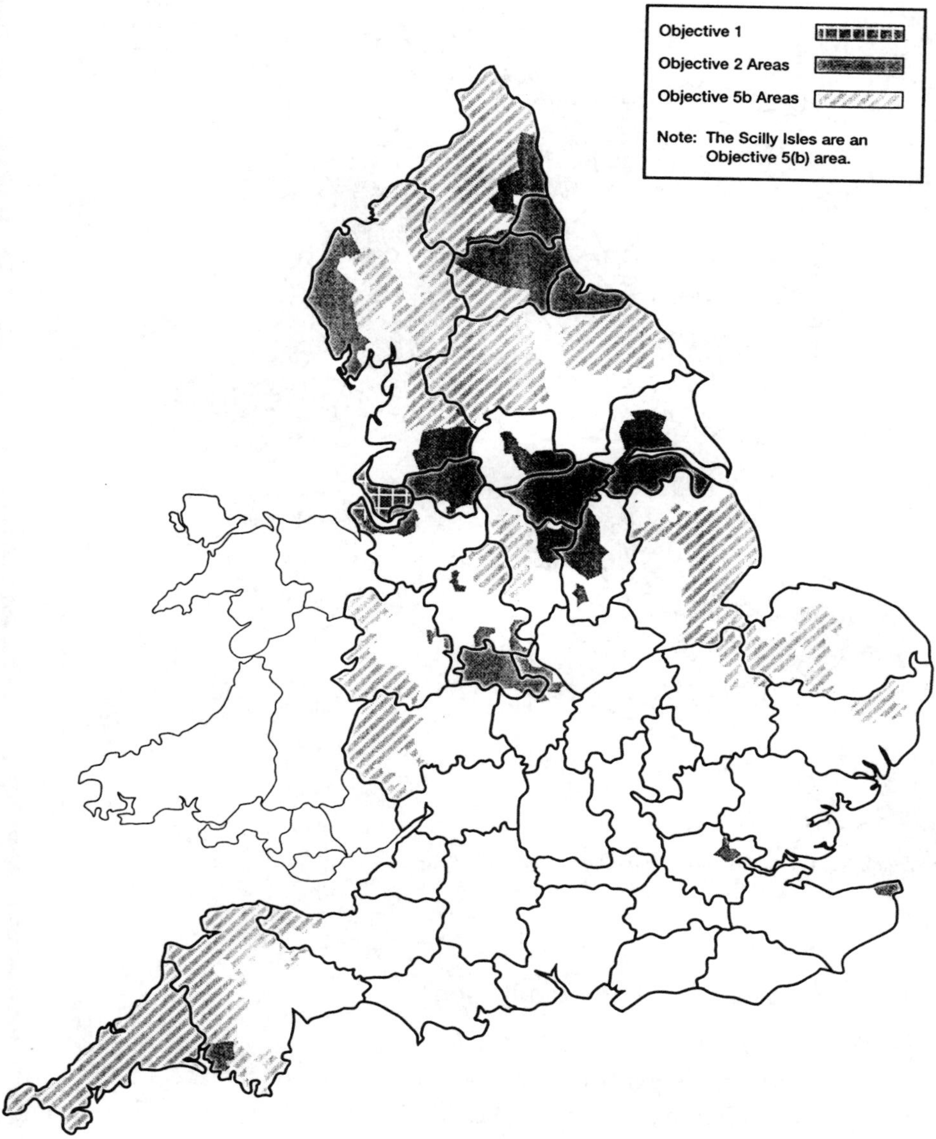

Source: LMU 1997

Figure 8.1 Objective 1, 2 and 5b areas in England (1994–1999)

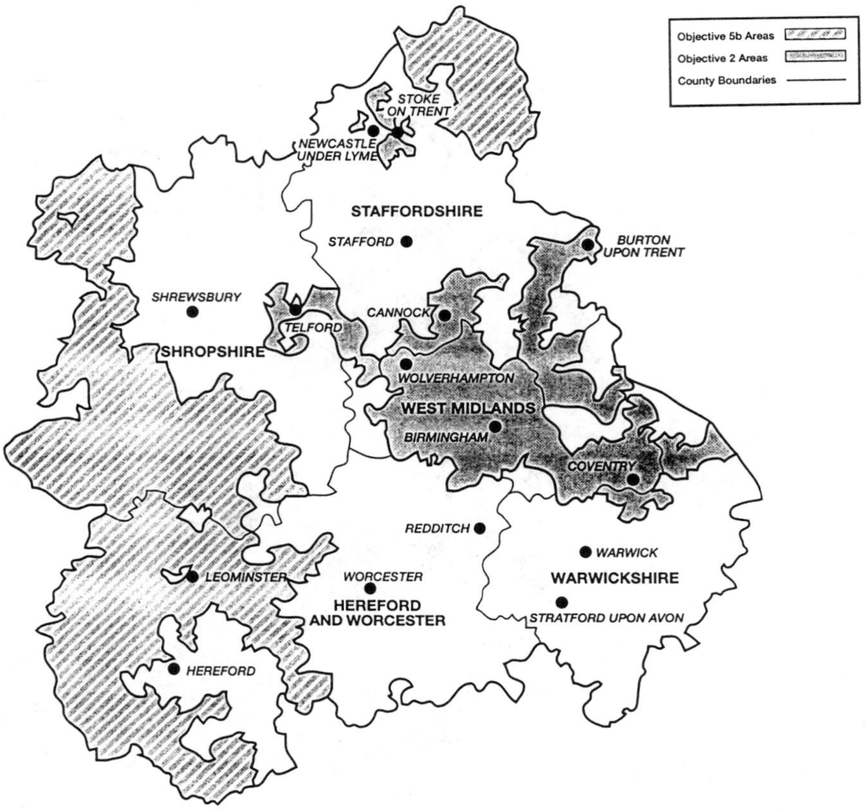

Source: CEC (1994d)

Figure 8.2 West Midlands region Objective 2 and 5b areas

The West Midlands: a European Region?

Partners in Europe in drawing up the strategy

The West Midlands, with its long-standing commitment and tradition of regional planning has strong regionally-based institutions and a strong European presence (Bentley and Mawson 1984), and it is a key player in the debate about a 'Europe of the Regions'. In the 1994 SPD, Objective 2 eligible areas include all or parts of Birmingham, Coventry, Warwickshire, southern Staffordshire/Telford, east Shropshire and Solihull. Burton and wards in Rugelely are eligible for the first time, as is the North Staffordshire area (see Figure 8.2).

Table 8.1 Birmingham City Council key events (1984–1994)

1984	European Unit established in the City Council
1984	Birmingham granted UK Assisted Area status
1985	City's Brussels Office opened
1986	Eurocities founded
1987	Single European Act ratified
1987	BIDO approved by EC (1987–1991)
1988	Birmingham granted Objective 2 Area status
1989	Structural Funds reforms
1989	City's centenary celebration
1991	Eurocities Conference (Birmingham)
Aug 1991	European Task Force established
Oct 1992	Special European Summit (Birmingham)
Jan 1993	Single European Market commenced
Jan 1993	BIOP one-year programme commenced
Feb 1993	Maastricht treaty on European Union signed
1993	European Committee of the Regions founded
1993	Birmingham granted UK Development Area status
Dec 1993	Maastricht Treaty ratified
1994	Structural Funds reforms
1994	City's Objective 2 Area Status reaffirmed

Source: Birmingham City Council 1994

Birmingham is a lead member of the Eurocities local authority network. Its proclaimed aspirations to become a great European City of the 21st Century are well set out in 'Birmingham 2010' and the 'City Strategy' and deserve to be a model and inspiration for all British cities. Birmingham is intent on maximising income from the European Commission, securing a place in the European policy practice and legislative process and securing the constitutional basis for local autonomy as well as enhancing Birmingham's ability to compete in the international economy (Birmingham City Council 1994). The city's achievements in the European arena are summarised in Table 8.1, which examines key European events for the city over the 1984–1994 period. Coventry and Wolverhampton have also been developing a strong awareness in relation to Europe recently.

Local authorities in the region are linked through the West Midlands Regional Forum of Local Authorities. Unlike the regional association for Yorkshire and Humberside, the Forum did not have a Brussels office of its own until 1996 but used the office of the Association of Regions of Industrial Technology (RETI). The forum nonetheless took a pro-active approach to

European matters. Prior to the SPD being finalised, it drew up an economic development strategy for the region – the West Midlands Region European Development Strategy [WMREDS] (WMRFLA 1993). Recognising that 'a joint input is essential to success', the strategy was written through a partnership of local authorities, the Regional Economic Consortium (the regional CBI, Chambers of Commerce, TECs, the TUC, MPs and MEPs), the Regional Development Agency (WMDA) and the Region's universities. The Regional Offices of Government Departments provided technical information and there were also detailed consultations with local agencies, including the voluntary sector.

This strategy was extremely comprehensive and ran to nine parts. It included an analysis of the problems of the region, the vision and strategy for economic recovery (including a sub-regional dimension), and it was intended that the WMREDS should form the basis for the SPD. In practice, however, the WMREDS was largely ignored in drawing up the SPD – whose priority objectives are very different from those of WMREDS. Nevertheless, despite their lack of input to the SPD, local authority partners were relatively satisfied with the SPD strategy. As they saw it, the SPD provided a framework for drawing down European cash for projects they wanted to see carried out. There was, though, concern about the extent of the involvement of local partners in the strategy formulation process and whether the SPD would enable local area priorities to be fulfilled. These issues remain relevant for the 1997–1999 period.

Problems and plan priorities

The SPD points out that the West Midlands is experiencing long-term structural employment decline of its key manufacturing industries, motor vehicles and engineering. Unemployment is above the average and it has some of the worst inner city deprivation in the UK. Nevertheless, the SPD's vision for the West Midlands is that of an advanced industrial region noted for the excellence of its engineering, its dynamic service sector and a highly skilled and flexible workforce. It also prioritised the revitalisation of urban cores, with help to go to less well off areas and dedication to a high-quality environment to pass on to future generations. The SPD identifies priorities for action, 'drivers for change', in the regional economy: support for research and development, support for indigenous business, diversification, urban regeneration and tourism development. Each priority has a number of measures (see Table 8.2) which follow a similar pattern: land and infrastructure, business development and infrastructure for human resource development.

In the period 1988–1993 some £300m was allocated to the West Midlands through Objectives 2, 3 and 4. This has been used to secure major investment in industrial sites, the transformation of Birmingham City Centre, tourism development and help for SMEs. The use of EU funds for property-led projects has not been without criticism, but the construction of the International Convention Centre in Birmingham and the expansion of the National Exhibition Centre and the Warwick Science Park would not have gone ahead in the absence of ERDF (Loftman and Nevin 1994; Turok 1992). It has been argued that the Structural Funds have so far failed to 'make inroads into combating the problems of inner city poverty' (WMRFLA 1993). There was also criticism of the failure to integrate ERDF and ESF in the 1988–1993 Community Support Frameworks (WMRFLA 1993). Formal evaluations of the CSF were carried out by PIEDA (1994a) which identified issues relating to the delivery of the CSF, including partnership and monitoring. The £286m allocated for the 1994–1996 period should address some of these issues.

Implementation and the Monitoring Committee

As in other regions, a Project Monitoring Committee (PMC) was established to oversee implementation of the SPD. Membership of such Committees has been one of the most contentious issues. EU Regulations stipulate that its membership is set within the terms of the partnership and should include the Government, European Commission, European Investment Bank (EIB), private sector, TECs, voluntary sector and local authorities (Commission of the European Communities 1993d). In the West Midlands, as elsewhere in England, the PMC is chaired by the Regional Director of the Government Office. Government agencies predominate, but the five local authorities in the region are represented. The individuals are all officers, not elected council members, a decision taken by the local authorities themselves. The social partners, in particular the trade unions and private sector representatives, are not members.

The Committee meets quarterly and, assisted by a secretariat, has set up an implementation sub-committee and local partnership groups in each sub-region. A project scoring system has been established to assist the decision-making process. Whereas in Yorkshire and Humberside project and bid assessment is an on-going process, in the West Midlands a bidding round process has been followed with discrete deadlines for project applications.

Table 8.2 The West Midlands Objective 2 programme (1994–1996)

	Priority heading		*Measures*
Priority 1	Developing research and development in the region and encouraging technologic innovation	**1.1**	Training in high-technology skills and environmental techniques.
		1.2	Developing environmental technology and encouraging use of best practice.
		1.3	Business support of innovation.
		1.4	Provision of premises and infrastructure necessary to accommodate R&D and innovative activity.
Priority 2	Support of indigenous enterprise and local business	**2.1**	Development of business.
		2.2	Training for business and skill in the workforce.
		2.3	Creating the infrastructure needed to stimulate the growth of enterprise.
Priority 3	Assisting diversification of the regional economy and creation of conditions for growth	**3.1**	Development of business enterprise in sectors with growth potential and support for business new to the area.
		3.2	Human resource development in skills needed for sectors with growth potential and by business new to the area.
		3.3	Creating the infrastructure required to assist diversification and new growth
Priority 4	Urban and community regeneration	**4.1**	Improvement of public transport.
		4.2	Delivery of localised training.
		4.3	Developing the infrastructure necessary to deliver localised training and support.
		4.4	Improving the image.
Priority 5	Building on the growth potential of the cultural, media and tourism industries	**5.1**	Supporting enterprise.
		5.2	Human resource development.
		5.3	Providing the infrastructure measures to secure the growth of priority industries.

Source: CEC 1994d

Local partnership groups consider all projects within their locality, but have few decision-making powers. Selection is made by the PMC on the basis of the extent to which projects contribute to the regional strategy. There are no sub-regional appraisal and allocation procedures, unlike the previous period when Integrated Development Operational Programmes (IDOPs) were prepared. At the end of 1995 one of the biggest issues was whether or not spend would take place at the pace originally envisaged.

Yorkshire and Humberside: On the European Periphery?

Drawing up the strategy: a fragmented partnership?

Yorkshire and Humberside has had a weaker commitment to regional planning and is a weaker actor in 'Europe of the Regions.' However, it has lobbied strongly for Community Initiatives, in particular RECHAR, which is most important to the coalfields in the region; as indicated in Chapter 7, the Coalfields Community Campaign has taken a key role in this. Humberside County Council has played a lead role in the Assembly of European Regions and North Sea Commission (O'Neill 1995).

Objective 2 assistance is concentrated in Yorkshire and Humberside in three areas: South Yorkshire, Humberside and West Yorkshire (see Figure 8.3). This encompasses key cities and urban areas like Sheffield, Doncaster, Wakefield, Grimsby and Scunthorpe, some of which are long-standing participants in the European policy scene, but not as leaders (financial crisis has reduced Sheffield's standing and capability in the 1990s). The redrawing of the map in 1994 brought a loss of Objective 2 status to parts of Bradford and Goole. Unlike Birmingham, Leeds – the regional capital – with a buoyant economy and the fastest growing regional financial centre, has never been eligible for Objective 2 support. It can be regarded as a 'late developer' on the European scene (Haughton and Williams 1995).

Local partnership arrangements in Yorkshire and Humberside are more fragmented and problematic than in the West Midlands. Whilst having a distinct culture, its traditions of regional co-operation and partnership building are not as strong as they might be (Shutt 1996) or as good as within the North-West region (see Peck and Tickell 1994). Nonetheless, there has been some partnership building at city, sub-region and regional level in the mid-1990s. The local authorities are linked through the Yorkshire and Humberside Regional Association (YHRA), which has an office in Brussels, and the Yorkshire and Humberside Partnership (YHP). The YHP was formed by the Trades Union Congress and the Confederation of British Industry, with the YHRA and the Yorkshire and Humberside Development Association

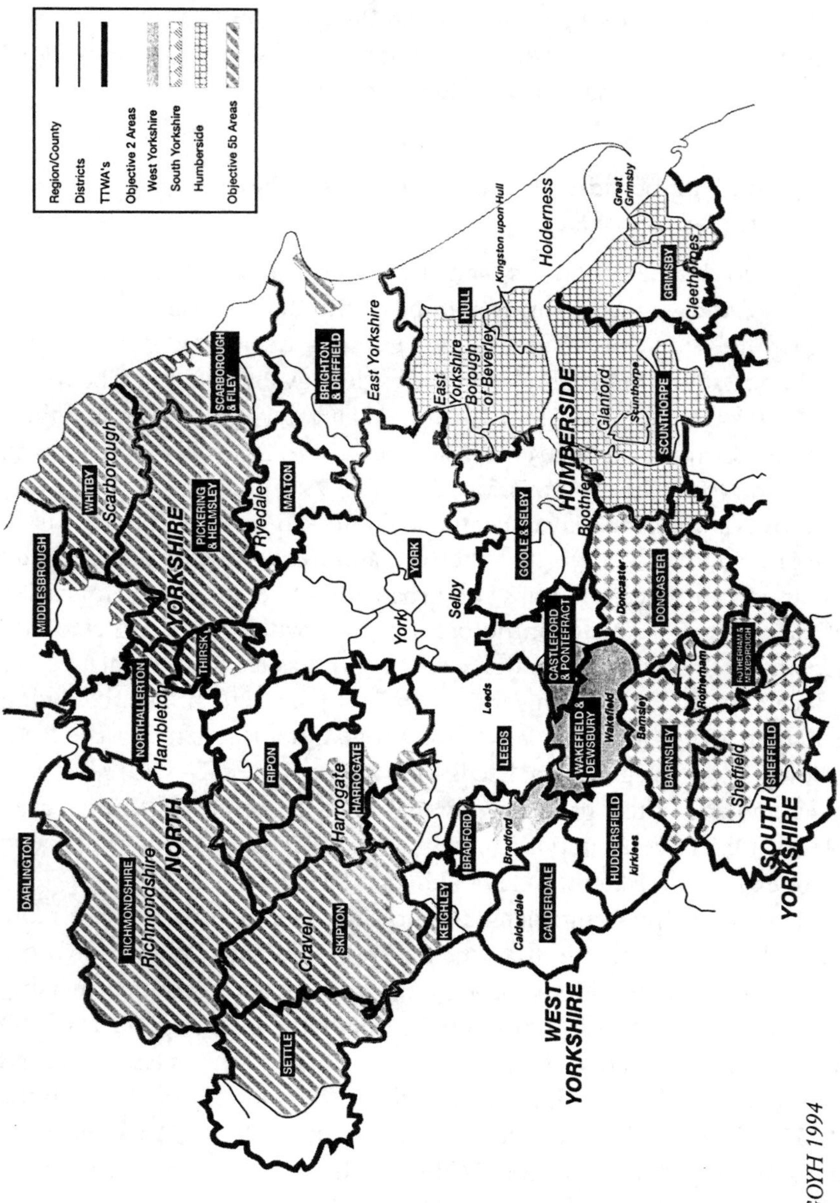

Source: GOYH 1994

Figure 8.3 Yorkshire and Humberside region

(YHDA) represented. This new public/private partnership did not include higher education institutions, TECs or regional government departments, but the Association of the Yorkshire and Humberside Chamber of Commerce was involved.

The YHP drew up a regional strategy in 1993 (YHP 1993) which provided a backcloth to the Objective 2 negotiating process but had no legal status in the EU and United Kingdom government regional planning process. Separate to the YHP strategy, the Yorkshire and Humberside office of the Department of the Environment prepared the SPD planning documents which provided the basis for negotiating Objective 2 funding.

The plan priorities

The problems facing Yorkshire and Humberside were seen by the SPD to be de-industrialisation and the collapse of the traditional coalfields and textile areas (GOYH 1994). Long-term structural decline has been underway and employment in its key industries – steel and coal mining, engineering, textiles and fishing – have been decimated. This has meant widespread regional deprivation and dereliction which is currently accelerating within the cities and outside in the coalfield and fishing areas. The region was allocated £243m from the Structural Funds for the 1994–1996 period.

The vision in the SPD for Yorkshire and Humberside is for the development of a self-sustaining, strong and environmentally sustainable economy with a modern technological base, a thriving SME sector able to compete nationally and internationally and to create good quality jobs for a workforce equipped with relevant skills training and enterprise. It also envisaged the creation of a pleasant environment in which people could live and work.

SPD plan priorities and supporting measures for the area are: support for SMEs, action to strengthen and diversify mature SMEs, strengthening of knowledge-based industries and development of advanced technology, attraction of new industry and services, support for tourist and cultural industries and targeted action in key deprived areas. A large proportion of the Funds has been earmarked for business support measures (see Table 8.3, p.137) which are designed to foster and strengthen the growth of SMEs, a focus which is very much in line with the emphasis at European level on SME policies. The measures are to help the weak SME sectors in the region to develop and to help start reconversion plans (Shutt, Robertson and Sear 1995).

As in the West Midlands, the Structural Funds have made a major contribution to the economic development of Yorkshire and Humberside in the 1980s. Community Initiatives are particularly important to the region, especially RECHAR and RESIDER. However, there has been a lack of systematic evaluation of previous achievements (Shutt 1996). A report by the Sheffield Business School (1992) found that some £436m of expenditure by the European Commission, United Kingdom authorities and private investors during the period 1988–1992 in South Yorkshire created 13,000 jobs, at an average cost to the Structural Funds of £10,000 per job. PIEDA (1994b) have also undertaken an evaluation of the East of England CSF, including the IDOPs for localities in the Yorkshire and Humberside region (although the results were not made publicly available). The SPD points to key flagship projects which the Structural Funds have supported, including bus interchanges, road improvements, the Sheffield Supertram and the construction of industrial floor space. As in the West Midlands, a number of comments were made on the management of the programmes prior to the establishment of the 1994 SPD. These included the need to establish a clear strategy and to communicate it to the partners, flexibility, proper monitoring systems, the lack of competition for funds, the need to ensure the best value for money, integration of the funds and the need for simpler administrative arrangements. Some concern was expressed about whether additionality was being achieved with spend on physical infrastructure.

Implementation and the Monitoring Committee

Membership of the PMC was contentious, as in the West Midlands. Government organisations predominate and the local authorities have only three places. These are also filled by officers and not members, but the participants were invited to the Committee by the Regional Director of the Government Office rather than nominated by the local authorities. The trade unions and voluntary sectors are similarly absent. There are no representatives of the utilities, although public transport interests are represented, and the private sector is barely represented through other interests.

The composition of the Committee highlights the tradition of fragmentation in the region. Business leaders have no real forum and rarely talk together above city level about regional regeneration. Significantly, there is no representation from the three major city local authorities: Hull, Sheffield and Bradford. The PMC is not in a strong position to facilitate linkage between these cities, which must be important to ensure regional strategy formation. This reflects one of the problems in the whole process – the SPDs are simply seen as documents for drawing down funds and the PMCs are not treated as fora where genuine regional plans can be developed and pursued.

Debate on the 1997 Objective 2 review was minimal. South Yorkshire set out its claim for Objective 1 status and discussions focused on how best to redraw the strategic regional plan in view of the multiplicity of players and changing position of key actors. At the same time, YHRA is to be restructured into the new Local Government Regional Assembly – whose regional constitution has been agreed in the context of the formation of the national Local Government Association which took effect from 1 April 1997.

GOYH and the mid-term position

The GOYH has made some progress in promoting a strategy for the region and stimulating programmatic development around the SPD. Its efforts at openness and development are indicated by the recent publication of a compendium of business support projects (GOYH 1996), one of the first regional offices to embark on such a venture, and its promotion of strategic business development forums to discuss project development. However, like all GORs, GOYH does not embrace all government departments in the region and faces a range of civil service management issues which make development of regional integration and planning difficult to follow through. It also had to start drafting the new 1997–1999 programme documents with only one year of operating experience. Project evaluation was difficult and the delivery process remains a key issue.

Strategic Issues and Lessons for 1997–1999

The negotiation and implementation of the English region SPDs in 1994–1996 raises a number of practical and theoretical issues regarding the formulation and implementation of regional development strategies. As the foregoing shows, there are differences between the two regional cases. However, elements of the SPD process also appear to be very similar. Issues relate to plan design and preparation, the content of the SPDs and approaches to regional development strategies.

Preparation and design of the SPDs

The European Commission expected the process of drawing up of the SPDs to involve the partners (Commission of European Communities 1993d). The case examples show that the GORs took the lead and virtually ignored prior work being carried out by the regional partnerships. Moreover, at each stage of the process there were difficulties over the involvement of partners, including the private sector. As the House of Commons Trade and Industry Select Committee report (1995) highlights, many witnesses complained that they had not been sufficiently involved in the preparation of the SPDs. A local authority witness, in particular, argued that the DoE consulted with the DTI and wrote an economic strategy for each region, despite the fact that very often partners were working on a regional strategy drawn up by a partnership of regional interests. The fact that the West Midlands displays a high degree of 'Europeanisation' among its local organisations appears to have made no difference to the outcome.

When the SPDs disappeared into the 'mincing machine' of the process of negotiation (Lloyd *et al.* 1995a), the Commission felt that the earlier lack of local involvement had been remedied by consultation with partners taking place at this stage (House of Commons 1995). While European Commission regulations meant that some changes had to be made to the SPDs and some account taken of local views, it can be argued that, in essence, the regional economic strategy drawn up by regional partners was still pushed aside. The final version of the SPDs was drawn up by central government and largely reflected their priorities and thinking with regard to regional economic regeneration.

As Peck and Tickell (1994) argue, partnership is rapidly becoming an overworked concept. Opportunities for synergy, budget enlargement and information sharing appear to be limited (Mackintosh 1992), and, at a practical level, there is much confusion about how it should be operated at a regional scale. While it is arguable that there was a 'multiplicity of ministrations' involved in the plan formulation process, and there was a fine line in the balance of power between the UK Government, local interests and the European Commission, the power to determine the plan content ultimately rested with the Government and not with any regional partnership. The Commission was unable to insist on the inclusion of the social partners, particularly the trade unions. This suggests the EU needs to consider whether the regulations need to be strengthened to allow full participation of all partners. There is also a question about whether central government or regional partnerships should draw up the SPDs.

Regional strategic approaches

There are other issues raised in relation to plan design and preparation. The change from CSF and IDOPs to the SPDs simplified the Structural Fund process and was a step towards a more strategic approach, given that the IDOPs were only a basis for drawing down ERDF. The SPDs need to fit within a region-wide view and the value of sub-regional perspectives in large diverse regions is always critical. The IDOPs encouraged local areas to understand what share of ERDF expenditure they would receive, which enabled the development of sub-regional strategies; Birmingham and Solihull even prepared such a plan this time round. Sub-regional plans were permitted in the EU regulations for SPDs but were rejected by the UK government, with the result that project selection in 1994–1996 is taking place on a region-wide basis. This means that some localities might end up with more ERDF than they might otherwise have received and others will end up with less and feel aggrieved. Some authorities were not unhappy with this situation as it provided the opportunity, at a time when budgets were being squeezed, to draw down as much ERDF as they could to carry out projects.

Overall, the process of regionalisation has weakened the focus on sub-regional strategies when both really need to be developed in tandem. The 1994 SPDs relate to parts of regions only, as do the 1997 SPDs. The 1994 SPDs were only partial and new attempts would need to be made to re-draw regional plans and fit the SPDs inside them for the 1997–1999 period, but thinking on this has barely started. A further point to be made is that the regional strategy linkages in the 1994 SPDs are relatively weak within and between regions – for example, there is no link made between Objective 2 and 5b areas in the SPDs. It can be argued, however, that the SPDs are not a 'plan' since the United Kingdom authorities do not see such an approach as appropriate (House of Commons 1995). Thus while project assessment is done on a region-wide basis, there is a suspicion that projects will come forward to be approved in such an *ad hoc* way that they will not add up to a coherent strategy.

Regional challenge

If the SPDs were supposed to result in a region-wide strategic approach, Regional Challenge cut across that process. Announced in May 1994, Regional Challenge was designed to run on similar lines to City Challenge. A competition for money from the Structural Funds, it was set up 'to encourage imaginative value for money proposals involving private sector funding'. Total 'prize' money was near to £200m, a sum created by top-slicing the funds.

While the Commission accepted Regional Challenge, the process raises important questions about control of the disbursement of the Structural Funds and about its impact on the process. Are funds controlled by the Commission or the Member State? The view put forward in the House of Commons Select Committee (1995) was that the 'EU regional funding the UK receives is effectively its own money being redistributed' and therefore the United Kingdom is making the best use of European funds. Regional Challenge, however, would seem to encourage further tensions between the different agencies in the regions without producing much added value, especially since failed projects simply go back into the regional 'pot'.

It can be argued that the competition hinders the development of region-wide innovation initiatives and cuts across the fulfilment of objectives for the priority measures in the regional strategy because projects are being considered against different criteria from the other measures. Furthermore, the question must be asked as to how many of the successful projects are actually strategic in regional terms. It would seem that a 'Regional Challenge' ought to have added to, not detracted from, such an emphasis.

Content of the Single Programming Documents

The problems of the West Midlands and Yorkshire and Humberside are fundamentally similar. Nonetheless, there is a specificity to their problems and one would expect their SPDs to reflect these differences. Yet they look very alike. Indeed, all five SPDs examined by Lloyd *et al.* (1995a) were remarkably similar in content and so similar that they could have come from a single template, with only the name of the locality changed. This was partly due to the relative speed with which the Objective 2 *ex ante* appraisal process was handled, compared with the Merseyside Objective 1. Criticism was made in the press at the time that delays in the process were resulting in some current projects, which could have expected further funding, being terminated. However, the SPDs were alike because they reflected national rather than local interests and were financial 'draw-down' documents rather than genuine plans.

If future SPDs are to constitute regional conversion strategies they must be more than frameworks for spending Structural Funds. The emphasis sought by the Commission was for soft infrastructure priorities, with support to business development in SMEs rather than physical infrastructure. Planned expenditure in the West Midlands and Yorkshire and Humberside SPDs reflects this (see Table 8.3 and Table 8.4), so they do demonstrate some coherence with EU objectives. However, this may be a constraint on local needs and priorities. Concern, therefore, extends to whether projects coming forward at implementation stage reflect local requirements. This raises a broader issue of what model of regional economic development the strategies are based on.

Table 8.3 Yorkshire and Humberside: Objective 2 priorities (1994–1996)

Percentage of resources by priority and fund	*ERDF (%)*	*ESF (%)*	*Total (%)*
1. Action to support SMEs	19.7	20.3	19.8
2. Action to strengthen and diversify mature SMES	12.4	17.7	13.7
3. Action knowledge-based industries and technological development	13.2	13.9	13.4
4. Action to attract new industry	17.5	12.01	16.1
5. Action to support tourist and culture industries	18.2	13.9	17.1
6. Targeted action for key deprived areas	18.3	20.3	18.8

Source: GOYH 1994

Table 8.4 The West Midlands: Objective 2 priorities (1994–1996)

Percentage of resources by priority and fund	*ERDF (%)*	*ESF (%)*	*Total (%)*
1. Research and development	12.0	15.0	12.7
2. Support for local business	14.2	45.0	20.8
3. Assisting diversification	22.6	18.2	21.7
4. Urban and community regeneration	39.5	10.7	33.2
5. Building on growth of media/ tourism	10.9	10.7	10.9
Technical assistance	0.8	0.2	0.6

Source: CEC (1994d)

Regional development strategies – competitive or comparative advantage?

During the negotiation stage the Objective 2 plans were strengthened by dialogue with Commission officials. The final SPDs were significantly influenced by thinking in the Delors White Paper *Growth, Competitiveness and Employment* (Commission of European Communities 1994c). This stressed the importance of SMEs for innovation and the links between investing in people, combating social exclusion and economic competitiveness.

It is clear the Commission believes that structural adjustment comes through an approach based on the notion of competitive advantage (Hirst and Zeitlin 1989). This focuses attention on a range of business development initiatives – for example, those relating to products and markets, new technologies, changes in methods of production, the labour process and changes in the management of organisations. The policy emphasis would vary according to the type of industry and demands a sophisticated sectoral approach. This is problematic for a UK government committed to achieving comparative advantage via deregulation, low labour costs, low corporate taxation and favourable exchange rates in a situation where regional sectoral analyses are weak and policy-making fora absent. While plan priorities made some concessions to Brussels, they reflect central government's own agenda.

The West Midlands and Yorkshire and Humberside SPDs prioritise support to business and innovation. This will mainly come through Business Links initiatives. Yet the achievement of competitive advantage requires more than a few more business advisers and counsellors, which is all that is offered by such an approach. A serious business development strategy would require a bolder vision of what could be achieved, more substantial institutional capacity to initiate projects and a more coherent regional network of business support agencies (Shutt, Robertson and Sear 1995; Turok 1995).

Synergy and integration

The evaluations of past programmes in the West Midlands and Yorkshire and Humberside stress the need to integrate the Structural Funds and the Community Initiatives. ERDF and ESF need better co-ordination and targeting too. Each have different time-scales and administrative procedures, which makes integration very difficult. The European Union needs to rethink the relation of the framework and timing of the Community Initiatives to the Structural Fund process (Shutt 1995).

Conclusions

This chapter has raised a wide range of strategic issues relating to the operation of European regional policy in the English regions, using the examples of the West Midlands and Yorkshire and Humberside. It shows that the SPD process has implications for the practice and theory of regional economic policy in the late 1990s. These need to be taken account of in reviewing the 1994–1996 Objective 2 SPDs and debated within the English regions and the European Commission. The issues concern regional strategic approaches and the institutional framework in which the SPDs are prepared and implemented.

It is clear that contested governance means that contrasting models of regional economic development are being pursued by Brussels and the UK (see Lloyd *et al.* 1995a). The regional strategies being pursued in England largely reflect central government priorities. There is a question mark over whether they will meet regional innovation and development needs.

The EU has sought to establish a broad framework for regional development priorities to be determined. Yet the SPDs may be no more than draw-down documents. This approach has created uncertainty for sub-regions about the amount of Structural Funds likely to be available for them. In addition, the top-slicing of Structural Funds through Regional Challenge gives rise to a number of concerns. It has adverse implications for long-term strategic policy and for the integration of European funding.

Key points for consideration are: whether sub-regional plans need to be established within improved regional frameworks to give greater certainty to the level of Structural Funds available in local areas, to develop the projects and the project selection criteria and to give greater weight to local priorities and realistic processes than to simple cost-per-job criteria. The question also arises about the sorts of projects that are prioritised for European funding. While the SPDs accord with EU emphases on soft infrastructure, there is a fear that underspending will see priorities steered back in favour of physical infrastructure at the expense of economic, social and community-based projects.

The Commission needs to respond to the complexity of programme delivery which it has created and which creates Euro-scepticism for those who have to operate them. In relation to project and capacity building, serious consideration needs to be given to training and to the capacity of agencies to deliver to newly emerging priorities. These points relate to the institutional framework in which the Structural Funds are managed.

Finally, the UK's institutional structure within which regional economic planning is taking place needs to be reformed. It is clear that the current situation is chaotic. Chaos may result in creativity but the multiplicity of administrations at both quasi-political and executive level means that the picture is extremely confused. The partnership arrangements create insiders and outsiders, which cause practical problems. There are simply too many agencies operating in the field of economic development, including the TECs, Business Links, local authorities, development associations, UDCs, City Challenge, Partnerships and the Chambers of Commerce. They are all leashed to the GORs, which act in the new contract culture as broker between the UK and Europe – adding to the complexity. The PMCs put key beneficiaries in the role of decision makers (House of Commons 1995), raising questions as to whether independent secretariats are required – as in Western Scotland.

In addition, an integrated Regional Planning Authority, a Regional Transport Authority and co-ordinated and strengthened Regional Development Agencies for each English region are needed to strengthen regional planning and development and to mediate between the local and national interests (Mawson 1995; Regional Policy Commission 1996). This is impossible for Brussels and Strasbourg to impose. Whether this can be grown from within the UK and the English regions remains to be seen, especially as regional government is not on the agenda of a first term Labour Government. At the very least, while strategy formulation remains in the hands of central government, to ensure ownership of the plan among regional interests Brussels needs to strengthen the role of the other partners in the process. The period 1997–1999 may well be the last chance for the English regions to use major tranches of Structural Funds to enhance their regional strategies. The need for these in an increasingly competitive European environment will remain a key task for the English regions, even if they lose out in the European fund-bidding game in the 21st century.

CHAPTER 9

The Implementation of Objective 1 in the Highlands and Islands of Scotland

John Bryden

Introduction

The Objective 1 programme for the Highlands and Islands of Scotland runs from 1994–1999. The area will receive about 311 million ecu (mecu) (£255m) of EU Structural Fund assistance over this period, to be matched by public sector contributions of 406 mecu from the UK and 295 mecu from the private sector. Although a substantial sum, the annual spend from the programme represents less than two per cent of regional GDP for the Highlands and Islands.

This programme has variously been described as a 'gold rush' for the region and a 'pork barrel' for the development agencies. The Highlands and Islands are a peripheral region of the UK and Europe. Until the accession of Sweden and Finland the area was the most sparsely populated region of the EU, with a 1991 population of 369,000 living in an area of 39,000 square kilometres. Large parts of the region, especially in the Islands and peripheral areas, exhibit many of the classic problems of a declining rural area, including population losses, unemployment and underemployment, a poorly developed manufacturing sector, and over-dependence on declining sectors such as agriculture and fisheries.

This chapter outlines the implementation of the Objective 1 programme in the Highlands and Islands and assesses the way in which the money has been invested so far. In particular, it focuses on the question as to whether money has been targeted on the most economically disadvantaged or 'fragile' areas of the region (see Figure 9.1). It concludes that whilst there has been some extra spending on the needy areas of the region, this has been because of a few large projects. Matching funding and the integration of projects at

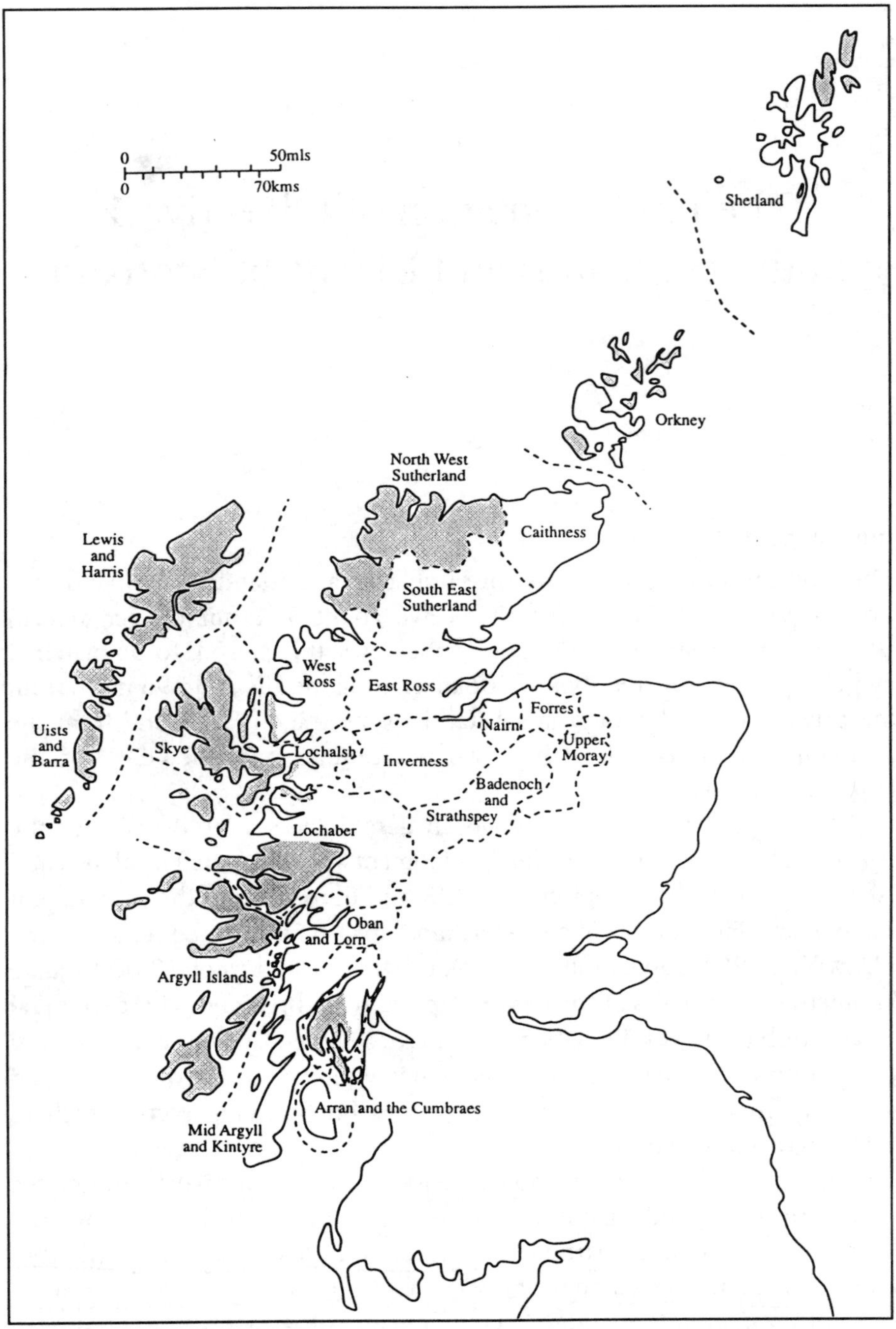

Source: HIE Inverness 1995

Figure 9.1 Fragile areas in the Highlands and Islands

the local level, as well as the functioning of the partnership, are serious problems with the programme. The chapter also assesses the distribution of EU funds amongst agencies in the region. It begins by outlining the background to the designation of the Highlands and Islands as an Objective 1 region in 1994 following the 1993 review of the Structural Funds.

Background to Objective 1 in the Highlands and Islands

European funding has played an important role in the Highlands and Islands since the 1970s through the provision of major infrastructure such as the up-grading of the main A9 trunk road and the Integrated Development Programme for the Western Isles in the early 1980s. The most recent programme prior to Objective 1 was the Highlands and Islands Community Support Framework (CSF) which led to the investment of £229.2m of public funds under Objective 5b status for declining rural areas over the period 1990–1993. An interim evaluation of this programme was carried out which is instructive in assessing Objective 1. This showed that the greatest effects of the CSF had been on reducing peripherality through investment in infrastructure, on strengthening the economies of some of the most remote areas and on improvements to the performance of marginal farming units. The report made four main recommendations:

- greater co-ordination of individual measures at the sub-regional level to achieve greater synergy between different aspects of the programme
- greater priority should be attached to business development
- ESF funds should be more focused on economic diversification and small business development
- the need to review and strengthen administrative resources, particularly monitoring.

Objective 1 status for the Highlands and Islands was announced in July 1993. Prior to this there had been a long campaign by local authorities, development agencies and politicians to upgrade the area from Objective 5b status. In November 1993 the Scottish Office submitted a regional development plan which had been drawn up in collaboration with local authorities, development agencies and others in the region. The drafting of the plan had involved several rounds of consultation with a range of interest groups in the region, but this fell short of anything which could be described as 'public consultation' and, in practice, the plan was compiled by a 'plan writing group'. This group comprised Scottish Office departments, Highlands and Islands Enterprise, Highland Regional Council, Strathclyde Regional Council, Scottish Natural Heritage, a representative of the three Island Councils and one representative from the 11 district councils in the Highlands and Islands area. The plan stated that the area had a GDP per capita of 76 per cent of the EC average and was the most sparsely populated and peripheral region in the European Community at the time (The Scottish Office 1993).

The plan drew attention to four strategic issues which had to be tackled for the region to move closer to the European average. These were, first, peripherality and insularity: the effects of remoteness contributed to economic, social and psychological problems exacerbated by the topography of the region, which makes internal communications difficult. Second, economic and social fragility caused by the sparsity of population and isolation, which made the area vulnerable to external forces and offered restricted development opportunities. In particular, the population was continuing to move away from the remoter areas. The third issue was the poor industrial structure of the region, with dependence on low-growth industries, the primary sector and tourism. Fourth, there was a need to safeguard the unique environment and heritage characteristics of the area, but also to capitalise on their economic potential (The Scottish Office 1993).

The plan submitted by The Scottish Office had an overall aim 'to promote the internal and external cohesion of the Highlands and Islands region over the period 1994–99, primarily by increasing and sustaining GDP growth rates and reducing unemployment and underemployment' (Commission of the European Communities 1995b, p.23). By these means it was considered that the programme would reduce the disparity between the Highlands and the rest of the EU and also reduce disparities within the region, for example between the more prosperous Inverness area and the less prosperous Western Isles where unemployment is typically 50 per cent above the regional average. This plan envisaged four sub-programmes relating to physical infrastructure (40% of funds), support for business (37%), human resources (15%) and environment and heritage (8%).

As required by the Structural Fund Regulations, the proposed plan was subjected to an *ex ante* appraisal, on behalf of the European Commission, carried out by a research team co-ordinated by the European Policies Research Centre (EPRC) at Strathclyde University. The evaluation criticised the plan because of its heavy emphasis on physical infrastructure such as roads, bridges, water and sewerage facilities. It also pointed to the lack of an industrial strategy behind the plan to provide a more coherent approach to the region's economic development. It further suggested that improvements in communications infrastructure could be counter-productive if they expose indigenous firms to increased competition from outwith the region. They may also allow firms to transport primary produce away from the region prior to processing, thereby losing local employment opportunities. In addition, training schemes may simply encourage people to leave the area once they are better qualified unless sufficient attention is paid to the demand-side for labour. Finally, the evaluators criticised the make-up of the 'plan writing group' who drew up the original document. The EPRC report stated that the process had placed too little emphasis on consultation with the district councils and local enterprise companies in the area and there had been no one to represent 'human resource development' needs. They also highlighted the lack of consultation between The Scottish Office, who submitted the plan, and the other partners who had little time to comment on the final version (Bachtler 1994; Turok 1994). Local politicians were also concerned about the issue of additionality, fearing that the Scottish Office may have been trying to substitute European aid for their own funding for infrastructure in the region (*The Scotsman* 20.1.94).

Protracted negotiations then took place between the Scottish Office and the European Commission over the final shape of the strategy. The effect was to delay approval of the Objective 1 strategy until July 1994, six months after the programme had supposedly started.

The Objective 1 Strategy for the Region

In addition to noting the problem of a too heavy emphasis in the past on infrastructure, this document placed greater emphasis on the region's economic strengths, notably tourism, the primary sector and related food industries. Further, the importance of local communities was recognised through a new community development priority, as was an increased emphasis on targeting resources to parts of the region with the greatest problems (discussed also in subsequent sections). The SPD set out six priorities for Objective 1 spending, compared to the four in the original plan, the amounts to be invested in each being set out in Table 9.1. The strategy is contained within the 'Single Programming Document 1994–99' (Commission of the European Communities 1995b).

The initial emphasis on physical infrastructure was reduced so that investment in communications and service networks (roads, ferries, water and sewerage) now accounted for 21.5 per cent of the programme. Within several of the other priorities, however, there is scope for physical infrastructure spending. Thus 25 per cent of the funds for business development measure

Table 9.1 EU Objective 1 assistance for the Highlands and Islands by priority measure 1994–99 (mecu at 1994 prices)

Priority	*Total funding*	*EU contribution*	*National contribution*	*Private sector contribution*
1. Business development	296.23 (29.3%)	72.10	72.10	152.03
2. Tourism, heritage and culture	91.95 (9.1%)	24.20	24.20	43.55
3. Enhancement of the environment	34.60 (3.4%)	16.30	16.30	2.00
4. Primary sector and food	274.13 (27.1%)	68.70	125.59	79.84
5. Community development	92.36 (9.1%)	46.90	45.46	0.00
6. Communications and service networks	216.95 (21.4%)	79.70	119.55	17.70
7. Technical assistance	6.20 (0.1%)	3.10	3.10	0.00
Total	**1012.42 (99.5%)**	**311.00**	**406.30**	**295.12**

Source: Highlands and Islands Single Programming Document 1994–99, p.123.

are allocated to the provision of new sites and premises for industry. Similarly, within tourism 41 per cent of the funds are allocated for the development of new attractions.

Three main indicators are proposed to assess the effectiveness of the programme. These are GDP per capita, employment growth and improvements to productivity and competitiveness. The programme is forecast to add between 2.5 per cent and 4 per cent overall to the GDP per capita of the region. At its most optimistic, therefore, with all other things being equal, the programme on its own would only increase the Highlands and Islands GDP to 80 per cent of the EU average if the latter remained static. A more realistic estimate, allowing for changes elsewhere, might be that the programme will enable the region to remain in roughly the same position as it was in 1993 in relation to the EU as a whole. Factors such as a substantial increase in tourism or a slowdown in growth elsewhere could, however, help the region grow faster than the EU average and hence improve its relative position. Employment growth forecast over the programme period is estimated to be in the order of 2500 full-time equivalents, or about 1.8 per cent above the 1991 employment level of 134,000. This compares with unemployment of over 16,000 at June 1993. It is also intended to measure employment growth at a sub-regional level. The third main measure is the effects of the programme on productivity and competitiveness in the region. The indicators are gross value-added per input cost and gross value-added per full time equivalent. Improvements in productivity will also be measured by comparing Highlands and Island's industries with those in other regions (Commission of the European Communities 1995b).

Implementation of the Objective 1 Programme

The Objective 1 programme is managed and delivered by the 'Objective 1 Partnership' through a series of committees involving a wide range of public sector and voluntary organisations, mostly chaired by the Scottish Office. The overall authority is the SPD Monitoring Committee chaired by a senior official of the Scottish Office Education and Industry Department (SOEID). This committee has around 18 members and meets every five months or so with responsibility for the overview of the programme and its policies. Membership of this committee includes representatives of the European Commission, three representatives from local authorities, and quangos such as HIE, Scottish Natural Heritage, the Scottish Tourist Board and the Local Enterprise Companies (LECs). The Scottish Council for Voluntary Organisations is also on the committee to represent the interests of the voluntary sector in the region, as is one of the local colleges to represent education and training interests (Claridge 1995).

Arguably, the most important role is played by the Programme Management Committee (PMC). This has around 28 members and is responsible for deciding on bids made for funds. It decides on all applications other than those for the primary sector and food priority, which are decided by the Scottish Office Agriculture and Fisheries Department. This committee is also chaired by the SOEID and meets on a quarterly basis. Its membership is similar to the overall monitoring committee with additional colleges, LECs and district council representatives. Its broader membership included organisations such as the Association of Community Enterprises for the Highlands and Islands (ACE-HI) (which ceased operating in 1996), Scottish Wildlife and Countryside Link and the ferry company Caledonian MacBrayne. Whilst the make-up of the partnership reflects a diverse range of interests, this may lead to problems of co-ordination and agreement on the selection and prioritisation of projects for funding. This committee is supported by three sectoral advisory groups which evaluate and prioritise applications relating to the three areas of Business Development, Tourism and the Primary Sector; Community Development and the Environment; and Communications and Basic Services. Each has a membership of 10 to 12 and is chaired by the Scottish Office.

The key agency administering the programme is the 'Programme Executive' based in Inverness. It undertakes initial assessments of bids prior to their discussion by the advisory groups. It has a staff of eight and is funded by a levy on all partners who receive Objective 1 funds. This level of staffing seems low, given the large volume of applications for assistance and restricts the Executive to an administrative rather than a development role. The bids are made by public sector bodies and voluntary organisations. The private sector has difficulties in making bids without public agency support due to European rules (Claridge 1995).

The initial experience of this innovative arrangement for the implementation of the programme has revealed a number of concerns. First, there have been difficulties in getting partners representing such disparate interests to work together. In addition, and linked also to the lack of an adequate strategic analysis in the Plan and SPD, there is an apparent lack of a shared understanding about the key challenges facing the region and what the appropriate policy responses should be. Although a large and diverse range of bodies are involved in the numerous committees and advisory groups, the whole partnership is heavily dominated by Scottish Office, not only because its officials chair the key committees, but, more importantly, because the Scottish Office is ultimately the main source of matching funding for most of the projects submitted. In addition, the European Commission had a substantial input into the final SPD. These two factors could mean that the local partners do not have a sense of ownership of the SPD. There have also been questions about the methods of evaluating projects submitted and the reasons for decisions taken, neither being 'transparent' to the public or applicants. Finally, although some improvements have been made to ESF funding mechanisms, problems still remain in supporting long-term projects through annual funding procedures.

Allocation of the Objective 1 Funds

In 1994 the delay in approval of the Objective 1 plan meant that there was only one bidding round. In 1995 there were two rounds, in March and June. Up to the time of writing there has been one round in 1996. The bids are appraised against a number of criteria for each of the priorities. Areas for evaluation are the justification for the project, the expected outcomes, the degree of environmental sustainability, additionality, innovation, integration, leverage and partnership. Each project is allocated a score against these criteria. Thereafter they are assessed on the basis of criteria specific to the type of project. A business development project, for example, seeking to provide finance for new ventures would be assessed on the basis of job creation, leverage, innovation, the extent to which new markets were being developed, synergy with other projects in the programme and a measure of peripherality. The screening process has been criticised as complex and bureaucratic by some partners, yet some form of evaluation is necessary to provide a logical basis for discriminating between projects and to ensure that the best projects, in terms of the SPD objectives and targets, are assisted. What is unclear, and far from transparent, is whether the existing procedures will, in fact, ensure this.

Other than through the media, there has been little attempt to assess the allocation of Objective 1 funds to date. Information on the bids for funds was provided recently by Claridge (1995). Table 9.2 sets out the pattern of bids and allocation of resources for the 1994 round of ERDF funding.

Table 9.2 Objective 1 bids and allocations for ERDF (1994)

Priority	*Number of bids*	*ERDF sought (£m)*	*ERDF available (£m)*	*ERDF spend (£m)*
1 Business development	40	17.6	4.8	4.4
2 Tourism, etc.	40	10.5	1.9	2.6
3 Environment	11	1.2	1.0	0.1
5 Community development	15	2.8	1.1	1.1
6 Infrastructure	106	47.8	8.4	6.9
Total	**212**	**79.9**	**17.1**	**15.1**

Source: Claridge 1995 and Objective 1 Programme Executive.

As the table shows, the largest number of bids was received for Priority 6. Projects funded under this priority were mainly physical infrastructure and the partner organisations were the Regional and Islands Councils. Of the £15.1m of ERDF allocated, 42 per cent went on road and bridge improvements under Priority 6. Major beneficiaries included Scalpay Bridge (£4.2m). The main problem for the Western Isles Islands Council was providing the matching funding. This apparently meant that the Council lacked funds to meet other road requirements in the Western Isles (*West Highland Free Press*, November 1994). Other projects to benefit from ERDF included a venture capital fund established by HIE (£1m), a new visitor restaurant by the National Trust for Scotland (£312k) and the Inverness Airport Control Tower for Highlands and Islands Airports Ltd (£320k).

The table also indicates a considerable disparity between bids and outcomes. There was a general impression that it was likely to be easier to get projects through in the early rounds, when procedures were likely to be less stringent. At the same time, the local authorities and organisations like

HIE were best placed to make bids due to their previous involvement with the Structural Funds and the preparation of the regional development plan.

In 1994 ESF bids were received for £7.2m of assistance. The total amount available was £6.26m, so the ESF was (relatively) only slightly oversubscribed at 15 per cent compared to the ERDF at 367 per cent. It is not possible to allocate the ESF awards geographically because they tend to go to educational institutions, training providers or to HIE for region-wide schemes. In total, £5.84m of ESF funds were allocated, slightly less than the sum available. The largest awards went to two national schemes administered by HIE: 'Training for Work' (£892k) and 'Youth Training' (£860k). Together, these awards accounted for almost 30 per cent of all ESF allocations. There have also been large sums of Objective 1 funding allocated to the national 'Investors in People' scheme.

There have been two rounds of Objective 1 funding in 1995 and a further round so far in 1996, although data on bids were not retained after 1994. These rounds are assessed in Table 9.3. Taking Table 9.2 and Table 9.3 together, it can be seen that allocations for infrastructure fell significantly in 1995 but increased again in the first round in 1996. Overall, this priority has remained substantially overspent compared with the allocation in the SPD. Allocations to business development increased slightly in 1995 and significantly in 1996, implying that this priority is well up to, and probably above, the SPD target. Tourism increased in 1995 but fell in 1996, although it also exceeds the SPD allocation. It is the allocations for the environment and community development which have fallen far short of the targets to date, and this must raise questions about both the content of these projects and the commitment of those involved to the two priorities. (Comparisons between allocations made and the SPD targets ignore Social Fund allocations, which are small by comparison. The figures in Table 9.1 are adjusted for Priority 4, agriculture.)

Objective 1 and Spatial Targeting

When the first round of ERDF was announced there was considerable controversy about the apparent lack of geographical targeting of the assistance. This reflected the fact that assistance appeared to be going to the Inverness area and not to the more needy parts of the Highlands (*The Herald*, 8.2.95). It was also shown that HIE and the LEC network had gained 34 per cent of the EU funds with the local authorities receiving 49 per cent, leading to criticism that Objective 1 was becoming a 'carve-up' between agencies in the region. The need for matching funds meant that development

Table 9.3 Objective 1 allocations for ERDF 1995 (2 rounds) and 1996 (round 1)

Priority	*ERDF allocated (£m) 1995*	*Percentage allocations 1995*	*ERDF allocated 1996 (first round) (£m)*	*Percentage allocations 1996*
1 Business development	6.79	29.9	9.56	34.4
2 Tourism, etc.	6.01	26.5	3.23	11.6
3 Environment	1.53	6.7	0.41	1.5
5 Community development	0.00	0.0	2.12	7.6
6 Infrastructure	5.76	25.4	12.11	43.5
Total	**20.09**	**88.5**	**27.43**	**98.6**

Source: Objective 1 Programme Executive.

agencies would inevitably receive large amounts of funding. The question remained, however, as to how much of the funds was being directed towards the neediest areas.

The SPD does not define the areas of greatest need in the region but stresses the need for targeting assistance on the basis of criteria such as unemployment rates and income levels. In particular, it notes that targeting should apply to Priority 5 for community development, which is directed to the poorest 15 per cent of the population. It also stresses that the criteria for, and implementation of, geographical targeting should be reviewed on a regular basis to 'ensure that the needs of the most disadvantaged areas are being tackled appropriately' (Commission of the European Communities 1995b, p.31). The targeting strategy was set out in a number of documents by the Objective 1 Partnership and was based on the HIE pattern of spending in the region. This moves funds from the more prosperous Inverness and Nairn LEC area to other LECs according to the level of need in fragile areas and areas of employment deficit (HIE 1992). This is done by splitting the annual HIE budget on a per capita basis and then redistributing three quarters of the funds from the Inverness area to other more needy parts of the region. The Objective 1 Partnership used the HIE formula in conjunction with the population data and a peripherality score to give targets for spending for each of 19 defined functional areas in the region. Other factors, such as unemployment rates and the pattern of HIE's training expenditure, were applied for particular measures. The peripherality measure scores each area into three bands, with the Western Isles, Orkney and Shetland in the most peripheral band. The targeting strategy was only intended to be temporary until research was conducted on the GDP for each of the sub-areas (Highlands and Islands Partnership Programme 1995a).

The Objective 1 Partnership decided that the targeting strategy should apply to 50 per cent of funds, a decision that met with criticism from some quarters – notably Calum Macdonald, MP for the Western Isles (*The Scotsman*, 20.9.94). The targeting also does not apply to Priority 3, for the environment, and Priority 4, agriculture and food, which is being implemented by the Scottish Office and where a separate method was to be developed. The main point to note is that the targeting strategy was poorly developed at the outset and that stop-gap measures had to be used largely in response to criticism. Moreover, whilst targeting applies to 50 per cent of funds, the reactive nature of the programme means that the Programme Management Executive (PME) is reliant on sufficient quality applications coming forward for the targeting strategy to be effective. A guide 'floor' level of assistance of 50 per cent of funds is allocated for each of the Priorities, with the exceptions of 3 and 4. As the report on targeting notes:

> Where a sub-area has generated insufficient quality projects in one year to reach the 'floor' the undercommitment will be carried forward. The PME will have a role in encouraging or assisting development projects to reach targets but the primary responsibility lies with the development organisations operating within these areas. (Highlands and Islands Partnership Programme 1994a, p.7)

It is not clear what would happen where the particular area continued to fail to generate sufficient demand for projects, due to the problem of raising matching funding, for example. Unless money was redistributed to less needy areas, there may be underspending on the programme as a whole. One way of encouraging projects in these areas might be to increase the rates of subsidy to projects, although there does not seem to be a mechanism for this at present.

Whilst the Objective 1 Partnership's strategy for targeting is complex, HIE has developed a policy of targeting assistance on readily identifiable fragile areas. These areas were drawn up on the basis of criteria such as low population density, the proportion of elderly people, demographic and economic trends and accessibility. This first appeared in the HIDB Corporate Plan for 1988, but is also used by HIE. It is instructive to assess the allocation of Objective 1 in relation to this definition. The areas are mainly in the north and west of the HIE area, the remotest and most sparsely populated areas of the region (see Figure 9.1, p.144). In 1991 these areas had a population of 69,000 or about 19 per cent of the HIE area total. The fragile areas provide a simple way of illustrating the impact of Objective 1 on the poorer areas of the region.

Since the ERDF funds are allocated to individual projects, it is possible to work out how much has gone to the fragile areas. It is important to treat these figures with some caution, however, as only those projects which are clearly in the HIE fragile areas have been included. Thus part of the Shetland Islands is classed as a fragile area, but where funds have been allocated to projects covering all of Shetland, the Shetland Business Enterprise scheme for example, these have been excluded. There are other elements of spending which are not geographically identified, such as the HIE venture capital programme mentioned earlier, but these are the exception. Taking account of these reservations, it appears that £5.8m, or 38 per cent of the first round ERDF allocations, went to the fragile areas in the Highlands. This figure includes Scalpay Bridge, which accounts for no less than 73 per cent of the ERDF allocation to the fragile areas.

It is not possible to compare bids against the sums allocated for each individual priority for awards in the two rounds in 1995. The fragile areas did relatively well out of the March 1995 allocation gaining 35 per cent (£6.8m) of the £19.6m of ERDF. This was largely due to the success of the Western Isles in gaining large infrastructure projects such as the Stornoway Ferry Terminal (Stornoway Pier and Harbour Commission £3.5m) and the Sound of Harris Ferry Vessel and Terminal (Caledonian MacBrayne £1.75m). The ESF awards for the first round in 1995 again showed that national training schemes operated by the LECs were major beneficiaries. The largest awards were for 'Youth Training' (HIE £894,404) and 'Training for Work' (HIE £300,000), together accounting for 18.5 per cent of the £6.45m approved under the ESF.

In the second round of ERDF in 1995 the HIE fragile areas fared less well, being allocated some 23 per cent (£2.1m) of the £9.3m total. The largest single grant of £2.2m went to HIE for the Hunters of Brora Woollen Mill project. In total, therefore, in the three rounds of spending, the fragile areas have gained approximately £14.7m from ERDF. This represents 33 per cent of all ERDF allocations, yet the fragile areas only contain about 19 per cent of the area's population in 1991 so they appear to have performed quite well. However, it should be noted that 64 per cent of the ERDF allocation to these areas was for three large projects (the Scalpay Bridge, the Sound of Harris Ferry and Stornoway Pier). There is also evidence of significant funds going to areas where the need may be less. Shetland, for example, has secured 6.6 per cent of EU funds to date, slightly above its population share of six per cent, yet Shetland has one of the lowest unemployment rates of any part of the region (3.7% compared to 8.8% for the HIE area at March 1995).

Which Agencies are Gaining Objective 1 Funding?

Concerns have also been raised that the bulk of funds are going to development agencies and local authorities. Calum MacDonald MP attacked Objective 1 as representing 'the politics of the pork barrel' (*The Scotsman*, 20.9.94). The need for matching funds means that it was always likely that development agencies and local authorities would be important. Table 9.4 shows the distribution of Objective 1 funding in the first three rounds in 1994 and 1995 (only those agencies gaining more than £1m of EU funds are shown).

Table 9.4 Distribution of Objective 1 funds by agency (1994–1995)

Agency	*Total grant award £m*	*Number of ESF projects*	*Number of ERDF projects*	*% of EU funds*
Highlands and Islands Enterprise	14.24	10	27	24.7%
Highland Regional Council	6.8	56	45	11.8%
Western Isles Islands Council	4.8	1	4	8.3%
Stornoway Pier and Harbour Comm.	3.5	0	1	6.1%
Shetland Islands Council	3.2	38	7	5.5%
Mallaig Harbour Authority	1.9	0	1	3.3%
Strathclyde Regional Council	1.8	15	14	3.1%
Caledonian MacBrayne Ltd	1.7	0	1	3.0%
Argyll and the Islands Enterprise	1.4	2	5	2.4%
Orkney Islands Council	1.2	7	7	2.0%
Loch Ness and Highland Horizon	1.1	0	1	1.9%
Lews Castle College	1.1	37	1	1.9%

Source: Highlands and Islands Partnership Programme 1995

The largest single beneficiary up to the end of 1995 was HIE. The HIE network has gained £18.06m, 31 per cent of all EU funds, including allocations to LECs such as Argyll and the Islands Enterprise. The three Regional and three Islands Councils have together gained the largest share of funding at £18.09m (31% of the total). The ten district councils have gained only £1.9m. The colleges have benefited to a large degree through ESF funding (£3.5m).

Conclusion

Although the main focus of this chapter has been the extent to which the fragile areas of the Highlands and Islands have so far benefited from ERDF spending under Objective 1, preliminary observations have also been made on the allocation of funds between Priorities, the functioning of the partnership and on other aspects of the implementation of the SPD.

With respect to the fragile areas, the figures suggest that to date they have outperformed the region as a whole on the basis of their population share with 33 per cent of ERDF – almost twice as much as their share of population (19%). However, this is largely due to three large projects which have accounted for nearly two-thirds of the assistance, and this must raise grounds for concern, especially as the availability of matching funding appears to be an increasing problem. One way of ensuring a continuing flow of good projects from the fragile areas in future would be to increase the rate of subsidy. It should be noted that this chapter has dealt mainly with the ERDF elements of Objective 1. The pattern of ESF spending and spending in the agricultural and food sector require further analysis, although it may be noted that spending on agriculture is largely on previous Objective 5a programmes including the Hill Livestock Compensatory Allowances and capital grants to farmers, both of which also apply outside the Objective 1 area. Although it is therefore possible that this analysis has understated the assistance to the fragile areas, this seems unlikely.

The reactive nature of the programme means that this pattern of spending has mainly reflected applications received rather than the results of a proactive policy. It could be argued that a more explicit policy of targeting assistance on the disadvantaged areas is required. This will ensure that funding reaches the areas which are most in need of assistance in the region and not simply those which are most able to provide matching funding or put forward the best projects. However, the small scale of the programme executive, together with the tasks of dealing with large numbers of spontaneous applications and with the numerous committees and advisory groups, limits their ability to be proactive.

Regarding the functioning of the partnership arrangements, it may be questioned whether there is a genuine partnership operating between those involved – either in terms of development strategy or project implementation. In terms of the 'vertical' partnership, it appears that the European Commission played a large part in writing the SPD whilst the Scottish Office is obviously by far the most powerful partner both because of its chairmanship of key committees and further because of its influence on access to matching public funding.

Turning to the allocation of funding between the different objectives of the SPD, it appears that allocations to infrastructure, business development and tourism are well ahead of target whilst those for environment and, in particular, community development are significantly behind target. The latter is of special concern, both because it was 'introduced' as a new priority during the negotiation stage (and at the behest of the European Commission) and because it is not clear that the partners know how to implement it in practice.

A further complex issue relates to the general objective of 'integration', both in terms of projects and programmes which are strategically focused and cut across sectoral divisions and in terms of the integration of the Structural Funds in this process. There is, so far, little sign of either of these dimensions in the implementation of the SPD. As PIEDA noted in their 1993 report, there appears to be a need for greater co-ordination of efforts at the sub-regional level between measures. But, for example, there are to date few examples of integrated programmes of support for business which combine ERDF and ESF funding. There is a need for more coherence and integration of projects as the *ad hoc* nature of the projects being submitted by a diverse range of partners to Objective 1 may fail to deliver the significant economic benefits required.

The Objective 1 programme for the region has only had four rounds of spending so far but up to the end of 1995 some £57.6m had been committed, excluding assistance to agriculture. Important questions arise about the extent to which this spending is additional. This requires further scrutiny but it is probable that some of the early rounds of projects would have gone ahead in the absence of Objective 1 because they were already in the pipeline. A further issue is the quality and strategic orientation of training provision being provided under the ESF. We can, however, note that significant sums are going to the further education colleges in the region. There are also issues relating to the business development programme where the main emphasis is on physical infrastructure and factory provision. One of the few examples of a project which allows SMEs in the region to benefit directly from the programme is the £1m HIE venture capital fund.

These preliminary observations raise doubts about the potential impact of the Objective 1 programme at the mid-point in the planning period 1994–1999. As the EU looks to expansion in Eastern Europe it is possible that the region will not qualify for such substantial funds, or indeed Objective

1 status, in future and so the maximum benefit must obviously be extracted over the next few years.

Despite these observations, it is important to stress that the chapter has not attempted to assess the effectiveness of the programme. This requires greater time for the projects to be implemented. External evaluation is a required part of EU assistance and it needs to be open and accountable. There is also a need for transparency to assess topics such as the geographical and sectoral distribution of funds. This will provide information to enable remedial action if support is failing to reach the areas which need it most. In this respect it is interesting that one of the main recommendations by PIEDA in their review of the 1990–1993 CSF was the need for effective monitoring.

Acknowledgements

Although accepting full responsibility for this chapter, the author acknowledges a considerable input by Dr Stuart Black during 1995 and early 1996 when the work was being prepared.

CHAPTER 10

Environmental Improvement within Regional Economic Development

Lessons from Clydeside

Vincent Goodstadt and Keith Clement

Introduction

Over the last ten years the perceived need to integrate economic development and environmental improvement has had a fundamental effect on assumptions underlying European regional development policy. Environmental issues have progressed incrementally up the EU policy agenda, their slow momentum reflecting the predominant economic orientation of EU regional policy and its focus on job creation.

Within EU Member States the practical integration of economic development and environmental policies has generally been limited to observing the principles of environmental impact assessment – particularly the need to safeguard significant ecological and heritage resources – and ensuring that the polluter pays, especially with regard to the treatment of effluent, discharges or emissions. This perspective has resulted in policies being expressed in reactive and protective (conservation) terms. However, there has also been a growing recognition that economic decline, social problems and environmental degradation experienced by European cities and regions are often part of the same dynamic, and initiatives tackling these themes are no longer viewed as reconciling competing objectives but are increasingly designed to support and develop identifiable inter-relationships between features that are central to strategies for renewing urban environments.

The focus of this chapter is on the interaction between economic development and environmental improvement in the context of EU structural policies. It draws on the specific experience of Clydeside in western Scotland, reviewing lessons from over a decade of experience with European programmes.

The chapter begins by considering two European perspectives comprising key features of EU environmental policy and the rise of environmental factors within EU regional policy. Following identification of strategic environmental issues in Clydeside, the chapter then describes experience of European programmes in the region and highlights specific issues of implementation and the difficulties encountered in tackling long-term environmental problems with short-term EU programmes. The chapter concludes by identifying lessons which have practical significance for the broader process of environmental improvement within regional economic development.

EU Environmental Policy

European environmental action programmes

Over the past two decades the European Commission's Environment Directorate-General – DG XI – has come to regard environmental protection as one of the Commission's success stories. The EU legislative programme on the environment has, to a large extent, been set down in the series of five-year Environmental Action Programmes which commenced in 1973 (Hildebrand 1993), initially adopting a reactive approach but subsequently becoming much more proactive.

The First Environmental Action Programme ran from 1973–1977. It listed the objectives and principles of Community environment policy and identified a number of remedial actions necessary at Community level. Its aim was to reconcile economic growth with the need to preserve the natural environment. The Second Programme, from 1977–1981, essentially updated and extended the first while supporting a special emphasis on measures such as the procedure of environmental impact assessment.

The Third Programme (1982–1986) adopted a different approach. Rather than presenting a detailed list of individual measures, it described a framework for EU environmental policy. Seeking an overall strategy which fully integrated environmental policy with socio-economic development through policies for agriculture, industry, energy, transport and tourism, it recognised that the environment was fundamental to economic growth. If this were ignored, sustainable development would be impossible. This approach was developed further in the Fourth Environmental Action Programme (1987–1992), which underlined the need for greater integration between environment and economic policies. However, integrating environmental requirements into other EU policies has been modest, with most advances taking place in the last three or four years. The individual Member States have proved reluctant to integrate environmental themes, their reasons including the required commitment in terms of resources and time to obtain relevant environmental information and to monitor the effects of policies (Baldock *et al.* 1992).

By the end of the Fourth Programme it was apparent that the environmental policy instruments and approaches being used were inadequate to deal with the extent of environmental degradation in Europe and they were seen as having even less chance of coping with the activity and environmental pressures expected from the Single European Market. A different strategy was required, subsequently crystallising in the Fifth Environmental Action Programme (Commission of the European Communities 1993e). Rather than relying on directives and regulations, the Fifth Programme – which commenced in 1993 – has sought to transform the 'throwaway consumer society' and initiate fundamental changes in values towards the environment and in patterns of behaviour and consumption (Ryan 1991).

In practice, the five Environmental Action Programmes have become five successively stronger pillars supporting EU environmental legislation and policy over the past 20 years. The last two programmes have been more focused, certainly in terms of time-scale, because of the impending Single European Market and they are perceived as significant steps in developing a long-term strategy for sustainable development.

The Single European Act and the Maastricht Treaty

The early stages of EU policy-making in the environmental field were characterised by initiatives mostly in the form of guidelines or non-statutory measures. These informal policy programmes were brought onto a legislative basis with the Single European Act (SEA) and the Maastricht Treaty of European Union.

The SEA in 1986 introduced environmental policy to the Treaty of Rome in Article 130-R. It basically reiterated policies which had appeared in the Environmental Action Programmes giving priority to prevention, rectifying damage at source and making the polluter pay. Significantly, it also stated that environmental protection requirements should become a component of the Community's other policies (paragraph 2) and that individual Member States could maintain or introduce more stringent protection measures if they wished, as long as they were compatible with EU legislation.

The Treaty of Maastricht added further environmental objectives to the Single European Act (Wilkinson 1992). These included the promotion of measures at international level to deal with regional or world-wide environmental problems and the fourth environmental principle of the Precautionary Principle, developed in Germany as the *Vorsorgeprinzip* (von Moltke 1987).

Significantly, the new provisions place environmental protection on an equal footing with economic development as one of the EU's objectives, and Community policy is now required to be sustainable. Whereas the Single European Act stated that environmental protection requirements should be a component of the Community's other policies, the Maastricht Treaty clarifies and extends this obligation: environmental protection must now be integrated into the definition and implementation of other Community policies.

EU Regional Policy and the Environment

Over the last ten years a number of factors have contributed to raise the importance of the issue of environment within the context of EU regional policy. Whereas the EU Environmental Action Programmes introduced the concept of environmental integration (Johnson and Corcelle 1995), parallel preparations for the Single European Market were considering the likely large-scale environmental consequences of the forthcoming reform in the Community's approach to European economic development. Attention was focused specifically on the Structural Funds, based on their perceived environmental impact through financial support for projects in manufacturing industry, transport, energy or tourism infrastructure. This resulted in the publication of a series of critical assessments focusing on this aspect of the interaction between environment and economic development (Baldock and Corrie 1989; Baldock and Wenning 1990).

As part of the gathering momentum, a report prepared by the European Court of Auditors in 1992 found little evidence to support any claims of environmental conformity within the Structural Funds: 'Following the reform of the Funds, the Community departments are seldom aware of the exact details of the individual operations funded by the structural instruments. Financing by programme makes it difficult to take account of their environmental implications' and (according to EU legislation) 'measures financed must be in conformity with Community policies, including those concerning the protection of the environment. Very little has been done towards effectively translating this obligation into operational terms' (Court of Auditors 1992, pp.7–8).

Subsequently, the Fifth Environmental Action Programme pointedly supported the further development of environmental protection in future regional development measures: 'it will be necessary to ensure that all Community funding operations and, in particular, those involving the Structural Funds, will be as sensitive as possible to environmental considerations and in conformity with environmental legislation' (Commission of the European Communities 1993e, p.16).

The Interim Review of the Fifth Environmental Action Programme was published in 1994. It noted that while there had been progress on the integration of environmental approaches both within the Community and individual Member States, sustainable development was basically still seen as the business of those who deal directly with the environment. Moreover, it observed that:

> '...strategic assessments of the impact of policy initiatives on the environment have yet to take root in most of the Member States...and...initiatives on the introduction and implementation of appropriate mechanisms to ensure that environment and sustainable development concerns are considered in new policy actions need to be speeded up...' (Commission of the European Communities 1994e)

However, environmental protection within EU regional policy still relies upon the Structural Funds Framework Regulation. A requirement for environmental appraisal was incorporated into this regulation in 1988 and Article 8.4 now states that, in preparing Regional Development Plans (RDPs) or Single Programming Documents (SPDs), Member States are obliged to carry out four environmental tasks (Commission of the European Communities 1992a; 1993e):

- prepare an appraisal of the state of the environment in the region
- evaluate the expected environmental impact of the Plan/SPD
- involve environmental authorities in Plan/SPD preparation and implementation
- comply with European Community environmental directives and regulations.

The degree of success in meeting these requirements has varied among the EU Member States. Regional Development Plans seeking ERDF support were first submitted by Member States in the late-1980s, superseding the earlier, mainly project-based, applications for EU regional and social funds. These plans indicated priority areas for EU assistance but were basically political documents with little reference to the environment (Woodford

1991). Among the Member States, the plans from Denmark were the most environmentally conscious with the Danish authorities advocating environmental appraisal for all development measures, whereas the Portuguese were at the other extreme with a minimalist approach which stated simply that development should conform to existing European law. Operational Programmes submitted in 1991 as a result of those Regional Development Plans had varying degrees of environmental significance, the production of environmental information often depending on the environmental awareness of individuals involved. Few of the programmes integrated environmental protection as a development objective; if this did happen it tended to be within infrastructure-based programmes or priorities. In this case the Spanish authorities proved the most reluctant to integrate environmental issues: they regarded the Funds as economic and social, not environmental, and they were much more interested in job creation and regional economic development.

When the second round of Regional Development Plans appeared in the early 1990s, *ex ante* appraisals revealed limited analyses of the state of the environment, only partial and very tentative appraisals of likely environmental impacts and very poor integration of environmental factors (even on the basis of the narrow definitions used) (Clement 1994). The Interim Review of the Fifth Environmental Action Programme subsequently commented that 'Integration of environmental concerns needs to be better reflected in the regional development plans and proposals for funding being developed by Member States' (Commission of the European Communities 1994e).

Clearly, on a Europe-wide scale, there is still a substantial distance to go before more rigorous and imaginative methodologies are put in place to integrate environmental factors into EU regional development.

Strategic Environmental Issues in Clydeside

To a certain extent, the environmental elements of the Structural Fund regulations are general and abstract. Like other aspects of the Regulations, their true impact emerges through their interpretation and application in practice. Clydeside, an area spanning the length of the River Clyde in western Scotland, provides a good example for reviewing the implementation of environmental considerations within economic development. The region encompasses some of the most urbanised and industrialised parts of the UK and, with a long history of industrial decline and reconversion, it has been eligible for integrated EU structural programmes for more than ten years.

In common with major urban areas across the European Union, Clydeside has a history in the post-war period of identifying and incrementally developing responses to environmental issues within the framework of regional economic development programmes:

- In 1946 the Clyde Valley Plan – the first development plan for the region – called for a long-term plan for land clearance and rehabilitation to attract industry and recognised that a piecemeal approach would make no impression on the problem (Abercrombie and Matthew 1949).
- In 1973 the White Paper, *Central Scotland – A Programme for Development and Growth (Cmnd 2188)*, recognised that more resources for environmental action were needed to facilitate new economic growth. This resulted in Exchequer grants for 85 per cent of the cost of acquiring and clearing derelict land being made available to local authorities in development districts.
- In 1975 the new Scottish Development Agency identified and exercised powers to treat derelict or neglected land. Its successor – Scottish Enterprise – has not shown the same level of commitment.

Within Clydeside there is currently a pressing need to recycle vacant and derelict land. The urban areas presently contain 5000 ha of vacant and derelict land and there are over 12,000 ha of underused land on the urban fringe, most of which needs remedial action. Looking ten years ahead, the likely scale of new urban development might require approximately 3000 ha for housing, industrial and commercial purposes. Even if all this new development were channelled to the available vacant land, the vast majority of sites would remain untreated and continue to blight the environment of the West of Scotland. Most of the land which needs to be enhanced has no immediate prospects of commercial development and is, therefore, unlikely to be funded through private investment. This is one of the clearest examples of market failure within the Region. The problem is compounded by the continued fall-out of industrial and commercial properties from economic use, and this factor has broadly off-set land renewed within the urban area (see Table 10.1). In effect, all the urban renewal over the last ten years has merely resulted in a standstill situation being achieved (Strathclyde Regional Council 1996).

Table 10.1 Land take-up (1) and land falling out of use (2) in the conurbation 1980–1994 (Hectares)

	1980	*81*	*82*	*83*	*84*	*85*	*86*	*87*	*88*	*89*	*90*	*91*	*92*	*93*
Take-up (all uses)	599	528	612	503	387	211	301	210	357	256	294	391	278	271
Fall-out	758	634	583	562	225	306	332	1016*	317	294	204	322	788**	260

* Due to changes in survey technique
** Including Ravenscraig

Source: Strathclyde Structure Plan 1995

The need for urban renewal has underpinned the planning policies of the Clydeside local authorities since 1975. Priority has been given to locating development on urban renewal sites with a general presumption against greenfield development. Consequently, over £2 billion-worth of additional investment has been harnessed to improve substantial tracts of Glasgow and surrounding towns by this strategy.

A framework of joint initiatives for 'Greening the Conurbation' currently provides a complementary environmental programme in Clydeside. This programme of action seeks to safeguard the rich natural heritage that exists in many parts of the region and to add quality to the process of urban regeneration, create new landscapes for the conurbation and create a more accessible and well-managed countryside (Strathclyde Regional Council 1993). Nine key projects each have a specific area focus within a partnership of public agencies and community groups, the voluntary sector and individuals. Their aim is to upgrade 3500 ha of underused and derelict land on the urban fringe, create a 200 km cycleway and walkway network, re-open the Forth and Clyde Canal for navigation across Scotland and bring 300 ha of threatened wildlife habitats under positive and sustainable management.

Experience of European Programmes in Clydeside: Environmental Elements

Development policy in Clydeside has been closely related to EU objectives since 1984 and there have been six programmes of European funding over this period: the NPCI, the SIDO, the RECHAR Programme, the RENAVAL Programme, the WSOP Programme and the Western Scotland Programme (see Table 10.2 for financial details). Each has shown varying levels of financial commitment and priority towards the task of environmental improvement (see Table 10.3).

Table 10.2 Environmental programme details

	Total programme	*Environment*		*SRC environmental contribution*		*Objective*
	Amount £m	*Total £m*	*% †*	*Amount £m*	*% ‡*	
Glasgow NPCI	140	7	5%	1.4	20%	Improve image and look of Glasgow
SIDO	56.40	14	25%	2.4	17%	Improve image for inward investment
RENAVAL	34	15	44%	1.2	8%	Economic conversion of shipbuilding areas
RECHAR	8.17	2	25%	0.35	18%	Conversion of former coal-mining areas
WSOP	71.3	14.2	20%	3.5	25%	Economic development and environmental sustainability
W S regional plan	516	74	14%	2*	3%	Economic regeneration of the West of Scotland

* relates to SRC contribution for a limited part of the programme period because of the impact of Local Government reorganisation
† as percentage of total programming cost
‡ as percentage of total ERDF grant

The National Programme of Community Interest (NPCI) (1985–1987) sought to co-ordinate efforts by the City of Glasgow District Council, Strathclyde Regional Council and the Scottish Development Agency with the objective of improving the appearance and image of Glasgow to make it more attractive to all types of inward investment and tourism. It established eight sub-programmes of investment, one of which was devoted to environmental improvements. Of the total £140m programme, five per cent was allocated to environmental projects on four specific themes. A modest target of 50 hectares was set for the treatment of land over a three-year period and £7m was committed by the three agencies mentioned above. Although only £5.02m was spent, a large number of beneficial small schemes were funded.

The Strathclyde Integrated Development Operation (SIDO) (1988–1992) also contained a specific environmental sub-programme in recognition of its significance and this formed 17 per cent of the total budget. Stressing the link to inward investment and tourism, the programme included refurbishment of landmark buildings in Glasgow (promoting the 'metropolitan

Table 10.3 Programme of environmental objectives

Glasgow (NPCI) (1985–87)	*SIDO (1988–92)*	*RECHAR (1990–93)*
Created sub-programmes for investment, 4 themes: • transport routes (M8, Clydeside Expressway, main rail links) • waterways (River Clyde frontage) • vacant land and buildings (over 800,000 m^3) • general image Target of 50 hectares treated over 3 years	• 1000 land improvements • 900 areas of land improved • 20 heritage and conservation projects • improvement of the environment for investment • complimentarity to EC directives • improved image relative to other parts of the UK	• environmental improvement • attract new investment and restore confidence • coal tip reclamation • clearing/reconversion of disused coal mining buildings • modernisation of premises for SMEs • creation of green areas • access to locations for new activities
RENAVAL (1990–93)	*WSOP (1993–96)*	*Western Scotland (SPD) (1994–96)*
• 20 environmental improvement projects • stabilisation of the shore-line • provision of public footpaths • tree planting • clearance of unsightly areas • improvement of the environment for investment • maintenance of significant buildings	• 122 kilometres of transport corridors improved • expand environmental training • 20 heritage/ conservation projects • improvements to fencing and boundary walls • 1787 hectares of land improved • 139 buildings enhanced	• derelict land reduced by 1500 hectares (100 ha require major work) • 50 hard/soft landscaping schemes • 50 environmental improvement schemes • 10 town centre improvement schemes • 5 environmental management initiatives • 5 urban fringe and river valley initiatives • general waterfront revitalisation • 30 tourist attractions improved • creation of 141 new jobs and 2778 jobs protected

heart' of the area) and other towns, the renewal of derelict land and the enhancement of waterways and walkways as tourist attractions.

The RECHAR Programme (1990–1993) included measures to tackle a series of environmental issues in former coal-mining areas, with just under 25 per cent (£2m) of the total budget to be spent directly on environmental renewal.

The RENAVAL Programme (1990–1993) to assist the 'economic conversion of shipbuilding areas' had three action programmes, one of which concerned environment and tourism. The RENAVAL Programme was more flexible in its interpretation of the scale and type of environmental action to be supported. The proportion of the Programme which included environmental and tourism action represented about 44 per cent of the overall Programme targets.

The West of Scotland Operational Programme (WSOP) (1993) recognised that, despite the advances made since 1986, derelict land improvements were not keeping pace with major closures in steel and shipbuilding industries. It identified about 6000 ha of derelict land remaining in the area and sought an increase in emphasis on environmental issues throughout the Programme. Twenty per cent of the budget was allocated to environment-related activities.

Finally, the Western Scotland Programme (1994–1996) reviewed the impact of previous programmes and sought to devise a more systematic framework to integrate environmental action. One consequence was that there was no specific environmental sub-programme and the type of projects which had previously been included under an environmental heading were integrated into a sub-programme dealing with the 'Creation of a High Quality Business Infrastructure'. Again, the Programme recognised that the upgrading of the natural environment was an important factor in attracting inward investment and promoting tourism. ERDF was proposed to be made available to projects tackling poor environments either in or surrounding industrial and commercial areas, transport corridors and tourism areas. Environmental pilot projects were proposed where a direct link to economic development was apparent.

In total, therefore, over the past 12 years, programmes to the scale of over £800m have been established in Clydeside for economic restructuring. Within this figure, the resources allocated to environmental action have increased from a base of five per cent to a level in excess of 20 per cent in several programmes. This incremental, but consistent, improvement indicates the more positive priority now being afforded to environmental factors. At the time of writing (June 1996), the successor to the Western Scotland

Programme was being prepared for the period 1997–1999, in common with other Objective 2 Programmes throughout the EU. Guidelines circulated by the European Commission illustrated how Structural Fund Programmes could undertake more integrative approaches to the environment.

Issues of Implementation

Common interests within the European programmes and the regional strategy of 'Greening the Conurbation' have made a range of important environmental initiatives possible, and these have brought together wealthy suburban and deprived peripheral communities, housing agencies and local communities, Local Enterprise Companies and natural heritage interests. Although this has harnessed European funds to benefit the West of Scotland, it has also highlighted lessons about the practicalities of this type of action.

Related strategic programmes

The EU Programmes have been implemented within a regional context including the Structure Plan of Strathclyde Regional Council, which set a clear framework for environmental action. However, the framework was not implemented consistently throughout the 1980s. Whereas the scale of improvement was approximately 300 ha per year at the beginning of the decade, this tailed off towards the end to fewer than 50 ha per year. This reflected the shift in policy by development agencies away from environmental enhancement in its own right. In effect, fewer resources were being devoted to treating land which had no immediate commercial after-use (Strathclyde Regional Council 1994). By contrast, between 1984 and 1995 the Regional Council increased its commitment to environmental action through other instruments and invested £9.8m annually in projects with a range of benefits including job creation and training programmes, indigenous business development, changing the perceptions of visitors and residents and establishing a more favourable climate for investment. European funds matched the commitment of the Council and other local agencies.

Additionality

The main environmental benefit of the European Programmes has been to increase the scale of enhancement on Clydeside. All programmes of action included major partnership initiatives, which meant that every £1m invested by the Regional Council generated £5m of money from the other local partners. ERDF effectively doubled the level of resource available. This was critical to the willingness of local authorities to make new resources available during a period of severe financial restrictions.

The changed rules of additionality and transparency in 1993/94 were particularly important. Prior to this, ERDF monies did not revert directly to the spending authority but were received by Central Government and the only real benefit to a local authority was a reduction in its interest charges on loans. The decision to ensure greater transparency in European funding meant that the local authority received European grants directly. The impact on Strathclyde's direct funding of projects was significant, with expenditure on Greening the Conurbation initiatives rising dramatically from £230,000 in 1992/93 to £924,000 in 1995/96. This transparency was also reflected in the Council policy, where a decision was taken to ensure that all European grants reverted to the department that generated the funding.

The benefit arising from the additionality generated by European programmes is exemplified by the roads budget. In this case, a new roads enhancement programme was established, complemented by landscape schemes considered in terms of wider environmental programmes and transport strategies rather than within infrastructure programmes. The rate of European funding for environmental schemes was set at 50 per cent – as opposed to 25 per cent for roads – and this resulted in higher quality environmental projects being brought forward.

Project eligibility

Throughout the European programmes in Clydeside the prime criterion for project eligibility has been that environmental enhancement should directly benefit regional economic development. However, eligibility has proved more difficult to establish when dealing with general environmental enhancement, partly because restructuring a conurbation's image is a long-term process compared to the time-scale of an ERDF programme. One scheme which has gained on-going support is the Regional Council's woodland creation programme. This costs approximately £1m per year and the European funding element amounts to £0.2m for implementing its strategic priorities. In comparison, ERDF has not been used for environmental initiatives in housing areas related to local recreational amenities or for the benefit of agricultural land which is not overtly related to wider economic development or urban regeneration initiatives.

In general, projects have been considered eligible for ERDF where they could demonstrate a link to a strategic planning framework for environmental action. This has been particularly important in view of the short time-scale of ERDF programmes which have ranged from one to five years. These time-scales cannot encompass the scale of action required to regenerate a conurbation or restructure its infrastructure and environment.

Environmental sub-programmes

The most recent ERDF Programmes in Clydeside have begun to integrate environmental considerations into regional economic policy implementation. Environmental works are now part of the same priority as industrial and commercial infrastructure and transport and communications. This has created difficulties in appraising project proposals because of their diversity, that is the benefits, cost profiles, implementation schemes and impact time-scales are very different for environmental enhancement schemes, business centres and traffic management schemes.

The European Commission's need for financial accountability has also created pressures for tighter project descriptions at the outset. This has posed problems for environmental programmes because of uncertainty about the speed at which individual schemes within them are implemented, the need for community participation and their final cost profile. From the point of view of local partners it would be more appropriate for a package of project proposals to be approved, allowing subsequent flexibility about which schemes are ultimately implemented, based on practical programming considerations.

Procedural features

In effect, European support has generated a higher level of partnership between local agencies. However, this has coincided with the EU's increasing concern with value for money and accountability and recent ERDF programmes have emphasised performance targets, monitoring and audit trails. Although desirable in principle, this has made the process increasingly complicated and placed additional burdens on local partners – normally three or four in the case of environmental projects.

In addition, the annuality problem associated with all public financing (i.e. the restrictions on carrying over funds between years) and the seasonality involved in implementing environmental schemes often create an acute log-jam in cash flow and processing in the latter months of the financial year. This is complicated by the need for authorities to fund all project costs up-front before receiving European aid and the risk of the aid being lost in the annuality programme. In effect, local authorities need to run in deficit in anticipation of grants being received and so risk overspending. Strathclyde Regional Council responded to this problem by creating a Joint Planning Projects Trust to deal with jointly funded projects. This Trust acts as a 'banker' for money and thereby ensures that it is not lost at the end of a financial year because of short-term slippages in programmes.

Impact

The facility to demonstrate the impact of European assistance is built into the programme evaluation criteria and monitoring arrangements. Where the impacts are direct and physical, measurements are possible, for example, in terms of the area of land improved. However, environmental initiatives often require a longer term for the full benefit to be realised and the nature of projects means that real impact emerges only with the cumulative outcome of many schemes being introduced over an extended time-scale. With regard to past environmental measures, their collective impacts are of a scale that if replicated over a 10–15-year period, they would allow the treatment of over 3000 ha of land and make a substantial contribution to the reduction of degraded environments.

Other impacts are less quantifiable but are also significant. In particular, the European programmes place a high priority upon partnership and this has resulted in a major increase in the level of co-operative action in environmental programmes, in effect allowing the participation of agencies and groups not traditionally thought of as natural partners. For example, Scottish Homes broadened its perspective in renewal programmes for deprived housing areas and worked with other institutions in more general environmental action; and the inner city and inner urban areas have become recognised within programmes as offering key opportunities for new investment following infrastructural and environmental improvement.

Conclusions

The implementation of regional economic development at European level and within EU initiatives in individual Member States is increasingly characterised by a concern for positive environmental impact. This transition in values is being realised in stages and an easy transfer of environmental criteria into one instrument or region does not imply that a similar facility will take place quickly at other levels. Nevertheless, it is clear that the relationship between economic development and environment no longer needs to be expressed in terms of the traditional dichotomy and that progressive regional strategies can deliver mutually-beneficial results.

Effectively addressing the complex issues arising in this field of environmental action and economic development requires a proactive and holistic approach, and this is best provided through a framework within which interactions are manageable and within which a sufficient degree of freedom allows flexibility in local responses. This means minimising factors such as bureaucracy, auditing and continual tests for value-for-money, and instead maximising the scope for local initiative and independent decision making. In this context, characteristic changes in policy priorities would increase the status of enhancing environments degraded from former economic activities while lowering the priority of urban regeneration initiatives linked only to direct economic after-uses.

In the west of Scotland, the perception of linkages between environmental and economic action is long-established. With the support of EU funding, Strathclyde Regional Council experienced both direct and indirect benefits in terms of the scale and type of action that can be achieved in renewing a conurbation and the level of local partnership has, to a large extent, been facilitated by a strategic planning framework which has established priorities for action and a framework for the joint management of projects. With regard to the benefits of Clydeside as a learning experience in the derivation of environmental improvement through regional development, several lessons are identifiable.

First, clear opportunities exist for environmental gain through regional development, and the European Structural Funds can be a very practical means to this end. It is evident that the expectation of European co-financing for economic development – even though frequently delayed in actual delivery – does facilitate funding generation and, ultimately, policy-effectiveness and realisation. In the process, it allows scope for the creation or positioning of dedicated environmental enhancement programmes which, as policy initiatives, can draw momentum from the framework regional strategies.

Second, a locally-based economic and environmental strategy may prove to be an essential component in realising policy continuation. In practice, EU programmes are too short term to solve long-term problems, and this includes tackling the scale of urban restructuring and regeneration required to transform the conditions of old industrial conurbations. The current Objective 2 programmes, for example, are of only three years' duration. Furthermore, decision makers cannot always rely on projects providing proof of supporting economic development, and under these conditions the physical environment becomes clearly disadvantaged without the vision provided by local frameworks and authorities such as the former Strathclyde Regional Council. In the absence of such guiding elements it is questionable whether EU-funded environmental improvement would be implemented in such a structured and committed manner.

Third, and related, in addition to the environmental approach of the Structural Funds benefiting from permitting a more local interpretation of eligibility criteria in cases where a strategic planning context has already been established, the effectiveness and efficiency of ERDF programmes would also benefit from simplified procedures – particularly relating to increased flexibility for bringing forward individual schemes within an agreed programme package.

Fourth, on a cautionary note, even when regional economic strategies do overtly incorporate environmental priorities, they must be monitored to ensure implementation. Although policy statements at the beginning of a programme may be well-founded and well-focused, the impetus may be lost during the life-span of the programme and economic concerns may come to predominate as environment slips quietly down the agenda. Accordingly, programme monitoring should be designed to secure against vulnerability to 'policy slippage' as priorities change.

Finally, substantial benefits can be gained from the creation of separate environmental programmes or sub-programmes. This allows not only the clearer identification and higher profile of environmental measures and targets but also facilitates the justification of financial allocations, makes the process more measurable in terms of monitoring and effectively promotes the environment to the status encouraged by the EU Environmental Action Programmes and consolidated through successive EU legislative measures.

CHAPTER 11

The Impact of the EU Structural Funds on Industrial Development Policy and Practice in Northern Ireland[1]

James McEldowney and Ronnie Scott

Introduction

The reform of the European Community's Structural Funds in 1988 represented a fundamental change in the administration of Community assistance towards economic and social cohesion. In particular, it emphasised the need for concentration of effort on those regions experiencing the greatest difficulties, improved co-ordination of the structural instruments and a greater partnership between the Commission and all relevant authorities at national, regional and local level within each Member State (Bachtler and Michie 1993). A key element in this reform was a switch from a project-based to a programme-based approach to financing over a five-year period 1989–1993 (Commission of the European Communities 1989). It has been estimated that this reform has involved almost a thousand individual operational-level programmes and global grants (Bachtler and Michie 1993). This chapter assesses the impact of one such programme – the Industrial Development Operational Programme (IDOP) for Northern Ireland (Department of Economic Development 1990a). Whilst much has been written about the methodology of evaluation (Foley 1992; Hart 1992) there is still a need for the dissemination of evaluation findings and on the lessons arising.

The chapter begins by setting out the background to the IDOP in the context of the implementation of the Community's Structural Funds and

1 The views expressed are those of the authors and should not be attributed either to the Northern Ireland Civil Service or the European Commission.

recent changes in industrial development policy within Northern Ireland (NI). The methodology adopted for this evaluation is briefly outlined. The Programme is then examined on a number of issues concerning the rationale for such intervention in the light of recent changes in industrial development policy in NI and the Programme's objectives. In terms of impacts and policy effectiveness, each of the Programme's principal measures is examined and the policy implications of these findings are then discussed.

Background

In March 1989 NI submitted a Regional Development Plan to the European Commission (Department of Finance and Personnel 1989). This comprised a strategy orientated towards strengthening the regional economy which focused on five key areas: image, infrastructure, expertise, enterprise and exports. Following this plan, a subsequent Community Support Framework (CSF) was drawn up which identified specific priorities for joint action between the Commission and the UK Government. The specific priorities identified included: the improvement of the physical and social environment, reducing the effects of peripherality, diversifying and strengthening of the industrial and tradeable services sector of the economy, the development of agriculture and tourism and human resources development (Commission of the European Communities 1989).

Over the period 1989–1993, NI was granted a total of 793 million ecu (mecu) from its CSF – involving nine Operational Programmes each with its own particular objectives and selection criteria. These programmes are listed in Table 11.1. Two points are worth noting. First, there is clearly a very strong commitment to the programme-based approach. In theory this should, at least in the Commission's view, facilitate a degree of decentralisation of the management of Community assistance and increase the predictability of such assistance as well as allowing for the adoption of 'a coherent overall medium-term view of the operations to be mounted in pursuit of each priority objective' (Commission of the European Communities 1989, p.21). Second, it can be seen that the Industrial Development Operational Programme (IDOP) was the third largest Operational Programme in funding terms during this period after the Transportation and an ESF-supported Programme aimed at facilitating the occupational integration of young people.

The IDOP was aimed at diversifying and strengthening the industrial and tradeable services sectors of the NI economy. The main thrust of the Programme was to raise the supply-side performance of the economy by

Table 11.1 Operational Programme allocation for Northern Ireland (1989–1993)

	Original allocation		*Current allocation*	
Operational Programmes	*EU funding (mecu)*	*EU funding (£m)*	*EU funding (mecu)*	*EU funding (£m)*
Physical and social environment	35.5	24.5	50.4	38.3
Transportation	127.0	95.0	165.5	123.0
Industrial development	122.5	85.0	127.8	93.5
Tourism	46.0	32.0	43.5	32.8
Unemployment (Objective 3)	34.5	24.0	34.6	25.3
Integration of young people (Objective 4)	148.0	103.0	153.3	112.7
Multi-priority	27.0	18.7	23.5	17.1
Special measures	5.0	3.5	11.0	8.2
Agricultural development	48.0	33.0	38.5	29.2
Horizontal measures – 5(a)	76.4	53.2	90.3	64.7

Source: Department of Finance and Personnel (NI), 1993, Table 1

raising the level of new firm formation, increasing the competitiveness of existing companies and attracting new investment. The Programme was broken down into three sub-programmes as follows: industrial development, human resource development and infrastructure for industrial development. The Programme was underpinned by a common strategy which focused on five broad themes:

1. Improving the competitiveness of indigenous industry.
2. Encouraging additional small enterprises.
3. Attracting inward investment projects.
4. Assisting the development of management and workforce skills.
5. Providing the infrastructure necessary for industrial development.

Overall, the Programme involved total expenditure of over 370 mecu, which included approximately 88.7 mecu from the ERDF and approximately 37 mecu of ESF assistance. Responsibility for the administration of the Programme rested with the Department of Economic Development (DED) for Northern Ireland. This operates through four agencies: the Industrial Development Board (IDB) whose remit covers those firms employing more than 50 employees, the Local Enterprise Development Unit (LEDU) responsible for companies employing under 50 employees, the Training and Employment Agency (T&EA) responsible for the delivery of relevant training for those in work and for those seeking work and the Industrial Research and Technology Unit (IRTU) which aims to encourage industrially relevant research and development and technology transfer.

Evaluation Methodology

Given the scale and range of the Programme and its constituent measures, the task of evaluating the IDOP initially may appear a formidable one. Certainly the analysis of the impact of the Structural Funds has been recognised as a difficult task (Gorecki 1993). However, the task of any evaluation must be to inform policy makers in order to improve the design and delivery of policies (Hogwood and Gunn 1984). In this respect the evaluation exercise must be made a manageable one tailored to the needs of the particular programme or project in question. In the case of the IDOP, the current study which forms the basis of this chapter was initiated at the request of the European Commission as a form of ongoing evaluation exercise running alongside the implementation of the Programme.

In more specific terms, the study involved two groups of activities in support of the Commission's requirements. The first group were essentially concerned with ensuring that the appropriate management and implementation procedures of the Programme had been adhered to. The second group involved a systematic qualitative assessment of each measure contained in the Programme. In terms of the process of evaluation, the first group of activities conform to the *in-itinere* phase of evaluation, which is principally concerned with both the monitoring of progress compared to the original Programme and the design of any corrective measures. This phase is probably of greatest concern to the administrator and day-to-day managers of the Programme. In contrast, the second group of activities corresponds with what is known as the *ex post* phase of the evaluation, which investigates the degree of effectiveness including the cost effectiveness of the Programme's measures and their impact over both the short and long terms. This chapter concentrates on an examination of the research findings arising from the second phase of the evaluation.

In terms of the methodology adopted, the study involved a macro-economic analysis of the NI economy complemented by an intensive quantitative and qualitative analysis involving a series of semi-structured interviews of companies, individuals and policy managers of each of the measures contained within the Operational Programme. The quantitative and qualitative analysis forms the basis of the current chapter. The methodology adopted for this evaluation study also had to be sufficiently flexible to allow for the incorporation of the results of any other parallel evaluations that had been commissioned by NI Government Departments or other bodies and institutions.

Taking account of the objectives of the Programme, these were combined to form an evaluation framework as shown in Figure 11.1. This lists the Programme's measures with their intended policy impacts, which, in theory, should directly contribute to improvements in the competitiveness of existing firms, the development of new firms and the attraction of industrial investment. In assessing the impact of the individual measures that comprised the Programme, two key areas were examined.

First, an attempt was made to assess the degree to which each measure addressed the various objectives of the programme. Table 11.2 summarises this analysis by identifying for each measure the actual areas of impact, as judged from the evaluation set against potential areas of impact. Clearly, where an individual measure manages to address more than one objective there is the distinct possibility that a degree of synergy will be achieved. This latter concept refers to the extent to which the eventual impact of any measure is greater than the sum of its individual parts. As a concept it has long been emphasised by the Commission. For example, if the objective is to encourage new firm formation or assist the development of entrepreneurship, one ought to consider this objective through a number of measures rather than the use of a single measure alone. In short, this would indicate that there are a number of ways in which the same objective can be achieved within a Programme. It is this concept of synergy on which the Commission places considerable emphasis as it indicates or implies a highly integrated cohesive programme.

Second, the principal areas of impact were identified for every programme measure. Each measure was then assessed on the basis of the following criteria: (a) the nature of the impact in terms of: timing – whether it was short term or long term; the degree to which the impact could be measured in quantitative or qualitative terms (or both); the number of programme objectives addressed; the degree of significance of each identified impact; (b) the degree to which each measure was targeted in terms of a broad or narrow focus; (c) the value for money of each measure; and (d) the additionality and leverage associated with each measure.

In assessing the economic impact and effectiveness of each of the IDOP policies and measures it was necessary to estimate, where possible, the level of dead-weight (or the extent to which the private sector would have undertaken activities in any case) and the level of displacement (or the extent to which companies assisted displace output and employment of other companies in the region).

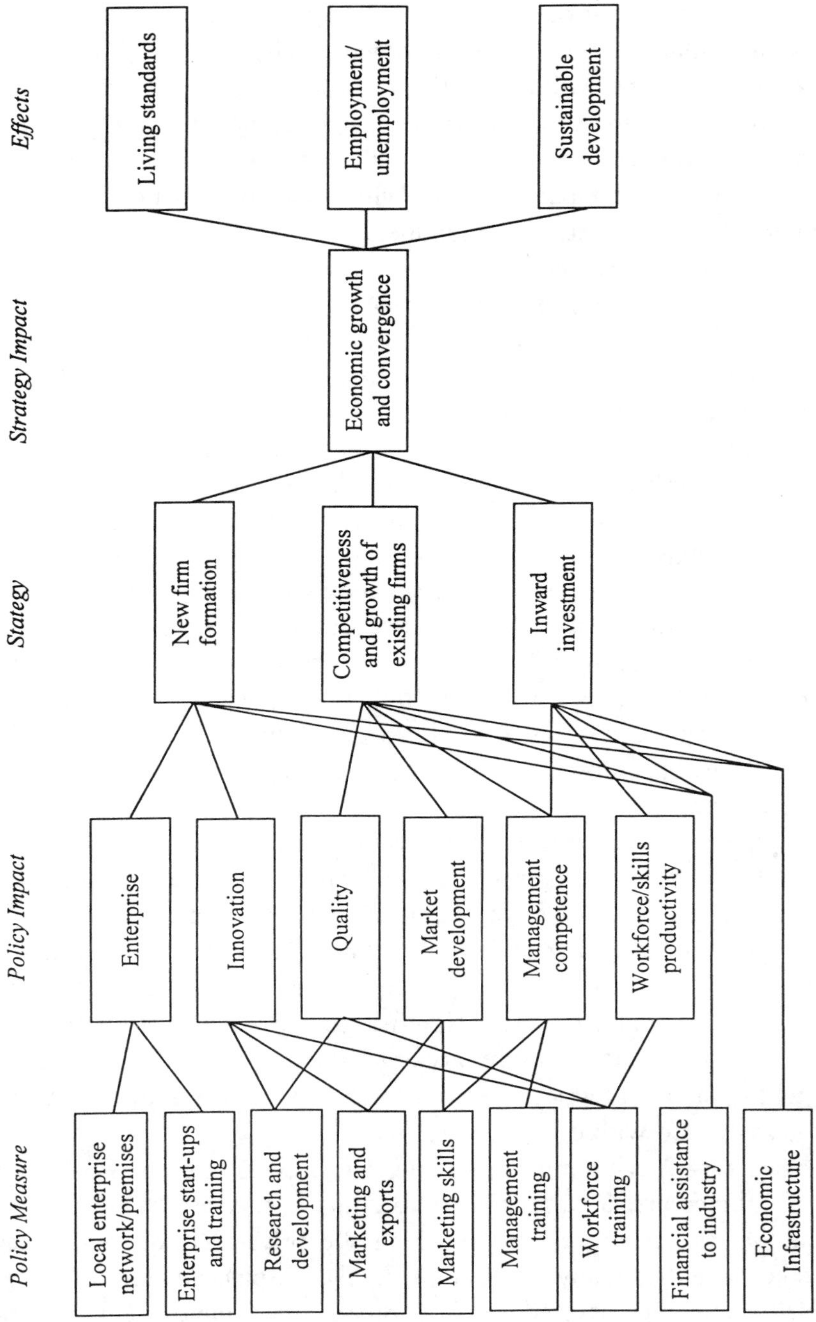

Figure 11.1 Evaluation framework

Table 11.2 Industrial Development Operational Programme: Strategy and Measures

Sub-programme measures	*Objectives* *To improve competitiveness of existing industry*	*To encourage additional small enterprises*	*To attract inward investment projects*	*To assist development of management and workforce skills*	*To provide the infrastructure necessary for industrial development*
Industrial development:					
• SFA	X	O	X		
• marketing	X	O	X	O	
• marketing development	X	O			
• R&D					
• LEN	X		X		
• LEP		X			
• information/ evaluation research		X			
Human resources:	O	O	O	O	O
• workforce					
• management			X	X	
• human resources in SMEs	X				
• marketing	X	X			
• enterprise training	X	X	X	X	
Supporting infrastructure					
• roads		X		X	
• electricity					
• facilities			O		X
•	O				X
•	O		O		X

X = actual areas of impact
O = possible areas of impact
SFA = Selective Financial Assistance
LEN = Local Enterprise Network
LEP = Local Enterprise Programme

Evaluation Findings

Rationale

Despite economic growth rates which have closely matched those obtaining for the UK as a whole since the 1950s, employment growth in NI has been insufficient to absorb the growing labour supply. The result has been a level of unemployment which has persistently been higher in NI than in any region of the UK and which is among one of the highest in the EU. Recent projections undertaken at the Northern Ireland Economic Research Centre (NIERC 1993a) indicate that this general situation will persist throughout the next decade. A combination of slow growth in the UK economy and an inability within NI to expand significantly faster than Great Britain means that job creation will be inadequate to reduce the region's already unacceptably high level of unemployment.

Against this background the case for the IDOP is simple. The private sector acting alone or in conjunction with traditional regional policy instruments has not demonstrated the ability to grow at a rate sufficient to create enough jobs to accommodate the rapid growth in labour supply. In addition, recent developments in industrial development policy in NI are consistent with, and represent a continued development of, the thinking behind the Regional Development Plan for NI presented to the Commission in March 1989 (Department of Finance and Personnel 1989) and were also reflected in the IDOP. In the past the prime objective of industrial development policy in NI was employment creation (Sheehan 1993). In 1990 the Department for Economic Development (NI) announced radical changes in industrial development policy, putting the future focus of policy on improving the competitiveness of NI industry to overcome specifically identified obstacles to growth (Department of Economic Development 1990b). The general implication of the new strategy for existing Northern Ireland firms was a reduction in traditional forms of assistance, particularly capital grants, and an increase in 'software' assistance for such areas as marketing, exporting, research and development as well as management and workforce skills.

Evaluation of Programme Objectives

From the surveys and analyses undertaken it is possible to draw out a series of observations concerning the extent to which the Programme's objectives have been achieved. First, virtually all of the Programme was directed at improving the competitiveness of existing NI industry – apart from measures such as local economic development, which involved the development of the region's extensive network of local enterprise agencies to provide workspace, common services and counselling for their small business tenants. Whilst such centres may well benefit many existing firms, much of their activity had been directed towards the promotion of new enterprise. Likewise, some of the measures under the Supporting Infrastructure Programme – for example, workshops for training of the disabled for open employment – either did not directly address competitiveness or did so only in a limited way.

Second, whilst virtually all measures addressed the competitiveness theme, the more detailed evaluations of individual measures indicated that some measures were more effective than others. For example, the evaluation raises serious questions over the contribution of direct financial assistance to industry in the form of capital grants. In the case of NI this assistance is provided under Selective Financial Assistance (SFA), which gave rise to several concerns related to its small contribution to the Programme compared to the overall amount spent on SFA within the region by Government, reported high levels of dead-weight and the nature of recent policy changes in the direction of assistance towards R&D, marketing and training rather than capital grant assistance. These arguments are outlined in more detail later in this chapter as they have implications for other regions that make use of such forms of assistance.

Third, Table 11.2 (p.183) shows that in addition to the principal objective of improving competitiveness, the Programme also had four other, more specific objectives. These concerned the promotion of enterprise, the attraction of inward investment, the development of management and workforce skills and the provision of infrastructure necessary for industrial development. These objectives were often addressed by a limited number of measures, as in the case of infrastructure provision, or by measures with ill-defined objectives – for example a market-research scheme to help indigenous businesses with export potential. In the case of the inward investment objective, the Programme can only claim to have had a limited impact – including the attraction to NI of the Post Office's return letter centre and the attraction of an American company. It should be noted, however, that NI's main industrial promotion activities overseas or throughout Europe were not funded through the IDOP.

Fourth, virtually all of the measures outlined in the Programme represented existing Government instruments available to local industry within NI. This over-reliance on pre-existing programmes, an issue already noted by other observers as a shortcoming of the Structural Funds arrangements for the region (Gorecki 1993), meant that the Programme generally lacked any form of experimental or innovative measure which could be applied to the overall objective of improving competitiveness. Arguably, the allocation of EU funding should provide an opportunity for the relevant regional or local authorities to put forward new initiatives or ideas or, alternatively, to focus efforts more directly on particular areas of need. Instead, the IDOP represented a compendium of existing Government schemes packaged together to meet the Commission's requirements for operational programmes. In effect, the Programme had been designed on the basis of pre-existing schemes combined to form a programme without justifying the efficacy or effectiveness of such schemes. The alternative procedure at the programme design stage would have involved the identification of industrial development priorities based on an assessment of the effectiveness of existing measures addressing identified policy gaps (e.g. the availability of venture capital) with relevant instruments.

A fifth issue concerned the degree of strategic integration within the Programme. The fact that almost all measures had at least some impact on industrial competitiveness does indicate that there had been some attempt at achieving integration between measures. Since the Programme had been compiled on the basis of existing NI support measures, a heavy burden was placed on those responsible for the selection of existing policy instruments for inclusion within the Programme. Evidence from this evaluation study suggests that the selection of measures had been undertaken in a somewhat arbitrary fashion. Several existing policy instruments, which had considerable relevance for the overall aim of industrial development policy or which were highly regarded as effective instruments, were omitted from policy – for example an IDB scheme oriented towards the promotion of strategic development planning within companies (Industrial Development Board 1991). In addition, a number of senior executive development programmes administered by the T&EA were not included within the Programme. There was little in the way of justification to support the inclusion or exclusion of particular measures within each sub-programme. While arguments outlining the rationale for intervention were presented, there was little evidence of a systematic prior appraisal of why some measures had been chosen and others had been excluded.

Impact of Individual Measures

In providing an overview of the findings of the impact of some of the Programme's principal measures, it must be appreciated that every scheme or policy instrument had its own organisational context which may have a bearing on the effectiveness or impact of the instrument concerned. Arguably, there is a case for considering NI as an extreme example of a peripheral region where there has been a long tradition of policy intervention and different forms of regional support measures for industry. Its administrative structure has a high degree of centralisation where the potential for co-ordination is high. Economic development policies have tended to follow trends in Great Britain but it would be wrong to see NI Departments as slavishly adopting what is formulated in 'Great Britain'. It has, therefore, been argued that NI accepts the general policy stance of the UK Government but implements it in a way appropriate to the circumstances of NI (Loughlin 1991).

In terms of industrial development policy, this position is reflected in a long tradition of industrial support measures (Harrison 1989; Harrison 1990a), a significant subvention from the UK Government (Hewitt 1990) and a separate range of industrial support agencies. In addition, there are industrial support measures offered within NI that have no directly comparable counterpart in the rest of the UK, for example various assistance packages offered by LEDU and a T&EA programme offering assistance to companies to assess their human resource development requirements. For the purposes of analysis, the measures have been regrouped under six headings which are addressed below. An attempt is made in each case to draw out the main implications arising from the use of these policy instruments.

Direct support to industry

Direct financial support to companies in NI is mainly in the form of capital grants, part of the SFA package offered by the region's industrial development agencies (IDB and LEDU) (Northern Ireland Audit Office 1990; 1993). The IDOP devoted an extremely small proportion of its expenditure to SFA – despite the fact that an average of £69.5m was incurred annually on this instrument over the four-year period 1990–1993 by the IDB (Industrial Development Board 1993). This would imply that there was little in the way of additionality associated with the measure as the spending on SFA would have probably occurred anyway. However, there were more serious reservations to be noted in respect of SFA: independent estimates of dead-weight associated with SFA were found to be relatively high. One study found that in the period 1989–1992, 49 per cent of companies would not have reduced investment expenditure levels in the absence of SFA whilst 56 per cent of companies reported that SFA had either 'no influence' or only 'some influence' on final investment (Sheehan 1993; Sheehan and Roper 1993). Evidence provided by a study of manufacturing profitability in NI companies also suggested that government grants such as SFA have had the effect of raising profit levels and retained earnings within firms without any impact on raising productivity or value-added per employee (Roper 1993).

Marketing assistance

The IDB makes provision within its measures for marketing assistance. Two postal surveys of recipients of assistance from each agency indicated that marketing assistance contributed to increases in sales, exports and profits, with relatively low levels of dead-weight. Survey responses, however, suggested that the more *ad hoc* schemes, involving relatively small amounts of assistance, were less effective in contributing to a planned approach to marketing within firms.

Research and development

Grant assistance was provided under the Programme towards research and development through the Product and Process Development Scheme (PPD). There was a strong rationale for the measure in view of NI's low level of GDP devoted to R&D (Harrison and Hart 1987; 1992; Northern Ireland Economic Council 1993). Privately funded R&D expenditure in NI was estimated at £44m or 0.4 per cent in 1990–1991 by the Northern Ireland Economic Council, compared with a figure of 1.09 per cent for the UK in 1990 and 2.24 per cent in Japan (NIEC 1993).

Evaluation found that the scheme had achieved the objective of stimulating companies to introduce new products and processes. Many good projects had gone ahead which would not have started without assistance and more than three-quarters of all projects assisted were technical successes. The gearing effect of overall company expenditure to overall grants for development was at least three to one, and, for those companies going into production, it was at least five to one. Set against these achievements, the evaluation indicated that the scheme was perceived by many of its users as a 'quasi-automatic subsidy' rather than as a programme primarily for encouraging technological innovation. A profusion of objectives for the original programme made it difficult to evaluate true achievements against all the objectives.

Quality

Support was also available within IDOP towards third-party certification of quality management systems as well as assistance for consultancy advice in respect of Total Quality Management (TQM) and manufacturing competitiveness. In the case of TQM, it has been viewed by some as probably representing 'the most fundamental reform of business organisation that the UK has experienced' (Whyte and Witcher 1992). Extensive postal questionnaire surveys of these measures indicated a high success rate for NI firms in respect of BS5750 certification and improved organisational efficiency, with some evidence to show increased employee commitment and increased labour flexibility.

The research findings in respect of TQM companies are less positive. Overall, two-thirds of survey respondents indicated they had difficulty in achieving their TQM objectives, whilst over 70 per cent admitted to difficulties in maintaining their TQM system. The policy implication here was that much greater efforts are required by both agencies and firms in the drive towards the promotion and incorporation of TQM concepts into company cultures.

Training and development

A recent NIERC study (1993) comparing skill levels in NI companies with a selection of matched plants in Germany identified a significant competitiveness gap between NI and German firms. Higher workforce and managerial skills were identified as a primary reason for the German firms' competitive advantage. These findings are consistent with those of earlier studies (Hitchens and Birnie 1989; Hitchens, Wagner and Birnie 1989). As a consequence, there was a strong justification for the inclusion of a measure within the IDOP aimed at encouraging companies to take a professional and structured approach to effective, company-wide training and to view investment in human capital as a key strategic decision to improve competitiveness. This measure made provision for the Company Development Programme (CDP), administered by the T&EA, which offered practical and financial assistance to companies to assess their human resource development requirements and to develop action plans. Grant assistance was then provided for the implementation of such plans over a three-year period.

The evaluation revealed that as the Programme unfolded, the Agency began to place a greater emphasis on supporting training which was realisable, increased efforts were being made to link training objectives with business objectives and more emphasis was being given to management development. The T&EA took seriously the question of evaluation, requiring new CDP participants to specify their key business objectives and, through a process of intermediate indicators, to identify training and development outcomes which would impact on critical aspects of their business performance.

Enterprise measures

Finally, a series of measures aimed at the promotion of enterprise and small firms was included within IDOP, including the Business Start Programme (BSP) designed to help those in self-employment as well as support for the region's network of local enterprise agencies. A survey of 100 start-up cases pointed to a reduction in levels of dead-weight from 50 per cent associated with the scheme's predecessor, the Enterprise Allowance Scheme, to around 36 per cent as a result of tighter eligibility conditions. High levels of displacement of other NI businesses arising from the scheme were recorded. The nature of the businesses supported under the scheme were such that few could demonstrate novelty while many were likely to be competing against similar small businesses. Thus for every job created, 36 per cent would have been created anyway and a further 32 per cent (50% of the remainder) would probably have displaced other jobs. The overall cost per job created, taking account of the implied level of dead-weight and displacement, was calculated to be £3964. The scheme as a whole appeared to be a relatively cost-efficient method of promoting self-employment and job creation despite high levels of dead-weight and displacement. However, the relatively low quality of some of the businesses supported under the scheme might suggest that there may be a high failure rate associated with the scheme.

Implications for Policy

Overall, the IDOP has been an unwieldy programme to evaluate, given the breadth of measures which the Programme encompassed. In response, a highly selective approach to evaluation was adopted focusing on the extent to which the Programme's strategy, objectives and measures were appropriate in terms of meeting the region's industrial development priorities and the impact of each measure in both quantitative and qualitative terms.

There are two principal conclusions arising from this evaluation study. First, serious questions have been raised concerning the appropriate mix of industrial policy instruments. In particular, strong evidence has been presented which raises serious doubts over the efficacy of direct financial assistance to firms in the form of quite generous capital grants. This must be seen against a background of the widespread use of regional incentive packages in the EU (Yuill *et al.* 1991), and the findings of this study should give cause for concern.

Second, the success of any programme depends on the adoption of a strategic overview of all relevant policy issues so that they can be presented as a coherent package of measures – essential for successful programme design. Such a co-ordinating role for EU programmes is made more difficult by the fact that the level of EU funding is so minor relative to the overall level of public expenditure on industrial development in the region (Harrison 1990b). Perhaps the greatest challenge to be faced in devising such programmes lies in achieving the necessary degree of integration between and within programmes (McEldowney 1991). This would tend to suggest a need for more focused programmes aimed at bringing a 'quantum' improvement in the area or sector concerned.

In the case of the IDOP, given the wide range of measures it covered (Table 11.2, p.183), there was a distinct danger that the programme itself was over-ambitious in the types of impact it is seeking to make. This 'shot-gun approach' to Programme formulation made the subsequent evaluation of the Programme difficult to undertake. The Programme made provision for all size ranges of companies from the sole proprietor to the multi-national enterprise. The measures included within the Programme were wide-ranging, covering, for example, capital grant assistance, assistance towards marketing, quality improvement, manufacturing competitiveness and research and development – including graduate placement, workforce skills and management development. On the one hand, the existence of such measures should be applauded as they reflect the existence of determined efforts on the part of government departments to address the region's industrial development problems.

On the other hand, if full advantage is to be made of EU funding, a more focused approach to programme design and content could result in a programme which is more capable of achieving better defined targets. For example, within the existing IDOP, one of the objectives of the IDOP was to encourage additional small enterprises in the region. This objective was addressed through a number of measures, such as the Business Start-Up Programme, as well as through the local enterprise agencies and related measures. These were worthwhile measures and, as the evaluations of these individual measures demonstrated, they resulted in benefits for the recipients concerned. As a consequence, it might have made more sense to have compiled an operational programme dedicated exclusively to the development of enterprise and the promotion of SMEs.

The implications for programme formulation is that programmes work best when they are drawn-up with well-defined objectives and the capability of successful implementation. Moreover, in view of the fact that the main areas of industrial development policy in NI concern the promotion of SMEs, as is also the case in many other European regions, future operational programmes of this kind should adopt a more integrated approach focusing in more specific terms on, for example, the development of an 'enterprise package'.

Finally, operational programmes based, as they are, on EU funds should be seen as offering an opportunity to experiment with new initiatives and schemes rather than simply relying on pre-existing programmes. Moreover, there is little to be gained by including such pre-existing schemes within operational programmes if doubts exist over the objectives or the effectiveness of such schemes.

CHAPTER 12

The Design and Implementation of European Programmes for Regional Development in the UK

A Comparative Review

Peter Roberts and Trevor Hart

Introduction

Most of the chapters in this section of the book have described and analysed the content and operation of regional development programmes in individual UK regions: western Scotland, London, the West Midlands, Yorkshire and Humberside, the Highlands and Islands and Northern Ireland. This last chapter of the UK part of the volume re-examines the key features of seven EU programmes from a comparative perspective. Reporting on the findings of a research project supported by the Joseph Rowntree Foundation, it explores some of the most important characteristics of the design, operation and management of regional development programmes in four regions: Scotland, Yorkshire and Humberside, the West Midlands and the South West. In each of these regions a selection of European programmes was examined in detail and the views of the partners responsible for the programmes were sought in order to identify the strengths and weaknesses evident in the procedures used for strategy formulation, the negotiation of a Single Programming Document (SPD) and the subsequent implementation of the agreed programme. A summary of the research design and the status of each of the programmes examined is provided in Table 12.1.

Research Issues

The research reported in this chapter made extensive use of the existing literature in order to trace the economic evolution of the regions investigated and to chart the emergence and application of European regional and structural policies. Following a literature and practice review, four categories of region were identified. Within these standard regions case-study areas were selected in order to allow for an investigation of the different challenges faced by regions and the various processes involved in the operation of the regional programmes. The case-study categories and the regions selected for study were:

- a region with established territorial management – Scotland
- a region with established regional structures – the West Midlands
- a region with emergent regional structures – Yorkshire and Humberside
- a region with a previous history of fragmented structures – the South West.

In each of the case-study regions a number of European programmes were selected for more detailed investigation and interviews were conducted with a sample of the partners to establish both a 'top-down' and a 'bottom-up' view of the design and operation of the programmes. Through the interviews and the study of existing literature, the research sought to address three key themes:

1. Strategy development and review, considering both the existing framework of regional and sub-regional strategies (for example, Regional Planning Guidance and local economic development strategies), the evolution of various strategies for European Union programmes and initiatives and the relationship between these two strands of strategy development.
2. Programme operation and management, considering matters such as committee structures and composition, roles of the committee members and the balance of influence on the committees when decisions are made on project proposals.
3. The impact of EU funds and programmes in the wider context, looking at the place of EU funds in the local regeneration process and how they complement or shape activity, as well as considering whether involvement in EU programmes helps to promote partnership and collaborative working among the involved agencies.

Table 12.1 lists the programmes investigated in each region; one Objective 1, three Objective 2 and three Objective 5b programmes were selected for study in order to identify any specific issues associated with particular types of programme. In addition, other European programmes and activities were investigated to explore the wider influence of the operation of European policies, including the operation of a programme outwith the mainstream of EU policy.

Table 12.1 Research design and case studies

Aspect of policy studied	*Objective 1*	*Objective 2*	*Objective 5b*	*Other programmes and European activities*
Scotland	The Highlands and Islands	Eastern Scotland*		North Sea Commission
Yorkshire and Humberside		Yorkshire and Humberside	Northern Uplands*	RECHAR
West Midlands		West Midlands	The Marches*	European Regional Partnership
South-West			South West England	KONVER

Note: * Signifies that the case study area is part of this SPD.
Sources: Various SPDs, Research undertaken by authors, Commission of the European Communities 1995c.

Table 12.2 Key features of the programmes

Programme	*Total investment (mecu)*	*Structural Funds contribution (mecu)*	*Population (millions)*	*Percentage of UK population*
Highlands and Islands (Objective 1)	1012	311	0.28	0.48
Eastern Scotland (Objective 2)	292	121	1.13	2.00
Yorkshire and Humberside (Objective 2)	814	313	2.60	4.50
Northern Uplands (Objective 5b)	262	108	0.37	0.65
West Midlands (Objective 2)	938	371	3.04	5.30
The Marches (Objective 5b)	91	40	0.15	0.26
South West England (Objective 5b)	515	219	0.80	1.38

Sources: Various SPDs, Commission of the European Communities 1995c.

As demonstrated in Table 12.2, the programmes studied represent a substantial proportion of Structural Fund activity in the UK (Commission of European Communities 1995c). The Highlands and Islands programme represents 17.8 per cent of the total investment in UK Objective 1 areas and 13.2 per cent of the contribution made by the Structural Funds. In the Objective 2 case study regions the overall level of investment is some 37.9 per cent of the UK total whilst the contribution from the Structural Funds represents 37.6 per cent of the national total. In the Objective 5b case studies investment is 43.1 per cent of the national total and 44.9 per cent of the Structural Funds contribution. Overall, the SPDs in the case-study regions have a combined level of investment of 3924 million ecu (mecu) (30% of the UK total), a total contribution from the Structural Funds of 1483 mecu (27.9%) and cover an area containing a population of 8.38 million, which represents 14.57 per cent of the total UK population.

One of the motivations for undertaking the research reported in this chapter was to identify the contribution of the experience of constructing and implementing European regional programmes to the more general revival of regional planning in the UK. The need to engage in a European level of strategic planning at the regional scale has been identified by a number of authors (Glasson 1992; Roberts 1996) as one of the factors which has helped to stimulate the resurgence of regional planning. Other factors include the rediscovery of the important role played by land-use strategies in helping to create the conditions necessary for economic, social and environmental reconstruction, the recent reorganisation of central government functions at regional level in England and the revival of local authority conference arrangements (Mawson 1996).

Reflecting the general chronology of the preparation and implementation of an SPD, and following the brief examination of the context for the current round of programmes which is presented in section two, the third section of the chapter focuses on a number of the more important factors which influenced and helped to determine both the content and the process of preparation of the initial European regional development strategies, the drafting of the programmes submitted by the UK Government to the European Commission and the negotiation of the final SPDs. Following this, the fourth section assesses a number of the major characteristics associated with the implementation of SPDs and provides an evaluation of the overall effectiveness of the management arrangements. In the final section some of the accompanying issues that have influenced, and which are likely to continue to influence, the planning and management of the regions are discussed. This discussion helps to inform the presentation of a number of preliminary conclusions regarding the operation of European programmes for regional development for the UK.

The Context for the Current Programmes

In a formal sense, regional policy is a relatively new area of activity for the European Union, but an interest in regional disparities and regional problems has a longer pedigree. The emergence of a formal regional policy was a slow process. During the 1960s research undertaken by, and on behalf of, the Commission identified the case for intervention, and this growing recognition of the need for a regional policy, together with the desirability of introducing a regional dimension into other areas of European policy, resulted in the establishment of the European Regional Development Fund (ERDF) at the Council meeting in December 1974 (Roberts, Hart and Thomas 1993).

As discussed in more detail in Chapter 2, in its early stages ERDF assistance was allocated on the basis of national quotas, emphasis was placed on the support of infrastructure provision and applications for assistance took the form of individual project submissions. The ERDF was established on the principle of additionality and also recognised the need to develop solutions to the particular problems experienced in individual regions. 'However, the quota system, which applied until the reforms introduced in 1985, prevented the EC from concentrating all the effort on the poorest regions' (Vickerman 1992, p.49). During the late 1980s the programme approach was elaborated, and, alongside this, increasing emphasis was placed on the role of partnership in the development and operation of programmes.

It is important to note that, at this point in time, a considerable degree of variation existed between UK regions in terms of their ability to respond to the shift in European funding towards a programme approach. The decline of regional planning and management activity from the late 1970s onwards had resulted in an absence of up-to-date regional strategies, a dearth of regional organisations capable of responding to the new challenges implied by the programme method of approach and a fragmented structure of central government departments with regional responsibilities (Wannop 1995; Roberts 1996). This neglect of strategic policy and institutions was reflected in the existence of a less than comprehensive foundation for the construction of European regional programmes.

Our purpose in rehearsing this brief history is to demonstrate the ways in which the Funds and their means of operation have evolved over the past 20 years, and to explain the origins of some of the preconceptions and prejudices that have survived successive reforms of the Funds. It is not uncommon, for example, for some of the participants involved in the operation of the Funds to carry with them notions of a 'golden age' of project-based funding whereby applications for assistance could be made as and when resources were needed, or to wish for a return to a period when the Commission staff exercised a looser control over matters enabling, it is claimed, a sub-national division of the funds available to be better integrated with other non-EU elements of regional assistance. These and other ideas continue to influence the attitudes of some actors and work against the strategic objectives of programmes.

An equally important influence from the more immediate past (the 1989–1993 round of programmes) is the extent to which programmes are regarded by some participants as 'local property'. In some regions, from 1994 onwards, a Single Programming Document (SPD) replaced a number of smaller programmes (National Programmes of Community Interest and Integrated Development Operations); the SPDs draw on, and are embedded in, a European regional development strategy. In such cases it is common to find that a number of the participants continue to argue that this has resulted in a dilution of local focus and that a spatial division of the regional programme would more directly match their local needs. This feature can be observed in a number of the case studies – the Highlands and Islands, West Midlands and the East of Scotland, for example – and the initial resistance to what is perceived as the unnecessary amalgamation of previous local programmes has continued to influence the operation of the SPDs.

Three other issues proved to be of particular importance in establishing the context for the preparation of the current round of programmes: the hazy nature of the guidance provided by the Commission regarding the required format and content of strategies and SPDs, the stance taken by the UK Government in relation to the allocation of responsibilities for various tasks associated with the preparation and submission of both the regional development strategies and the SPDs; and the difficulties associated with the definition of the scope and membership of the regional partnership. Each of these three issues is now considered in more detail.

A substantial number of participants observed that whilst the Commission provided general guidance on the expected overall structure and content of a strategy (in the form of the published Regulations and other contextual material), it proved to be more difficult to obtain a detailed description of what was required and in what form a strategy should be presented. This reflects both the absence of institutionalised mechanisms for dialogue between the regions and the Commission (Greenwood, Levy and Stewart

1995), the desire on the part of the Commission to avoid providing too much detailed guidance – for fear of encouraging the preparation of formulaic strategies – and, perhaps, some uncertainty on their part as to what an 'ideal' strategy might look like. One Commission official who was interviewed alleged that the previous round of draft regional development strategies had all been put through the 'Whitehall washing machine' and one of the steps taken by the Commission in order to avoid a repetition of this bland uniformity was to emphasise the need for a grassroots approach.

The general level of preparedness in the UK in 1993 – both in central government and in the regions – represented a marked improvement compared with the previous round of strategy and programme preparation, if only because they had learned from previous experience. Wannop (1995, p.197) typifies previous UK submissions to the Commission as being 'scrambled from the hands of civil servants without any depth of reflection'. Alongside the burgeoning revival of regional and strategic planning (Roberts 1996), a greater degree of responsibility for the preparation of the regional development strategy was claimed by local and regional actors.

In addition, the central government departments associated with the operation of the Structural Funds attempted to refine and streamline their structures; this was generally more successful in Scotland and Wales than in the English regions. Most of the activities associated with the preparation of regional development strategies and draft SPDs had been completed prior to the formation of the Government Offices for the Regions (GORs) in April 1994, although these new integrated offices were involved in the subsequent revisions to the drafts. One of the reasons given for the establishment of GORs was the need to ensure greater inter-departmental co-ordination in relation to the operation of the Structural Funds (Mawson 1996); in the previous round of programmes differences of approach were clearly evident between programmes managed by the DTI and those managed by the DoE.

Regional partners have a role to play in strategy and programme development, and in programme implementation. In addition to representatives of national government and the Commission, partners are mostly drawn from a range of actors active in economic development and regeneration. While all bring some resources to the partnership, a major motivation for involvement is the desire to gain access to European funds to support projects they are promoting or projects which are complementary to or in support of their objectives. So, partnerships are mainly composed of organisations which have a primary interest in taking from the programmes, and the factor that often contributes to their qualification for membership of the partnership is that they are experienced or aspirant applicants for European funding.

A final point of importance in a number of the case studies is related to the restricted scope and narrow membership of regional partnerships. Amongst other factors, the restricted nature of partnerships reflects the absence of a formal regional tier of governance in the UK – a situation which, in the view of Wiehler and Stumm (1995, p.245), can prove to be a 'growing obstacle to the economic development of regions' – and the dominance of central government. This dominance can be seen to be reflected in the absence of the 'social partners' in many of the regional partnerships and in the precise specification of the procedures to be followed by partnerships in the preparation of regional development strategies.

All of the above points of context can be seen to have influenced the preparation of regional development strategies and SPDs in all of the case-study regions. Past experience, together with false expectations in some cases, helped to shape both the structure and content of strategies and SPDs. A number of these themes recur throughout the following analysis and, in addition, they provide the basis for the specification of broad criteria against which the performance of the SPDs can be measured.

The Preparation of Programmes

The regional development strategy

In chronological order, the processes leading to the agreement of SPDs include the preparation of European regional development strategies, the drafting of SPDs and the negotiation of final SPDs. The observations in this section are drawn from a study of the relevant documents, from interviews conducted with participants involved in the processes and from the views expressed by a number of external observers. The starting point in the process of developing and negotiating a European programme is the preparation of a regional development strategy. In theory, though not always in practice, a regional development strategy should be informed by an *ex post* evaluation of the performance of any pre-existing programmes, prepared at an early point in the planning cycle in order to allow for reflection and subsequent modification, and developed in response to explicit guidelines that specify the expected output in terms of both structure and content. However, in reality, many of the regional development strategies were prepared in the absence of a comprehensive evaluation, were hastily developed and were drafted and submitted without the benefit of clear and detailed guidance from the Commission as to their expected structure and content.

It is important to note at this point that, reflecting the general condition of regional planning reported in the previous section, there was a considerable degree of variation between regions in terms of the level of pre-existing plans available. In some regions and sub-regions the level of sophistication and nature of regional planning arrangements allowed partners to move forward rapidly in the preparation of a strategy; this was the case in the West Midlands where the partnership was able to build upon the foundation of joint working on regional issues established in the 1960s. In other regions a less substantial basis of prior regional strategic agreement existed.

In some regions the situation proved to be even more complex and potentially confusing owing to the relatively late designation and notification of the areas' eligibility to receive assistance from the Structural Funds. Although in most regions there was a substantial degree of continuity between the areas which were designated as eligible for assistance under the 1989–1993 programmes and the 1994–1999 programmes, there were a number of modifications to boundaries or, more significantly, to the status accorded to certain regions. The Highlands and Islands, for example, was designated as an Objective 1 area at a relatively late point in the planning cycle. This late designation caused a number of operational and structural difficulties in relation to the drafting of the objectives and measures proposed in the regional development strategy; the original work in this region had been targeted towards the production of an Objective 5b strategy.

An equally difficult issue for many local partners was the absence of sufficiently clear and detailed guidance from the Commission in relation to the expected or required scope and content of a regional development strategy. This problem was compounded in some areas and programmes by the lack of any previous tradition or experience of drafting a regional development strategy. A typical response in most regions to the task of preparing a strategy was to nominate a small group of (mainly) local authority officers and to charge it with the task of producing an initial evaluation of strategic parameters. Although the work of such a group was managed and guided by a wider partnership, there is some evidence that detailed consultations were restricted to an inner group of partners. Owing to a shortage of staff and other resources, and the presumption in most cases that the majority of tasks could and should be undertaken within the resources of the partnership, some of the initial draft strategies were hurried, incomplete or lacking in detail. A propensity for partners to focus on projects rather than on strategy was evident in some of the initial drafts. One observer of the process (who was involved in a number of partnerships) noted a tendency for some strategies to be built from the 'inside outwards' rather than starting from an 'outside' strategic perspective.

Although the Commission avoided providing detailed guidance on the scope, structure and content of strategies, the stated intention was not to confuse or confound but rather to discourage the partnership from adopting a 'standard' solution; the aim was to encourage the partners to adopt an approach that was appropriate to the needs of the region and, perhaps, innovatory. This desire to avoid mechanical or formulaic responses did not prevent partnerships from seeking and gaining advice from the Commission and from the UK Government; unfortunately, advice from these sources was not always consistent. Experienced partners and actors working at the grass roots generally found it to be relatively easy to obtain the advice and assistance they sought, but this was not always the case. Inexperienced actors found the lack of detailed written guidance unhelpful and lacked the experience or contact network necessary to make maximum use of the more informal channels of communication and sources of advice.

The range of participation in the partnerships responsible for producing the regional development strategies varied between regions. In the West Midlands long-standing arrangements for regional planning and management provided the core of the partnership. The other 'Partners in Europe' were drawn from the Regional Economic Consortium (Regional CBI, Chambers of Commerce, Training and Enterprise Councils (TECs), Trades Union Congress (TUC), MPs and MEPs), the regional development agency (the West Midlands Development Agency) and the region's universities (West Midlands Regional Forum of Local Authorities 1993). Additional technical support for the preparation of the strategy was provided by the regional offices of central government and other contributions and specialist advice were provided by the voluntary sector and other agencies. Overall, this was a local authority-led, but widely-based, partnership and process.

In other regions different arrangements were put in place. The Yorkshire and Humberside Partnership – chaired by a member of the regional TUC – brought together a number of regional actors and agencies, including the local authority regional association, CBI, TUC, Chambers of Commerce, TECs, universities and regional offices of government. The secretariat was provided by the local authority regional association – the Yorkshire and Humberside Regional Association – while the regional analysis and assessment was prepared by a regional academic network through the Regional Research Observatory (Yorkshire and Humberside Partnership 1993).

The East of Scotland strategy was prepared in-house by a small core team of officers drawn from the partner organisations; the partnership itself obtained most of the resources necessary to support the process of strategy preparation from local authorities and Local Enterprise Companies (LECs).

Additional support to the partnership was provided by a specialist unit within the Scottish Office.

In the South West the lead on the development of the strategy for the Objective 5b area was taken by the local authorities, and by Cornwall County Council in particular. Other partners also made a number of significant contributions, for example the agriculture section of the draft SPD was drafted by Ministry of Agriculture, Fisheries and Food staff in the region and financial assistance in the latter stages of SPD development was provided by Devon and Cornwall TEC.

Overall, the methods used for the preparation of regional development strategies reflected the pre-existing distribution of skills, knowledge and experience of previous rounds of European programmes, the availability of information on regional indicators and the willingness of the regional offices of government to contribute to the process. In many cases the local authorities led or dominated the process. This could arouse suspicion among less well-informed partners, but in most areas this diminished as it became clear that the work was for the common good and as other partners' knowledge and understanding improved. However, it is likely that few, if any, of the other partners in the programmes could marshall the resources or expertise provided by the local authorities, and in most cases this was recognised. Thus a significant factor was the sensitivity with which the local authorities exercised their potential dominance of the process. Many of the partners, and especially those new to the process, used their involvement in the preparation of the strategy as a learning experience.

A number of conclusions can be drawn from this evaluation of the first stage of the preparation of a SPD. Earlier designation of the areas eligible for assistance (especially in cases where the status of assistance had changed) would have helped to create greater certainty as to the nature of the task to be undertaken; this was particularly important in those areas subject to discontinuity in the boundaries for the old programmes and those for the new strategies. In addition, more detailed and explicit guidance on the scope, structure and content expected of a strategy would have helped to speed the process. Arrangements for consultation between grassroots actors and the Commission were in general satisfactory, but tended to rely on personal contacts and prior knowledge; actors new to the process were somewhat disadvantaged by this situation. The role performed by the regional offices of government varied between regions: the existence of a single main point of contact in the Scottish Office helped to structure dialogue and the flow of information, whilst arrangements in the English regions were less consistent.

Drafting the Single Programming Document

Following the development of the regional development strategies, formal responsibility for the preparation of draft SPDs fell to central government. During the process of drafting the SPD a number of different agendas emerged. Participants in several of the case-study regions have noted the existence of what could be referred to as a national-European agenda, with the Commission playing an increasingly important role which, over time, converged with or diverged from local-national agendas and expectations. Whilst some commentators have observed that the resulting SPDs were broadly similar in appearance and content (Bentley and Shutt 1995), it would appear from our research that, compared with the previous round of programmes, the alleged 'Whitehall washing machine' effect was less pronounced. Although the SPDs which emerged in early 1994 followed a similar pattern, this was due in part to the desire of the UK Government to be consistent in terms of the calculation and presentation of the non-Structural Fund financial implications of the programmes. It also, perhaps, reflects the fact that the emerging revival of strategic planning in central government was still at a relatively early stage and that the integration of the regional offices of government did not occur until after the preparation of the regional development strategies and the initial stages of the SPD process were completed. Equally, some participants have suggested that the shortage of time towards the end of the process of SPD preparation and approval forced partnerships towards the adoption of a standard model; others have suggested that there was a desire to avoid substantial differences between programmes to avoid the possibility of the Commission 'playing one area off against another'.

Nevertheless, the substance of the critique holds true. It would appear that in some regions the national-European agenda tended to dominate local and regional distinctiveness and that, in the view of one South West regional partner, the programme was considered to be chiefly a national matter within which other participants 'did what they were told'. Arrangements for consultation and the participation of partners varied between regions and between programmes. The consultative exercise for the South West, for example, went through various stages of the evolution of the SPD (some 20 drafts) and up to 50 people or organisations were involved in an Objective 5b interest group. Elsewhere the arrangements for consultation and involvement were more limited, causing the House of Commons Trade and Industry Select Committee report on Regional Policy to note that many witnesses complained that they had not been sufficiently involved in the process

(House of Commons 1995). Social partners tended to be absent from the process, despite the active participation of the CBI and the TUC in a number of the exercises which had led to the production of the initial regional development strategies. There was also an absence of direct local political input, with local authorities being represented in the process by officers rather than elected members. Perhaps the most balanced judgement that is available is that of a non-government participant in a number of programmes who has observed that there was generally a greater involvement of partners in the drafting of SPDs in 1993–1994 than there had been during the preparation of the previous round of programmes. However, this judgement does not cover the circumstances evident in all of the case-study regions and programmes and does not deny the restricted nature of some of the partnerships.

As has been pointed out above, programmes are subject to *ex post* evaluation and the evaluation of a pre-existing programme is clearly a valuable input to the preparation of the next programme. However, the SPDs were planned to cover a period which followed on immediately from the completion of the previous round of programmes, and in reality the preparation of the SPDs had begun before the 1989–1993 programmes had been completed and before the evaluations had been started. So, for example, the *ex post* evaluations of the 1989–1993 Objective 2 programmes did not commence until early 1996, and at that date spending on some projects was only just being completed and the impact of such projects was far from clearly established. The solution adopted was to rely on interim evaluations. While these can yield some interesting indications of progress, a large part of the programme has often still to become established and the impact of the programme as a whole remains a matter of speculation.

The negotiation of a SPD

The features observable in the transition from the preparation of a draft SPD to the negotiation of a final SPD reflects and reinforces many of the points made above, together with the further complications that inevitably accompanied the entry of an additional main actor – the Commission. During this final stage of preparation it appeared that there was a substantial degree of policy iteration and that a number of changes were made to the content of policy agendas. Policy iteration took the form of the introduction of new elements of policy and additional strategic objectives into SPDs by the Commission, and this can be traced to the fact that their idea of what a 'good' programme should look like was evolving as they worked with the developing programmes across the EU. Some of these new elements unbalanced strategies previously agreed by the partners. Other factors encouraging policy iteration related to the desire of the UK Government to produce balanced programmes which avoided the introduction of elements into the SPDs which were seen as being inconsistent with other areas of national policy, and to the transfer of experience between local and regional partners working through, for example, local authority formal and informal networks. Changes in the content of policy agendas also occurred, reflecting both the policy iteration process described above and recognising the requirement to introduce new elements and procedures into the programmes in order to emphasise local needs.

Taking a longer time perspective, the impact of the changes introduced by the revisions to the Structural Fund Regulations can be seen to have developed in a number of ways. In addition to the move to a programme approach, there has been a gradual change in the balance of the projects included in the programmes with a change in emphasis from hard infrastructure to soft infrastructure becoming more evident over time. It is also the case that there has been a growing emphasis on strategy. Generally, the Operational Programmes from 1989–1993 were more project-focused and partners and programme secretariats seemed to pay little attention to the strategic envelope provided by the CSF once the programme was approved, whereas under the current round the SPD holds a more significant place in the minds of applicants and those responsible for programme management.

One of the major problems encountered by all participants was the tight time-scale within which negotiations took place. This combination of a tight overall time-scale, the lack of time to evaluate the introduction of new elements, the difficulties inherent in working with a large group of actors and the great range of local and regional interests and requirements, created a feeling amongst many participants that the overall process was not as well managed as it might have been. Local and regional participants, the UK Government and the Commission were all, at one stage or another, guilty of a degree of laxity or inconsistency. With a more generous (but tightly defined) timetable, a dedicated strategy team working full-time on the preparation and negotiation of an SPD and a greater degree of clarity at the outset regarding the scope, structure and content of a SPD, many of the problems experienced during the 1993–1994 period would have been reduced or resolved. These and other points are discussed further in the final section of this chapter.

In spite of the Commission's wish to avoid the production of a 'standard' response (in terms of either the regional development strategy or the SPD), a number of factors conspired to move programmes in this direction. Drawing on *ex ante* assessments and knowledge of approaches adopted in programmes elsewhere in Europe, the Commission offered guidance and comments on draft SPDs – some of which sought significant (as they saw it) improvements. When such belated guidance was added to the pressure of time to complete the process and a shortage of resources to complete the task, there was a tendency to follow a 'preferred route'.

The Implementation and Management of the Programmes

Three aspects of implementation and management are of particular interest: the structure of the management arrangements, the membership of the various bodies within the structure and the operation of the programmes. Each of these issues reflects, to a certain extent, the aims and content of the agreed SPD. However, the outcome of national policy decisions, together with the Regulations which govern the operation of the Structural Funds, also exercise considerable influence over the arrangements for implementation and management.

Management arrangements and structures

In general terms, the organisational structure and assignment of management responsibilities follows a standard pattern in most regions and for most programmes. A Programme Monitoring Committee (PMC) superintends the overall operation of the programme and is advised by a number of Advisory or Working Groups. The role of the PMC is seen as strategic, being primarily concerned with ensuring that the implementation is firmly focused on the defined objectives and that these objectives remain relevant to the needs of the area. Each programme is provided with administrative support by a Secretariat. In England this function is discharged by the relevant government office, whilst in Scotland Programme Executives largely undertake many of these responsibilities. These Executives have the particular virtue, in the eyes of some partners, of operating at arm's length from central government. Two further additions to the management arrangements in Scotland are the existence of Programme Management Committees, which are responsible for decisions on individual applications based on recommendations from the Advisory Groups, and Joint Management Boards which oversee the technical assistance budget for programme management and the work of the Programme Executives (Russell 1995).

These management arrangements are not, in themselves, a matter of general dispute or disquiet in all programmes, although in some cases there is a degree of disquiet. However, the detailed operation and discharge of particular functions is the subject of contention. In part, such contentions relate to the membership structure of the various groups, but they also reflect certain concerns about the efficiency and effectiveness of the arrangements. A further source of disquiet reflects a residual dissatisfaction with the delays experienced in establishing programmes, which is said by some participants to reflect the time taken to negotiate agreed programmes.

One of the evident sources of tension has its origins in the transition from the smaller programmes of the 1989–1993 period to the present arrangements. Smaller, locally-based groups, it is claimed, were able to focus attention on particular local needs and opportunities and could expedite decision making with regard to individual project applications. This previous arrangement, in the view of one participant, encouraged a 'cosy' atmosphere in which the scoring of projects (against a set of criteria which sought to identify the contribution of projects to the achievement of the strategic objectives and therefore their priority for funding) was often undertaken by non-experts; the same participant considers the current arrangements to be more rigorous and satisfactory. This view is generally shared by other participants, although in the previous round of programmes differences of approach were evident depending on whether the programme was the responsibility of the Department of the Environment or the Department of Trade and Industry. A further source of tension evident in some programmes is the absence of a sub-regional tier of management. Once again this reflects, in part, the cultural change between the previous and present programmes, but it also reflects the concerns of some partners, especially those involved in programmes which cover large geographical areas, regarding the level of spatial specificity of the SPD and the appropriateness of the management arrangements. In the Highlands and Islands programme this has led to a call for greater spatial targeting and the establishment of area advisory groups. In the West Midlands five local partnership groups provide sub-regional advice, and this tier of spatial management is generally considered to have been helpful.

Committee membership

Matters of structure and management are closely related to the selection of members and the roles which they perform in the various committees. The membership of the PMC is specified in the Regulations which govern the operation of the Structural Funds. Members of the PMC should represent a partnership between the Commission, the Member State concerned and the competent authorities and bodies in a region. It is the PMC which is charged with the management of a SPD. Local and regional members of a PMC are selected in accordance with these Regulations and almost always include representatives from the local authorities, TECs or LECs, the voluntary sector and the private sector. In addition, many PMCs include members from further and higher education, environmental organisations and other local and regional special interest groups. The PMC is chaired by the Regional Director of the appropriate Government Office; in Scotland the PMC is chaired by the Scottish Office.

There are three important issues with regard to the selection and operation of the membership. First, the 'social partners' are not represented, at least directly, on the various PMCs. This is the result of a decision taken by the UK Government based on an interpretation of Article 9 of Council Regulation 2083/93, which specifies that arrangements for the involvement of the economic and social partners shall be 'within the framework of the Member State's national rules and practices' (Commission of the European Communities 1996c, p.72). The exclusion of the social partners reflects the view held by the UK Government and other members of some partnerships that the PMC should be composed of partners who actually have a role in implementing programmes at the local level. The UK Government states that it has made appropriate alternative arrangements for the involvement of the social partners, including the provision of briefings. Briefings are also provided for local authority elected members in some regions.

The second issue relates to the methods used for the selection of members of the various committees. Although it is usually apparent why certain organisations are selected to be represented, there is a lack of transparency regarding the methods used in selecting local authority representatives. Elected members are generally excluded and officers serve on the committees. In some programmes the decision to establish representation by officers was taken by the local authorities themselves (this occurred in the West Midlands), whilst in other cases there was little or no discussion of the method of representation and officers were invited to serve by the government office rather than through nomination by the local authorities (as in Yorkshire and Humberside).

The third issue of importance with regard to membership reflects the uncertainty experienced by some members of PMCs or other committees concerning the roles which they are expected to perform. In theory, members represent the partnership and work together in order to arrive at the best collective decision in accord with the agreed SPD; in this capacity they act as guardians of the strategy. However, in reality, some participants have argued that there is a danger that they may be seen to perform a dual role: as an objective evaluator of project proposals and, in some cases, as an advocate for a particular project. It is not suggested that the research highlighted any evidence of irregularity or collusion, rather it would appear that the difficulty experienced by individuals results from having to apply specific local or subject knowledge in what is frequently a complex and time-constrained system for the evaluation of proposals in a strategic context. One of the benefits of involving the social partners would be their greater distance from individual projects.

The operation of programmes

The above point is linked to the third aspect of administration and management: the operation of the programmes. A number of participants have expressed concern that the procedures used for the management and administration of the programmes are overly complex and bureaucratic. In part, this is a consequence and a reflection of the complexity of the SPDs themselves – they are multi-topic and frequently cover large geographical areas – but it also reflects the inherent limitations of the management structures adopted. Procedures for guiding and encouraging project submissions and for the scoring of proposals vary between programmes. In general, the Secretariats are responsible for the initial scoring of project submissions but this task can prove to be beyond the technical capabilities of the staff if the procedures specified are over-complex or, with the benefit of hindsight, ill-advised. In the West Midlands, for example, a procedure which specified a single bidding round for 1994 and 1995 was adopted with the result that 850 outline applications were submitted in early 1995. This massive influx of outline applications was reduced in scale following a lengthy period of initial appraisal but, even so, some 250 full applications were received in September 1995, which then had to be scored. Whilst this protracted process of decision making may have stimulated greater competition between projects, the delay which resulted generated a considerable degree of frustration both within the partnership and amongst the proposers of potential projects. In other programmes a more regular, quarterly or bi-annual bidding process is used; in Yorkshire and Humberside project and bid assessment is a rolling process.

Two other features of the implementation of programmes are of particular significance: the difficulty experienced in achieving and maintaining a strategic or programmatic stance in the operation of a SPD and the extent to which flexibility exists within a programme. On the first point there is evidence that some partnerships continue to be 'project driven'. In such cases it can become difficult to instil a sense of strategic purpose and, especially amongst new partners and applicants lacking any previous experience of programmes, to convince participants that a successful application is one which demonstrates how it meets the objectives of the programme and makes a contribution to environmental, economic and social improvement. This difficulty was experienced in the South West, particularly in those parts of the programme area which were receiving European assistance for the first time and in new sectors of activity such as community regeneration. Here the lack of availability of technical assistance from the programme disadvantaged some applicants and forced them into a project-specific approach. In other cases experienced players continue to regard the programmes as simply another source of funds and operate with the objective of maximising income. Even in those partnerships where there is a strong desire to maintain a programmatic approach the drive for Structural Fund support for projects increases competition and makes it difficult to maintain a consensual and co-operative approach. In part, this situation reflects the competition inherent in any partnership-based programme, but it also reflects the difficulties of the financial situation in the UK public sector.

The second feature relates to the extent to which programmes are sufficiently flexible in terms of either their ability to respond to opportunities or to meet specific requests for funding. There have been some complaints that the Commission, despite having failed to produce detailed guidance at the outset, imposed a high level of financial detail on some programmes and also introduced what was seen as an unnecessary and inappropriate level of sectoral specificity. As a consequence, there has been a slow rate of expenditure on certain SPD priorities. In the Highlands and Islands the Tourism priority was separated from that for Business Development; by November 1995, 51 per cent of funds available under the Tourism priority had been committed but only 27 per cent of those under Business Development. This, a number of local participants observe, reflects their original view that many businesses in the Highlands are tourism-centred and that the division of the original single priority has hindered the implementation of the programme. In other cases there have been disputes between some members of the partnership and the Commission about the degree of financial freedom allowed. In part, this results from disagreements between the UK Government and the Commission about the status of the financial tables, with the UK Government favouring the view that the tables are at the indicative end of a spectrum of specificity whilst the Commission favours the opposite view.

Some Preliminary Conclusions

The preceding discussion of some of the main features of the origin, development and operation of seven European programmes for the UK regions has identified a series of issues which require attention in order to help correct any faults in the operation of the current round of programmes and to ensure the production of better programmes in the future. Most of the points discussed have been experienced and observed in all four of the case-study regions and many of the conclusions are consistent with the conclusions of the single-region studies undertaken by other independent researchers and are also reflected in the preceding chapters of this volume. It is important to note that in this field of research a number of studies, some of which have resulted in published papers, are based upon consultancy exercises undertaken for specific clients and have concentrated on particular aspects of the programmes.

A significant feature identified in the research is the importance of encouraging discourse as the basis for establishing policy and developing programmes. The uneven pattern of central-local relations in the UK fits uneasily within a system of regional planning and management that is designed for use throughout Europe. In the UK the absence of strong regional administration (monitored by a supervisory representative body with or without some degree of democratic legitimacy) or some form of regional government places considerable power in the hands of central government and this almost inevitably increases the likelihood of conflict. In a situation where there was a wider range of partners with a more even distribution of power it is likely that the potential for conflict between the UK Government and the Commission would be reduced.

Discourse is also an essential element in creating and encouraging a learning environment both within and outwith a partnership. Learning within a partnership is essential in order to drive home the benefits and importance of a strategic and programmatic approach, especially if the eligibility status of an area is likely to be subject to doubt in future. These messages are also important for the wider regional policy community in the UK as it seeks to re-establish regional planning and management as a more permanent feature.

One of the factors that has hindered the preparation, negotiation and implementation of programmes in the UK has been the lack of any permanent arrangements for regional planning. This resulted in some partnerships having only a weak basis upon which to construct their European strategy. With the formation of the GORs and the revival of regional and strategic thinking and planning, a basis now exists for the monitoring of the development of regions and for the production of generic regional strategies which can be applied in a multitude of situations, including European programmes, land use planning, regional innovation plans, urban funding bids and other purposes. If draft and final SPDs were based upon a generic strategy, then the potential for conflict with other areas of national and regional policy would be minimised and the opportunity for integrated development would be enhanced (Roberts 1996). There are indications that, in some regions, there are now moves to develop a single strategy for a region.

The above point reflects the benefits which arise from the adoption of a strategic programmatic view. Owing to their strategic role and wide experience in relation to many aspects of regional development, the greater involvement of other partners in a region would add considerably to the strategic capabilities of partnerships. In particular, a greater involvement of partners from the voluntary and environmental sectors would help to ensure that programmes are better able to meet the increasingly important sustainable development and social cohesion objectives of the European Union.

The emphasis placed in a SPD on strategy and the programmatic approach is balanced by a precise definition of the priorities of a programme and the details contained in the financial tables. It is often difficult to strike a balance between strategic vision and operational detail without sacrificing the ability to respond to new challenges and opportunities. A move towards the delivery of a greater proportion of funds in the form of global grants may help achieve a better balanced and more robust alternative, but this could only be implemented in a situation where partnerships operated with a more even balance of power and influence and where strategy leads the implementation process.

Better strategy is unlikely to emerge without additional detailed guidance at the outset from the Commission and it is evident that the Commission has responded to this request (Wulf-Mathies 1996). Whilst accepting that the Commission does not wish to encourage the production of formulaic strategies and SPDs, local and regional partners welcome greater certainty and they have expressed the view that this would help to empower them. In addition, learning from the improvements made in the current round of programmes compared to the previous round, there is the generally held view that the provision of a longer period of time for the final polishing of strategies, especially at regional level, would be beneficial. However, there is evidence of a degree of tension between the Commission and local actors (especially the local authorities) in the operational phase of the programmes. This tension stems from the growing level of involvement of Commission officials in matters of detail seen as more appropriate for local determination. This change can be seen to follow from the requirement for better-focused programmes under the current round, but a range of other explanations were also offered by local partners, including the fact that the greater-output focus of current programmes more readily lent itself to detailed monitoring, the impact of changes in personnel within the Commission and the increasing tendency for government offices to defer to Commission officials on matters of detail.

A further observation relates to the definition of the roles performed by the partners and the ways in which the partners are engaged in the process of developing and managing programmes. The general view is that partnerships should aim to be representative of regional interests, should build upon other pre-existing partnership arrangements in a region and should aim to define the role or roles to be performed by partners at an early stage. There is a less well-developed literature (Bailey 1995) and less widely-diffused experience and understanding of the operation of strategic partnerships than there is of the more sharply-focused development partnerships (here the roles are more clearly defined, if only because it is clear what each partner is bringing to the table and what it hopes to take away). Such a clear definition is hard to achieve in the European partnerships and political realities dictate that it is also difficult to ensure that tension or confusion never arises between the interests of the strategy and the partnership, and the interests of the partner. An enhanced Secretariat – and there are good reasons to suggest that this function is better carried out by a body at arm's length from any partner or group of partners, as is the case in Scotland – would assist in the definition and the development of roles that are performed by partners. This, in turn, would help to ensure the smooth operation of programmes through the provision of clarity with respect to the functions to be undertaken and the development of the skills necessary to the discharge of functions.

Finally, it is important to acknowledge the important contribution made by the European programmes to the rediscovery of regional and strategic planning in the UK. Despite their relatively restricted time horizons, the programmes have injected a degree of strategic purpose and vision into the process of local and regional development. The longer-term strategic spatial policy aspirations espoused by the Commission have provided encouragement and support for regional actors and, when considered alongside the other initiatives discussed in the introduction to this chapter, these aspirations have assisted in the rediscovery of regional capability and competence. There is also some – albeit limited – evidence from the research that participation in European programmes has encouraged the development of partnership working between organisations outside the confines of the programme. In this context it is possible to see a longer-lasting and wider benefit flowing from the programmes. For these reasons, whilst it is tempting to focus on the weaknesses evident in the process of designing and implementing complex regional programmes, the strategic empowerment provided by such programmes is likely to be of more enduring value.

Acknowledgement

Support for the research upon which this chapter is based was provided by the Joseph Rowntree Foundation as part of its Central – Local Government Relations Programme.

PART THREE

Regional Development Strategies in the Wider Europe

CHAPTER 13

EU Regional Development Strategies

Comparisons and Contrasts Among Objective 2 Programmes

John Bachtler and Sandra Taylor

Introduction

Previous chapters have examined the detailed characteristics of Objective 1, 2 and 5b programmes across the UK, focusing on the internal and external coherence of regional development strategies. The contributions highlight several important concerns with respect to the appropriateness of EU-funded regional development responses as well as questions regarding the effectiveness of implementation arrangements. In considering the broader relevance of these issues it is important to be aware of how the British approach compares with experiences elsewhere in the Union. In Britain, for example, the intensity and persistence of inner-city problems have given a higher profile to integrated area-based regeneration strategies than in other Member States. The British approach to project selection, through a competitive bidding process, is also different from the practices of Member States, such as Spain, which prefer to control expenditure allocation more closely at the strategy design stage. Further, other EU countries have different institutional structures, notably stronger regional authorities.

In this second part of the book the chapters provide insights into the design and implementation of strategies in other parts of the EU – Germany, Austria, the Netherlands and Finland. As a prelude to these national contributions, this chapter provides an overview of Objective 2 areas across the Union and a comparative assessment of their development strategies. Based on a detailed study of the 82[1] current Objective 2 Single Programming Documents/Operational Programmes (SPDs/OPs)[2], the chapter has three main sections: the first examining the nature of Objective 2 areas as a group, the second discussing the overall content of the reconversion strategies and the third illustrating a selection of strategic approaches.

Three main caveats should be raised prior to the discussion, the first concerning the meaning of 'strategy' in the context of Objective 2. SPDs are required to contain a 'description of an appropriate strategy' to achieve industrial reconversion (Commission of the European Communities 1993b). This encourages the various elements of Objective 2 programmes to be presented coherently, with a description of the problems faced leading to the identification of overall objectives and a range of actions through which they may be achieved. However, these programmes of activity account for only a small part of public and private economic development expenditure. Interpreting them as free-standing strategies – even if they are *genuinely* coherent in content, structure and presentation – is misleading. The strategic direction proposed is instead a construct to draw together a range of components which, in practice, are only small parts of the wider operations of a large number of economic development agencies.

A second issue is that the strategies represent the outcome of an often long and fraught negotiation process in which the priorities of the Commission and Member State authorities also play a significant role – as previous chapters in the book have illustrated. They do not, therefore, necessarily reflect entirely the priorities of given eligible areas or of the whole partnership in these areas. A third, related issue is that the documents only offer a snapshot of intentions agreed among the most significant partners and may not be an accurate reflection of what actually takes place. As Structural Fund evaluation reports clearly demonstrate, during the implementation of programmes there is frequently a reallocation of expenditure between priorities and measures reflecting factors such as changing economic conditions, absorption difficulties and the quality of bids for funding.

---

1 The 82 programming documents cover 88 eligible Objective 2 areas. Finland has eight eligible areas covered by one Single Programming Document. Spain has seven eligible areas but eight programming documents, including a pluriregional ESF programme.

2 Spain submitted Operational Programmes while the other relevant Member States opted for the new, simplified, Single Programming Document format.

The Characteristics of Objective 2 Areas

Objective 2 areas share a common need for regional economic adaptation and conversion in the face of industrial restructuring or decline, but they are, in fact, an extremely diverse group of areas (Bachtler and Taylor 1996a). This diversity is reflected in the designation criteria. The main selection criteria for Objective 2 zones, as defined in 1988, are NUTS III areas with an unemployment rate above the Community average in the last three years, a level of industrial employment as a percentage of total employment above the Community average and an observable fall in industrial employment. However, in the 1993 reforms a set of secondary eligibility criteria were introduced to reflect better the complexity of regional problems. These enabled urban problem areas to be proposed, as well as zones facing the sharp decline of key sectors (including fishing) and those facing serious problems in the rehabilitation of derelict industrial sites.

Incorporating 16.5 per cent of the EU population, the 88 Objective 2 areas are spread across 12 of the EU's 15 Member States, reflecting the widespread nature of industrial reconversion problems. Around 20 areas, such as Limburg and Turnhout, are situated within the 'central and capital cities region' (Commission of the European Communities 1996a), enjoying some of the highest levels of accessibility, centrality and economic performance in the EU. Others are located in the remoter parts of the Union, such as Norra Norrlandskusten, Styria, the Balearic Islands and along Finland's eastern border with Russia. Several Objective 2 areas are part of capital cities (Berlin, London and Madrid), within commuting distance of a national capital (Lower Austria, Lazio, Lolland) or contain large urban/industrial centres (Cataluña, western Scotland, Greater Manchester, West Midlands, Bremen, Blekinge).

France currently has the largest number of eligible areas (19), followed by the UK (13) and Italy (11). At the other end of the spectrum, Luxembourg has just one and Denmark two. An additional ten programmes were added with the accession to the Union of Austria, Finland and Sweden (or 17 if the regional sub-programmes are counted for Finland rather than the single national SPD). Not all the designated areas form coherent regions: the designated parts of some comprise two or more non-contiguous areas. The Bourgogne Objective 2 area, for example, comprises two separate zones 50km apart and located in two different *départements*; the Lower Saxony and Lazio areas each consist of six fragmented sub-zones. Further, most do not correspond with the boundaries of the territorial administrative unit in which they are located. Although a few designated areas (e.g. Zuid Limburg,

Fyrstad, Eastern Gulf of Finland, western Scotland) are wholly or largely congruent with administrative regions, the majority of Objective 2 areas encompass varying proportions of the administrative unit within which they are situated (ranging from 20 to 80% of the regional population).

The eligible zones vary in size – this variation being reflected in the financial allocation of each programme. They range from tiny areas such as Aubange (46km^2), Thanet (104km^2) or Hessen (145km^2) to the extensive designated areas of the East Midlands (15,630km^2), Cataluña (12,582km^2) or Lolland (11,242km^2). Population densities vary substantially. While most eligible areas have 100–500 inhabitants per square kilometre, densities range between less than 100 per km^2 in the Nordic regions and, at the other extreme, over a thousand inhabitants per km^2 in the metropolitan Objective 2 areas. Demographic trends in the Objective 2 areas show a similar degree of variety. According to SPD information, almost half of the designated areas are experiencing population growth, a further sixth have a static population level and around one-quarter have a declining population. Population decline is raised as a problem of particular concern in some of the French and Finnish areas.

More fundamentally, the eligible areas differ in the nature of their industrial past, the character and timing of their decline and in their current prospects for reconversion. If the unemployment rate is used as an indicator of the severity of problems, experience is very different across the Union. According to the SPDs, most Objective 2 areas were experiencing unemployment rates in the range of 10–14 per cent in 1993–1994. Almost one-fifth had lower rates but at least one-quarter of the designated areas had higher unemployment levels, in several cases exceeding 20 per cent (South Karelia, Satakunta, Päijät-Häme, Kokkola, Central Finland, East London/Lee Valley). Other than in Spain, the unemployment rates of Objective 2 areas were generally in the range of 1 to 4 percentage points higher than their national average, although sub-zones of the designated areas were much worse off. In Greater Manchester unemployment rates were up to 30 per cent in some parts of the conurbation, some 20 percentage points higher than the national average.

The variety of circumstances in Objective 2 areas can usefully be conceptualised by placing them on two continua or axes, the first measuring the duration of industrial decline which they have been experiencing and the second the stage which they have reached in economic regeneration.

Turning first to the duration of industrial decline, some Objective 2 areas are fortunate in that, while their decline presents serious problems, it has only occurred recently. A good example is Zuid Limburg which had a positive economic situation and a diversifying industrial structure until the end of the 1980s. Here increasing international competitiveness, a world-wide economic recession and overcapacity resulted in a fall in investment, rising unemployment and a halt in productivity growth in the early 1990s. In some cases of more recent decline, prolonged maintenance of high levels of manufacturing employment was attributable to protection by government subsidy or regulation. This category includes numerous areas in the new Member States as well as in Germany and the Netherlands.

The problems are more entrenched in regions which have experienced decline since the early 1980s in sectors such as pharmaceuticals, chemicals, mechanical engineering and metalworking, or which have fallen victim to the more recent rationalisation of shipbuilding capacity. Typical of these areas is the Dutch area of Arnhem-Nijmegen where a large decrease in manufacturing employment since the start of the 1980s has not been sufficiently counteracted, either by subsequent recovery or growth of the service sector.

At the furthest end of the continuum are the 'core' Objective 2 areas which have experienced successive waves of deindustrialisation dating back to the 1970s or even earlier. In most cases these are areas formerly reliant on traditional, resource-based and often heavy industries such as coal mining, iron and steel production, metalworking, mechanical engineering and shipbuilding. In some cases deindustrialisation has been a feature of these areas for up to two generations, beginning with the rationalisation of coal and steel capacity during the 1920s and 1930s, a further downturn in coal and steel during the 1960s and 1970s and then accelerating over the 1975–1985 period supplemented by the reduction/relocation of shipbuilding capacity. A classic example of these regions is Nordrhein-Westfalen which has been undergoing economic restructuring for over 40 years. Long-term declines in output in traditional sectors have seen mining employment fall from 600,000 in 1957 to 83,000 in 1993, together with a similar fall in the steel sector and, more recently, major job losses in chemicals and mechanical engineering.

The second key issue which helps to illuminate the diversity of areas is the progress they have made towards reconversion or their prospects for achieving this.

The most positive position is enjoyed by the category of Objective 2 areas where the decline of traditional activities has been significantly counter-balanced by the development of new activities in manufacturing or services. In these areas traditional industries have been largely re-structured, downsized or modernised. Among the few areas exhibiting these characteristics is Blekinge in Sweden, where reconversion is perceived to have reached an advanced stage. Despite the loss of the naval shipyard at Karlskrona, the region's agro-business and automobile plants are competitive and new information technology, telecommunications and conference-related activities are developing. Zuidoost Brabant, Twente and Valle d'Aosta also appear to have achieved an advanced stage of reconversion – in the Dutch cases through diversification in alternative manufacturing and service employment and in Valle d'Aosta through strong growth in tourism. Other areas in the category are those where decline has been recent and the elements are already in place which, with appropriate support, should enable regeneration to progress fairly rapidly (e.g. good environment with little industrial dereliction and pollution, high level of social and cultural services, high skill levels, good knowledge infrastructure, a core of firms in growth sectors). Zuid Limburg and Zuidoost Brabant are two examples.

More frequently, an 'intermediate' position has been reached in the process of structural change. Most Objective 2 areas with a longer history of industrial decline have been the focus of active regional development and labour market initiatives for some time at national, regional and local levels (in addition to EU intervention), and this has brought some success in many cases. In Cataluña, for instance, diversification was progressing during the 1980s and the area had above-average growth rates with an increasingly important service sector. The recession has impeded progress substantially but the area has a significant number of SMEs to build on if important competitive weaknesses can be addressed effectively.

There are two main groups of areas in which limited progress towards readjustment has been made. The first are areas in which decline is fairly recent but recovery is likely to be slow as there are only limited elements in place to drive regeneration. Franche Comté is one example. Previously specialising in automobiles and mechanical and electrical engineering, large firms have dominated the employment structure and influenced the SME population, leading to a vulnerable economy. Faced with restructuring, the SME base (especially in mechanical engineering, electronics and plastics) has the potential for reconversion but firms lack the culture, organisation or financial means to diversify markets. In such areas small firms tend to be 'followers' rather than leaders, relying on traditional markets and lacking the resources or ability to innovate, and with relatively low survival rates. The inability of existing SMEs or the service sector to compensate for further rationalisation among large employers means that further job losses are likely.

The second group of areas which are failing to progress in reconversion are those with the longer histories of industrial decline, where progress in economic regeneration has been counteracted by successive waves of restructuring or recession. The Saarland has already experienced severe economic and labour market problems but the employment losses in mining and steel are likely to continue for some time. The growth in new industries has not resolved the unemployment problem, nor has the service sector compensated for manufacturing employment losses. Recovery has been further impeded by Europe-wide recession.

Amidst the diversity of Objective 2 areas there is a range of characteristic challenges which most face in some form. These include:

- eradicating the negative physical and environmental legacy of past industrial activity, thereby enhancing the quality of life an area offers and its attractiveness for investment
- diversifying the economy away from a few formerly dominant, declining sectors
- encouraging entrepreneurship and enabling new and existing firms to compete
- adapting both the employed and unemployed to the changing skill requirements of the labour market
- reducing economic and social disparities, especially where they entail exclusion of part of the population from the mainstream labour force
- adapting transport, communications, environmental and economic infrastructure to the changing demands of the evolving economy
- rebuilding and redefining a region's external image (often tarnished by the negative connotations of industrial decline).

Objective 2 Regional Development Programmes

As previously noted, the content of Objective 2 programmes is determined by a complex process of interaction between a range of factors. These include: the economic situation of the region and the resources available for regeneration, the priorities and influence of the different partners (which are in turn influenced by their understanding of the mechanisms for economic regeneration), the implementation structures in place at the regional level and existing economic development policies in the region and progress made by former activities.

The content and role of Objective 2 strategies

Each Objective 2 strategy consists of a range of proposed activities, each addressing a particular deficiency or seeking to exploit a particular asset of the regional economic context. At the same time, synergy is theoretically sought between the different actions. Strategies are meant to be derived from a thorough analysis of the economy and prospects of the eligible area and are translated into action through development axes or 'priorities', each consisting of a number of individual actions or 'measures', which are either all in the same expenditure field or, more frequently, contribute to the same ends.

Whilst all the strategies outlined in the SPDs are presented in a broadly similar way, their content and role varies depending on the size of the eligible area and the resources available. The largest programme has over 300 times more resources than the smallest. The larger programmes tend to encompass a broader range of activities, and consequently have the potential to play a strategic role in regional development, by co-ordinating the strands of what might otherwise be a fragmented economic development picture and by encouraging awareness of how the different elements complement and support each other in achieving common goals. Many of the smaller strategies, by contrast, pursue a narrower range of activities and may nest within and complement the economic development framework operating in their areas.

Typical of the larger, broad-based programmes of action is Piemonte, receiving 205 million ecu (mecu) in Structural Funds support. Here, SME development is used as the indigenous 'motor' for regeneration, tourism promotion as a means to diversify using existing potential, technology transfer and innovation to bring the local economy competitive advantage, improvements to the living and productive environment to remove traces of former industry and attract investment and human resource development to complement the other economic changes taking place. This combination of action is echoed in other large programmes, such as Greater Manchester and Nord Pas de Calais.

The smaller programmes typically focus their activities more on specific activities. Two-thirds of the programmes allocated less than 15 mecu per year concentrate at least 40 per cent of their Structural Funds expenditure on a single theme (see Table 13.1). Clear national preferences in terms of the investment foci also emerge. For instance, business development predominates in Italy and Sweden and economic infrastructure is prioritised in Belgium and Germany (discussed in more detail below).

Table 13.1 Small, focused Objective 2 programmes

Theme	*Programme*	*Country*
Tourism	• Gibraltar	UK
	• Val d'Aosta	Italy
Economic Infrastructure	• Aubange, Turnhout	Belguim
	• Valle d'Aosta, Lombardy	Italy
	• Bayern, Schleswig Holstein, Hessen, Rheinland Pfalz, Lower Saxony	Germany
Business Development	• Vorarlberg, Styria	Austria
	• Balearics	Spain
	• Angermanlandskusten, Norra Norrlandskusten, Fyrstad, Bergslagen	Sweden
	• Marches, Friuli-Venezia-Giulia, Umbria, Emilia Romagna	Italy
R&TD/innovation	• Upper Austria	Austria
Regeneration	• Aubange	Belguim
	• Valle d'Aosta,	Italy
	• Lower Austria	Austria
	• Schleswig Holstein	Germany
Human resources	• Pluriregional programme	Spain

Source: Bachtler and Taylor 1996a

The argument used for focusing resources in this way is the potential derivation of efficiency benefits, maximising what may be achieved by ensuring that at least one priority of substance can be pursued and minimising programme running costs. A good example is Gibraltar, which has dedicated most of its resources to tourism development, with the other elements – basic infrastructure and training – also reinforcing this aim. Tourism is seen as the most promising prospect for the area since it exploits its assets and is more feasible than manufacturing, given Gibraltar's remote, isolated trading location and limited size.

In Emilia Romagna the accent is on developing weak SMEs. In the context of a wider region which has an extremely dense and dynamic SME population, this seems to offer good prospects of success. The creation of new firms and the development of existing ones are being encouraged – an effort reinforced through support for advanced-level training, innovation and the diversification of production.

Policy options for Objective 2

Measures are the most detailed level at which the strategies can conveniently be broken down, and analysis of these provides an effective overview of the activities and emphasis of Objective 2 programmes. The 1200 measures collectively contained in the SPDs are classified in Figure 13.1 under a number of expenditure headings: training, business development, economic and basic infrastructure, tourism, environment-related activities, RTD and innovation, community economic development and technical assistance (for programme management). The black columns represent the aggregate amounts of Structural Funds dedicated to each main theme. Since 20 per cent of Structural Funds allocations are equally relevant to two of the chosen headings (e.g. training in tourism), these measures have been counted under

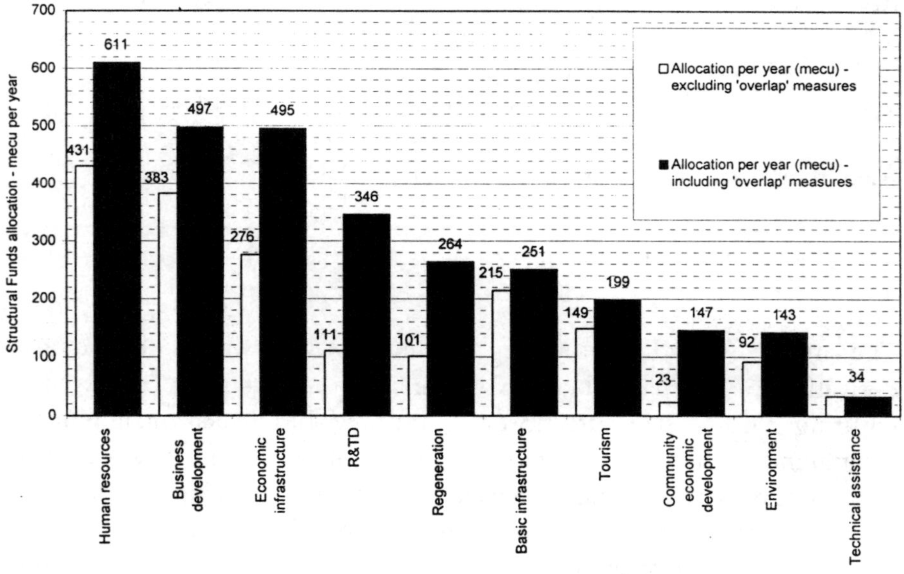

Figure 13.1 Overview of Structural Fund allocations in Objective 2 zones to main 'action areas' (mecu)

both headings to give a full picture of the extent of activity to be undertaken under each (for reference only, the white bars illustrate expenditure excluding these overlapping measures).

The figure shows that the main areas to which resources will be channelled in Objective 2 areas across the EU are training, direct business development and economic infrastructure. Together, these activities account for almost two-thirds of Structural Funds expenditure. Other themes each account for less than 15 per cent of the total (for a fuller description of the activities being supported see Bachtler and Taylor 1996b).

Commission influence on policy content

The balance of expenditure proposed is, in part, a reflection of the priorities of the Commission. The Commission services generally indicate their preferences prior to SPDs being drawn up and can then use the negotiation stage to ensure that full account is taken of them. The patterns of expenditure illustrated in Figure 13.1 reflect the fact that Objective 2 funding is increasingly being steered away from major capital projects such as transport infrastructure (and, to a lesser extent, basic environmental and economic infrastructure) and encouraged to place greater emphasis on revenue-based services or 'soft' projects supporting business development more directly. Initiatives promoting increased innovation and greater exploitation of RTD in the old industrial areas are also highly favoured. The reason for this evolution in priorities lies partly in the belief that Objective 2 areas are already endowed with adequate infrastructure and more impact can be made through direct approaches to economic development and job creation.

The Commission's policy preference for developing human capital as the 'driver for successful restructuring' (Commission of the European Communities 1995d) is also translated into Objective 2 strategies. The development of human resources is an element of every programme and is the largest spending category, receiving over a quarter of the allocations to Objective 2 areas (611 mecu per year). It forms between 15 and 30 per cent of the expenditure of most programmes and reaches 41 per cent in Schleswig Holstein. In addition, at a superficial level at least, ESF-funded action is being co-ordinated with ERDF-funded action in a way which should produce synergy in the pursuit of common goals. In the Plymouth programme, for instance, training is listed in the SPD as an element of all four priorities – complementing the development of industry, knowledge-based sectors and tourism – and the reduction of internal spatial disparities.

European funding is also being used in Objective 2 areas to strengthen their economic development framework. The impetus for this lies, in part, in increasing Commission concern for value for money in economic development activities and the considerable information demands it makes at all stages of programming. Principal activities involve enhancing the mechanisms for policy design and delivery.

In terms of policy design, initiatives are being proposed which deepen understanding of the local economy and contribute to building up relevant long-term databanks and analytical tools. This is driven by the requirement to demonstrate the demand for, and relevance of, proposed measures and to design policies which target an area's prime economic constraints and so have maximum economic impact. One of the most frequent examples is labour market surveys. These potentially improve the cost-effectiveness of regional training provision by enabling improved targeting of courses to specific skills deficits. Labour market surveys also form ten per cent of the ESF allocation in Liége, 21 per cent in Bretagne and 17 per cent in Aquitaine. The dissemination of any effective systems of ongoing monitoring and analysis which are developed is to be encouraged, as is co-ordination of effort within regions to avoid duplication of research effort (e.g. between Objective 2 and 3 programmes). A further area for which monitoring systems are being developed relates to the supply and demand of business property, as in Hessen in Germany.

Policy delivery frameworks are also being improved with EU support, a field of particular relevance to Objective 2 regions which lack established expertise in areas such as business development. Specialised delivery mechanisms able to liaise with the local business population are not universally present, especially where direct support to SMEs is an emerging element of the local economic development mosaic. In such cases measures occasionally propose the establishment or enhancement of development organisations – as in the case of the Balearic strategy, which proposes infrastructure and equipment for a regional development agency. In Emilia Romagna a business information centre is being set up to support a strategy focused on SME development, while in the Veneto economic development personnel will be trained. EU funding is also being used to enhance agencies to expand area promotion activities aimed at attracting inward investment (e.g. the Veneto, Italy).

Among the aspects of the policy delivery system, mechanisms are being set up to help in the delivery of training. Enterprise-related training support is being provided to help firms define their training needs, for example through training plans in Madrid or training databanks identifying relevant training providers in Vorarlberg (Austria). Measures focused on the unemployed also include a range of support mechanisms: a complementary element is often the provision of vocational counselling and reorientation programmes to enable those affected by industrial decline to make informed training and career development choices (e.g. in Vorarlberg or the Balearics).

In defining its priorities for Objective 2, the Commission does not operate in a vacuum but is influenced by input from the Member States and regions: the stress on monitoring and evaluation of expenditure is partly the result of Member State lobbying, as was the broadening of the eligibility criteria for Objective 2 areas. Commission priorities, however, do not always coincide with those of Member State authorities, as is evident from a comparison of the draft SPDs and final approved strategies. Some Member States and regions clearly would have preferred greater emphasis on basic infrastructure, for example, although the Commission maintains that its priorities are not applied indiscriminately. Basic infrastructure measures have been supported where it could be shown that they would 'directly create jobs, or provide direct access to areas with economic development potential' (Commission of the European Communities 1995d, p.26). Thus, in Finland, basic infrastructure is being supported to contribute to a 'gateway strategy' enhancing transport and trading links with Russia.

National level trends

Despite strong Commission influence, the SPDs display diverse approaches to industrial reconversion. National development cultures emerge clearly from a comparison of the balance of funding between different activities (see Table 13.2 and Table 13.3), indicating also the degree of influence of national over regional authorities in setting a framework for the content of Objective 2 strategies. Tables 13.2 and 13.3 provide a breakdown of SPD spending by activity (and by Member State) as a proportion of total programme expenditure and total Structural Fund expenditure respectively.

Human resources and business development are the most common themes, incorporated in virtually all of programmes. Business development is especially prominent in the new Member States, accounting for 57 per cent of the resources of the Swedish programmes, 42 per cent of the Finnish ones and 40 per cent of those in Austria. It is also prominent in Denmark (51%) and in Italy (40%). This contrasts with Spain where it accounts for only 13 per cent, Germany (12%) and Luxembourg (4%).

Table 13.2 Percentage of eligible Objective 2 SPDs supporting specific activities

Country	*Human resources*	*Business development*	*Economic infrastructure*	*Research and development*	*Physical regeneration*	*Basic infrastructure*	*Tourism and cultural industries*	*Community economic development*	*Environment-related measures*
Austria	100	100	100	100	50	0	50	25	25
Belgium	100	75	100	100	100	25	75	0	75
Denmark	100	100	100	100	0	0	100	0	50
Finland	100	100	100	100	100	100	100	0	100
France	100	100	95	84	100	53	95	37	95
Germany	100	67	100	100	56	11	56	11	89
Italy	100	100	73	82	73	45	82	0	73
Luxembourg	100	100	100	100	100	0	100	0	100
Netherlands	100	100	100	100	40	80	100	0	40
Spain	100	88	88	88	88	75	50	13	75
Sweden	100	100	80	100	60	40	100	40	40
UK	100	100	92	85	92	100	92	85	77
Total	**100**	**94**	**91**	**90**	**78**	**52**	**82**	**28**	**74**

Source: Bachtler and Taylor 1996a

Table 13.3 Percentage of Structural Funds resources dedicated to each action area*

Country	*Human resources*	*Business development*	*Economic infrastructure*	*Research and development*	*Physical regeneration*	*Basic infrastructure*	*Tourism and cultural industries*	*Community economic development*	*Environment-related measures*
Austria	29.2	39.6	17.0	16.5	15.4	0.0	7.9	1.0	0.0
Belgium	17.9	21.7	36.4	16	11.8	3.1	6.3	0.0	5.8
Denmark	20.5	51.4	14.3	yes†	0.0	0.0	14.7	0.0	2.9
Finland	27.5	41.5	yes†	4.9	10.0	10.0	6.9	0.0	0.4
France	22.7	21.2	18.4	15.2	18.5	5.8	8.5	1.8	5.9
Germany	36.0	11.8	31.7	12.8	13.8	2.7	2.8	1.2	11.9
Italy	20.2	40.1	21.7	13.1	9.1	3.1	11.1	0.0	8.9
Luxembourg	13.2	3.6	35.9	12.0	37.7	0.0	1.9	0.0	31.5
Netherlands	31.3	22.4	20.8	18.4	4.8	11.4	11.2	0.0	1.7
Spain	23.6	12.6	17.8	14.9	6.7	29.9	yes†	yes†	9.7
Sweden	24.4	56.5	5.6	15.8	3.9	yes†	7.1	6.6	0.4
UK	26.1	16.9	20.1	14.2	7.7	10.4	13.1	18.3	2.0
Total	**25.3**	**20.6**	**20.5**	**14.3**	**10.9**	**10.4**	**8.3**	**6.1**	**5.9**

* Measures are counted under all categories relevant to them, hence totals of percentage allocations sum to 122 per cent.
† Indicates where action will be undertaken in a field, but financial information could not be disaggregated.

Source: Bachtler and Taylor 1996a

Economic infrastructure measures are prominent in the strategies of Germany (32% overall), Belgium (36%) and that of Luxembourg (36%). There is less emphasis in Italy and Sweden (where direct business development is to the fore) and in Spain (where physical infrastructure is more significant). There are marked patterns, too, in general regeneration measures, which are principally found in France, Finland, the UK and Spain, and community economic development measures, which are a feature of the UK programmes. Basic infrastructure measures show further distinct national patterns, with the greatest allocations in Spain (30%), followed by the Netherlands, Finland and UK (each at c.10%). In most other countries the allocations to basic infrastructure are very limited, with nothing in Denmark or Luxembourg and just three per cent in Italy and Germany.

Some of these expenditure patterns find their roots in the different policy contexts and approaches to economic development of Member States. The 'community economic development' policies present in almost all UK Objective 2 programmes reflect serious urban problems and a history of area-based regeneration strategies (see Chapter 5). The high percentage of resources allocated to transport and environmental infrastructure in Spain is explained by inadequate basic infrastructure provision in the Spanish Objective 2 areas. Since Objective 2 programmes form only part of the economic development policy framework for any area, however, it cannot be assumed that their patterns of expenditure always match those of the wider policy environment. The emphasis of the smaller German programmes on economic infrastructure has emerged as a complement to a federal and regional framework which already prioritises direct business development support. In particular, this also reflects the Commission's concern to avoid substituting EU funds for projects that would otherwise have been financed from domestic sources.

The influence of the region and its actors

In terms of policy content, there is, superficially, considerable similarity between strategies. Most SPDs include elements of training, business development and economic infrastructure development and use them to pursue economic regeneration through a limited number of aims – principally diversification, increasing competitiveness and improving the investment environment. Broad economic development themes such as business development are, in a sense, universally applicable: they encompass an extensive set of policy options which may be tailored to a wide range of specific circumstances. The true relevance of strategies, and the differences between them, do not emerge from broad-brush analysis but require closer inspection of what exactly is proposed, how it was agreed and how it relates to the specific context.

Some interesting area-specific cases can be identified which demonstrate how the particular assets and opportunities of individual areas form the inspiration for elements of their strategies. The potential presented by West Berlin's restored status as a capital city has led to policies assisting the development of high-level services, while its role as a potential 'driver' for the regeneration of the surrounding hinterland of eastern Germany has engendered policies promoting improvements in RTD capability. Arnhem-Nijmegen in the Netherlands and, to a lesser extent, Limburg in Belgium are pursuing the development of the logistics sector, interpreting their location at the heart of the Single European Market as their principal regeneration asset. In Groningen-Drenthe in the Netherlands a cluster strategy is being built around an existing group of environment, energy, recycling and waste-related companies which offer a useful building block in economic regeneration.

Where a strong regional economic development framework is already in place it tends to exert a pronounced influence on the strategic aims and programme details set out in the SPD. The programme for West Cumbria and Furness (UK) clearly reflects the goals and initiatives being pursued under the North-West Regional Economic Strategy; Lower Saxony's tourism policies build upon the region's 1992–1996 Strategy for Tourism and North-East England is prioritising technology support in the context of a new Regional Innovation and Technology Strategy (RITS). The existence of such a framework provides stronger continuity of action and strategic direction than is potentially available in the three-year Objective 2 programming periods. It also simplifies the SPD preparation stage since established partnerships and widely-agreed strategic goals are already in place, and it may strengthen the robustness of the strategy proposed and the reasoning behind it since it is drawing on a wider and longer term strategic development and policy design effort. Proposed SPD actions would complement, supplement or reinforce existing policies.

Approaches to Industrial Reconversion in Objective 2 Strategies

The measures proposed by most Objective 2 areas are designed to pursue a limited number of economic objectives. The four main strategic goals, presented in various forms, are: diversification (by indigenous and exogenous means), enhancing the competitiveness of the company base, improving the competitiveness of the area as a location for economic activity and reducing economic disparities within Objective 2 zones.

Diversification

Many old industrial areas are characterised by a long-running reliance on a narrow range of mature and declining sectors vulnerable to structural change. In some cases this has led to sudden and catastrophic economic collapse when the main firms and sectors have failed. Diversification through indigenous and, to a lesser extent, exogenous potential is, therefore, a frequent element of Objective 2 strategies, aiming to steer the local economy towards growth sectors and broaden the economic base more generally.

Diversification by developing indigenous potential is the primary approach, either through new firm formation or by encouraging the further growth or reorientation of existing, locally-based firms. There is some form of explicit sectoral focus in most strategies pursuing diversification, the main activities to be targeted being: tourism (featured in four-fifths of strategies), cultural industries (e.g. East London and West Berlin), logistics (the Netherlands), environment-related activities (e.g. 'eco' products and services in Picardie and Saarland) and producer services (Bremen, North Jutland).

Tourism is considered to offer direct short-term benefits of job creation and revenue generation and is a relatively straightforward option in that it requires low levels of technology and the workforce can be (re)trained relatively rapidly. Thus the sector is being promoted in the Plymouth SPD as part of the first phase of diversification away from the naval dockyard. Tourism also offers indirect and longer term benefits in promoting a change in the physical appearance and image of areas. Few SPDs explicitly recognise the potential contradiction between the quality of jobs provided by tourism (low salaries and low stability) and the sustainable economic regeneration of problem areas.

In some cases SPD-funded diversification is to be achieved through reorienting existing firms in mature and declining sectors, moving them from mass production to flexible and specialised production for niche markets. Examples include support for textiles firms to develop new and more specialised product ranges (as in Lombardy, Italy) or the reorientation of defence firms to civilian markets (Hessen, Germany). Defence-related firms whose military markets have recently experienced steep decline are often seen as having particular potential for reorientation: many are technological leaders, have research and design capabilities, maintain high and consistent quality standards and have systems equipped to respond rapidly and effectively to market opportunities.

The focus of some diversification initiatives is on the processes involved rather than the target sectors. The French and Italian strategies frequently encourage new firm formation through measures including advice to potential entrepreneurs, access to start-up finance and property tailored to the needs of micro-firms. Such initiatives may be inadequate alone as they are most likely to create micro-firms in low growth, low value-added, locally-oriented sectors with high displacement effects.

An alternative and more sophisticated approach is to encourage diversification through technology transfer and innovation initiatives targeted at existing or potential new firms. Such measures frequently build on the research infrastructure present in Objective 2 areas, typically encouraging the development of new or improved products and services or means of service delivery.

Diversification through inward investment offers more rapid job creation potential than is usually achieved through the development of indigenous firms, especially where entrepreneurship has been inhibited by the prolonged dominance of a few large companies in a narrow range of sectors. Relevant policy options include the development of prestige or specialised economic infrastructure, targeted human resource development, image building through regeneration and promotion of the region as an investment location. Targeted training is proposed in Piemonte, Hessen, the East and West Midlands and Yorkshire and Humberside. In Greater Manchester this training (which is also to enable the growth of key local firms) is combined with area promotion initiatives and the provision of appropriate sites, services and communications networks.

The rapid potential of inward investment helps to explain the strategic choices made in Schleswig Holstein, Germany. Here indigenous potential was seen as too slow a route to economic regeneration, especially given that economic decline had been recent but steep. Instead, resources have been focused on exploiting assets able to attract external investment – including waterfront sites in Kiel, which are being developed to accommodate high-level service activities.

Some programmes, particularly the larger ones, have dual diversification strategies addressing both exogenous and indigenous potential. An exclusive reliance on one or the other presents well-known disadvantages. Inward investment strategies may not be successful and, even if they achieve results, the incoming economic activities may only embed themselves superficially in the locality, so bringing minimal multiplier benefits to local suppliers and prolonging economic vulnerability. At the same time, the development of indigenous potential may be slow – especially where the stock of small and medium firms is restricted in number and dynamism and entrepreneurship rates are low. In north-east England the first priority targets inward investment and the development of firms of strategic importance, while the second addresses SME development. This balances the need to create jobs and diversify with a concern to create a self-reliant economy which is less vulnerable to shifts in the location of externally-owned firms.

The competitiveness of the regional economy

A second key focus of Objective 2 strategies is enhancing the competitiveness of the local economy. There are two foci: the companies themselves and the business environment in which they operate.

The existing business population of (usually small- and medium-sized) firms offers a basis upon which to build an economic renewal strategy if they can be turned from 'followers' into 'leaders'. Many rely on traditional markets and lack the resources or ability to innovate, reorganise their activities, diversify or market more vigorously and imaginatively. They lag in their awareness of and compliance with environmental legislation and many fail to benefit from advances in technology.

The circumstances of the indigenous business population vary among Objective 2 areas. In some cases the size, independence and degree of vigour of SMEs has been adversely affected by the former dominance of monostructures now in decline. The example of Franche-Comté is typical. As its main plants undergo restructuring, the SME base is needed to drive the regeneration process, but these firms need to develop the culture, organisation, technological capacity and financial means to diversify and increase their market access and value. In other areas the, albeit large, population of SMEs may be too focused on declining sectors such as textiles, furniture, leather and metalworking. In La Rioja these sectors account for one-third of industrial employment. Since firms are small, and often family owned and managed, they struggle to acquire new skills, invest in new technology, develop new products, gain access to wider markets and train personnel. Whatever the reasons for the weakness in the SME base, the inability of indigenous firms to compete impedes their potential for enabling major employment growth or export-led recovery.

A variety of measures have been proposed to enable businesses to raise their competitiveness from within. The most frequent services offered are: training for employees, business advice and information services, finance and investment support, and access to expertise in fields such as technology or the environment. At best, these are tailored and combined to enable firms to pursue objectives including diversification, modernisation and internationalisation. Measures enhancing firms' access to finance or investment funds appear most frequently and prominently in Italy. Investment measures support the modernisation of productive or administrative systems and may raise a firm's technological level or reduce costs through minimising waste or improving efficiency. Some projects also assist firms in achieving environmental accreditation, opening up the possibility of new markets.

Where SMEs are under-competitive, the issue is often as much one of business culture as resource availability. Advice and consultancy support have a critical role in enabling new outlooks and approaches, sensitising firms to issues, then helping them to address them. SPD measures propose support in areas like international marketing, modern management techniques (such as total quality management), organisational approaches and joint ventures. More specialised information and support services are also being made available for environmental and technological questions. In Saarland environmental measures include energy efficiency advice for firms and the promotion of 'green' commercial opportunities. Other programmes raise awareness of environmental legislation and help firms to comply with it. Information is also critical in encouraging firms to consider innovating and increasing their technology levels, responding to the questions of who to approach, what a project might involve in financial and resource terms and what the benefits might be.

Projects aiming to enhance company competitiveness are reliant, to an increasing extent, on the capacities of the workforce and require human resource development as an essential complementary element. In Emilia Romagna the reorientation of SMEs in sectors such as textiles and mechanical engineering is being supported by management training programmes helping firms to regenerate from within.

The extent, type and quality of infrastructure available in a locality impacts on firms' efficiency, and so their competitiveness. In broad terms, a suitable mix of business premises is required whose type, number, size, cost and degree of accessibility answer the needs of the local company base and which are complemented by an appropriate communications network. Current infrastructure provision is poor in many of the Spanish eligible areas compared with Objective 2 zones elsewhere in Western Europe. They have been characterised by a history of under-investment in many types of public good and also by patterns of unplanned urban development which impede the functioning of existing infrastructure. In Aragon, for example, only 15 per cent of firms are on industrial estates and have access to the services they require, three-quarters are housed in buildings which also have a residential use and many have problems meeting EU standards. Some Spanish programmes, therefore, aim to raise the competitiveness of existing locally-based firms by moving them to better accommodation.

Improving the functioning of existing infrastructure may be an appropriate solution. Some SMEs in East London were found to be constrained by prohibitively high overheads associated with their premises. Measures have been proposed to enhance security and so reduce high insurance charges and costly losses through burglaries. In turn, a service is being offered which enables firms to organise their activities more efficiently within their existing premises or to reduce the size of premises they require. Further examples are available in transport infrastructure where the focus is sometimes on improving the linkages between existing networks. In Tuscany multimodal transport nodes are planned in Prato and Guasticcel, while in Friuli-Venezia-Giulia 2.67 mecu is dedicated to modernising a regional transport interchange to support the development of a modern internationally-oriented economy.

The competitiveness of areas in attracting and retaining investment

The ability of an area to attract and retain investment and qualified personnel is a further aspect of regional competitiveness. Principal activities include regeneration of the physical and cultural environment to enhance the quality of life and renewing their image as locations for modern services and industry.

The decaying and neglected urban and industrial fabric characterising many former heavily-industrialised areas is seen as one of the key barriers to economic revival. As a result, urban regeneration appears in four out of five strategies. Some is associated with the creation or improvement of economic infrastructure (as in Luxembourg and Poitou Charentes) or with enabling tourism development (e.g. Valle d'Aosta, Marches and West Cumbria). These SPDs link regeneration directly with an ultimate objective of job creation.

This link is less direct in many other regeneration measures, especially in France where more general urban renewal or *requalification du territoire* is taking place to improve the image of certain areas and the quality of life offered to inhabitants. The ultimate aim is usually to halt depopulation through out-migration and so retain qualified personnel or to support efforts to attract and retain investment. There may be a time lag between such regeneration activities and the economic rewards they reap (other than in temporary job creation terms). Furthermore, the impact on the economy, being indirect, may be difficult to quantify.

Areas improving their living environment can usefully accompany such efforts with appropriate image-building publicity to ensure that their reputation is progressively reoriented from a region of decline to one of dynamism, opportunities and a high quality of life. Tourism initiatives, such as those in Franche Comté and Lorraine in France, frequently have such a dual purpose.

Reducing disparity within Objective 2 areas

The SPDs illustrate a growing concern with the reduction of disparities within Objective 2 zones. Relevant measures are targeted at better integrating specific groups of individuals into the labour market whose employment prospects are worse than the rest of the population. The most frequently highlighted groups are the long-term unemployed, ethnic minorities, young people, women and those nearing retirement. Measures include: skills development for women in problem areas (Lower Austria); support for women (including from ethnic minorities) to enter the mainstream labour market, through child care provision and training and the integration of homeworkers into the formal economy (East London and the Lee Valley, UK); entrepreneurship support for young people and women (Norra Norrlandskusten, Sweden); and work experience to increase the employment prospects of the jobless (Pais Vasco, Spain; Fyrstad, Sweden).

This approach is developed more fully in the UK, where specific geographic sub-zones of greatest disadvantage are targeted with additional resources (see Chapter 5). Among those UK programmes including what has become known as 'community economic development', this tranche of activities accounts for between 9 and 26 per cent of Structural Funds allocations. Taking the form of a programme within a programme, 'mini-strategies' – comprising a collection of mutually-supporting measures – are put in place for specific zones facing especially serious difficulties and are embedded within the wider programme which addresses the whole of the eligible area. In the West Midlands one-quarter of the programme is dedicated to measures supporting 'Urban and Community Regeneration', including public transport to enhance access to job opportunities outside the zones, vocational training, training infrastructure and improvement of the environment. In Greater Manchester, where community economic development receives 17 per cent of the allocation, the strategy also includes the development of community businesses.

Discussion

This chapter has demonstrated how the Structural Fund regulations are being translated into practice within Objective 2 regions. It has analysed in detail the form and content of Objective 2 SPDs and has attempted to explain some of the differences between regional development strategies. The analysis clearly shows the diverse range of factors influencing programmes – factors which go well beyond the nature of the regional problems. Strategies are influenced by national economic development cultures, the scale of Structural Fund expenditure, the attitude of Commission services, the economic development history of the area, the relationship between the major economic/political partners and the interrelationships between Structural Fund expenditure and other national, regional and local policies.

As an information source, the SPDs provide considerable insight into the above issues. They are sometimes less helpful in assessing the appropriateness of proposed measures to the problems faced, especially in answering the following questions:

- Are the proposals coherent with the region's wider economic development framework and based on sound economic development principles?
- Are they closely tailored to the specific problems, threats, strengths and opportunities of their region and do they address them appropriately?
- Do they have the commitment of the region's economic development agencies and other related bodies and have they emerged from a partnership approach?
- Is there genuine demand for the measures proposed and are appropriate agencies in place, with the requisite expertise and resources, to ensure their implementation?
- Does the strategy promise impacts commensurate with the resources deployed?

The primary criticism of SPDs is that the information required for an effective appraisal of the strategies along these lines is frequently missing or presented in an inconsistent fashion. Without an adequate presentation of the context in which they are embedded, their appropriateness cannot be properly assessed – except by individual and detailed area-specific analysis. There is a requirement for SPDs to place their 'structural' strategies, priorities and measures in their wider context and to demonstrate in what way they are additional or complementary to the existing policy framework.

This comparison of Objective 2 SPDs has enabled several other specific conclusions for improving the structure and content of SPDs to be identified. A detailed, focused and up-to-date analysis of the local economy is a prerequisite to understanding the rationale behind any strategy. This information needs to be exploited to its best advantage in elaborating the strategy. It is also necessary for strategies to take account of the wider geographical context, especially where the eligible area is not a self-contained economic unit.

Descriptions of the relationships between problems and strategic priorities, and between the proposed strategies and other national, regional and local policies, could be improved. There is considerable difficulty, in many cases, in relating the strategy to the profile of the Objective 2 area and, more particularly, to the assets which could be further exploited and the constraints to industrial reconversion which need to be addressed. The approach of Languedoc Roussillon is exemplary. Here the proposed measures are presented in a clear matrix which illustrates their relevance to the area's strengths and weaknesses and the opportunities and threats it faces. Such approaches to demonstrating the coherence of strategies would benefit Objective 2 areas not just at the stage of final strategy presentation but also in the developmental phase, enabling a more coherent choice of measures and priorities to be made and permitting comparison of alternative approaches.

There could also be more evidence of lessons learned from former rounds of Objective 2 support and the fuller incorporation of these into new programmes. The apparent reluctance to highlight problematic aspects of programmes or their administration is understandable, but also unfortunate, since identification of the reasons would afford insights from which programmes might benefit in subsequent rounds.

These conclusions relate primarily to the presentation of SPDs and their ability to demonstrate that they are proposing coherent strategies that are appropriate to their areas. However, such recommendations assume that the Member State authorities responsible for preparing programmes are committed to the SPD process beyond its function as a mechanism for drawing down EU funding. Improvements to the information content of SPDs cannot fully answer the questions of whether strategies really do guide the implementation of programmes, whether there is true additionality, whether 'partnership' really exists and whether there is coherence, in practice, between individual measures and projects. Such questions can only be addressed by analysing the implementation of SPDs.

The 1997–1999 Round of Objective 2 Programming

The implementation of the 1994–1996 Objective 2 programmes has now drawn to a close and the 1997–1999 round is underway. Changes to Objective 2 geographic coverage have already been decided and strategies reformulated.

The review of eligible Objective 2 areas, completed in May 1996 in preparation for the 1997–1999 programming round, only led to very limited changes in an effort to ensure continuity in the process of regeneration and to avoid delays in approving programmes. Some minor modifications were approved for Spain, Italy and the Netherlands, involving reductions in the eligible population of certain zones, in order to extend others within the same Member State.

Detailed guidelines were released by DG XVI to support the next round of programme development (Commission of the European Communities 1996b), emphasising the Commission's current priorities for Objective 2 and suggesting some possible approaches which areas could explore. In spite of these guidelines, it is unlikely that there will be substantial changes in the strategies implemented. First, the guidelines reinforce trends apparent during the previous programming period, including the emphasis on revenue rather than capital-based projects and the promotion of a higher profile for research, technological development and innovation. Second, areas will be endeavouring to maintain continuity of action. This is an efficient approach in the tight time scale, acknowledging (if partially) the need to develop stable frameworks for economic development and maximising the benefits of efforts made in the current round to establish effective formats and procedures.

However, the process has enabled areas to modify their programme content in the light of experience locally and elsewhere by redefining measures, adding new ones or altering the balance of expenditure allocations on the basis of demand. The review has also provided an opportunity for Objective 2 areas to improve the presentation and coherence of strategy documents. This would include adding to the description of economic problems and assets, giving further consideration to the wider geographic context, setting out the impact of former programmes more effectively, improving output and impact indicators and, perhaps most importantly, placing strategies more clearly in the context of the wider economic development policy framework.

Acknowledgements

This chapter is based on research funded by DGXVI of the European Commission and undertaken by the European Policies Research Centre (in part together with ACT, Paris) during 1995–1996. Apart from the authors, the EPRC research team included Conor Kearney and Geraldine McBride, Rona Michie, Patricia Noble, Anne Mette Hjalager, Maria Vigers and Mary Louise Rooney – all of whose contributions are gratefully acknowledged. Any errors of fact or interpretation are the responsibility of the authors alone.

CHAPTER 14

The Effects of European Regional Policy on the Federal Republic of Germany

Heinz Schrumpf

Introduction

Regional policy has a long tradition in Germany. Until the early 1970s, apart from a few emergency measures, regional policy was essentially a function of the federal states (*Länder*). As in other countries, German governmental administration is traditionally organised by policy divisions, with individual ministries assigned to the areas of transport, telecommunications, agriculture, urban planning, research and development and the environment; there is only loose co-ordination of these policy areas by regional planning policy, which has a so-called 'policy cross-section' function. Regional planning policy has been kept consciously weak in relation to the specialist ministries and to the governments of the federal states in order to allow the 'policy cross-section' principle to be applied on the one hand while abiding by the principle of federalism and subsidiarity on the other. As a result of this strict division between fields of activity, regional policy has had to restrict itself to the field of regional investment aid.

As in some other EU countries, German regional policy is based on regional incentive support – in which a uniform regional aid scheme is applied in designated areas across the nation as a whole. Regional labour markets are demarcated as designated assisted areas with the aid of accessibility analyses and travel-to-work patterns (Eckey, Horn and Klemmer 1990). Designation operates through a uniform system of indicators (covering regional income, unemployment, infrastructure endowment, etc) and the indicators are then grouped together to form an overall synthetic designation indicator permitting a ranking of all German regions by level of disparity and thus the need for regional aid. The federal and state governments jointly determine the limit up to which regions are to be assisted and aid is targeted exclusively at job-creating investments in businesses with inter-regional sales (export base theory) as well as local authority investments, which are regarded as complementary to these private investments.

It is important to note that for over two decades regional policy in Germany has been a *Gemeinschaftsaufgabe* – a Joint Task for the 'improvement of the regional economic structure' undertaken by both the federal and the state governments. Both levels of government work together in a Planning Committee, collectively establishing the framework regulations and assisted areas and award criteria under which regional aid can be provided to companies and local authorities (see also Chapter 21).

The German approach to regional policy has been affected in various ways by the EU competition and structural policies operated through the European Commission. On the one hand, the Commission has successfully exerted pressure on the German administration to reduce the assisted areas in western Germany. On the other hand, there are now two competing concepts of regional policy in Germany, each following a very different philosophy.

This chapter examines the effects of EU structural policies on regional policy in Germany. The influences of the EU, through its regional and competition policies, on regional development in Germany can be considered at three levels: it has considerably restricted the extent of national regional aid, has forced the German administration to bring its regional policy concept more into line with the EU concept and, with the promotion of the eastern German regions (Objective 1), former industrialised areas (Objective 2) and rural regions (Objective 5b), EU policy itself has had effects on regional development in Germany. Each of these issues is considered in turn, concluding with some critical observations on the relationship between German and EU approaches to regional development.

EU Regional Policy and German Regional Policy

By means of the aid controls under Article 3 of the EU Treaty, the Commission has persuaded the German administration to reduce the size of the national assisted areas. In 1980 more than 40 per cent of the West German population was living in designated areas, but the figure today is only 22 per cent. In comparison, the Commission's assisted areas for EU structural policy include over 30 per cent of the German population.

It is the Commission's intention to prevent the success of aid measures in relatively weak member countries being endangered by the promotion of regions in the richer Member States. Nevertheless, the Commission approves national aid areas when either per capita income is below 75 per cent of the national average or the unemployment rate exceeds the national average by 50 per cent. In doing so, the Commission recognises that the population of a region still compares its standard of living with national and not EU averages. There may, therefore, be a need for regional policy action in the relatively rich Member States, even if the assisted regions appear strong in an EU context.

The Commission has not been successful in cutting down its own aid under Objective 2 and Objective 5b. In the case of Objective 2 promotion in particular, there is a suspicion that the main aim is to have funds flow back into certain Member States rather than to combat serious problems. This is reinforced by references to the Structural Funds being 'side payments' to compensate for the effects of other EU policies.

As areas with declining industrial development play a significant role in individual federal states (e.g. North-Rhine Westphalia and Bremen), EU regional policy is now more important to these federal states than national policy, which is predominantly targeted at rural areas. One of the consequences of this has been that North-Rhine Westphalia has systematically brought its own concept of regional economic policy into line with the Commission's concept in recent years.

For Germany as a whole, it has to be noted that the existence of two different concepts of regional policy is leading to a split between the federal states. States with predominantly rural problem regions are interested first and foremost in the national concept of regional policy. States whose problem regions predominantly consist of conurbations with declining industrial development tend towards the concept of the Commission. From the point of view of the Federal Government, there is, therefore, a risk of the consensus approach to regional policy under the Joint Task (*Gemeinschaftsaufgabe*) breaking down in the long term. As will be shown, this risk is increased by the Objective 1 promotion in the new federal states of eastern Germany.

As a result of the reunification of Germany, regional policy has experienced an enormous increase in status with regard to the funds being made available for regional development and its strategic importance to the restructuring process in the new eastern German states. Following the surprisingly rapid course of reunification, for which not even the West German politicians were prepared, it was initially resolved that the West German system of regional aid promotion should be applied to East Germany with no changes apart from considerably higher amounts of aid. At the same time, the new German states were all recognised by the Commission as designated areas under Objective 1. The process of co-ordination between national and European policy thus required was, in the view of the Federal Government, to be resolved as follows:

- Promotion of productive investment in the new federal states was to take place through the Joint Task 'Improvement of the Regional Economic Structure'. This was to be co-financed by European Regional Development Fund (RDF).
- Investments in human capital in Germany, in so far as these were not made by the companies themselves, were considered a function of the Federal Employment Office. Such investments were to be co-financed by the European Social Fund (ESF).
- Aid measures for rural settlement renewal and agriculture in Germany were to be a function of a second Federal-State Joint Task 'Improvement of Agricultural Structure and Coastal Protection'. Co-financing was to take place through the European Agricultural Guarnatee and Guidance Fund (AGFF)-Guidance Section.

This concept met with resistance within the German administration. Several ministries (e.g. transport, environment, research and technology) had recognised that this arrangement would exclude them from any possible co-financing of their measures by the EU. The same applied to the German federal states, whose supplementary programmes on regional policy – particularly aid measures for small and medium-sized businesses and for research and technology – had also been excluded from co-financing by the EU.

The concept was also questioned by the Commission, which was concerned that the importance of European aid for reconstruction in Eastern Germany was not sufficiently clear. In addition, no account was taken of certain requirements of the Commission: measures for small and medium-sized businesses, environmental protection, special promotion of jobs for women and acceleration of technical progress were not (or only just) included in the original concept for German regional policy. In the subsequent negotiations between the Commission and the Federal Government a compromise was reached: up to and including 1996 the procedure was to follow the Federal Government's proposal and re-negotiations would take place for the period 1997–1999.

This agreement forced a major reform of German regional policy in 1995, effectively bringing the German approach much more in line with the Commission's ideas. It involved a radical restructuring of the formerly complex matrix of award rates, graduated according to the intensity of regional problems, and it overhauled the types of support to be financed through regional policy. For instance, German regional policy now provides special aid to small and medium-sized businesses and technology investment also qualifies for aid; the purpose was to ensure that EU regional policy expenditure could be more readily co-financed from German regional policy budgets. It is notable in this regard that these adjustments apply to the entire territory of the Federal Republic of Germany and not just to East Germany.

For Germany, therefore, the existence of EU regional policy has forced the governmental administration to move closer to EU concepts of regional development. This has a political consequence of reducing the independent room for manoeuvre of national policy. In addition, in the medium term, closer co-ordination between the various ministries will be necessary. National policy in Germany, therefore, now also promotes the establishment of regional development plans. At a regional level at least, this will require integrated planning by individual divisional ministries – which will at least have to be co-ordinated with the policy of the relevant federal state.

Effects of EU Regional Policy in the German Regions

The second major influence of the Structural Funds on regional development in Germany concerns the impact on the regions of the Federal Republic. The following section examines the problems and successes of EU regional policy using an Objective 1 region (Sachsen Anhalt) and an Objective 2 region (the Ruhr District) as examples.

Objective 1 (Sachsen Anhalt)

The five new federal states of eastern Germany are all Objective 1 areas. As throughout central and eastern Europe, the transition of eastern Germany from a planned to a market economy led to a breakdown of the industrial system and enormous job losses. This caused the Commission to make funds available of around DM 27 billion (c.14 becu) for the period from 1994–1999, that is DM 1636 (c.860 ecu) per head of population. This sum is put into perspective when one considers that the West German public budgets provide around DM 150 billion per year in net transfers for East Germany. These funds flow, for instance, into a massive improvement of the infrastructure, house building and support for the budgets of local authorities and the federal states. The size of these transfers reflects the severity of the problems arising from the collapse of industry – attributable to obsolete production processes and products, productivity of only one-third of that in West

Germany, isolation from western European markets, lack of skills in managing companies in a market economy and loss of markets in eastern Europe.

The regrouping which has resulted within the last five years in Sachsen-Anhalt alone is reflected by the following diagram:

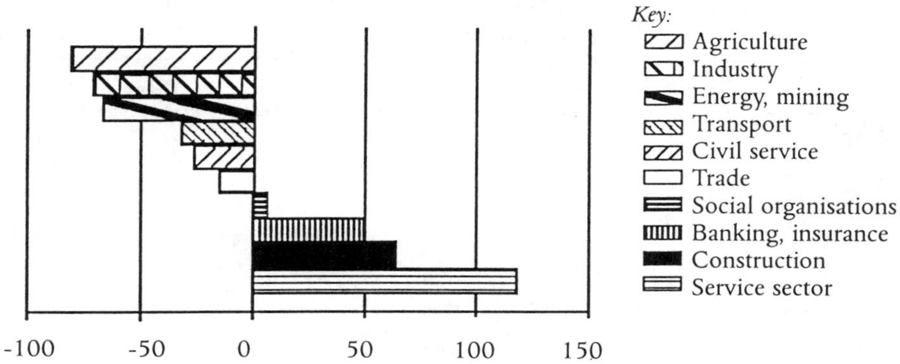

Source: Federal Statistical Office

Figure 14.1 Employment in Sachsen-Anhalt by sector, per cent (1989–1994)

As the annual average for 1995, an unemployment rate of 15.6 per cent was registered in Sachsen-Anhalt. It is to be assumed that approximately 400,000 jobs are lacking in this federal state with a population of around 2.8 million (the unemployment rate only reflects around 60% of the actual requirement for jobs as employees over 55 took early retirement as an emergency measure and a large number of people are undergoing temporary training courses or are engaged in government employment programmes). A further problem is that a major expansion of the construction industry is being supported by government investment programmes which cannot be maintained in the long term. Within industry there is also expansion, particularly in fields which are suppliers to the construction industry or predominantly serve regional markets. The more strongly a sector is exposed to international competition, the worse has been its development. Industry in Sachsen-Anhalt is narrowly based: in the case of mining and chemicals industry regions this has led to considerable environmental pollution.

In contrast to other federal states, for example Thuringia or Saxony, Sachsen-Anhalt restricts itself to the regular support provided under national German regional policy which is co-financed by the EU. The aid is provided on a State-wide basis without discrimination by type of area. The State government has not, in principle, established any regional focal points for regional promotion; this is justified on the grounds that all regions suffer from a major disparity relative to the federal average. For Sachsen-Anhalt, the financial plan provided for expenditure amounting to 2.5 billion ecu (becu) from 1991 to 1993. These funds came from various sources (see Table 14.1).

Table 14.1 Finance plan for promotion in Sachsen-Anhalt, mecu, (1991–1993)

Source	*Amount*	%
ERDF	268.2	10.84
ESF	114.5	4.64
EAGFF	122.3	4.94
EU, total	505.0	20.42
Federal and state	644.8	26.07
Local authorities	127.5	5.15
Government total	772.3	31.22
Private	1196	48.35
Total	**2473.7**	**100.00**

Source: Commission of the European Communities, Community Support Framework 1991–1993. Bundesrepublik Deutschland. p.35.

These investments are divided between nine priority areas (see Table 14.2).

Table 14.2 Priority areas in the Community promotion concept for Sachsen-Anhalt (1991–1993)

Focal areas	*Investments*	%
Infrastructure	333.3	13.47
Industrial investments	1147.6	46.39
Development of human resources	143	5.78
Long-term unemployed	21.6	0.87
Youth unemployment	54.2	2.19
Agriculture	504	20.37
Agriculture and environment	261.7	10.58
Technical assistance	8.3	0.34
Total	**2473.7**	**100.00**

Source: Commission of the European Communities, Community Support Framework 1991–1993. Bundesrepublik Deutschland, p.35.

Studies on the results of EU assistance – undertaken mainly by the Institut für Wirtschaftsforschung in Halle – provide a fundamentally favourable view from the perspective of the communities receiving aid. Attention was drawn to the contribution of aid in modernising the existing production basis and creating new employment potential, particularly by small and medium-sized businesses. It was, however, also noted that aid particularly strengthens those counties which already had a differentiated industrial structure in the past (the counties *(Kreise)* represent the NUTS III regions in Germany). At the NUTS I level, EU aid appears to have had a favourable effect on the region as a whole but to have contributed to polarisation at the level of the smaller NUTS III regions.

The evaluations performed to date for East Germany and for the specific case of Sachsen-Anhalt draw attention to a number of fundamental problems. First, when a massive amount of funds are provided by the national government in addition to the programme co-financed by the Community for the expansion of infrastructure, housing, the tertiary sector and the establishment of general administration, the effects of promotion can no longer be clearly assigned to any particular programme. For example, is the high growth rate in individual industries induced by the expansion of infrastructure by the national government or by the promotion of productive investments? Second, the same problem occurs when joint initiatives are carried out in addition to the aid programmes of the Community in the same area. If the evaluation is only intended to be related to the programmes or to the joint initiatives, the results must necessarily be distorted.

Third, each evaluation presupposes two scenarios: what would development in the region have been like without the existence of the promotion programme? and what was the development really like? The evaluators argued that this classic problem of identifying the 'counterfactual' meant that no precise results could be deduced in the evaluation because a simulation of a regional development situation without the existence of a promotion programme was considered impossible. This is further exacerbated in that superimposed effects of the economic cycle considerably distort the results. Fourth, the very large number of programme components, for example the development of new industrial areas or measures to improve human resources, only have a favourable effect on the regional structure after several years. The same applies to efforts made in the field of research and development. Evaluation directly after the end of an operational programme will not, therefore, be in a position to permit a final judgement on the success or failure of that programme.

Objective 2 (North-Rhine Westphalia)

North-Rhine Westphalia was historically the core area for industrialisation in Germany. The economic basis was the coal and steel industry, itself based on the coal mined in the Ruhr. From 1956 onwards, this energy base was increasingly displaced by cheap petroleum on world markets and later also by natural gas. At the same time, from 1972 onwards, the steel industry throughout Europe underwent periodic crises which had a serious effect on the Ruhr with its emphasis on coal and steel. The consequence of this development in the region was a high base of unemployment (which is approximately 50% above the national average in most years), a very low earnings rate (particularly among women), initial decline in population resulting from emigration and a major reduction in the financial resources of local authorities.

Restructuring faced the difficulty that the Ruhr is a densely populated polycentric conurbation and the individual cities in the region are not in a good position to establish relationships with their surrounding areas. Furthermore, large parts of the area used by the coal and steel industries were highly polluted and located in the middle of residential areas. Further considerable structural change is unavoidable because hard coal mining still employs around 70,000 people, current subsidies for the mining industry may not continue and the steel industry also faces increasing pressure to adjust. The German government subsidises mining with approximately 10 billion DM per year. At the same time, the price of German hard coal is four times the world market price. The difference can only be maintained by a relatively rigorous import ban and purchasing agreements with the (predominantly governmentally owned) electricity companies. The EU has, therefore, been assisting the Ruhr region as an Objective 2 area since 1989. The priorities and funding allocations are shown in Tables 14.3 and 14.4.

The promotion of the Ruhr since 1989 makes it clear that the restructuring process of conurbations with a significant decline in employment in industry can only be measured after decades and not a period of years, is highly dependent on the development of the economy as a whole and is exposed to competitive pressure from Objective 1 and Objective 5b promotion.

There is a systematic link between macro-economic development and the opportunities for regional restructuring insofar as the Ruhr regularly exhibits growth rates in employment (even if these are below average) in years of economic upswing and declines (above average) in periods of recession for the economy as a whole. The real problem is that it has not been possible,

Table 14.3 Ruhr region Objective 2 priorities

1.	Diversification of the economic structure by assistance to the small and medium-sized enterprises in particular
1.1	Promotion of industrial investment, above all for SMEs and new businesses
1.2	Promotion of technology and innovation, consultancy and 'other' software activities for SMEs
2	Creation and expansion of infrastructure, above all for SMEs and new businesses
2.1	Creation and expansion of facilities in technological infrastructure, new business centres and similar facilities
2.2	Creation and expansion of initial and further training facilities
2.3	Creation of transport infrastructure in conjunction with the demand for SME development
2.4	Tourism infrastructure
2.5	Cross border co-operation
3	Restoration of abandoned industrial and military sites, improvement of their surroundings and environmental quality and removal of the consequences of earlier industrialisation
3.1	Restoration of abandoned industrial and military sites for commercial purposes (especially SMEs)
3.2	Restoration of old factory buildings on abandoned industrial sites and areas formerly used by the military
3.3	Improvement of the environmental situation and measures for environmental protection
3.4	Promotion of infrastructure investment for rational use of energy and the use of inexhaustible energy sources
4	Promotion of human resources
4.1/4.2	Promotion of human resources for industrial diversification structure/promotion of human resources for ecological and social renewal of the Objective 2 regions
4.3	Transnational and cross-border measures
4.4	Programme infrastructure and studies
5	Evaluation, technical assistance

Source: Commission of the European Communities, Community Support Framework 1991–1993. Bundesrepublik Deutschland, p.35.

in the last 15 years, to reduce the high base of permanent unemployment. To this extent, the promotion of job-creating industrial investments is understandable as the first priority. There is, however, a considerable difficulty here, as with all programmes which pursue this priority. They are not successful when the national economy as a whole is in a downswing or recession. Investments in expansion presuppose a growth in demand which will fully utilise the new capacities in the long term. From this point of view,

Table 14.4 Distribution of the Structural Fund allocations in North-Rhine Westphalia, mecu (1994–1996)

Priorities	*Structural Fund contribution*	*National financing*	*Private financing*	*Total*
Priority 1	56.176	64.51	461.085	581.771
Priority 2	114.452	153.312	–	267.764
Priority 3	91.877	91.877	–	183.754
Priority 4	97.57	119.252	46.064	262.886
Technical assistance	1.295	1.295	–	2.59
Total	**361.37**	**430.246**	**507.149**	**1298.765**

Source: Inforegio

it may be understandable that promotion focuses on small- and medium-sized enterprises in the region.

An initial evaluation of the Objective 2 programme for the ERDF component has been performed by the research institute of the Friedrich-Ebert-Foundation (1993). The evaluation encountered several difficulties: for several parts of the programme the number of cases receiving aid was too small to permit any generalised statement, other programmes beside ERDF were applied at the same time in the region and the overlap effects could not be quantified and there were considerable uncertainties as to the aid contribution above which a programme can be assessed as 'successful' – part of the region was, for example, also promoted by RESIDER and RECHAR programmes. Nevertheless, the reviewers arrived at a positive general result. The instruments were judged to be adequate and progressive with regard to synergy effects, co-ordination of aid instruments and inclusion of target groups previously not involved. Assessments of the quantitative results of the programme were more cautious. Investment support involved 1156 cases, associated with an investment volume of c.1.1 billion DM, the creation of 3921 new jobs and 6301 secured jobs. If one assumes that the investments would not have been made without this aid, the job deficit in the Objective 2 region would have been 4.8 per cent higher.

In addition, investment grants were paid to small and medium-sized enterprises, supporting 43 investments with a volume of c.640,000 DM (c.336,842 ecu), creating 1031 new jobs and securing a further 57. Three-quarters of the promoted investment volume and almost two-thirds of the jobs were attributable to the establishment of new plants. One remarkable factor is the high capital intensity of the assisted investments; amounting to approximately 583,000 DM (c.306,842 ecu) per job created (excluding one major project from the calculation gives a result of 343,000 DM), in part associated with a high level of technology intensity.

Assessment

By comparison with the Objective 1 programme, the more targeted application of EU support in North-Rhine Westphalia allows a more conclusive assessment of the effects of the Structural Funds. With regard to the priority areas specified by the Commission (SMEs, environmental protection, research and development, integration of ERDF and ESF), the programme can be considered a success. However, the programme also confirms the reservations made at the start of the previous section: the promotion of productive investments, particularly where the area of small and medium-sized enterprises is concerned, is dependent to a high degree on the development of the economy as a whole. By contrast, the specifications of the operational programmes are always based on a macro-economic 'normal situation', with the consequence that it is almost impossible, in an *ex post* evaluation, to determine whether an inadequate degree of objective fulfilment is attributable to weaknesses in the programme or to a decline in the economic cycle during the period under review. In addition, the question arises as to whether the Commission and the Member States do not overestimate the potential of small and medium-sized enterprises. A recent study for Lower Saxony, for instance, arrives at the conclusion:

> ...that net job creation rates and firm size are not systematically related when firms are classified according to their average number of employees in the base and end year. Small firms create (destroy) quite a large share of all new (lost) jobs...size alone should not be a cause for concern in establishing industrial policy programmes to promote firms. (Wagner 1995, pp.469–474)

The promotion of small and medium-sized enterprises does, of course, represent a focal area in all Objective 2 programmes. It must, however, be asked – and here there is a considerable need for research – to what extent this focus does not represent an impermissible extrapolation of trends from the 1980s. Under the motto of 'lean production', a significant reduction in manufacturing depth occurred in almost all large companies – that is components previously manufactured within the organisation were bought in from predominantly small and medium-sized businesses. At the same time, service operations were demerged from the companies and either given an independent legal identity or sold. The background to this strategy was the fact that it had become almost impossible for central management of major companies to monitor the efficiency of these service operations effectively. This control function was, so to speak, transferred to the market. Both effects together led to considerable reductions in employment in the major companies and to increases in employment among the small and medium-sized businesses. The employment balance of this particular form of rationalisation remained negative. It was however, at least in Germany, covered by the growth in the service sector.

Whether this trend is to continue appears doubtful. On the one hand, the process of restructuring in industry, as described above, is predominantly finished and, on the other hand, the trend today is more towards 'global sourcing' for supplies. Thus the state of North-Rhine Westphalia has been losing around 10,000 jobs per month in industry since 1991 – predominantly outside the Objective 2 region (characterised by the coal and steel sector) – mainly in the component supply industries for mechanical engineering, electrical engineering and automotive engineering.

It is not disputed that newly-founded small and medium-sized enterprises, in particular, can make a fundamental contribution to the recovery of the assisted regions in the long term when they are active in relatively fast-growing markets or in profitable market niches. This is, however, an extremely time-consuming process. In the Ruhr from 1985 to 1996, according to a survey by the Ruhr Local Authority Association, 26 technology centres were founded. These accommodate 602 businesses with 4595 employees. Subsidy funds from the EU were also used in part for these centres. If one considers that the closure of a steelworks or a mine in the Ruhr leads to the loss of around 3500 jobs, it becomes clear that these centres will only be able to assist in alleviating the employment deficits in the region in the very long term.

This point draws attention to a fundamental aspect of the evaluation problem. The success of programme items such as the improvement of infrastructure for small and medium-sized enterprises, measures to improve human resources and development or recycling of industrial areas can only be assessed after a number of years. Then, however, under changed background conditions, it becomes difficult to draw conclusions for the continuation of programmes from this experience.

A further point of criticism is the promotion of investments aimed at the 'preservation' of jobs. If subsidies for the establishment of plants can be justified by the argument that this has a favourable effect on the selection of locations by businesses, the question arises here with particular clarity as to whether the investments would not have been made without government subsidies. Even this is highly disputed in German literature, particularly with regard to small and medium-sized enterprises. In location studies, the availability of qualified labour, the existing infrastructure and the size of the accessible sales market are regularly emphasised. Subsidies, on the other hand, play a subordinate role in the results of all surveys. The relative merits of 3900 newly-created jobs and 6300 secured jobs makes this question important.

Finally, evaluation is made very difficult by the regional designation of the assisted areas. The Commission's procedure, starting in principle with NUTS III in order not to exceed the politically stipulated limit of 15 per cent of the Community population in Objective 2 areas but also to permit designation at the level of parts of cities, is extremely problematic. On the basis of such designation, Objective 2 support can be extended almost arbitrarily and an assessment of the success of the programmes is also prevented.

CHAPTER 15

Integrated Regional Development under EU Regional Policy

The Dutch Experience

Willem H. Kleyn and Martin Bekker

Introduction

To understand the development of a country's regional policy it is important to appreciate its internal regional geography as well as its position in the international economy. This is clear in the Netherlands, given its open economy and location on Europe's largest river delta. The processes of global trade liberalisation and convergence of macro-economic policy on the road to EMU reinforce the importance of region-specific factors in international competition and impose fresh requirements on the conduct of regional policy (Kleyn and Oosterwijk 1992).

This chapter starts with a short portrait of regional development in the Netherlands. It then looks at Dutch regional policy and its relationship with European regional policy. The third part of the chapter assesses the various EU programmes in the Netherlands. Finally, the chapter considers the lessons for national and European policy development. A central thesis is that European policies should be more flexible and allow for a wider range of policy approaches among Member States and regions. Compatibility of European and national regional policies is a *conditio sine qua non* for fruitful policies. Integration of politicies should take place at the regional level.

Dutch Regions in the International Context

The Dutch economy has always been relatively open with a large proportion of national income generated through exporting. Very substantial investments are made in other countries and the level of inward investment is high.

This strong integration with the world economy is attributable to the size of the Dutch market and the country's location. Being on the Rhine Delta and the North Sea has strongly influenced the pattern of economic development for centuries. There is intensive trade with other EU Member States and other continents too. The seaport of Rotterdam and Schiphol-Amsterdam airport act as gateways for trade between north-west Europe and the economies of Asia and America. International trends such as trade liberalisation and shifts in the international division of labour have a rapid and powerful impact on the Dutch economy and the position of its regions, presenting both new opportunities and threats (Kleyn and Oosterwijk 1992; De Groene, Heijs and Kleyn 1995). The economic future of the regions depends on their position *vis-à-vis* evolving networks and their ability to mobilise local assets and resources to exploit these opportunities.

Before discussing the way government policy responds to these new challenges, we consider the changing spatial pattern of economic activities.

Put simply, there has been growing convergence in the economic performance of different parts of the country. For instance, over the past decade employment has increased more strongly in the east and south than the national average. These regions have become less peripheral in an international context and have benefited from spillover effects from the western conurbation (the Randstad) and proximity to Germany and Belgium. Development in the western part of the country, where about half of the national population and economic activities are concentrated, has lagged somewhat, while the north continues to stagnate (TNO-INRO 1994). Unemployment in the north remains persistently high compared with the declining national average. However, the situation in the west asks for concern too. Half the country's number of unemployed is concentrated in this part of the country. About a quarter of the unemployed are concentrated in the four major cities of the Randstad (Amsterdam, Rotterdam, The Hague and Utrecht).

In the south and east there has been particularly strong growth in Gelderland, Noord-Brabant and Limburg and the transport axes connecting them with major economic concentrations in Germany, Belgium and northern France. Economic dynamism within this area is fuelled by the continuing development of the main ports, the urban economic concentrations and transport axes (De Groene, Heijs and Kleyn 1995).

The Development of Dutch Regional Policies

Spatial policies have a long tradition in the Netherlands and have always had two broad objectives. They have been concerned with 'efficiency', or the promotion of regional economic development as a contribution to national growth by tapping unused potential, and with 'equity', or the pursuit of a physically more balanced spread of population, services and economic activities. The emphasis between these has changed over time, just as the strategy, policy instruments, resources and designated regions have been altered in the light of experience. In the period of economic reconstruction following World War II, promotion of industrialisation was a priority. In the second Government White Paper on industrialisation (Ministry of Economic Affairs 1950), nine peripheral regions were designated as development areas with more than forty centres of industrialisation. Resources were also made available for the development of industrial estates and infrastructure, housing construction and education, workers migrating from those areas and financial support to locating and expanding industrial enterprise (Bartels and Van Duijn 1981).

From the end of the 1950s, when physical planning started to take shape, the equity objective became more prominent. The strong migration to the west continued. Population growth elsewhere and rising costs of concentrated development in the west prompted interest in a more balanced distribution of population and economic activity. Key themes of physical planning have been the maximum absorption of population growth and development of economic activity within existing urban areas, protection of rural areas from further urbanisation and diversion of growth from the west to adjacent areas in Noord-Brabant, Gelderland and Flevoland.

The rather defensive character of regional policies which became dominant during the 1970s was subsequently turned into a more offensive approach. This shift in orientation embraced several aspects of regional policy, like the relationship with other government policies, the criteria for designating regions and the policy instruments and powers of administrative tiers. This shift occurred over about two decades and involved several inter-related developments.

One of the instruments of defensive policies was the relocation of central government services to the assisted regions, which stopped in the late-1980s. Another example of the strongly defensive approach was the Selective Investment Regulation (SIR), introduced in 1974. This imposed levies on investment and requirements for licences in some parts of the west. Complementary to this, the Investment Premium Regulation (IPR) was applied in the north, in Twente and the southern part of Limburg. Later it was extended to areas in Noord-Brabant, Flevoland and the northern part of Holland.

This combination of 'stick and carrot' was motivated by increasing unemployment in many parts of the country and by the need to align regional policies with physical planning and environmental policies. However, growing criticism of the strong directive features of this approach, coupled with increasing unemployment in the west and decreasing migration from the west to Noord Brabant and Gelderland, led to the SIR being abolished. The search for an integrated approach continued, at least as far as the indirect policy instruments were concerned. The regional programmes for the north (Integraal Structuur Plan) and south (Perspectieven Nota Limburg) gave most emphasis to the integration of government policies towards the economy, labour market, education, cultural facilities and so on. Integration also has a geographical dimension. There is a growing recognition that the effectiveness of regional policies depends on the geographical scale at which they are applied and their coherence. Discretionary policies at a small scale and diverse investment grant schemes are believed to be ineffective. When a reassessment of national regional policies took place at the end of the 1980s (Ministry of Economic Affairs 1988) the IPR scheme was radically simplified.

There has been a commensurate shift in emphasis in the objectives of Dutch regional and spatial policies. Partly as a consequence of regional convergence and a growing concern about the economic viability of the core regions in the west, more emphasis was put on efficiency. A more structural approach was also taken in policy thinking, whereby the disparities between regions have become less important to national government than the economic relationships between them and their position in the international economy.

An example of the shift towards a more offensive approach is in the development of physical planning policies. Dutch physical planning has traditionally been characterised by strong top-down control by the State. However, during the 1980s, under the influence of the economic recession and the waning belief in the idea that society could be moved towards preconceived blueprints, more attention was paid to the international economic context and the spatial processes related to it (De Groene, Heijs and Kleyn 1995). In addition, increasingly strict application of the principle of subsidiarity has moved policy from a centralised top-down approach towards a more decentralised bottom-up approach. This development has gone hand in hand with a conviction that regions should primarily utilise their 'own' endogenous potential rather than depend on geographical redistribution of national resources. Moreover, the region is increasingly regarded as the most appropriate level to implement national policies and to develop 'tailor-made' solutions in areas like SMEs, technology-diffusion, the labour market and physical planning. Integration of policy measures is easier at regional than at the national level.

There has also been a movement from direct towards indirect policy instruments. In view of the Single European Market, the government decided in 1990 to restrict financial support for the IPR and the extent of the eligible areas. Instead, more attention is being paid to the conditions or environment for regional development. The introduction of the business environment policy within the framework of the White Paper on Regional Economic Policy 1991–1994 focused attention on the physical accommodation of economic activities in an internationally-competitive business environment, which, at the same time, can be justified in terms of physical planning and the environment (Ministry of Economic Affairs 1990; Clement 1991). The business environment policy concentrates on large and medium-sized urban centres and other economic concentrations throughout the country.

This reorientation in policy was prompted by pressures of internationalisation and the imminent completion of the Single Market, which focused attention within regional policy on the physical business environment – including the need for accessible business locations, high-quality living and working conditions and uncongested communications between seaports, airports, other economic concentrations and the hinterland (Kleyn and Oosterwijk 1992). Influenced by research – for example, DATAR (1989) and Netherlands Economic Research Institute (1989) – and by major projects such as Docklands in London, La Defense in Paris, the Channel Tunnel and development of high-speed railways in France and Germany, the Ministry of Economic Affairs developed a strong interest in major infrastructure projects for regional development. Particular examples include the upgrading of Schiphol into a main port, the expansion of Rotterdam seaport, the connection to the international high-speed railway network and the construction of a goods railway between Rotterdam and the German hinterland.

The change in thinking is particularly clear in the latest government White Paper on Spatial Economic Policy to the Year 2000 (Ministry of Economic Affairs 1995). This policy document considers the regions not as self-contained units but in their inter-relationships and in the broader economic and spatial context (Heijs, Kleyn and de Groene 1996). It is argued that there is a threat that there will be insufficient space for business activities throughout the country, especially for heavy industries, distribution activities and high-quality activities (BCI and NEI 1994; Ministry of Economic Affairs 1994; Kleyn and De Vet 1994). The shortage of business locations that satisfy contemporary requirements is also a key theme of the Fourth National White Paper on physical planning (De Groene, Heijs and Kleyn 1995). This proceeds on the principle of an integrated approach – in other words the development of residential and working infrastructure and other service provisions should be co-ordinated within the 'own' region, allowing for 'tailor-made' solutions. The primary responsibility for quality business sites stays with regional and local government. This approach is consistent with the adage 'regions under their own power', which began to catch on in the policy sphere towards the end of the 1980s. The concept is that regional development is defined primarily by the development and utilisation of endogenous potential (Ministry of Economic Affairs 1990). A more integrated approach at the regional level also counteracts the growth of travel and congestion on the main infrastructure.

The Implementation of the Structural Funds

The policy shift in the Netherlands towards a more offensive and decentralised approach, with a greater emphasis on spatial elements, could be expected to generate tensions with European regional policies. Indeed, since the reform of the Structural Funds in 1988, the relationship between Dutch and European policies has become rather complicated. Although there was some experience of an integrated approach, the combination of European and national funds within a Single Programming Document was new for the Netherlands. For example, the national integrated programme for the northern provinces had been guided more by a philosophy of co-ordination than by a fully integrated approach. At the political level, various national ministries and the regional authorities co-ordinated their policies for the northern provinces and tried to give them special emphasis. However, only the Ministry of Economic Affairs had a specific policy and budget for these regions. In practice, the objectives and programmes of the various ministries were not really integrated in the strict sense of the word, but fulfilled the requirement that they had to be aligned with national policies. There were no consistent time horizons, individual projects had their own planning systems and the budget of the Ministry of Economic Affairs was set annually.

The Structural Funds programmes were, in many respects, completely different. The programmatic approach, with one budget, clearly defined objectives, a limited programme period and substantial contributions from the ERDF and ESF, constituted a major change for the implementation of regional policies in the Netherlands. This was not apparent in 1988, when the parties concerned considered these programmes to be additional to the existing national regional programmes. However, it soon became clear that a different approach was required, especially with respect to the role and structure of programme management and the monitoring and evaluation of the programme and projects. In addition, things were complicated by the reorientation of Dutch policies described earlier, especially the shift to more uniform regimes, the decentralisation aimed at tailor-made solutions and the greater emphasis on efficiency as the overriding objective. This meant that the requirements and technical guidelines of the Structural Funds programmes were not easy to meet.

One particular problem arose because the Ministry of Economic Affairs was in the process of curtailing spending on regional aid to the peripheral regions and focusing more on the business environment throughout the country. In addition, the new approach of integrated ERDF and ESF programmes forced the national authorities to expand their regional policies, create new organisational structures and set different goals and priorities. Establishing a new structure for labour market policy was particularly complicated because policy became a shared responsibility of employers' organisations, trade unions and the Ministry of Social Affairs. It took several years for the role of this organisation in the regions to be clearly established. Meanwhile, the regional programmes had to be formulated and implemented. The role of the labour market organisations – given by the Ministry of Social Affairs – was targeted at the unemployed. This role interfered with the RBA's responisbility for the Social Funds, that also targets at the employed. This made it more difficult to integrate ERDF and ESF and meant that training for people in jobs has received little attention.

The Structural Funds required decentralisation of decision making on national co-funding. This meant that the regional authorities became the central players in implementing the CSFs. National government restricted its involvement to the monitoring and steering committees. The national authorities remained formally responsible for the programmes and pursued an important co-ordinating, controlling and financial role in their development and implementation. Consequently, the Ministry of Economic Affairs wanted a clear overview of decentralised spending decisions and the need for evaluation became stronger. Before 1992 there was no systematic assessment of effectiveness and efficiency in the EU programmes. Control was exercised through progress reports, external audits and general democratic control. The financial flows to beneficiaries and the amount of co-financing were the main concerns, explained by the strong emphasis the Commission put on financial deadlines, additionality and costs eligible for subsidy. This practice became more and more unsatisfactory and the call for policy evaluation grew stronger. The Ministry of Economic Affairs took the initiative to develop an evaluation framework (TERP/CBEA 1993) to enable programmes to be evaluated in a structured and standard way in the *ex ante*, ongoing and *ex post* phases. This framework had to meet several requirements, including consistency with the views of the Commission and flexibility to be adapted to different types of programmes in the various regions, thereby enabling general lessons to be drawn.

The Evaluation of Regional Programmes

From the outset it was recognised that a pragmatic approach was necessary. It is impossible to separate the impact of a programme from other factors in a completely objective way because of its relatively small scale and because of the long time gaps that may occur between actions and their structural effects. Moreover, the overall objectives of regional policies are formulated in general terms, such as reinforcing the regional economic structure or lowering unemployment rates. They cannot be linked unambiguously with measures in different fields such as infrastructure and training. However, if there is agreement about certain operational or intermediate goals – like improving external access or diffusion of technical knowledge – in pursuing the objective of strengthening regional structures, it may be possible to establish relationships between means and goals. This suggests a way of measuring effectiveness based on plausibility and intersubjectivity.

Evaluations seek to analyse both the effectiveness and efficiency of the regional programmes. Judgements about complete programmes containing various projects and measures are reached by combining top-down and bottom-up approaches and accepting quantitative and qualitative data. The top-down approaches analyse changes at the regional level, comparing assisted region performance with nation-wide results and emphasising effectiveness. The bottom-up approaches assess the physical and intermediate effects at the level of projects, which are then aggregated to the level of measures and priorities emphasising efficiency issues. Following the plausibility approach, programme effects and autonomous external influences are separated in qualitative terms. The resulting evaluations analyse the appropriateness of the strategies that have been implemented and quantify their impacts.

The Dutch evaluation framework integrates the European vision of evaluation with national demands, taking into account the needs of the regional authorities as well. The European Commission puts great emphasis upon impact assessment and 'value for money'. The Ministry of Economic Affairs formulated three basic requirements: compatibility, in the sense that the approach had to be consistent with Commission demands and aspirations; comparability, making possible cross-regional comparisons; and flexibility, to allow for specific regional features and conditions. For the regions, validation of the chosen strategy and its translation into concrete actions was of greatest interest. The efficiency of programme management and learning from experience and other regional programmes were also major issues. The framework was an important step forward in assessment practices. Before this, evaluations were merely descriptive and concerned with financial accounting.

In 1994 a first round of evaluations was carried out comprising *ex post* studies of three older Objective 2 programmes and *ex ante* studies of five new programmes. In 1996 a second round of studies was completed, including ongoing (1994–1996) and *ex ante* evaluations (1997–1999) of all five Objective 2 programmes. Drawing on the results of these evaluations, some useful conclusions can be drawn.

Concentrating first on a regional top-down perspective, it appears that inter-regional imbalances in employment and unemployment have gradually diminished. In the three Objective 2 regions established since 1989, unemployment rates have fallen more than the national average. Only the northern regions still have very high unemployment: almost 12 per cent compared with a national average of 7.5 per cent. In regions like Twente and Southern-Limburg, regional unemployment disparities have fallen to about one per cent. The strongest effects were experienced between 1989–1992. Since then progress has been limited.

One of the reasons for the progress made has been the growth of the service sector. In Twente the increase in service sector employment at the beginning of the 1990s was more than enough to compensate for job losses in industry. Since 1993 this has slowed down, resulting in some divergence from the national average. Overall, one conclusion is that economic structures in the Objective 2 regions have shifted towards the national pattern. Industrial employment is still decreasing while sectors such as transport and tourism have begun to play a more important role. However, most assisted regions are still more vulnerable to cyclical economic movements than other regions.

The most positive structural changes have been in the provinces of Limburg and Brabant. These regions have developed a strong internationally-oriented industrial sector, which has not lost jobs, and simultaneously have succeeded in establishing a modern service sector. Yet the changing character of employment has meant a considerable loss of less-qualified jobs and resulted in unacceptably high unemployment rates. Large parts of the labour force, especially older people, women and immigrants in traditional industrial regions such as Limburg and Twente, have not benefited from the employment opportunities created.

Table 15.1 Regional unemployment rates in The Netherlands

	1989	*1990*	*1991*	*1992*	*1993*	*1994*	*1995*
Oost Groningen	12.5	11.6	10.0	8.0	8.2	9.1	8.8
Delfzijl	13.3	12.5	8.7	7.3	6.3	8.1	7.8
Overig Groningen	16.1	13.0	10.4	8.2	8.6	9.3	9.0
Zuid Oost Drenthe	10.3	10.5	9.8	8.8	8.9	8.2	7.9
Twente	9.6	9.4	8.2	6.0	7.0	8.2	7.9
Arnhem/Nijmegen	13.6	10.4	9.3	6.9	7.9	8.0	7.8
ZO-Noord Brabant	8.9	7.2	7.4	5.6	6.8	6.4	6.3
Zuid-Limburg	11.5	8.6	7.9	6.2	7.1	7.0	6.8
Netherlands	9.8	7.4	7.0	5.6	6.3	7.0	6.7
EU-12	9.3	8.4	8.5	9.1	10.6	11.3	10.83

Note: Since 1992, another definition for unemployment is used based on the strict ILO-definition.
Source: Eurostat 1996

In other respects, such as R&D efforts and export performance, the Objective 2 regions seem to have caught up. In Limburg, Brabant and Twente the number of SMEs investing in process innovations is significantly higher than in other parts of the Netherlands. The number of ISO-certified firms also shows continuous and faster growth in the Objective 2 regions than the national average. The improved export performance may be partly attributable to the changing position of the border regions as a result of the Single Market. Regions with well-developed industrial and transport sectors, like Twente and Limburg, have shown very good results. The northern regions, which are less well situated, have not been able to improve their overall export position.

A key question is to what extent programme measures have contributed to these positive developments. In the *ex post* evaluations, attempts have been made to assess the impact of the three programmes on employment. Distinctions have been drawn between several categories of jobs: direct versus indirect, permanent versus temporary and newly-created versus preserved. According to the assessments, the direct and indirect impact is in the order of 4000 permanent jobs created and preserved and additional private-public investment of approximately 700 million guilders (TERP.V.Run 1994).

The central objectives of the programmes have not been changed fundamentally during the period considered. Strengthening the regional economic structures is still the priority. However, since 1994, more attention has been paid to environmental matters. Sustainable growth is defined in economic and ecological terms. Apart from this, the character of the programmes has hardly changed. Since 1989, infrastructure, human capital, SME support and technology transfer have been central themes, although priorities have shifted. In the period 1989–1993 infrastructure investments had the highest priority in all three programmes. Since 1994, the Commission has forced the regions to give higher priority to support for SMEs – especially in combination with innovation and technology policies. For example, in 1994 Groningen/Drenthe planned to support four times as many firms, compared with the period 1989–1993, through advisory and investment schemes. These measures have a stronger market orientation than infrastructure. New, promising sectors, such as the medical sector and mechatronics, have received substantial attention. High priority is also given to start-ups and upgrading the skills of workers and the unemployed. In the period 1994–1996 about 25,000 people in the five regions were trained by ESF-supported actions. The *ex post* evaluations also examined the number of firms assisted in terms of technology and innovation, exporting and management development. These schemes have had quite a high take-up, bearing in mind the relatively low level of investment (approximately 2% of the programme budget). In the advisory schemes in the northern regions, six per cent of eligible firms were participating. In Twente the figure was ten per cent and in Limburg 2.5 per cent.

The evaluations have resulted in much more attention being paid to issues of efficiency and effectiveness. In the first programmes quantified objectives were almost non-existent. Since then a complete set of indicators and quantified objectives have been embedded within the programming process. They are taken very seriously by the regional programme managers and have proved that intermediate measurable effects of the programmes are not difficult to establish. This has resulted not simply in a more efficient way of operating the programmes but also in wider support for the Structural Fund actions.

Conclusions

What lessons can be drawn from the Dutch experience for regional policies in Europe? There are several international trends which are extremely important for the future of the regions, offering both opportunities and threats. First, technological developments and changes in the organisation of production and distribution mean that the international division of labour has become less dependent on natural comparative advantages. The location of economic activities is more and more footloose and man-made location factors, such as infrastructure, quality business-sites and an attractive physical environment, are becoming more important. Second, the free movement of people, goods and capital within the EU and the creation of the World Trade Organisation lead to an intensification of economic traffic and a growing dependence of regions on the world market. Changes in international markets work their way more rapidly and comprehensively through regional economies and make them increasingly interdependent. Third, the convergence of macro-economic policies between Member States will further reinforce the importance of optimal regional conditions to attract, retain and expand business activities.

These trends are associated with new spatial patterns of activity. Future growth in countries such as China and Indonesia, and central and eastern Europe, will create new gravitational fields, new development poles and development axes. Gateway towns and cities will get new opportunities whilst former centrally-situated regions may become more peripheral. Many traditional urban industrial regions may have to go through extensive restructuring processes to develop new positions in the emerging economic networks. They will have to tackle the costly legacy of industrial decline in derelict and contaminated land and out-dated skills, otherwise people and businesses will leave the cities and the economic base of the regions will be undermined.

In the Netherlands the two classic objectives of regional policy have been influential from the outset, with gradually more emphasis being put on the efficiency/development objective with policies increasingly designed to achieve both. This is unlikely to change in the future. Broadly speaking, inter-regional differences in income and unemployment have been diminishing, caused mainly by a convergence of production structures of central and peripheral regions. Moreover, the more market-oriented, offensive approach to policy, which emphasises strong points in the regions rather than the distribution of growth, will become more important because of growing international competition and evidence that it is more effective. This approach leaves no room, except in cases of severe stagnation and backwardness, for investment subsidies and other defensive strategies.

Population growth, rising incomes and the expansion of economic activity will make new demands on space and the physical environment – so one can expect physical planning policies aimed at more evenly distributed activities and a high-quality environment for housing and business to become more important. As long as these policies are well co-ordinated with development policies, they may contribute positively to economic development.

The case for integrating the various policy fields seems strong at first sight. It should enhance the legitimacy and efficacy of measures and lead to more value for money. Early regional policies in the Netherlands were co-ordinated rather than fully integrated. The European Commission advocates integration of objectives, budgets and policy programmes. In practice, serious doubts have emerged in the Netherlands about the feasibility and effects of this. Full integration presupposes a common hierarchy of objectives and targets. It is a huge task to set priorities, develop a common strategy and procedures and align measures. Many people need to be involved in developing a coherent programme, implying a large bureaucracy and a big loss of flexibility, leaving little room for 'tailor-made' solutions. All things considered, a co-ordinated but piece-meal approach would be better than a fully integrated approach based on a grand design.

The call for evaluation has been growing in recent years. Much has been achieved thanks to efforts of the Commission, the Member States and the regions. A common language and, to a certain extent, a common methodology have been developed. Many lessons can be learnt from evaluation, provided that certain conditions are fulfilled. One is that there is agreement about what measures contribute to the attainment of programme objectives which are usually couched in very general terms. This has been called the plausibility principle, since there is no way of proving a direct relationship between concrete measures and the achievement of broad objectives. One has to accept that the efficiency and effectiveness of actions can only be measured quantitatively in terms of a set of intermediate goals, which we have to agree upon as contributing to the main programme objectives. One also has to realise that regional development policies require a long time horizon and some measures may only prove to be effective in the long run.

Eligibility is a complex and multi-dimensional problem demanding compromises between different, often contradictory, indicators. Budget constraints mean restricting the number of qualifying regions to prevent dissipation of scarce resources. High thresholds imply designating rather small eligible areas. However, there are several economic arguments in favour of supporting relatively big regions, including sufficient critical mass to reach self-sustaining growth. To develop an offensive development strategy there should also be strong points within the boundaries of designated regions. Consistency with the scale of administration and the coherence of the labour market should also influence regional boundaries; mechanistic designations based on clinical indicators tend to ignore crucial realities on the ground.

This brings us to one last issue, the role of the different tiers of administration. A gradual devolution of powers has taken place in the

Netherlands from central government to the provinces and municipalities. There has been some scaling-up of administration at the local level as a result of the increased scale of spatial, economic, labour market and other policy issues. This rearrangement of powers between administrative levels is an example of subsidiarity being applied at a national scale, leaving enough room for region-specific approaches to solve region-specific problems. The design of future European regional policy should recognise and take into account such trends, which extend beyond the Netherlands.

CHAPTER 16

Perspectives on EU Regional Policy from a New Member State

Austria

Markus Gruber

Austria's accession to the European Union had an important impact on regional development and regional policies in Austria. Both the implementation of the Structural Funds framework and adaptation to EU competition policies had major repercussions on the political system in Austria, particularly with respect to the organisational framework of Austria's regional policy. This chapter attempts to show how the characteristics of Austria's regional policy have changed, which coherent or even distinct domains of the policy approach between the Austrian and the EU framework exist, which important changes occurred and – last but not least – which tasks are still open for the future.

Regional Policy in Austria[1]

For a long time, regional policy was of minor significance in Austria, with regard both to the level of financial support and the political priority given to the policy. This is not really surprising in a small country with relatively few disparities. In spite of recent changes in the importance of regional policy, the insitutional framework still is very fragmented due to a variety of factors.

1 An excellent overview of Austrian regional policy, its development, organisation and tasks in the future is given by Downes (1995). For further information see also ÖROK (1991).

First, Austria is a federal state consisting of nine regions (*Länder*). Therefore, responsibility for economic policy, including regional policy, is distributed between federal, regional and local levels. Apart from the classical tasks of nations like defence, security, etc, other policy domains like science and research, as well as higher education, social policy and a large part of labour market policy, is the responsibility of the federal government. Health, primary education and other policy fields are exclusively in the hands of the *Länder*. Transport and industrial policy are examples of shared responsibility. Every *Land* carries out economic development policies for its specific area. But, as Downes (1995) stressed, this is clearly not regional policy in the sense of social equity as it does not concentrate on underdeveloped areas or attempt to counteract regional disparities. Many of the main regional policy assistance schemes are joint measures, co-financed between the federal and *Länder* governments. Second, regional policy is, in fact, often carried out by other policy areas (Downes 1995). Even at federal level, at least four ministries (plus the Federal Chancellery) and numerous funding organisations are involved in the regional development process. Third, the Austrian policy approach is consensus oriented. The non-governmental 'social partners' (trades unions, labour chamber, chamber of commerce and industry and chambers of agriculture are all protagonists in the Austrian corporate policy making system) and other interest groups are involved and various inter-ministerial committees co-ordinate different tasks (Sturn 1994). Fourth, the two main regional policy co-ordinating bodies – the Department for Regional Policy and Spatial Planning of the Federal Chancellery and the ÖROK[2] are both too small and have too many tasks at European, national and regional levels.

Until the 1980s, the Austrian regional policy system was characterised by a traditional view of economic development. Disparities between regions were primarily explained in terms of the lack of capital, market imperfections and the existence of barriers restricting the import of resources required for production. The increasing ineffectiveness of traditional regional policy and the progress in regional economic research caused a shift from the old policies to a new philosophy of regional development. This was combined with a shift from a static concept, emphasising the reduction of regional disparities, to a concept of structural policy – which implies a more dynamic view of

2 *Österreichishe Raumordnungskonferenz* (Austrian Conference on Regional Planning) was created in 1971 to act as a forum for co-operation between the different actors in the field of regional policy. It has a membership comprising the federal government, the *Länder* governments, representatives from the city associations and social partners.

regional development. The new philosophy concentrates more strongly on the promotion of the indigenous potential of regions and their integration into regional, national and international networks rather than on the mere transfer of capital into poorer regions. At federal and regional levels a great change occurred with respect to the target of policy and the financial support provided. Support schemes now focus on aiding comprehensive innovation, infrastructure, modernisation, internationalisation or application-oriented R&D projects (Jud and Steiner 1995). The 1980s also marked the re-emergence of regions as economic entities and as promoters of economic development in Austria. For the first time, concepts were developed that were adapted to the individual regional situations.

Commonalities and Contrasts between EU and Austrian Approaches to Regional Policy

Austria's membership of the EU had a significant impact on regional development and regional policy in Austria. In part, accession reinforced several existing trends underway in Austrian regional policy since the beginning of the 1990s. First, the EU principle of partnership complies with the Austrian consensus-oriented policy. The traditionally wide integration of non-governmental 'social partners' into the decision making process at federal as well as regional levels means that the basis for the fulfilment of partnership requirements already existed. Often, however, the appropriate structures were not formalised in Austria.

Second, there was coherence between the EU and Austria as regards the thematic focus of regional policy. The new orientation of Austria's economic and regional policies at the start of the 1980s placed greater concentration on endogenous development (including a major focus on SMEs) and stress was put on innovation, networking and qualification as well as research and development. These issues were addressed in conjunction with the maintenance and enhancement of living conditions and the environment. Given that, since the 1980s and early 1990s, the content of Austrian regional policy complied with the main features of the Structural Funds, adoption of the regional policies of the EU did not result in any major alterations in the focus of regional development. As Austrian regional assistance is diverse but not overly significant in financial terms, relatively little change was required with regard to award rate maxima (ÖIR 1992; Downes 1995).

Although there are major parallels between the Austrian and EU approaches to regional policy, there are also significant differences in the regional policy philosophy (see Downes 1995; Huber 1995a; 1995b;

ÖROK 1991). One contrast relates to the importance of quantitative versus qualitative factors. In the EU the Structural Funds framework, with its five-year programmes and the massive input of resources, places great emphasis on objective, quantitative outputs and impacts. The EU approach, which emphasises 'regional planning', is confronted with a rather systemic understanding of regional policies in Austria. According to Huber (1995a), successful regional development is mainly based on the co-ordination of numerous public and private actors, the behaviour of which will be adapted to the changing framework conditions in a continuous process of learning. This point of view has also changed the understanding of planning and of the role of planners: 'Planning now has more to do with moderation or arbitration of negotiation processes and with building of communication networks' (Huber 1995b, p.36). This flexible alignment of regional policies and the minor volume of financial support led to a relative lack of evaluation competence in Austria. Consequently, the evaluation-oriented EU programme structures are a challenge for Austria's regional political actors, as the first experiences with *ex ante* appraisals have shown – programme evaluation was interpreted more as a form of 'control' than as an opportunity for the further development of the programmes.

A second contrast is that while the EU addresses 'problem regions', Austria traditionally gave more emphasis to 'regional problems'. For Austrian regional policy makers the designation of problem regions according to economic indicators and exact boundaries reduces the flexibility of the system: there is no longer the possibility to encourage the development of peripheral regions in an indirect way by promoting centres with possible 'spread effects' to neighbouring regions (e.g. by establishing supplier links). This entails the risk that financial resources are transferred exclusively to regions with a relatively weak potential for purely endogenous development. On the other hand, neighbouring regions which could act as motors for the development of these regions are excluded from promotion/support. For example, high-profile projects were promoted in central locations of Austria, such as the provincial capitals Graz and Klagenfurt, as positive effects were expected for the surrounding areas too, particularly the peripheral regions.

Apart from the issue of thematic coherence and philosophical differences in regional policy, there is the challenge of implementing the Funds. Adopting the Structural Funds framework, and its principles of concentration, partnership, programming, additionality and an improved monitoring and evaluation, entailed new structures (BKA 1992; ÖIR 1996). Innovations in organisation and reorganisation of the entire development system were necessary due to the requirement for multi-annual, cross-sector programme planning (BKA 1992). By adopting the Structural Funds framework it was hoped that it would be possible to surmount traditional bureaucratic structures among the strictly separate areas of competence of the federal government, *Länder* and local authorities, and also individual sectoral departments, ending up with a flexibly networked, co-operative structure (Huber 1995a; 1995b).

EU Regional Policy and its Impact on Austria

Austria's accession to the EU has clearly upgraded regional policy in the country with respect to its political priority and volume of resources. Each year, additional EU funds amounting to 135 million ecu (mecu) are available for Objective 1, 2 and 5b regions. In addition, a series of national budget items are included that were previously not allocated (specifically) for the objectives of regional policy in order to ensure the necessary co-financing of the Funds and entailing regional, strategic reorientations to these areas of responsibility (ÖIR 1996). Thus it is not surprising that access to Structural Funds has been of great political importance in internal Austrian negotiations. Political pressure and the growing distributional struggle was aggravated by two factors:

- EU regional policy required development areas to be identified and, of course, no region wanted to be excluded
- there were exaggerated expectations of the Structural Funds, both with regard to the amount of funds available and the overall problem-solving capacity of EU regional policy.

Area Designation

With regard to the designation of assisted areas, the consensus-orientated policy approach in Austria led to the maximum number of municipalities being adopted into the assisted area map – with the result that 41 per cent of the population (far more than in comparable Member States) currently live in Objective 1, 2 and 5b regions. As Downes (1995) noted, 'the extensive coverage of the assisted areas map for EU regional policy could have the potential danger of distributing resources too thinly' (p.50). Partly due to the extensive coverage of the assisted areas map, regional policy in Austria is now, to a large extent, synonymous with EU regional policy. Two further critical points should be mentioned with respect to the designation of assisted areas.

First, some areas have the same economic and structural problems but different award priorities. The *Land* of Burgenland (NUTS II level) has been designated as an Objective 1 area and now can offer substantially higher award rates than the neighbouring region Eastern Styria (NUTS III level), which is as large as Burgenland (both in terms of population and area) and faces the same economic and structural problems but is 'only' an Objective 5b area. This encourages the danger of a divergent development of regions with a similar starting position. This also partly results from the fact that NUTS regions are usually created from administrative units and therefore differ from so-called 'economic regions' (Thöni 1995). Second, it is questionable whether the system of designation of areas assisted under Structural Funds really follows objective criteria. There is obviously substantial scope and discretion involved in the EU system of area designation based on objective criteria, considering that several areas in Austria were actually accepted as Objective 5b after having been rejected as Objective 2 areas.

Programming

The complex nature of the preparatory work required for the EU programmes was recognised early on. In order to avert the time pressure that was to be expected – there were barely six months to get the programmes finished after the referendum on joining the EU – Austria was 'covered' with a total of 17 Regional Development Plans (RDPs), excluding only the largest agglomerations. The characteristic features of the RDPs were: limitation to relatively small spatial units (20,000–470,000 inhabitants), a powerful 'bottom-up approach' and elaboration and operation by external experts.

The RDPs elaborated at sub-regional level provided the basis for the Single Programming Documents (SPDs). In some cases, however, the degree of integration of the RDPs into the SPDs was relatively small; the external experts who created the regional economic concepts were only marginally integrated into elaborating the SPDs and there was often a clear break between the concepts elaborated at sub-regional level and the strategies and measures set out in the SPDs. Within the scope of EU regional policy, a wide variety of programmes was created. Due to the federal structure of Austria, one SPD per *Land* and per Structural Fund objective has been agreed. This led to 15 programmes related to the objectives of EU regional policy and 20 programmes for Community Initiatives, seven of them for the Interreg II-Programme alone. In all, 35 SPDs were developed plus the 17 RDPs elaborated at sub-regional level during the preparatory phase (without any allocation of money). The vast number of concepts for a relatively small nation such as Austria (it is important to keep in mind that some of the German *Länder* are more than twice as big as Austria) means an enormous amount of administration. It is doubtful whether this can possibly justify the low amount of funding for some of the programmes (especially the Community Initiatives).

Partnership

A new model of partnership, the so-called *Programmgruppen auf der Länderebene*, was installed to elaborate the SPDs. The programme groups comprised representatives of the federal ministries, *Länder*, social partners and representatives of the municipalities. Co-ordination was carried out by the Federal Chancellery for the government and by the respective co-ordination office for the *Länder*. The competent *Land* authorities elaborated proposals for the SPD, which were then fine-tuned in the programme group and by regular informal contacts between federal and local authorities. The programme group certainly made a major contribution to improving horizontal co-operation (between the ministries) and vertical co-operation (between federal and local authorities) and endeavours are being made to continue this programme group in future.

Implementation

As noted earlier, the system for government support in Austria is extremely fragmented with a wide range of small policy measures at federal, *Land* and sometimes local level. Nevertheless, the decision was made not to install any separate organisations for EU Structural Funds but rather to have the existing authorities at federal and local levels implement the programmes. The objectives of EU regional policy have, in part, contributed to a material/conceptual reorientation of existing Austrian assistance, extending the 'regional component' of a number of schemes with the aim of enhancing their suitability for EU co-financing. Basically, however, the existing assistance instruments are employed for EU co-financing (BKA 1995).

Vertical co-ordination between project sponsors and aid authorities and horizontal co-operation between complementary projects is carried out by new regional management offices. In the past, regional managers were employed in certain 'focus' regions – an approach which has been expanded by installing a regional management office in all designated areas at the NUTS III level. Alongside efficient programme operation, the regional management offices are entrusted with the task of constantly developing the

RDPs, stimulating promising new development projects in a 'bottom-up' approach, and accompanying these projects to the implementation stage. Decisions concerning awards are, however, still the responsibility of the individual assistance institutions. If more than one state office is involved in a decision (e.g. federal and local authorities), they make the decision on the basis of informal contacts. It is not planned to install any new co-ordination mechanisms for this purpose. The selection of EU co-financed projects is thus basically the responsibility of the aid authorities, who decide on the co-financing of individual projects within their own area of responsibility. Finally, co-ordination at the level of the three European Structural Funds (financial co-ordination) is performed via the ministries assigned in each case, who provide the advisory committees with appropriate information on the status of implementation. Overall co-ordination is the responsibility of the Federal Chancellery.

Case Study of Styria

Styria is one of the nine Austrian *Länder* with about 1.2 million inhabitants. Except for the agglomeration of Graz, Styria is wholly covered by designated areas under Structural Funds, comprising a large Objective 5b area on the border with Slovenia and Austria's largest Objective 2 area. The approach taken to EU regional policy in Styria involves four main problems.

First, while Graz is of importance for the economic development of huge parts of Styria's rural areas, it is now excluded from the assisted areas map – although its economic performance has been relatively weak in the past. The exclusion of Graz can hinder development processes not only with respect to the Objective 2 and 5b areas; under the Interreg II Programme, aside from the cross-border activities of the neighbouring districts, an improved co-operation of the regional centres (Graz, Maribor) is important to encourage the development of the whole region.

Second, the eastern part of Styria, an Objective 5b region, might be affected by the higher award rates of the neighbouring region Burgenland. Due to a lack of tradition of inter-regional co-operation in Austria, no effective relations have been established yet as a stabilising factor – even though both regions have similarities in economic structure and almost the same regional development focus (e.g. spa tourism).

Third, an innovation in the Objective 2 SPD is the emphasis on soft measures such as consultancy and technology transfer, which will be enforced by the Community Initiative Resider II. One deficiency, which can be observed in many SPDs, is the lack of integration of ERDF and ESF measures. In this respect, the SPD measures are clearly not well tuned.

Fourth, a wide range of instruments is used in the SPDs but, as mentioned above, there are only slight changes of level and no changes in award rates. Thus there is some disappointment among applicants for financial support, who expected to get more money for their projects from the Structural Funds than before.

Conclusions and Questions

EU regional policy has had several clear positive effects on the Austrian regional policy approach but there are still some unanswered questions. In particular, the decision simply to increase the funds going to existing authorities is a source of grievance. It means that the only consequence of EU regional policy is that more money is available for more projects. For the individual, it is irrelevant whether the beneficiary receives EU co-financing for the project or not. The awards thus lack a certain European dimension. In addition, the award system is highly fragmented and needs to be reorganised but this has not happened: the Objective 2 programme in Styria designated a total of 46 award instruments and 19 award institutions.

Installing programme groups at *Länder* level has improved horizontal and vertical co-operation in programme elaboration. But whether EU regional policy can contribute to surmounting traditional bureaucratic structures with the strictly separate areas of competence of the federal government, *Länder*, municipalities and individual sectoral departments, as often hoped for, is doubtful due to the organisation of structures currently selected. The focus has been on safeguarding the existing competencies of the federal ministries and *Länder* authorities.

There is also a question about whether the increased use of money and relatively rigid system of the Structural Funds framework represents a step backwards for Austria. The relatively flexible and innovative approach to regional policy in the past was not orientated towards achieving 'measurable success' in the short term. It is now facing a rigid 'five-year plan', greater financial resources and the challenge of achieving measurable success within the next years. Austrians hope that qualitative aspects can also be emphasised in monitoring and evaluation so that the standard of Austria's regional policy can be safeguarded. There is also a tension between the objective-driven approach of the Structural Funds and the decentralisation and fragmentation of delivery.

By getting support from EU regional policy, Austria has gained access to numerous programmes and regional networks. The regions, however, have a great deal to learn about using international know-how to consolidate endogenous processes of development. The current lack of know-how at local and sometimes even regional levels has created a big market for regional consultants.

The EU programmes have a strong focus on assistance for individual firms. Some Austrians believe that support should be redirected to encouraging inter-firm co-operation and strengthening the business environment. ERDF and ESF measures also need to be better integrated.

Finally, the Austrian partnership approach may be a model for the EU. As Thöni (1995) stressed, the notion of partnership is not well defined in many of the regional development programmes and its nature differs between Member States depending on the degree of centralisation or decentralisation. The Austrian 'social partnership' may be a useful model for the EU and other countries.

Table 16.1 Structural Fund expenditure in Austria (1995–1999)

Objective	*mecu*	*As % of all Structural Fund expenditure*
Objective 1	165.6	10.2
Objective 2	101.4	6.2
Objectives 3/4	395	24.3
Objective 5a	388	23.9
Objective 5b	411	25.3
Community Initiatives and pilot projects	162	10.0

Source: BKA (1995)

Table 16.2 Co-Financing of Structural Funds in Austria

EU funds	*mecu*	*As % of all Structural Funds*	*As % of public expenditure (national and EU)*	*Co-financing funds*	*mecu*	*As a % of public expenditure (national and EU)*
ERDF	352.84	52	19.27	Federal	609.20	33.26
ESF	135.68	20	7.41	*Land*	488.00	26.65
EAGGF	189.08	28	10.32	Other	56.52	3.09

Source: BKA (1995)

Table 16.3 EU regional policy and its effects on Austria

The Austrian approach	*Similarities – differences*	*Consequences of EU accession*	*Conclusions and open questions*
• Regional policy has for a long time had a relatively low (political) profile; the institutional structures are very fragmented and often dominated by more informal than formal structures. • The policy approach is usually very consensus-orientated, enforced by the Austrian 'social partnership'. • The lower profile and the lack of formal structures allowed a more flexible and innovative approach. • A shift from a concept emphasising the reduction of regional disparities to a concept of structural policy (more dynamic stance) occurred at the end of the 1990s. • The new philosophy concentrates more strongly on promotion of the indigenous potential of regions by supporting comprehensive innovation, infrastructure, modernisation, internationalisation and applied R&D.	• Coherence with EU approach: ○ the consensus-orientated policy and the 'social partnership' form the basis to fulfil the partnership requirements ○ coherence in thematic focus exists due to the reorientation of Austrian economic and regional policy in the 1980s and 1990s ○ EU competition policy: As regional assistance is diverse but not overly significant in financial terms, relatively little change was required with regard to award rate maxima. • Distinctions in the philosophy behind: ○ the planning approach of EU versus Austria's more systemic approach to regional policy ○ concentration on problem regions versus regional problems ○ lack of tradition in programme appraisals in Austria.	• The awareness and importance of regional policy was heightened in general. • Substantially more money is available for regional policy: ○ additional EU money ○ additional budgets that had not been allocated under regional policy aspects up until now had to be considered to secure national co-financing; thus the regional focus of these measures has increased. • For the first time, legally-binding assisted area maps and award rate maxima had to be designated. • Improved co-ordination in the field of regional policy, both in a horizontal (between ministries) and vertical (between federal, *Land*, local level) direction, has been achieved. • For the implementation of the EU regional policy the consulting capacity at regional level was enlarged by the establishment of Regional Management offices at NUTS III level. • Austria is almost wholly covered by RDPs, which were elaborated by a strong bottom-up approach. • Besides 17 RDPs (at sub-regional level), 15 SPDs for Structural Funds objectives and 20 Programmes for Community Initiatives were elaborated. It is often doubtful whether the amount of administration connected with this justifies the available means.	• Improved co-ordination but no real innovative organisational approach was achieved. The expected chance of re-organisation of the Austrian economic promotion landscape and of changes in organisation of regional policy have not been achieved. • A future task will be the reduction of supporting instruments and a further shift from supporting individual firms to inter-firm co-operation and the business environment as a whole. • Does the increased deployment of money and the relatively rigid system of the Structural Funds framework lead to a step backwards in qualitative terms? • Can a target-orientated deployment of the Structural Funds money be guaranteed despite such a strong decentralisation in the decision for EU co-financing and such a great number of programmes? • How to use the now open access to European knowledge effectively for the endogenous development processes in Austria? • How to achieve an improved integration of EFRE and ESF measures? • The Austrian partnership as a model for the Commission?

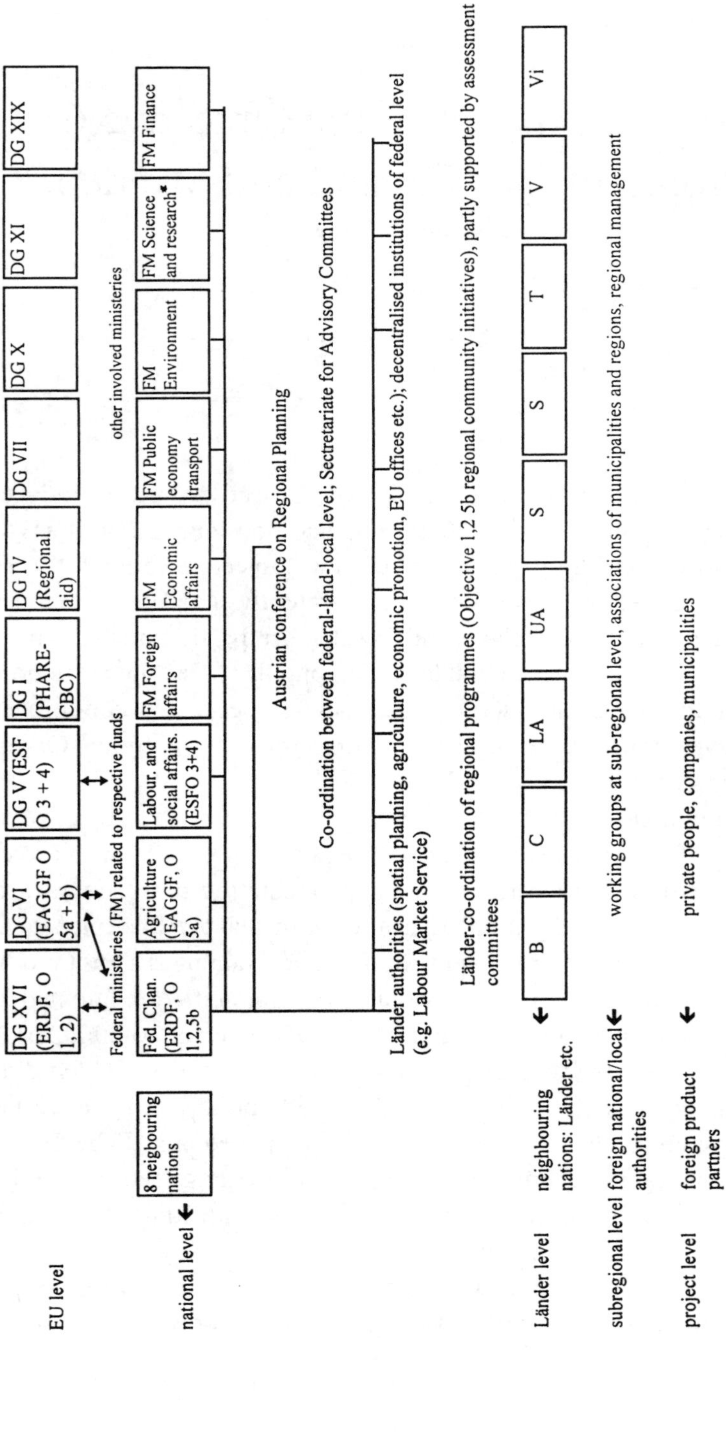

Source: Federal Chancellery, dept. IV/4 September 26th 1995

Figure 16.1 EU Structural Funds Programme in Austria: public authorities involved.

CHAPTER 17

Implementation of the Objective 6 Programme in Finland and Sweden

Mårten Johansson

Introduction

When Finland and Sweden joined the Union, Objective 6 was introduced as a new regional policy instrument to enhance development in areas with extremely low population density. The new Objective follows the same regulation as Objective 1 but is defined differently. The special features of the Objective 6 areas in Finland and Sweden are harsh climate, extremely low population density, peripheral location, long distances and small domestic markets for goods and services. In these respects, the conditions for regional development differ significantly from those in traditional Objective 1 or 5b areas.

The Commission approved the SPD for the Finnish Objective 6 in November 1995. As the management of the programme was not able to draw on earlier experience, the first year of implementation has been a learning process and a time for different parties to work out practical management procedures. The organisational context of the programme is a joint monitoring structure (one SPD and one Monitoring Committee) combined with regionalised implementation (eight separate management committees). The programming process was pushed through in a short period, which did not allow much time for designing new tailor-made policy measures to tackle the development problems of these sparsely populated areas. The European principle of partnership, however, brought new working methods which, in the long run, may bring together the different administrations at regional level to work towards common goals.

The future of a separate Objective 6 beyond the year 1999 is partly dependent on how strong a priority Sweden and Finland give to maintaining it and partly on how future EU policies will be structured. The Nordic Member States argue that the EU has to show solidarity with this northern periphery and its people, who had the most negative attitude toward membership in the referendum. Expenditure is rather low as there are few inhabitants and the risk of misusing the funds is minimal. There may also be an opportunity to enlarge the Objective 6 concept to include existing Objective 1 regions such as Scotland or Ireland, both having features in common with the Nordic Objective 6 area.

This chapter examines these issues in more detail. It reviews the context for regional development in Finland and the characteristics of the Objective 6 area, drawing comparisons with the situation in Sweden. It then discusses the content and implementation of the Objective 6 programme, again highlighting the differences with Sweden. Finally, the chapter assesses the implications of EU structural policies in Sweden, notably the coherence with, and lessons for, national regional policy.

Context

The accession of Finland and Sweden to the EU in 1995 significantly enlarged the territory and introduced a new type of sparsely populated large region. Nordic geographic conditions (harsh climate and long internal distances) in combination with extremely low population density create quite distinctive handicaps for regional development (OJ No C 364/06, 20.12.1994). Consequently these conditions were not included in the *aquis communitaire* for State aid or regional policy before negotiations on enlargement of the Union started.

The first adjustment of EU regional policy to Nordic regional conditions was made in the context of the European Economic Area. In June 1994 the Commission introduced low population density (below 12.5 persons per km^2) alongside low GDP and high unemployment as a third criterion in the method of assessing regional aid eligibility under Article 92.3(c) of the Treaty (changes to the method for the application of Article 92 (3) (c) of the EC Treaty to regional aid, 1 June 1994, OJ No C 364/06, 20.12.1994). Use of transport aid for compensating domestic transport costs in areas with low population density was recognised under some specific conditions.

Invention of a separate Objective 6 programme for the development of sparsely populated areas is, perhaps, the most notable adaptation of EU structural policies to the Nordic reality. The Finnish position in the membership negotiations in late 1993 was to have the most sparsely populated eastern and northern parts of the country eligible under Objective 1. The major part of these areas had a GDP per capita below 75 per cent of the Union average and unemployment was above 20 per cent. This claim was met with understanding from the regional policy Commissioner, Bruce Millan, who was also inclined to approve the same status for northern Norway. However, it was impossible for the Member States to accept Objective 1 status for the equivalent parts of northern Sweden due to the significantly higher levels of GDP per capita (close to the EU average). It could have led to further claims from other Member States to include new areas above the 75 per cent GDP ceiling into Objective 1.

The Member States and Sweden (Liikanen 1995) argued that all three Nordic applicants should be treated in the same manner, so the Council of Ministers invented a new Objective 6 tailor-made for the northern parts of Finland, Norway and Sweden. The new objective follows the regulation for Objective 1. The aid intensities (108 ecu per head in the Finnish Objective 6) are equal to the levels approved for Dutch, Belgian and French Objective 1 areas. The difference is only in the criteria for eligibility, that is areas with population density below eight persons per km2. This new Objective 6 was finally agreed and the allocations were included in the Accession Treaties of the new Member States. As Norway rejected the result of the negotiations in its referendum on November 28 1994, the new Objective 6 became a policy instrument for only two Member States.

Characteristics of Objective 6

The Finnish Objective 6 area covers 206,000 km^2 (61% of Finland's land area) and a population of 804,000 (16.6% of Finland's population). The area stretches over a 1000 km-long belt from sub-arctic northern Lapland along the eastern border to the lake district in the southern interior parts of Finland. The population density of the area is, on average, four persons per km2 and the biggest conurbations are Rovaniemi (56,000), Kemi (25,000), Tornio (24,000), Kajaani (36,000), Joensuu (50,000) and Mikkeli (44,000). The Swedish Objective 6 area is even more sparsely populated (two person/km2). Only two conurbations (Östersund and Kiruna) have more than 20,000 inhabitants.

Sparse population and a strong emphasis on agriculture and forestry distinguishes the Objective 6 area from the rest of Finland. Nearly 30 per cent of all Finnish farmers and over half of all cattle farmers live in the area. In several areas more than half of the total labour force earn their income from agriculture and forestry. The competitive position of agriculture is rather weak as the growing season is only 100–170 days (EU12: 200–300 days)

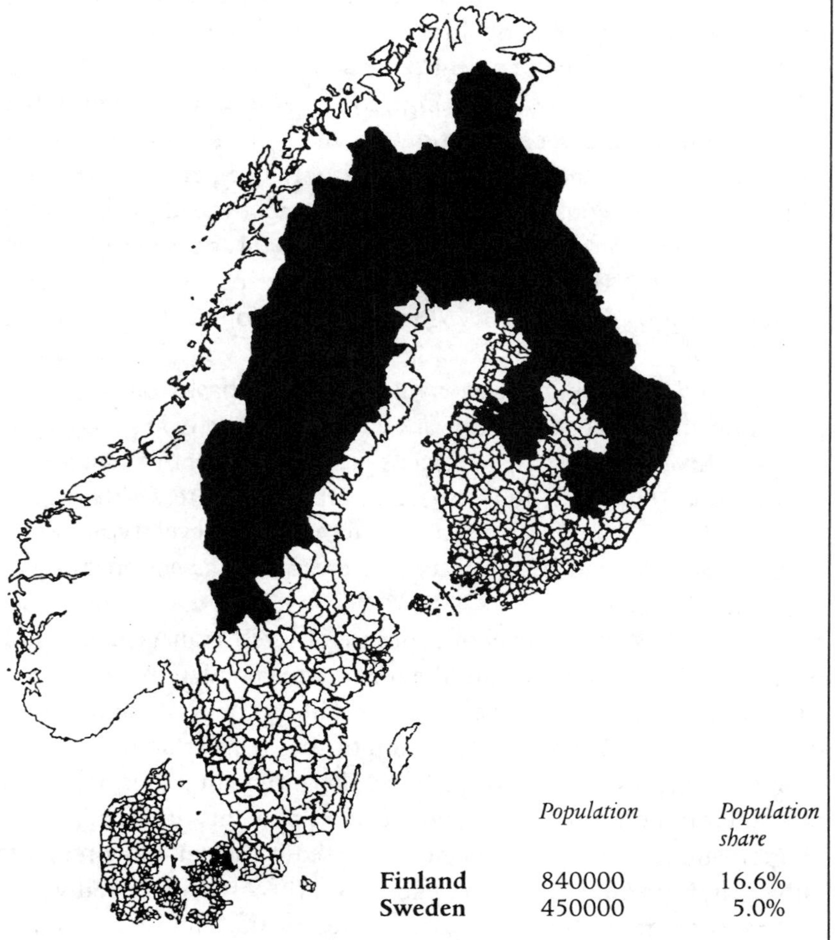

	Finland	*Sweden*
Total population (000)	5099	8816
Population of Objective 6 (000)	840	450
Population share	16.6%	5.0%
Total land area(000 km^2)	305	411
Land area of Objective 6 (000km^2)	206	272

Source: NOGRAN 1995

Figure 17.1 Objective 6 in Finland and Sweden (population and coverage)

and the average farm size is small. Long travel distances add substantially to the production costs of agriculture and the food industry.

The public sector employs 34 per cent of the work-force in the Finnish Objective 6 area. It has been a long-term creator of job opportunities and a stabiliser during the deep recession Finland went through in 1990–1994. The loss of jobs in the public sector was only five per cent over the period 1988–1993, while loss of jobs in manufacturing was 25 per cent. In 1994 the unemployment rate in the Objective 6 area was 24 per cent, compared to an average of 20 per cent for Finland and 11 per cent for the EU12.

According to the Objective 6 regional development plan, the region is over-dependent on agriculture, large corporations with limited new employment potential and a public sector vulnerable to cutbacks. Basic infrastructure, education and social and health care services are largely in good order. There are two universities in the area (Joensuu and Rovaniemi) and a good supply of vocational training. In that respect the Objective 6 areas differ significantly from the traditional Objective 1 areas but they share several common features with the Scottish and Irish Objective 1 areas, such as peripherality and low population density.

The area has a high level of expertise in forest management and the use of timber. Other strengths are the area's attractive landscape, proximity to Russian markets and long-established traditions of co-operation with Sweden, Norway and Russia. Exploitation of these opportunities, however, is a long-term process (much longer than the programme period) heavily dependent on political and economic developments in Russia. The most tangible infrastructure improvement planned is the completion of a missing railway link (Ledmozero to Kochkoma) on the Archanglsk railway, making the transport route from the Barents area to the Finnish harbours in the Bothnian Gulf 500km shorter.

Many of the constraints and thresholds of the Objective 6 area are permanent. The long distances can be overcome but there is always extra time to be spent travelling and extra costs in meeting colleagues and customers and getting products and services to consumers. As the domestic market is only five million people, exporting is the main way for most firms to grow. The Objective 6 area does not constitute a functional region with a single centre but cuts through eight administrative regions (*maakunta*). Several regional centres in northern and central Finland, such as Oulu, Jyväskylä and Kuopio, are not included in the eligible area. The area has no joint regional administration other than the joint Monitoring Committee for the Objective 6 programme.

Programme Content and Implementation

The overall objective of the programme is to stimulate new activity in order to create jobs. It comprises two main strategies: to develop business activity and improve the competitiveness of enterprise and to maintain acceptable living conditions in remote areas whilst taking into account the impact of EU membership and macro-economic adjustments taking place in the Finnish economy. More specifically, the objective is formulated in terms of four measurable targets:

- annual reduction of unemployment by 2.1 per cent and 8000 unemployed (the unemployment rate in 1994 was 3.8%, i.e. 90,600 unemployed people)
- increase the number of jobs in private services and manufacturing by 17,500 from 117,500 to 135,000 (the reference level is for 1992)
- narrow the gap between GDP per capita in the area and the national average by five percentage points
- increase the number of jobs for women and young people.

The new jobs are expected to come from diversification of the economy within small local businesses based on the natural resources of the region and private services. Established industrial clusters that have potential for growth and exploitation of the re-emerging business opportunities with Russia are also expected to generate new jobs. The aim of the plan was to reduce unemployment by 10,000 by creating 17,500 new jobs. How this would be feasible without significant out-migration was not explained in the programme. The prior appraisal of the regional development plan of the Objective 6 regions in Finland, undertaken by the Nordland Research Institute in Bødø, Norway in 1995, stated that it was dangerous to ignore the resources available in large firms and to overestimate the potential for employment growth within smaller firms.

The total estimated costs of the programme amount to 1326.1 million ecu (mecu), of which 991.2 mecu is public and 334.9 mecu is private funding. EU funding comprises 459.9 mecu (ERDF 37.5%, ESF 23%, EAGGF 38.6% and FIFG 0.9%). The Structural Fund resources are concentrated on three priorities: business development and company competitiveness – 33 per cent of EU spending; development of human resources and expertise – 19 per cent; agriculture, forestry, fishing, rural development and the environment – 46 per cent.

One might have expected that a stronger focus would have been given to measures aimed at reducing the effects of long distances, such as information technology, and measures providing social services in sparsely populated areas. There are three measures promoting information network services, expertise and human resources for development of an information culture but they have only five per cent of total public spending. Agricultural adjustment and business development get more emphasis. Investment in road infrastructure is totally excluded from the programme.

Implementation of the Funds

The organisational context of the programme is a joint monitoring structure (one Monitoring Committee) combined with regionalised implementation. The regional dimension indicates that the planning process is carried out bottom-up. The eight regions drew up their own regional plans which were processed further in partnership with the relevant ministries to one SPD for the whole area. The regional plans were submitted to the Commission as appendices to the national plan. Estimates of expenditure are given in the SPD broken down by individual region at the level of priorities and funds (see Table 17.1).

The regional dimension means that the selection of projects and decisions on funding are taken by authorities at regional level, even in cases when ministries take the formal decisions on funding at central level. This means that every region makes its choice from the *à la carte* menu consisting of 26 measures, in the context of the restrictions set in the indicative financial table.

The national perspective means that the same authorities that are taking decisions on national public co-funding also take the formal decisions on EU funding. As more than 90 per cent of the public co-funding comes from the State budget, the ministries have maintained their role in the implementation of the Objective 6 programme as in all the other EU programmes. The difference from purely national regional policy (i.e. without EU co-funding) is that implementation is carried out in close co-operation between several national and regional partners according to jointly agreed targets.

The national and regional perspectives meet in the Monitoring Committee. It consists of two members from each region and representatives from ministries and the Commission (31 members in all). It is chaired by the lead ministry (Ministry of the Interior) and its operations are prepared by officials from the different ministries responsible for the Structural Funds. Every region has its own management structure, composed of State district authorities, social partners and municipalities, with the regional council as the lead

Table 17.1 EU resources and population by region

			EU funding (1995–1999)			
Sub-region	*Population in eligible areas (000)*	*Total public funding*	*in mecu*	*by priority as share of EU funding (%) Priority:*		
				1	*2*	*3*
Etelä-Savo	176	202.5	94.2	35	20	45
Pohjois-Karjala	178	206.3	95.3	33	19	47
Kainuu	96	108.6	51.6	39	22	38
Lappi	203	223.8	108.6	43	25	32
Pohjois-Savo	25	30.3	13.2	21	12	67
Keski-Suomi	39	48.6	21.3	23	13	65
Keski-Pohjanmaa	20	26.5	10.8	6	4	91
Pohjois-Pohjanmaa	104	126.1	55.7	24	14	62
Objective 6 total*	**841**	**972.7**	**450.7**	**34**	**20**	**46**

Priority 1: Business development and company competitiveness.
Priority 2: Development of human resources and expertise.
Priority 3: Agriculture, forestry, fisheries, rural development and the environment.
* excluding 9.2 mecu technical

Source: SPD for Finnish Objective 6 area 1995–99

organisation. Two committees supervise the management of the SPD in each region: a regional management committee and a working group on business aid. The management committee works under the auspices of the regional councils and the working group on business aid under the auspices of the Ministry of Trade and Industry district office.

The regional management committee gives guidance on how the programme should be implemented in the region, follows up on operations and gives opinions on aid decisions. Some regions, such as Lapland, have established a working party to prepare decisions for the management committee. The management committee is the regional partnership and has between 21 and 60 members. The Lappish committee is the smallest. It meets four or five times per year and its working party roughly every six weeks. Individual project applications for business aid are assessed by the working group on business aid and are rarely reviewed by the management committee. Confidential treatment of business information has been the main argument for handling business aid applications in a separate group. The members of this group are mostly members of the management committee as well. Core organisations are the district offices of the Ministry of Trade and Industry,

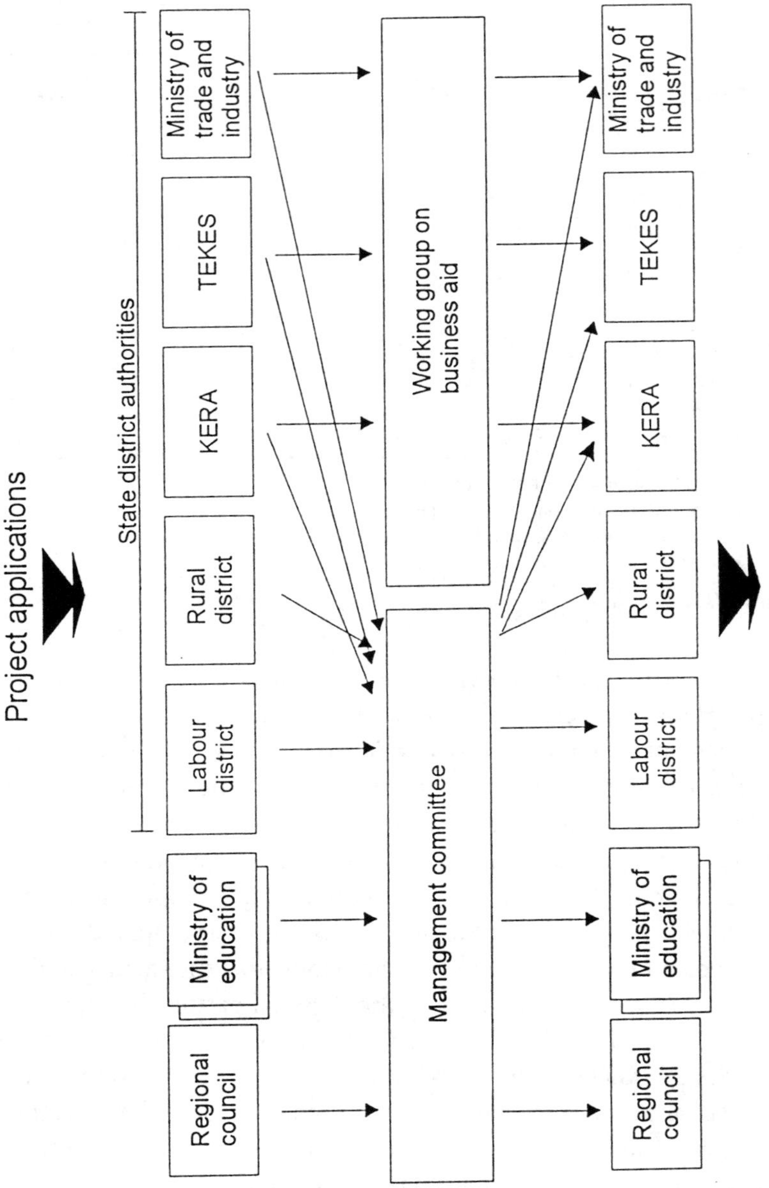

Source: Nogran 1996

Figure 17.2 Decision making process in Finnish Objective 6 regions

TEKES (Technology Development Centre), KERA Ltd (development bank), Ministry of Agriculture, Ministry of Labour, the regional council and the Finnish Foreign Trade Association (FFTA).

Individual applicants submit their project plans to the district office (State authority) responsible for public national co-funding or to the regional council. Applications can also be submitted directly to the Ministry of Education, which does not have any district organisation. Assessment of the application according to eligibility criteria and the regional strategy is made by the same authority that formally approves national co-funding. As a subsequent step, the co-funding authority asks the management committee for its opinion on the project. In the case of aid to individual firms, the application is reviewed by the working group on business aid.

If the management committee/working group approves the proposal, the co-funding authority can take a formal decision to grant the project. If the committee/working group rejects the proposal, the co-funding partner cannot grant EU funding but can still consider whether or not to support it from national sources. The co-funding authority then takes a two-fold decision, on EU-funding and on national aid. The whole process from submission of an application to decision generally takes no longer than two months.

All Objective 6 regions have ongoing application processes with no fixed deadlines. In some regions, such as Lapland, similar training projects are gathered and reviewed jointly some three or four times per year. The ongoing application process means, in practice, that those actors (universities, educational institutes) producing good plans with spending committed over several years at the beginning of the plan period secure a significant share of the allocation at an early stage.

Budgeting

The use of funds is an ongoing dialogue between regional ambitions and initiatives on the one hand and the national budgeting system on the other. Every region has an indicative financial framework responding to the regional strategy approved annually at priority level by the Monitoring Committee. Some 90–95 per cent of all EU funds are allocated to seven or eight ministries according to the national plan and use of national public co-funding. EU funds are distributed annually between ministries in a slightly different way. The ERDF allocation is distributed between ministries at priority level and the ESF at measure level. Matching national funds were in the State budget of 1995, allocated to 33 different budget lines managed by eight different ministries.

Differences between Finnish and Swedish Objective 6

The Swedish model differs significantly from Finland in several respects. First, there is a difference in terms of programme content. Agriculture is less important in the Swedish area: only 59,200 Least Favourable Areas (LFA) have eligible cattle units against 255,000 in Finland and only 16,600 hectares of arable land against 340,000 hectares in Finland. Consequently, expenditure on aid to LFA takes only a small share (11%) of total public expenditure in Sweden but nearly one-third (31%) of public expenditure in the Finnish programme area.

Business development schemes are also less significant in the Swedish programme, restricted to joint development actions (a minimum of two companies) and small aid packages (below the EU *de minimis* ceilings), while a significant share of the Finnish programme is development and investment aid to individual firms up to approved aid ceilings. There are several Swedish measures targeted at specific industries (tourism, food processing, wood processing, mining and mineral industry), while the Finnish programme (with the exception of agriculture, fisheries and forestry) is neutral in relation to sectoral support.

Sweden has a specific priority with public spending of 15.1 mecu (3%) for the development of Sami culture and reindeer husbandry. The Swedish programme is more focused on labour-force-related measures (24% of EU funding) than in Finland (14%). Surprisingly, enterprises are the main group of final beneficiaries in the Swedish programme, despite the reluctance to include development measures targeted at single firms. Finally, local development measures are a stronger focus in the Finnish programme than in Sweden (Aalbu, Sommerseth and Pedersen 1996).

The second set of differences concerns implementation – the management structure of EU funds in Finland is completely different from Sweden. While decisions in Finland are taken by the same national authorities which provide the national public co-funding, decisions in Sweden are taken by a separate body. A Swedish applicant has to find national public co-funding from relevant sources, whereafter the application for EU funding is submitted to a county management committee (one in each of the seven counties). Some 60 per cent of all EU funds, including Objective 3 and 4 type measures, are managed this way.

Projects in the field of R&D, tourism and IT are reviewed by a separate regional management committee for the whole area (roughly 20% of the funding). Decision making on EU funds for the Sami priority (3%) is delegated to the Assembly of Sami People (*Sametinget*); the national public co-funding is also given as a lump sum allocation to be distributed by the Sami Assembly. EU funding for Objective 5a type agricultural measures (14%) are managed through the National Board of Agriculture *(Jordbruksverket)* and fisheries measures (2%) by the National Board of Fisheries *(Fiskeriverket)*.

The seven county management committees have between five and thirteen members, of which a majority represents the elected regional and local administration (county council, municipalities). The secretariat is held by the State county administration. The regional management committee has 16 members, with a clear majority of representatives from municipalities and county councils. Its administration is located at the State county administration of Jämtland. In Sweden the State county administration is responsible for co-ordination of most national development measures, including business aid. The secretariat for EU funds is, therefore, in most cases, the same body that grants the national co-funding of the projects. While all funds in the Finnish model are allocated to sub-regions, the Swedish model allows, at least in theory, some competition between projects from the whole area. In practice, the competition element is significantly smaller than 20 per cent of all funds due to the fact that two big projects were already agreed in the SPD.

Sweden has given the elected local and regional administrations a strong position (majority) in the decision making on EU funds, while more than 95 per cent of decisions on EU funds in the Finnish system are taken by district authorities of State administration.

Third, the Swedish budgeting system is much simpler than the rigid Finnish approach. There are only two specific budget lines for co-funding the Objective 6 programme in the Swedish state budget, one for the agricultural and fisheries measures and one for the Sami measures. All relevant budget lines in the Swedish state budget (as well as funding from municipalities and county councils) can be used as national public co-funding, while all potential budget lines (some 30 in 1995 budget) providing national co-funding are specified according to fund and amount in the Finnish State budget.

The advantage (Aalbu, Sommerseth and Pedersen 1996) of the Finnish model is that all co-funding partners know in advance their financial responsibility and can contribute to the realisation of the programme. The disadvantage is that budget planning is extremely rigid. It has also proved to be difficult to find national co-funding for activities which are not on the State budget. By contrast, the Swedish model contains huge flexibility and simple budgeting procedures. There is no need to identify allocations for national co-funding before projects are approved. The main disadvantage is that the identification of need for the allocation of funds is significantly slower than in the Finnish system and the need for reallocation of funds is predicted to be bigger (Aalbu, Sommerseth and Pedersen 1996).

Implications for Finnish Regional Development Policies and Institutions

Finland revised its national regional policies at the beginning of 1994. One objective was to establish greater coherence between national regional policy and EU procedures. The revision brought in partnership and programming as new working methods. The co-ordination of regional policy in the regions was moved from the State province administrations (12) to joint municipal boards, called regional councils (18). Six sets of objective programmes were launched, of which two were designated for the traditional support areas: programmes for development areas (model Objective 1 areas) and structural change areas (model Objective 2). A third set of programmes was targeted at rural areas (model Objective 5b) and a fourth at lake districts and the archipelago. These programme targets are familiar from earlier legislation. Two new sets of programmes were added to the policy arsenal, for centres of expertise and for border regions. The new objectives did not, however, add any new budget lines or support measures to the policy arsenal.

Regional development programmes were not an innovation as such. Such programmes had been carried out for decades by the provincial State offices. The new element was the partnership and the new lead organisation. The programmes were to be worked out in partnership between State district authorities (Ministry of Trade and Industry, Ministry of Labour, Ministry of Agriculture) under the lead of a joint municipal board (the regional council). The ambition from the very beginning was to create programme commitments where partners would sign binding agreements on the funding of concrete measures/projects, similar to a letter of intent.

The regional councils received 10 mecu in 1994 and 19 mecu in 1995 from the State budget to strengthen their negotiating position with the State district authorities and to part-finance their own projects. To ease the implementation of regional development programmes the Government has earmarked a number of budget-lines in the national budgets since 1994, intended to be used mainly for the financing of regional programmes. These allocations from the field of administration of the Trade and Industry, Transport, Labour and Agriculture Ministries amount to some 700–900 mecu.

Nevertheless, the ambition to agree on binding co-operation agreements proved difficult to put into practice. By the start of May 1995 only 7 of the 19 regional councils had signed some form of co-operation agreement with one or more State district authorities. The reasons are several. First, the different ministries were not willing to regionalise their budget allocations according to other than their own priorities. Second, the regional councils have very limited budgetary resources. Third, 1994–1995 was a transitional period with new players and working methods. The regional councils gradually took over the leadership for regional development co-ordination from the provincial State offices during 1994. Some of the regional councils only recruited key staff in 1995. The negotiations for EU membership in early 1994 totally overran the interest in the new programme-based national regional policy. All the partners, as well as the regional councils and Ministries, were busy finding out how they could use the Structural Funds to enlarge their power bases.

EU Programmes as a Door-Opener for Regional Programming

While the revision of the national regional policy from the beginning of 1994 was planned as an introduction to the EU way of working in partnership and with committed programmes, the reality seems to have worked the other way around. The Commission has urged different State authorities to set common objectives, agree on priorities and measures, and implement the programmes in partnership within strict deadlines.

The regional programme produced during Autumn 1994 turned out to be the basis for the planning of EU regional programmes (Objective 2, 5b, 6 and INTERREG). The working methods agreed in the framework of the EU programmes should have been applied to purely national funded policies as well. However, it is questionable whether there is a scope for any other regional policy than the national implementation and co-financing of EU programmes, for several reasons.

First, it is difficult to get different authorities to commit themselves to joint strategies and decision making voluntarily. Only the extra resources from the Structural Funds and the negotiation power of the Commission has made this possible.

Second, a large share of national regional policy measures and many other budget-lines are used as co-funding of EU programmes. In 1996 some 36 per cent of the main regional policy incentives (investment and development grants) totalling 80 mecu is national co-funding of ERDF. Only two minor incentives, transport aid (8.4 mecu) and tax relief for development areas (valued at 10 mecu), are left outside the EU programmes.

Third, of the six regional policy programmes introduced in 1994, only the one for centres of expertise has maintained transparency and avoided being integrated into the EU programmes. Its future financing beyond 1996 is uncertain.

Fourth, from a regional point of view, more than 90 per cent of the regional council's available resources in the Objective 6 area are tied up as co-funding of EU programmes. As the main part of all development officers' work involves implementation of the regional programme, there are few funds or human resources available for other policy efforts. From an Objective 6 perspective, the coherence between EU programming and national policy seems to be almost complete. The coherence between national regional policy and EU programmes is weaker in southern Finland, where the coverage of Objective 2 and 5b is smaller. The regional councils in these areas (Tampere region, Helsinki area) are, however, actively using other EU measures (pilot projects) to promote regional development in their areas.

Finally, at ministerial level, EU programming and implementation engage a great deal of operational staff, so other planning efforts play a secondary role.

Conclusions

Finland's membership of the EU has strengthened the role of the Ministry of the Interior as the lead ministry for co-ordination of regional policy, co-ordinating Objectives 2, 5b and 6, INTERREG and the ERDF, while the management of funds/incentives mainly lies with other ministries. The concept of regional policy, that is the content of EU programmes, has been broadened in terms of incentives and activity from some three or four ministries to eight. However, the balance of power between ministries and central and regional levels is still settling down. The aim of the regional councils in the programming of Objective 2, 5b and 6 was to get a large share of funds as a global grant managed by themselves. The ministries, with the Ministry of Trade and Industry to the fore, opposed this view. The Commission introduced a rural development grants package of measures to be managed by the regional councils. Until recently, even these local development measures were channelled through the State district authorities.

Even though the ministries have managed to maintain their influence, the new partnership, with roots in the 1980s, has led to a better co-ordination of development actions in the regions. The different district authorities are more aware of potential development activities going on. They are able to avoid duplication of resources and they seem to be committed to achieve the targets jointly set in the planning documents.

Is there a rationale to maintain Objective 6 as a separate EU objective or should the needs in these areas be met in a different way, for instance by including it in Objective 5b? The rationale for maintaining Objective 6 can be discussed both from a political and an analytical point of view. From a political perspective, Objective 6 was introduced as a result of the membership negotiations. This can be seen as a parallel to the invention of Objective 1 when Spain and Portugal joined the Union. Objective 6 covers the northernmost corner of the Union territory, with a long border with Russia. Its population voted strongly against membership in the referenda in autumn 1994, and Objective 6 could be seen as a confidence-building measure. If Finland and Sweden consider Objective 6 as crucial, it is likely to survive the next reform of the structural policies.

From an analytical point of view, the Objective 6 area has several geographical obstacles that cannot be overcome through the development of infrastructure: the long external and internal distances, harsh climate and small domestic markets. These specificities have been recognised by the Commission and operationalised in the *aquis communautaire* as low population density. Some of the Objective 1 areas, such as the Scottish Highlands and Islands and Ireland, share several of these features. They are on the periphery of the Union territory, have good physical infrastructure and rather low population density. They differ at least in one respect. They have a large native-speaking market of some 50 million people within convenient reach. As similarities between the Nordic Objective 6 and some Objective 1 areas exist, the latter may see Objective 6 as a realistic alternative if their Objective 1 status is threatened.

PART FOUR

Lessons and Challenges

CHAPTER 18

Development Programming, Negotiation and Evaluation

Lessons for the Future

Conor Kearney

Introduction

The two preceding sections of this volume have examined the coherence of the Structural Funds mainly from the perspective of *researchers* analysing the implementation of EU Structural Policies across a range of UK regions as well as the experiences of other EU Member States, focusing in particular on Germany, the Netherlands, Austria and Finland. This final part of the book turns to the viewpoints of *policymakers*, with a series of four contributions from current or former government officials from the European Commission, Department of Trade and Industry (UK), Federal Ministry of Economics (Germany) and DATAR – Delegation for Spatial Management and Territorial Action (France). In each case the chapter authors draw on their experience of working with the preparation, negotiation, implementation, monitoring and evaluation of EU structural programmes.

In introducing the 'policy perspectives' section, this chapter considers the processes of development programming, negotiation and evaluation from the standpoint of a former Commission official working in the Evaluation Unit of the Directorate-General for Regional Policy and Cohesion (DG XVI). It begins by rehearsing some of the issues presented in Chapter 2 with respect to the changing policy context of EU structural policies – a necessary reference point in developing an adequate appreciation of the policies and their implementation. The chapter then describes the practical experiences of programming, negotiation, monitoring and evaluation and concludes with a discussion of the principal lessons learned.

The Recent Context

The regulations which are the basis of the EU's authority and activities are defined by a complex process in which the governments of the EU's individual Member States, acting in the Council of Ministers, are by far the dominant influence. Amongst other things, these regulations specify the responsibilities which the Commission and the various Member State authorities must meet in the allocation and expenditure of the assistance for promoting social and economic cohesion provided under the EU's structural policies.

After the adoption of the Single European Act in 1986 it was generally recognised that the establishment of a single market would put increased pressure on economic and social cohesion. In response, a first reform of the Structural Funds was implemented in 1988. The clearest and most complete statement of the rationale for this reform is that provided in Padoa-Schioppa (1987). This reform entailed the doubling of the Funds' resources between 1987 and 1993 (both in absolute terms and in relation to the Community budget as a whole). It also authorised the Commission to launch Community Initiatives as a further means of promoting structural development. Finally, four principles (concentration, programming, additionality and partnership) were introduced, which have fundamentally shaped the subsequent development of the structural policies and which are discussed in more detail below.

In 1992 the Treaty of Union set a range of new objectives for both the Member States and the European institutions. Perhaps the most significant of these was the establishment of a three-stage timetable for the achievement of economic and monetary union (Articles 102 – 109). Just as the polarising effects of the transition towards a Single Market had been balanced by the first reform of the Structural Funds, the potential for social and economic polarisation which was inherent in the transition towards EMU was balanced by a number of actions. These actions included: the establishment of a Cohesion Fund; the ratification of the Treaty's Social Chapter (Article 130) by all of the Member States except the United Kingdom; an increase in the budget for the structural policies to over 141 becu (1992 prices) for the period 1994–1999 (this amount excludes the budget for the new Cohesion Fund and the Community Initiatives); and a further revision of the regulations which govern the administration and use of the Structural Funds (last revised in 1988).

The Principles

Channelling a large amount of public expenditure through a variety of multi-national, national and regional institutions to meet identified needs in an effective manner is a complex process. It might be best to describe how this process has evolved by referring to the four principles for the reform of the Funds which were mentioned above.

The principle of *concentration* has been pursued by targeting the Structural Funds on specific global Objectives. Objective 1 was to promote the structural adjustment of those regions where development was lagging behind the Community average and, in practice, went to those Member States or regions where GDP per capita was below a specified level. Objective 2 was the conversion of regions seriously affected by industrial decline and, in practice, these regions tended to be smaller areas of high unemployment. Objectives 3 and 4 were not spatially targeted but focused instead on specific population groups: the long-term unemployed and unemployed young people respectively. Objective 5 was split into two components, only one of which was spatially targeted; Objective 5a was to assist the general adjustment of agricultural structures while Objective 5b was the development of specific rural areas.

After the 1993 reforms Objectives 1 and 2 remained unchanged, the old Objectives 3 and 4 were combined as Objective 3 and a new Objective 4 was introduced 'to facilitate the adaptation of workers...to industrial change and to changes in production systems in particular' (Council Regulation 2084/93, article 1§2). Objective 5 remained essentially the same but with a new, explicit reference to the needs of fisheries. A new Objective 6 was established later, on the accession of Sweden and Finland to the Union, to promote employment and development in areas of extremely low population density. Finally, the Funds were concentrated between the various Objectives with almost 70 per cent going to the pursuit of Objective 1. It should be borne in mind that the definition of the Objectives themselves, the selection of those regions or Member States which are to be eligible for assistance under each of the Objectives and the broad allocation of resources between both the various Objectives and the Member States is decided for each programming period by a process in which governments of the Member States are once again the dominant influence.

The 1988 reforms had identified *partnership* as involving officials from both the Commission and from the national, regional or local administrations (the latter being chosen by the relevant Member State) in all stages of the programming of the Structural Funds. The 1993 reform extended this principle to cover other 'competent authorities and bodies' as designated by the Member State concerned. In practice, partnership is, perhaps, most evident in the constitution of the Monitoring Committees, which manage the use of the Structural Funds allocated to each Objective in each region (or in each Member State in the case of the non-regional Objectives and the many Objective 1 programmes which cover entire national territories).

Until the principle of *programming* was adopted in the 1988 reforms, assistance had, in most instances, been provided to discrete projects. Under the reformed regulations, the intended use of the Funds over a multi-annual period had to be set out in formal documents for each region receiving assistance under the spatially targeted Objectives and for each Member State under the other Objectives. For all Objectives, except Objective 2, the original programming period was five years (1989–1993); in view of the perceived potential for quicker change in relation to industrial conversion, Objective 2 programmes covered the periods 1989–1991 and 1992–1993. The 1993 reforms specified a new six-year programming period (1994–1999), again except for Objective 2 – for which the period was split into two three-year phases, although the second phase of Objective 2 programming has proven to be largely a continuation of the approaches adopted in the first phase.

Finally, the principle of *additionality* was introduced by the 1988 reform in an effort to ensure that assistance from the Structural Funds was not simply used to replace national public expenditure which would have been made in the absence of assistance from the EU. Observance of the principle of additionality is notoriously difficult to confirm in practice since such confirmation depends on establishing what might have happened if support from the Structural Funds had not been available. In some instances the approaches adopted in various Member States have clearly not respected this principle and the Commission has been obliged to respond accordingly (e.g. by blocking payments) but in many cases it is virtually impossible to judge the precise extent to which Structural Funds assistance is genuinely additional. An effort was made in the 1993 reforms to make the requirements regarding additionality more explicit and detailed but arguably less demanding (Council Regulation 2082/93, article 9); whether this re-formulation will in fact promote more rigorous observation of the principle remains to be seen.

The Practice

Programming

Application of the four principles of the Structural Policies should result in measures with specific, concentrated objectives being combined and implemented through coherent, multi-annual programmes which are negotiated and implemented in partnership and clearly additional to pre-existing efforts. Just as the principles and objectives of the EU's structural policies have been shaped by the successive reforms of the relevant regulations, so too has the process of design and approval of these programmes.

For the 1989–1993 programming period, development plans were first presented by each Member State for each Objective or for each eligible region under the spatially targeted Objectives. On the basis of each development plan, groups of officials from the Commission and the relevant Member State then negotiated a Community Support Framework (CSF) which included financial information in addition to a description of the regional conditions and policy responses. Based on the CSF, the Member State concerned then made applications for individual forms of assistance – most frequently operational programmes.

Following the reform of the regulations in 1993, the Member State authorities were required to include more detailed information in their development plans for the 1994–1999 or 1994–1996 programming periods. The new requirements for programme content and design are set out most clearly in Articles 8§4, 9§8 and 11a§5 of Council Regulation 2081/93 and Article 8 of Regulation 2082/93, which stipulate that each document should contain:

- a description of the current situation and the scale and main results of any previous development efforts supported by the Structural Funds in the region
- a description of a development strategy formulated in response to this situation, related to the overall Objectives of the Funds and specifying more detailed priorities and objectives (quantified where possible)
- a prior appraisal of the expected impact of the operations described, including impact on employment and the environment
- an indicative overall table summarising both national and Structural Fund resources by development priority and an indication of the planned use of these and any other EU funds in implementing the plan.

These requirements emerged from negotiations in the Council of Ministers and reflect a desire to improve the management of the increasingly substantial amount of EU resources devoted to the structural policies. Improved management was sought in order to enhance the effectiveness of the programmes both in respect of the benefits each programme would bring to the region concerned and in respect of the overall positive impact of the policies on the cohesion of the Union. To balance the requirements for the development plans to contain more detailed information, the procedure was also simplified by allowing Member States to submit the development plan and all related applications for assistance simultaneously to the Commission as the basis for negotiation of a single programming document.

The timetable for the delivery of the development plans to the Commission by the Member States was also specified in the regulations. The responsible Commission services were given six months from the date of delivery of the plans in which to check each of them and verify that they: met the regulatory requirements summarised above; they provided for appraisal, monitoring and eventual *ex post* evaluation of the actions proposed; and, the actions which they proposed were compatible with wider Union policies relating to such subjects as competition and equal opportunities. Moreover, the Commission services were obliged to examine each of the applications for forms of assistance contained within each development plan to ensure that: they too conformed with Union policy: contributed to the overall strategy of the relevant plan and the achievement of its specific objectives: and their constituent measures were coherent (Council Regulation 2082, Article 14§3).

The regulations referred to above were agreed in late July 1993. The Objective 1 plans were expected to be submitted within three months of this agreement and the plans for Objectives 2 and 5b three months after the lists of areas eligible for assistance under these Objectives were finally agreed (in the case of Objective 2 the list was officially adopted in late January 1994). The outcome of this process is summarised in Table 18.1.

Table 18.1 Programme documents under Objectives 1, 2 and 5b

Type of programme	*Number of programme documents*	*Number of Member States*	*Amount of SFs: (billion ecu)*
Objective 1:	42	10	102
Objective 2:	70	9	16.2
Objective 5b:	69	9	6.7

Source: European Commission

These figures refer only to the twelve Member States which made up the Union at the start of the 1994–1999 programming period; all increased when Austria, Finland and Sweden subsequently joined the Union. It should also be noted that in some instances under Objectives 2 and 5b, a Single Programming Document covered a number of separate regions. In the course of less than one year, 181 development plans were received for the geographically targeted Objectives alone and these plans provided information on activity which was to receive almost 125 becu of assistance over six years. In some exceptional cases individual documents ran to over 1000 pages, although the length of a document was not necessarily proportionate to the adequacy of its response to the requirements of the regulations.

Negotiation

Even if we ignore the time and resources which had to be devoted to those aspects of the structural policies which are not targeted geographically, it is obvious that the preparation of development plans and negotiation of programmes under Objectives 1, 2 and 5b was itself a substantial task. It was also a task which was carried out under the double time pressures of the calendar set out in the regulations on the one hand and, on the other hand, the fact that this programming period actually started at the beginning of 1994 and absorption of the allocations was expected to commence as soon as possible after that date. In this situation the negotiations tended to focus on ensuring that three key elements were present in each submission:

- all necessary administrative and financial information
- sufficient information on the substance of the strategies proposed – particularly in terms of clear descriptions of the specific activities to be assisted, the projections of impact likely to be achieved and the specification of baseline values for key indicators to be used in the monitoring and evaluation of the programmes
- a distinctive and coherent overall strategy which responded clearly to identified local needs.

Each of the plans was evaluated by external experts and, on the basis of both the reports of these experts and the relevant Commission services' own readings of the documents, a series of negotiation meetings took place between Commission, national and regional officials before agreed programming documents were submitted to, and approved by, the Commission. The programming documents which emerged from these negotiations were expected to contain much of the information which should have been included in the original plans as well as covering 'the progress to be achieved during the period concerned compared to the current situation' (2081/93 articles 8§5, 9§9 and 11a§6). There was also an ambition that the coherence of all elements within each programme should not only allow each element to be fully effective but also enhance the overall level of effectiveness of the programme by promoting synergy (the effect of the overall impact of a programme being more than the sum of the impacts of its constitutive elements).

Two further practical considerations deserve mention at this point. First, the regulations governing the Structural Funds are quite complex and were relatively novel when the negotiations of the programming documents took place – officials in both the Commission and the Member States had to come to terms with new 'rules of the game' as well as maintaining an awareness of the changing and complicated situations in the regions. Second, the human resources available for carrying out this work were limited in terms of numbers, experience and expertise. In the Commission, for example, many of the officials involved in negotiating technically quite demanding programmes were able to call neither on directly relevant experience or on immediate support. Similarly, not all Member State officials shared either a uniform understanding of, or degree of commitment to, EU policy – as may be evident from a comparative reading of other chapters of this book.

Such practical constraints further complicated the already complex and sensitive process of negotiation between representatives of Member States and the Commission. The programming documents for the delivery of the Union's structural policies were developed in partnership, but in a partnership which worked under considerable pressure. On one side, Member State officials were naturally concerned to ease the almost universal restrictions on national public expenditure allocations to existing policy commitments. On the other side, Commission officials were trying to respect ambitious deadlines for the agreement of programmes which met demanding (and sometimes less than completely clear) requirements. They were also aware of the need to maintain and develop working relations with their partners in the national and regional administrations – partners who, in many ways, were closer to the realities of the regions and who were expected to play a vital role in the eventual implementation of the programmes.

Moreover, it should be acknowledged that there was not always a completely coherent set of views expressed on individual programmes, either among the Commission officials involved in these negotiations or among their counterparts from the regions and Member States. On the Member State side, differences in priorities and preferences would occasionally emerge between representatives from the regional and national levels or between representatives of different government departments. On the Commission side, different services with different responsibilities also occasionally expressed different preferences and priorities. Since the Commission is a relatively young and open institution, with a less well-established hierarchy of authority than is the case in Member State administrations, internal differences may have been more evident on the Commission side during the negotiations.

In spite of the difficulties listed above, there appears to be a general agreement among Commission officials that the programmes finally agreed for the period starting in 1994 contain more detailed and relevant information than those used for the previous programming period. However, it is also likely that most participants in the negotiation process would acknowledge that, in more propitious circumstances (e.g. had time been available to both provide and respond to a detailed and clear set of requirements for each document), the negotiation process could have been still more useful and the substance of the programmes might have been refined in ways that would promise a better ultimate impact (e.g. by including more precise information on the key characteristics of the regions covered and the activities being implemented in an effort to improve them).

Monitoring and evaluation

The outline of recent patterns of evaluation of European structural policies which follows is, like the outlines of programming and negotiation given above, very brief. Further details are contained in the report of the MEANS pilot programme (CEOPS/European Commission 1993) and in the output of the current MEANS programme (to which further reference is made below). A concise but reasonably detailed overview of relevant developments is provided by Bachtler and Michie (1995).

Before examining the practice of evaluation in the management of the EU's structural policies, it is important to distinguish between the need for programmes to meet conditions with regard to additionality and financial management on the one hand and with regard to their design and delivery on the other. The practice of ensuring that financial conditions are met and regulations observed in the management of the Structural Funds is generally referred to as 'control'. Assessing and providing judgements and feedback on the design, delivery and impact of each programme has been known as 'evaluation'. Both practices rely, to a large extent, on data provided by monitoring. The distinction between these activities is made for both methodological and practical reasons.

With regard to control, and contrary to the impression that is sometimes given in the media, the EU has devoted quite formidable resources to the task of ensuring that expenditure is legitimate. A specific European institution, the Court of Auditors, is complemented within the Commission by a Financial Control service – DGXX – while other services of the Commission (most notably Competition – DG IV – but also, if to a lesser extent, Economic and Financial Policy – DG II) have a natural inclination and considerable scope to encourage parsimony.

Monitoring is the responsibility of the Monitoring Committees which oversee each programme. In practice, monitoring has ranged from supplementing information on the actual expenditure of a programme with minimal information on the consequences of that expenditure to sophisticated systems which make later payments conditional on managers providing detailed information on the outputs which have actually been achieved from preceding payments.

Evaluation is best considered in relation to the point in the programming period at which it is carried out. In the process of designing and agreeing programmes, prior appraisals of individual measures and *ex ante* evaluations of each programme take place. Given the technical difficulty of making accurate prior appraisals and the different traditions of the various administrations involved, it is hardly surprising that the responses to this particular requirement have displayed considerable variation in approach and quality, not only between Member States but also between the different plans submitted by individual Member States. This variation was obvious in the different degrees of detail provided in projections of the results of the proposed programmes. These ranged from general aspirations for improvement to detailed, specific and quantified projections of impact for many of a given programme's component measures, although it must be acknowledged that the basis for the latter type of projection was often not specified.

A more significant cause for concern was that, in many instances, comprehensive baseline data (which are absolutely necessary if actual impact is ever to be calculated) were not fully specified in many development plans. In almost every instance the negotiation process was used to strengthen the response to the requirements for both prior appraisal and the provision of such baseline data (usually drawing on the reports of the *ex ante* evaluations carried out by external experts on each plan). Regardless of this effort, it should be acknowledged that *ex ante* evaluation of even relatively substantial, narrowly targeted and self-evidently influential policies is inevitably imperfect. When the subjects of such evaluation are complex combinations of activities which seek to influence variables that in most cases are open to other, and often more significant, influences then the task can quickly slip beyond the reach of established analytical methodologies and data sources. The continuing commitment to *ex ante* evaluation of European structural policies is based on a realistic acceptance of these limitations and the likely imperfections of the projections of impact which they produce. Such weaknesses are seen as being more than compensated for by the fact that *ex ante* evaluation encourages a much more systematic and open (or in Commission parlance 'transparent') approach to programming.

Intermediate evaluation is intended to ensure that any weaknesses in programme management information which remain after the programme's launch are remedied. It is also meant to provide a solid basis of information for any necessary re-programming decisions (due to either changing policy priorities or to the fact that circumstances have not in fact evolved as was foreseen at the start of the programming period) and to help consolidate a solid foundation for the eventual *ex post* evaluation of actual impact. Efforts in intermediate evaluation have produced mixed results to date. The value of a formal requirement to evaluate in the course of a programme has been contested by many of those involved in implementation. This applies especially in the case of those programmes which are of short duration (e.g. Objective 2) and may have, in fact, really only begun to be implemented half-way through the theoretical programming period and so have little to show in terms of immediate outputs. Intermediate evaluation is increasingly being presented, therefore, as an activity which should be viewed less as a formal, bureaucratic requirement and more as an integral element of ongoing programme management.

Ex post evaluation is intended to inform both the re-definition of individual programmes for subsequent programming periods and the overall re-formulation of the structural policies by providing accurate information on the effects of current policy. Two main problems must be overcome for *ex post* evaluation performing its intended role. First, many standard statistical time-series are subject to considerable time-lag, so that the latest available information often refers to the situation as it was two or three years previously. *Ex post* evaluation attempts to minimise this particular obstacle by the use of customised surveys and projections based on monitoring information when this is appropriate. Second, there is a difficulty in the case of the structural policies of attributing causality to policies which are often only one of a number of influences on the characteristics in which change is sought. Responding to this problem has demanded efforts to ensure that the full range of available evaluation methodologies is explored and that these methodologies are further developed when necessary.

Various Commission services have made contributions to evaluation methodology and practice, including not only the three services which are responsible for the Structural Funds (DGs V, VI and XVI) but also the service responsible for overseas aid (DG VIII), the service responsible for science, research and development (DG XII), and the service responsible for environmental matters (DG XI). However, in part because the overall role of the Commission and the nature of the policies for which it has been responsible has been subject to much more rapid change than has been the case in most national administrations, there has been less evidence in the past of a sustained pattern of building on established areas of technical competence, less of an institutional memory, than one might have expected.

In recent years the relevant Commission services have made increased efforts to promote a more widespread, common appreciation of evaluation concepts, approaches and methodologies among the partners. Two significant examples of such efforts are the Technical Working Group on Evaluation, which involves evaluation specialists from both the relevant Commission services and national administrations, and the current MEANS programme, which has the objective of developing evaluation methodologies specifically suited to the needs of the structural policies by building on the best practices of all levels of policy evaluation within the European Union.

The Principal Lessons Learned

The still-evolving process of programming and managing activities which are supported by the Structural Funds is but one element in the overall development of EU. Moreover, despite the results of the variety of activities mentioned above and the availability of thorough and substantial reports on related matters (see, e.g. Commission of the European Communities 1994b; 1996d), the complexity of the subject matter and the limitations of the existing level of relevant information combine to make it impossible to draw definitive conclusions on many points of detail. In these circumstances, there is, naturally, a variety of interpretations of the lessons learned from this particular experience. A personal interpretation is set out below.

First, there is an increasingly widespread acknowledgement that timing considerations can have a significant effect on the quality of programming. This is, perhaps, most evident in the severe time constraints which apply to agreeing development programmes in the first place. It is also evident in the recent emphasis placed by the Commission on the importance of intermediate evaluation, not just for re-allocation decisions within ongoing programmes but also to inform any re-formulation of overall policy approaches from one programming period to another. Given the inevitable time-lags before conclusive *ex post* evaluations can be carried out, and the need to formulate and agree each generation of programmes in a relatively short period, the adoption of a more ongoing and synchronised approach to both policy formulation and evaluation feedback would have obvious advantages.

Second, the need for clear communication can scarcely be overemphasised in this context. Real miscommunication can cause serious difficulties, and anything but the clearest level of communication allows scope for wilful misinterpretation if there is not a uniformity of interest or commitment among the actors concerned. The political sensitivity and technical difficulties of the subject matter are enough in themselves to demand exemplary levels of communication, and this need is compounded when the policy area involves a wide variety of linguistic, political and administrative traditions. The fact that both policies, and the socio-economic conditions to which they are a response, change over time does not make the communication of policy rationale any easier. Together with the fact that the precise nature of the Commission's responsibilities and authority has often been challenged, this may explain some of the Commission's previous shortcomings in this respect. Recent efforts to meet this need, in relation to some technically difficult topics (e.g. through the activities of the Technical Working Group on evaluation and the output of the current MEANS programme referred to above), are, therefore, particularly encouraging.

There is a growing appreciation of the need for appropriate data to be used for the management of activities supported by the Structural Funds and a growing awareness of the types of data which are most likely to be useful. The availability of absolutely comprehensive information for the rigorous monitoring and evaluation of the programmes supported by the Structural Funds remains the exception rather than the rule, but the situation is significantly better now than it was during the previous programming period and is probably well able to stand comparison with management information systems used for the national policies of the Member States.

Third, the joint activities of the Commission and the Member States in relation to this subject show increasing awareness of weaknesses in existing levels of information and of the need to define carefully and to collect a limited number of key indicators which can provide the most important information on a programme's implementation and impact in a cost-effective way. This task is of fundamental importance since the most sophisticated policy implementation and evaluation techniques are virtually worthless if it is not possible to obtain the basic information, which specifies in a precise fashion: existing needs, the policy response to those needs and the changes which have subsequently taken place.

Finally, systematic evaluation is becoming increasingly accepted as a practice which promises significantly to enhance the effectiveness and efficiency of the activities supported by the Structural Funds to the benefit of all concerned. Misgivings persist in some quarters concerning: the fact that the results of evaluation can always be used selectively for partisan political interests; whether the policy level on which evaluation is focused at present is appropriately defined; and, the appropriate level of effort and resources which are required for effective evaluation. None of these issues either outweigh the benefits of the practice or are beyond resolution. Abuse of evaluation results is less likely if they are presented in a professional fashion which includes a clear statement of the exact purpose and limitations of each exercise. Clarifying the relative roles and responsibilities of the partners and the focus of evaluation are complementary activities and, over time, the relationship between the costs and benefits of evaluation should become clearer.

Appropriate and fully-developed evaluation methodologies may not always be readily available to deal adequately with the particular problems which inevitably arise from time to time but there is ample evidence both of sustained effort on the part of the Commission systematically to review and make available existing methodologies and of attempts being made to develop more advanced methodological responses to key problems which have been identified.

Even if definitive quantified evidence of their value is not easily produced, it is clear that the principles of the reform of the Structural Funds have served a useful purpose in the past and are likely to continue to be used, with some modification, in future.

Concentration has given a necessary focus to the structural policies and is likely to become more important in a context where increasing demands on the resources of the EU (e.g. in relation to assistance to the countries of Central and Eastern Europe which have applied for membership of the Union) are unlikely to be matched by a commensurate increase of the resources themselves, particularly in view of the fiscal restraint required in preparation for EMU and the absence of a dramatic economic recovery across the Union. The development of this principle in future is most likely to be evident in an increasing focus of the structural policies on particular themes (e.g. specific employment or urban issues).

Programming has been useful in both assuring the coherence and complementarity of activities assisted by the Structural Funds and developing the abilities of the Commission to work effectively with the administrations of the 15 different Member States (and vice versa). However, it has also resulted in quite demanding administrative procedures. Some simplification of these procedures can be expected to come about naturally with increasing experience but this is likely to be complemented by conscious efforts to simplify programming through concentrating more assistance on larger projects or through global grants than has been the case recently.

Additionality is an inevitable requirement if the Structural Funds are to perform their intended function but, in light of the continued likelihood of resource constraints, it is possible that in future we will see a more active approach to generating private sector co-financing of activities supported by the Structural Funds.

Partnership has allowed the establishment of the European identity of the programmes assisted by the Structural Funds while assuring national and regional ownership. Despite the establishment of the principle of subsidiarity in the affairs of the EU in general, the development of partnerships in response to the particular needs of the EU's structural policies is likely to continue in future and such development is likely to be both challenging and potentially very valuable, for reasons related to the next point.

The overall political nature of the Union at any point in time reflects the dominant political tendencies at the inter-Member State, national and even regional level. The relative political authority of, and roles played by, the various EU institutions, the Member State governments and regional and local authorities have a critical influence on both the formulation of the Union's structural policies in general and the types of partnerships which are entrusted with translating those policies into development programmes and implementing those programmes. However, if structural policy is to be effective, partnerships need to allow the different partners from the Commission, Member States and regions to meet their responsibilities regardless of the immediate political context. For example, despite the principle of subsidiarity, it is difficult to see how the Commission will not continue to be responsible for overall financial control, and a much greater degree of harmonisation than exists at present, of the information related to the monitoring and evaluation of policies which are fundamentally aimed at improving the cohesion of the Union as a whole. The challenge is to develop modes of partnership which are effective vehicles for the design and implementation of development programmes while reflecting the changing and sometimes contested relationships of EU, national, regional and local actors. In general, it seems that adopting approaches to management and even evaluation techniques which frankly acknowledge the different interests and responsibilities of the different partners involved is ultimately more productive than proceeding as if these differences do not exist.

Conclusions

Although the results of evaluation are as yet far from definitive, they do provide a basis for both cautious optimism and acceptance of the advantages of much of the overall approach taken to the implementation of the structural policies in terms of:

- enhancing their impact
- enhancing the range of tested strategic policy responses available to national/regional authorities across the EU through the exchange of experience
- and developing administrative skills. The adoption of the programming approach has proven itself to be flexible enough to adapt to a wide variety of regional circumstances, administrative structures and traditions, yet demanding enough to encourage increasing standards of design and delivery.

Nonetheless, it should be borne in mind that the effectiveness of the structural policies is determined on three distinct levels:

(1) the way in which resources are used to deliver the policies through specific programmes

(2) the broad nature of the policies themselves

(3) and the overall amount of resources allocated to the policies and the broad pattern of the allocation of these resources between Member States and Objectives.

In the management of the Structural Funds, evaluation has, in recent years, tended to focus on the relationship between the design, implementation and impact of programmes (essentially the first of the levels mentioned above). While continued efforts are definitely needed on this level, significant progress has been made. As the findings of such efforts become more robust and representative they should become increasingly useful, not only for improving the implementation of policy but also in the broader formulation of policy and the general allocation of resources. However, the development of the structural policies also needs to be informed on the other two levels mentioned above and, in conclusion, three steps might be taken in this respect.

First, to the extent that there is any overall socio-economic model or vision of development for the Union as a whole, it has, arguably, included only a partially explicit depiction of the regional patterns likely to constitute and result from this overall dynamic. The overall formulation of European structural policy would benefit from the articulation of an explicit and clear general development perspective for the Union, to include detailed references to regional development.

Second, in recent years a development perspective for the Union has been implicit in two major projects: the Single Market and, more recently, economic and monetary union. The deflationary strategy chosen for completing the second project is not only provoking considerable political disquiet but also beginning to undermine the significance of national cohesion policies which are even more influential than the structural policies. In this context, there is a need for a much more sustained and explicit evaluation than is available at present of the adequacy of the overall level of allocations to, and the appropriateness of, broad patterns of distribution within EU structural policies (including patterns of distribution between Member States).

Finally, while it is increasingly clear that the expansion of the EU to incorporate even the stronger applicants for membership from Central and Eastern Europe will demand years of preparatory work, some form of further geographical expansion of the Union is likely over the next decade. Any such enlargement will have profound effects on the type of structural policies pursued by the Union and the level of resources which is needed to pursue them. An authoritative statement of the various enlargement options and an analysis of their implications would be timely.

CHAPTER 19

UK Policy Perspectives

Richard Wells

Introduction

In recent years, while so many other items of public expenditure in the European countries have been under severe restraint, the European Structural Funds have grown astonishingly fast. They now amount to one-third of the Community's budget. In some Member States they are now of major financial – and therefore political – importance. Even in the UK and other northern European countries, their grants have become sufficiently large, compared with corresponding national expenditure, to have a significant influence on a range of domestic policies.

The ERDF was created in 1975 under the leadership of Commissioner George Thomson in Brussels, on whose personal staff I then served. Its initial annual budget was 250 million units of account. By 1987, when, in London, I returned to work in this field, this Fund alone had 3700 million ecu (mecu). The three Structural Funds together amounted to 8 billion ecu (becu). Shortly after this, the major reform of the Community's Structural Funds negotiated in 1987/88 included a real-terms doubling of the funds between 1987 and 1993. Within this, the appropriations for the poorest, 'Objective 1', areas were to double faster, by 1992, to 10 becu in cash terms.

Later, the decisions at the 1992 Edinburgh summit included a further doubling of grants for the four poorest Member States from Objective 1 and a new Cohesion Fund and an increase in total expenditure on the Funds to 30 becu (in 1992 prices) by 1999. The British Government secured Objective 1 status for Merseyside and the whole of the Highlands and Islands Enterprise area, in addition to Northern Ireland. Including now allocations for the three newest Member States, in 1999 the Funds will amount (in 1999 prices) to 37 becu. The disproportionate rise in the financial allocations to Objective 1 (and now 6) areas means that they are the only clear net beneficiaries. Objective 2 and 5(b) areas contribute to the Funds in taxes roughly as much as they receive.

The Funds have achieved, in the name of the European Community, a great deal. They are now contributing up to four per cent of the national income of the poorest Member States. The physical endowment of the poorest regions has already been transformed, and by 1999 still more will have been done. At the same time, there has been much to criticise in the management of the Funds and no convincing demonstration that such a hugely expensive system of public expenditure transfers has given the European economy quite the stimulus it needs.

By the Community's own standards, the management of the Structural Funds has been distinguished by an unusual degree of Commission influence, hardly fettered by the Council's usual supervision and political control. Council discussion of the Funds is, in fact, extremely rare. The finance is administered bilaterally between the Commission and each Member State. The administration of the Cohesion Fund, uniquely, is not overseen by any committee of Member States at all. In contrast, CAP (Common Agricultural Policy) expenditure is subject to an elaborate system of Council decisions and frequent management committee meetings, as are other, relatively minor, items of Community expenditure.

'Community Initiatives'

The Funds' 'Community Initiatives' would be better called 'Commission Initiatives'. Their budget, now nine per cent of the Funds or three per cent of the entire Community budget, is effectively at the Commission's disposal for expenditure on purposes of its own choice. The increase in the Initiatives' percentage from six per cent to nine per cent agreed in 1993 was unjustified; the Commission's proposal to increase it to 15 per cent had, rightly, been strongly opposed by the Member States. But the Community Initiatives were, naturally, of special interest to the Commission.

The Edinburgh European Council sought to limit the role of the Community Initiatives mainly to promoting cross-border and inter-regional co-operation, on the principle of subsidiarity. On this basis, the INTERREG Initiative and the more recent Peace and Reconciliation Initiative for Northern Ireland are the most apt of all the current programmes.

Popular though they have naturally been with their beneficiaries, the other Initiatives are not so easy to justify in resource allocation terms. Nearly all the Community Initiatives consist of measures that could have been financed instead by general Structural Funds programmes. They therefore either duplicate measures foreseen at the time of the Single Programming Documents (SPDs) and Community Support Frameworks (CSFs) or distort the priorities that were agreed in the latter. In addition, a special management procedure has to be set up for each programme under each Initiative, making the administration of small Initiatives, in particular, disproportionately heavy and increasing the bureaucratic burden on a system that is already overloaded.

Moreover, as the national shares of Community Initiatives grants are similar to the national shares of the rest of the Funds, there is no overall additional benefit for Member States to receive money through the Initiatives rather than through their SPDs or CSFs. Without the Community Initiatives, the SPDs and CSFs could have been ten per cent bigger.

Selection of Areas

Not surprisingly, the Community has had much trouble with the selection of areas for Objectives 1, 2, 5(b) and 6. Though the selection criteria are apparently objective, in practice this is far from the case. Several of the Objective 2 and 5(b) criteria leave room for subjectivity and inconsistency in their application across the Community.

A further difficulty, for Objectives 1, 2 and 6, arises from the 'NUTS' classification of territorial units. The NUTS was invented for the purpose of statistical returns. It is now used for the entirely different purpose of helping to determine the allocation of huge sums of money. The unequal size of NUTS areas, while perhaps unimportant in statistical compilations, becomes significant when money is allocated according to the application of a uniform criterion to non-uniform areas. Some NUTS III regions have larger populations than some NUTS II – notably Greater London, which has a higher population than all but a handful of NUTS II areas. With the accession of Finland, there is now a NUTS II area with a 25,000 population – less than Gibraltar, which, anomalously, is not classified in the NUTS at all, although a worthy recipient of its share of the Structural Funds.

At the time of the last review of the Regulations an alternative method of determining Objective 2 and 5(b) eligibility was advocated by several Member States, including the UK. National-level statistics would have been used to fix each Member State's entitlement. Within this, each State would have been able to determine its own areas. This method would have had the advantage of being more objective, as national-level statistics tend to be more reliable, and it would have accorded with the principle of subsidiarity. It would also have facilitated concordance with national regional policies.

The current method did not, in the UK view, achieve in 1994 a fully appropriate coverage for Objective 2 of English urban areas – in London, for example, the Commission agreed to include only a small area in the north and east, and that only after heavy pressure from the UK Government.

Appraisal, Monitoring and Evaluation

Whatever the result of the eligibility process, the business of managing Structural Funds programmes is now more demanding than prior to 1994. At the UK's initiative, and as agreed by the European Council at Edinburgh, the 1993 Regulations include enhanced appraisal, monitoring and evaluation requirements. The Commission, through its operational and financial control services, is implementing them with increasing thoroughness.

The UK's approach to the appraisal, monitoring and evaluation of Structural Funds expenditure is broadly the same as that applied to its domestic programmes. Its main features can be summed up as:

- comprehensiveness: all programmes of expenditure to be evaluated
- independence: from those responsible for the programme's administration
- proportionality: to the value and importance of the programme
- timeliness: to allow evaluation results to influence policy decisions
- transparency: the prompt publication of all studies.

In essence, the Commission have adopted most of these broad principles, as well as other important features of UK evaluation practice. They (and other EU institutions) have largely conceded the impossibility of a comprehensive 'top-down' approach and have adopted, for most purposes, a pragmatic 'bottom-up' approach. While it is true that this renders more difficult the assessment of broad cost-effectiveness at Community or Member State level, it facilitates useful analysis, at local and regional levels, of effectiveness and value for money.

Thus, largely at British insistence, Structural Funds evaluation has progressed from the vague commitment to 'assessment' contained in the 1988 Regulations to the status of an inherent part of the Funds' administration. 'Value for money' is no longer seen as an odd 'Anglo-Saxon' hobby. It has, increasingly, become an indispensable element of sound management. And if the distance that the Commission and Member States alike have traversed in this relatively short period has depended on a realisation of the political attention focused on 'cohesion' measures, it is not less notable.

The journey is not, of course, complete throughout the Community. Some Member States are still in the process of acquiring the national resources and experience to put in place adequate monitoring systems; and evaluation crucially depends on the availability of monitoring data. But the legal requirements for systematic appraisal, monitoring and evaluation that the UK secured in the negotiation of the 1993 Regulations have ensured that, in the Commission and Member States alike, the will exists to remedy such gaps. The UK will, of course, continue to press for the resolution of these and other outstanding problems.

The Environment

The operations of the Funds have a significant influence on the environment. At the time of the last review of the Regulations there was a need to put an end to serious environmental concerns that some Community programmes had caused. The UK and many other Member States accepted that environmental considerations should be given a higher profile in the Regulations and were keen to see an element of environmental conditionality incorporated into the Structural Funds. Others argued that special mention was unnecessary since Structural Funds measures had, in any case, to comply with all Community legislation.

Above all, the UK sought to ensure that there was effective implementation and enforcement of existing Community environmental law and that environmental aspects should be covered by the monitoring and evaluation processes. The UK Government succeeded in having inserted into the Regulations a number of provisions relating to environmental appraisal which are already bearing fruit.

Administration

The other great achievement of the 1993 review of the Regulations was the simplification of the programming procedure, from three stages to two, by the amalgamation of the previously separate stages of negotiation of CSF and individual Operational Programmes (OPs). When they were introduced in 1988, CSFs were, in effect, the counterpart of the doubling of the budget, presented as a means of improving the management and effectiveness of the Funds. The CSF system was inspired by the French model of '*contrats de plan*', instituted in 1982, between the French Government and the then newly created regional councils. At the Community level it had the effect of increasing the Commission's influence on the way the Funds were spent.

The 1993 revision meant that there need be only one decision stage on the part of the Commission. This was at first resisted on the basis that only through separate negotiation of OPs could the Commission have sufficient detail to ensure that money was appropriately spent on behalf of the Community's taxpayers. The Commission's concerns were particularly centred on effective control of funding in the main recipient countries. In the event, these countries have largely retained the CSF system, which remains as an option.

The new SPDs were initially controversial in parts of the UK, especially in some small areas that had been running their own programme, but they have now been accepted as the standard procedure, as they are in all other northern European countries.

The reduction of the old three-stage process through the introduction of the SPD system has also cut the number of committees and the volume of paperwork required. Nevertheless, due to the extensive regionalisation of the programmes in the UK, there are 30 British SPDs and monitoring committees. The picture is similar in France, but Germany, by contrast, has only a single Objective 2 monitoring committee. Spain has only a single monitoring committee for its Objective 1 CSF, providing for ten times the money of the largest British SPD.

The procedures remain far too complex. The Structural Funds have become a by-word for arcane complexities and remain difficult for people to understand. This cannot improve their economic effectiveness or their political impact. And the contraction in the procedure for programme adoption has not eliminated the endemic delays. One of the major drawbacks in the system remains the delays that beset the adoption, and consequently the implementation, of the programmes throughout Europe. Delays have, unfortunately, become the rule rather than the exception with the Structural Funds. Objective 2 and 5(b) areas were not decided until the beginning of 1994, leading to delays in the preparation of SPDs. Objective 1, 2 and 5(b) programmes started between 7 and 16 months late and the new Community Initiatives have experienced even longer delays. Domestic programmes could have been implemented much quicker.

It is important that the Community's objective of reducing the level of state aids is not undermined by excessive use of the Structural Funds to subsidise industry. In the UK the use of the Funds broadly follows the priorities of the UK Government and the other British authorities and agencies concerned. There are, however, exceptions. Good infrastructure, for example, is vital to economic development in Objective 2 areas as well as Objective 1 and the UK clearly attaches higher priority to it than the

Commission. A Danish Government report on regional policy published in 1995 (Erhvervsministeriet 1995) makes a similar point. After explaining the disadvantages of subsidies to firms, it calls instead for more projects to improve areas' 'framework conditions' or underlying competitiveness.

By coincidence, the revision of the Regulations to include the promotion of partnership has been implemented at the same time as UK domestic moves towards a similar approach, both in terms of its business support infrastructure and its administration of regional funding. Regional and local authorities in some other Member States have, in several respects, more to complain of than UK authorities have in their Government's 'partnership' policies as there are instances where regional partnerships play no significant part in the negotiation of the programmes or in some aspects of their implementation. But partnership need not include every conceivable interest group and the UK continues to oppose Commission advocacy of the inclusion of the 'social partners' whose role in economic development in the UK is not comparable to that in some other Member States.

Negotiation of the current UK SPDs concentrated to a surprising extent not on what the Funds were to be spent on, but on the administrative arrangements. There was particular interest in the constitution and composition of committees through which interested parties perhaps hoped to influence the subsequent disbursement of the Funds. There has been a common, but erroneous, belief that grant approval decisions are taken by monitoring committees or their working groups. In fact, grants are decided and offered by Government Departments, after a procedure, agreed by the monitoring committee, which includes local consultations.

This preoccupation with institutional rather than substantive issues surprisingly seemed to extend to the Commission in Brussels. It appears that this has been more the case in Britain than elsewhere.

Private Sector Participation

On the other hand, the involvement of the private sector in the Funds has gone further in the UK than anywhere else. The UK SPDs include demanding targets for private sector participation. However, despite repeated requests over a period of two years, the Commission was unable to agree rules on the participation of the private sector in ERDF-grant-aided projects. New criteria for facilitating private sector contributions were finally introduced by the UK Government in May 1995. The new criteria allow reasonable profit levels to be achieved from ERDF-supported projects.

Regional Challenge was launched by the then President of the Board of Trade and Secretary of State for Trade and Industry, Mr Michael Heseltine, in February 1995 to stimulate greater competition for Structural Funds grants and encourage wider participation in the Structural Funds programmes, particularly from the private sector. Its competitive approach to the allocation of grants had its origins in the pioneering City Challenge and other successful Challenge competitions. The Challenge approach aims to promote innovation, increase the value for money and attract more private sector participation, and has already had a radical effect on the conventional approaches to urban and rural development. The first round of Regional Challenge is now bringing these benefits to the use of the European Structural Funds.

The projects are of a higher quality and involve more comprehensive regeneration schemes than previous Structural Funds projects. In many areas the Challenge has been effective in getting programmes going faster by the early encouragement of some especially good large projects. The winning projects, chosen directly by Ministers after recommendations by monitoring committees, will be the 'cream' of Structural Funds projects. The UK hopes to see the spread of the Challenge approach throughout the rest of the Community.

The Future

Before very long, the European Union is due to enlarge to take in countries to the East. This enlargement will have profound effects on the EU's cohesion policy. In 1999, when the Structural and Cohesion Funds are due for review, the annual cohesion budget will be approximately 37 becu, with the four poorest countries receiving, on average, 368 ecu per capita. The Central and Eastern European states are, on average, considerably poorer than these countries. It is, therefore, widely accepted that the Structural and Cohesion Funds cannot continue in an enlarged Community without substantial reform to make them affordable. The next review of the Funds can be expected to be much more radical than those in 1988 and 1993.

CHAPTER 20

French Policy Perspectives

Richard Lagrange

Introduction

Since the mid-1980s the main objective of European regional policy has been to support regions whose level of development is lagging behind that of more dynamic regions. For the latter, setting up the Single European Market may be a source of new opportunities and resources. Despite a common terminology (economic and social cohesion) and identical administrative and financial instruments (the Structural Funds) the implementation of European regional policy varies greatly from one Member State to another. One reason is that it is not possible to take the same approach when the Funds represent two, three or even four per cent of GDP to that when they are only a small complement to national policies and interventions.

For France, the Funds have become a decisive element of regional development policy and the so-called *aménagement du territoire.* Unknown by the general public, and unlike the Common Agricultural Policy, the Structural Funds are the daily concern of central government and local and regional authorities. Their economic and social impact is related to their financial importance and the regions can no longer conceive their development without considering the Funds. French regions benefit from them at different levels and for the 1994–1999 period more than 100 programmes co-financed by the Structural Funds will be implemented in France. Before trying briefly to evaluate their effects and the problems they raise, it is important first to appreciate what they represent in financial terms for the French regions.

Community Intervention in France

The 'planning contracts', or '*contrats de plan*' (development programmes negotiated by the State with the regions), for the 1994–1998 period represent about FF 75 billion. The Structural Funds for the same period will represent about FF 50 billion (regionalised objectives only). In areas eligible for Funds assistance, they represent, on average, about 15 per cent of the overall public aid budget. This figure encompasses great regional variations: for ten out of 26 French regions the figure is above 25 per cent, and for five out of the ten it is above 50 per cent.

Objective 1

France was allocated 2.19 billion ecu (becu) for Objective 1 for the 1994–1999 period, amounting to two per cent of the overall European budget for the Structural Funds. The Commission adopted the six Objective 1 programmes for France on 29 July 1994 following partnership negotiations. The French Hainaut (districts of Douai, Valenciennes and Avesnes) and, as exceptional cases, Corsica and the overseas *départements*, are eligible for the 1994–1999 period. The main types of expenditure can be grouped into six categories: economic action (which includes assistance for SMEs, craft, trade and research and development), agricultural development (including rural development), tourism, opening up and regenerating areas (infrastructure and the environment), human resources (training, employment, etc) and technical assistance. The largest categories of expenditure are economic action, development of the rural economy and territorial regeneration. Tourism is only a small part of the overall budget.

Objective 2

The Objective 2 SPDs for 1994–1996 were drawn up by the *préfet de région* (which, with the *préfet de département*, forms the central government representative within the decentralised levels of authority) in consultation with all the partners concerned and, after a few months of negotiations, they were adopted by the Commission in December 1994. As European regional policy is conceived as being complementary to French national policy implemented in the same areas, the SPDs for Objective 2 are consistent with the State-regional planning contracts. Their content and the financial balance between types of action differ slightly from one to another but, in all of them, absolute priority is given to projects which create jobs.

The main fields of intervention covered by the Objective 2 programmes are tangible and intangible investments in SMEs, the business environment (enterprise zones, services to firms), research and technological development, regeneration of derelict industrial estates and urban areas, urban policy and cultural facilities, the tourism economy and environmental protection. Exceptionally, investments in the fields of transport infrastructure (roads, railways, airports and harbours) and in further education can also be financed when a positive impact on employment has been demonstrated. Finally, training and access to employment measures constitute a significant part of Objective 2 strategies with an average 17.5 per cent share of ESF.

The Monitoring Committees include all financial partners, representatives of the socio-economic sectors, central government and the Commission. The *préfet de région* chairs these committees, which seek to ensure satisfactory progress in implementing the programmes.

Objective 5b

Objective 5b deals with support for the development of the most fragile rural areas and is of particular interest to France since it benefits most from this objective, with 36 per cent of the total allocation (2238 million ecu (mecu) for six years (1994–1999) out of a total of 6134 mecu). Except for Picardie, Ile de France, Nord-Pas de Calais, Corsica and the overseas *départements*, all French regions benefit from this objective to different extents throughout their territory on the basis of the population and size of the area.

One SPD was negotiated for each eligible area. After lengthy negotiations the Commission finally agreed the financial breakdown for the SPDs and, during the first quarter of 1995, the programmes were able to start with the first meeting of the Monitoring Committees. Common features of the Objective 5 programmes are: development aid to SMEs, support for diversification and adaptation of agricultural activity, assistance to trade and craft industries, support to tourism and action promoting environmental protection which improves the region's attractiveness.

Special inter-regional mountain programmes provide support for the Pyrenees, Alps, Jura Mountains, Vosges and Massif Central. They amount to 28 mecu, 1.4 per cent of the French Objective 5b endowment; their measures are inter-regional and financed by the regional SPDs.

Implementation

The implementation of European regional policy is the responsibility of the *préfet de région* (SGAR); central government has only a co-ordination role. At national level, the Delegation for Spatial Management and Regional Action (DATAR) is responsible for the co-ordination of regional programmes for Objectives 1 (except for the overseas *départements*), 2 and 5b, as well as for the Community Initiatives LEADER, INTERREG, SME, RECHAR, RESIDER, RETEX, KONVER (jointly with the Ministry of Defence) and URBAN (jointly with the inter-ministerial bureau for towns and cities).

DATAR is also in charge of co-ordination between different ministries, liaising on the negotiation of the 1993 Regulations, the definition of eligible areas and the financial allocations. The definition of national priorities in the programmes and their negotiation were also undertaken by DATAR. Finally, DATAR undertakes nation-wide 'animation' of the programmes (information, training, exchange of experience, evaluation and technical assistance). Given its national co-ordination role, DATAR participates in the group of the Council of the Union competent in the field of Structural Funds (the 'structural action' group) and represents French authorities in the consultative committees of the Commission dealing with the implementation of the Structural Funds (the Committee for the development and reconversion of regions (for Objective 1 and 2) and the Management Committee for the Community Initiatives).

At regional level, in line with current regulations, the 'implementing authority' is embodied in the *préfet de région* (SGAR). The *préfet* led the consultations among the various partners (local and regional authorities, economic and social partners) in order to prepare the regional programmes and it also conducted the negotiations with the Commission (with central government). The *préfet* is responsible for implementation of the programme (assessment of applications, selection of projects, etc) while respecting the principles of partnership and procedures set out in the SPD through close involvement of all the local and regional authorities co-financing the programme.

The *préfet* also has responsibility for financial management of the programme and the legality of expenditure undertaken. European funds are delegated to the *préfet* by the Ministry for the Interior for ERDF, the Ministry of Agriculture for EAGGF and the Ministry of Labour and Employment for ESF. In practice, although the *préfet de région* has a central role in implementation, the local and regional authorities also play an important part, particularly the regions and *départements* at all stages of the procedure (definition of the strategy and measures, financial plans, negotiations with the Commission, implementation, monitoring and evaluation). The *préfet* represents a kind of 'fulcrum' point in the system.

Experience

The Structural Funds have undoubtedly contributed to economic and social cohesion in the Union. They have enabled the least-favoured regions and states to develop significantly and anyone travelling in Europe cannot help but notice the major infrastructure projects that have been co-funded. The outcome has been very positive in many respects for France.

First, the reasonable time-scale of regional programmes and the predictability of financing is a great advantage. Without the constraints of a yearly budget, the Funds have enabled the partners to implement strategic development policies. Continuity and the guarantee of funding has enabled thorough-going action to address the economic and social situation in targeted regions.

Second, the emphasis attached to evaluation in the Council Regulations has had a useful educational role, contributing to more coherent public policies. There is less of a tradition of systematic evaluation in France than in other countries so the Commission's requirements helped to improve the effectiveness of the programmes and the better targeting of the measures, and made the selection criteria more objective.

Third, partnership is one of the most interesting aspects of the Structural Funds, particularly because of the large number of French local authorities. Of course, consultation between the different public partners existed prior to the introduction of the EU programmes but the latter has imposed greater transparency and, to some extent, an obligation to 'succeed together', which has created new, more efficient and more dispassionate work habits on the part of organisations.

These aspects probably vary in importance depending on the type of region and its political situation; the economic partners are, perhaps, too often absent from the partnership, which gives the public authorities undue influence. Finally, one cannot deny that the partnerships are sometimes more apparent than real; EU funding has, in some cases, reinforced institutional or political division, leaving the partnership nothing but an empty shell.

Perhaps the worst features of the Funds concern the complex procedures and delays in decision making. They give rise to justified criticisms that the rules are unnecessarily complicated and the bureaucracy is overzealous and lacks practical common sense. Complexity affects the administrative and financial procedures – EU systems add to national ones – but also relates to the number of programmes. There are more than 100 programmes in France, partly because of the large number of Community Initiatives. Unfortunately, only a few of these have genuine added value compared to the measures undertaken under Objectives 1, 2 or 5b. Paradoxically, when the Regulations offer some flexibility, as in the case of eligible measures, the Commission strove to make the whole mechanism obscure and uncertain. Questions to the Commission were often answered very late or not at all. The Commission's motives for interfering in local priorities, and insisting on certain measures rather than others, were unclear and controversial: who can say for sure that this or that measure is more or less effective? The effects were very disruptive. In addition, administrative costs for the smallest programmes are prohibitive because of the bureaucracy required.

The demanding Commission rules and procedures do not seem to be implemented consistently throughout the EU. Every country has difficulties but they seem to be standardised and consistent. Why was Denmark forced to have two SPDs for Objective 2? Why was it possible to create one national Monitoring Committee in some Member States but not in others?

Some of the difficulties experienced stem from the policies and processes advocated by the Commission. One cannot criticise the Commission for seeking to promote certain views: it is required to ensure some coherence at Community level and the Council agrees principles and objectives that should be reflected on the ground, partly through Community funding. Part of the difficulty lies with the generality of these views, which lead to different interpretations: in some cases they appear to stem from the training and culture of the civil servant in charge of the problem rather than from a well-founded policy. The Commission always expects the partners to demonstrate the economic efficiency of their proposals but does not fully justify its own positions. A simple illustration occurred in France in 1994 during the elaboration of the Objective 2 SPDs. Proposals regarding airport infrastructure were rejected by the Commission because 'they could not contribute to the development of these regions'. However, the Commission was forced to reconsider its position after the French authorities discovered that such types of infrastructure had been accepted in another Member State.

Finally, one particularly complex aspect concerns the designation of eligible areas: the objective criteria in the Regulation are not followed in practice. There are numerous cases of incoherence and inconsistency between and within Member States. The same NUTS level is not always used, the assisted areas under the Structural Funds do not coincide with those in receipt of regional aid (in the sense of Article 93 of the Treaty), some designated areas are too small to be viable and zoning has had perverse effects in some cases – encouraging competition between territories.

All the above points deserve to be further developed and, probably, balanced more evenly. It is difficult to get a precise understanding of some aspects, such as the likely efficiency of some measures and their impact on development. Community programmes have sometimes given rise to changes in the approach to regional development; in other cases they arose through spontaneous evolution. In a country such as France, where the European debate has become more tense and less consensual, the Structural Funds demonstrate an action of solidarity in favour of the most economically disadvantaged regions. In general, this Community-wide form of financial solidarity is one of the most positive aspects of Europe.

People are now looking towards the post-1999 period; the future enlargements of the Union are without precedent both in their scope and in the nature of the economic problems facing future Member States. Furthermore, they will occur in a European context which will be deeply altered by economic and monetary union. In these circumstances, solidarity action in favour of those facing the greatest difficulties will be more necessary than ever. At the same time, the economic and financial conditions of all the current Member States means that this effort will not be able to take place without a fundamental reform of the Structural Funds.

CHAPTER 21

German Policy Perspectives

Dieter Drerup

Introduction

Some of the future challenges facing regional policy in Europe are vividly illustrated by recent developments in Germany. Here reunification has resulted in disparities on a scale quite different from those that existed prior to 1990. The integration of Central and Eastern European countries into the EU will pose similar difficulties to European regional policy, albeit on a much larger scale.

Structural Fund assistance for Germany will reach approximately 20 billion ecu (becu) over the period 1994–1999, or some 14 to 15 per cent of the total budget. Two-thirds (68%) of the EU's regional aid for Germany is for the Objective 1 area encompassing the new German *Länder* (states) of eastern Germany. The scale of EU expenditure in Germany reflects the problems and disparities brought about by unification. From a Federal government perspective, it is extremely important that the aid is spent effectively and efficiently and that it reflects regional requirements. This chapter discusses the objectives and structure of regional policy in Germany, the contribution of European programmes and explores some of the key emerging issues.

German Regional Policy – the 'Gemeinschaftsaufgabe'

The federal structure of Germany means that responsibilities for regional policy are shared by the Federal Government and *Land* (state) governments. Prime responsibility lies with the 16 *Länder*. The main instrument of regional policy is the so-called 'Joint Task for the Improvement of Regional Structures' (*Gemeinschaftsaufgabe, Verbesserung der regionalen Wirtschaftsstruktur, GA*) where the financing of, and decisions concerning, programmes are divided equally between the Federal Government and the *Länder*. A Planning Committee is responsible for the approval of programmes and assistance and financing modalities; the Federal Government has the same number of votes on this Committee as all the *Länder* together and decisions require a significant majority. The implementation of programmes and approval of projects within the Joint Task is the exclusive responsibility of the *Länder*. They decide on the basis of agreed rules and regulations whether assistance is to be given to an individual project and how much.

Regional policy in the Federal Republic is part of national economic policy and has three main objectives. First, it aims to mobilise the growth potential of structurally weak regions in order to improve their contribution to national economic growth. Second, regional policy has a 'stabilisation' function intended to reduce the susceptibility of problem regions to fluctuations in the economy and structural changes, particularly through the removal of industrial mono-structures. Third, policy aims to reduce inter-regional disparities in relation to the regional potential for income generation and, to a certain extent, the provision of public and private services. Regional policy thereby contributes to the equalisation of living conditions throughout the Federal Republic, based on its Basic Law (*Grundgesetz*).

The new *Länder* continue to be the top spatial priority of German regional policy. Regional expenditure in eastern Germany amounted to DM 7 billion in 1996, compared to DM 700 million in the 'old' German *Länder* of western Germany. Policy instruments give preferential treatment to the new *Länder*; the maximum award ceiling for the regional investment grant programme is 35 per cent here (plus 15 percentage points for SMEs), compared to an award ceiling of 18 per cent in western Germany (plus ten percentage points for SMEs). Non-regional aid can also be used to increase the award rate by 10 per cent in western Germany for firms which do not meet the SME definition.

EU Regional Policy in Germany – Objective 1

Germany first received assistance from ERDF in 1975. Since reunification the amount of assistance has increased greatly because of the needs of eastern Germany. The new *Länder* and eastern Berlin became Objective 1 regions on 1 January 1994. GDP per capita in these areas was as low as in the poorest regions of the EU and they, therefore, met the criteria for Objective 1 status according to the Framework Regulation. In addition, since 1990 they have been undergoing profound social and economic change as a result of their transition to democracy and a market-based economy. The transformation of a planned economy into a social market economy has involved massive reconstruction. For instance, one in three jobs has disappeared since 1990. Despite a massive effort to retrain the labour force and large numbers of workers taking early retirement, there are still more than a million people looking for work. In addition, more than 13,000 enterprises have been largely transferred to the private sector and industry is being totally re-equipped because productivity was only about a third of that in West Germany. There is also a catastrophic inheritance of pollution and land contamination to be overcome.

The situation of the new *Länder* is not really comparable to the problems in other poor EU regions. The transformation process has required a unique concept and activities of special quality and scope.

Although serious problems still exist, structural changes are well under way and significant progress has been made – mainly through considerable investment. The restructuring is supported by massive public financial transfers. The Federal Government's gross contribution amounted to some 400 billion DM over the period 1991–1994 and transfers in 1995 are estimated to exceed 150 billion DM. The Federal Government's policy is strongly growth-oriented and aims to create competitive regions focusing on several priorities.

Having privatised most of the former state-owned enterprises, private investment has a decisive role to play in creating a modern and competitive economic structure. Economic research institutes estimate that private investment in eastern Germany totalled some 420 billion DM between 1991 and 1994 (Institut für Wirtschaftsforschung 1995). By the end of 1994 private investment of more than 130 billion DM was granted financial assistance within the Joint Task (*Gemeinschaftsaufgabe*).

It is also important to continue the process of creating a modern infrastructure. The Federal Transport Plan (Bundesministerium für Verkehr 1993) envisages 540 billion DM for investments in the construction and extension of transport infrastructure up to the year 2012, of which 180 billion DM is earmarked for the new *Länder*. Major improvements are also foreseen in telecommunications. In 1990 there were 12 telephone connections per hundred inhabitants in the new *Länder*. According to Germany's 'Telekom 2000' plan (Deutsche Bundespost Telekom 1994), which involves a total investment of some 60 billion DM in the new *Länder* over the period 1990–1997, it is expected that the number of telephone connections will rise to 48 per hundred inhabitants by 1999. By the end of 1994, 34 per hundred had already been achieved. Production-related infrastructure projects are supported by the Joint Task (16.3 billion DM of regional aid was granted up to the end of 1994 for investments totalling 22.5 billion DM).

Other important activities of the Federal Government with substantial financial transfers are related to the environment, innovation and technology, SMEs, social security, human resources and agriculture.

In 1991 the European Union gave a special ERDF grant of 1.5 becu to the new *Länder* and eastern Berlin for a three-year period. A further 1.5 becu was committed through the European Social Fund (ESF) and the European Agricultural Guarantee and Guidance Fund (EAGGF). The ERDF contribution was entirely spent on productive investment and production-related infrastructure.

For 1994–1999 Structural Fund assistance will be 13.64 becu for Objective 1 in Germany. Of this, 6.82 becu will be provided by the ERDF for the following purposes:

- support for productive investment and accompanying investment in production-related infrastructure
- measures to support SMEs
- measures to promote R&D and innovation
- measures to protect and improve the environment
- measures to combat unemployment, through vocational training and temporary employment experience
- measures to promote agriculture, rural development and fisheries.

These priorities contrast with the narrower, preferred approach by the German authorities. Originally, the Federal Government's Regional Development Plan for eastern Germany, agreed with the new *Länder* and eastern Berlin, had foreseen the continuation of the 1991–1993 arrangements for using ERDF. Investment would have been concentrated on the two priorities of German regional policy under the Joint Task, that is productive investment and local economic infrastructure. However, the European Commission preferred a broader-based approach. The Community Support Framework finally agreed with the Commission, following protracted negotiations and containing the above six priorities, had two important implications. First, it created opportunities for EU regional aid to be spent according to EU priorities rather than the preferences of the German authorities responsible for regional policy. Second, the administrative arrangements are much more burdensome.

Objectives 2 and 5b

In western Germany support from the Structural Funds continues under Objectives 2 and 5b. For Objective 2 regions, 733 million ecu (mecu) are available during the period 1994–1996, while Objective 5b assistance will amount to 1227 mecu during 1994–1999. As in the other Member States, new lists of eligible Objective 2 and 5b areas were established by the Commission and became effective from January 1994. The number of inhabitants in all German Objective 2 and 5b regions is 14.7 million, or 22.7 per cent of the total population of western Germany. The corresponding percentage for eligible GA-regions (Germany's own regional policy) is 22 per cent. A number of regions eligible for EU assistance are not covered by the latter and vice-versa.

Community Initiatives

The regulations governing the EU Structural Funds provide that nine per cent of the appropriations between 1994 and 1999 will be devoted to Community Initiatives. The initiatives are intended to complement the measures included in CSFs for Objectives 1 to 5b. However, part of the funds allocated to Initiatives, even if these are of a regional nature, can be spent outside the eligible Objective 1, 2 and 5b areas. So far, a total amount of 1893 mecu has been allocated for Community Initiative programmes in Germany.

The *Länder*, rather than the Federal Government, have principal responsibility for the German programmes. Consequently, the total number of German programmes for the 11 Community Initiatives is more than 100 (in addition to programmes for Objectives 1 to 5b). Most of the funds available under Community Initiatives have to be spent in Objective 1, 2 and 5b areas. So individual regions have received EU assistance from three or four programmes, adding to the complexity of implementation. In rural areas there is usually a clear overlap between Objective 5b and the LEADER initiative.

The large number of ERDF programmes is a huge administrative burden at all levels – regional, national and Community. Guidelines for Community Initiatives starting at the beginning of 1994 were only published on 1 July 1994. Delays also arose from the late decision on the eligibility of areas. By the end of July 1995 decisions had been taken on programmes covering about 66 per cent of the total amount allocated to Community Initiatives in Germany. While the areas covered by Objectives 1, 2 and 5b, in terms of population figures, correspond broadly to assisted areas under the GA scheme, Community Initiative programmes go far beyond this area. The major initiatives of a regional nature (RECHAR, KONVER and RESIDER) together with Objective 2 and 5b programmes in the western *Länder* (including western Berlin) cover areas having a population of 33.7 per cent, compared to only 22 per cent in GA areas.

Wider Issues

Having dealt with aspects related to specific programmes in Germany, it is also important to touch on some general aspects of EU regional policy, taking into account decisions made by the European Council in Edinburgh in 1992. First, it appears that there is no controversy about the fundamental objectives of regional and cohesion policy. The reduction of spatial disparities is an objective laid down in Article 130a of the Maastricht Treaty. This is not the only objective. At the Third Informal Meeting of OECD Ministers Responsible for Regional Policy (April 1994) most of the delegations explicitly agreed that regional policy should also – and as an equally important goal – aim to promote competitiveness and economic growth. When the Commission submitted a document to the Informal EU Meeting of Ministers responsible for Regional Policy in Strasbourg (March 1995), stressing the importance of the Structural Funds for growth and employment and emphasising the employment goal, this was also generally welcomed. The growth priority cannot be separated from the employment imperative. If opportunities for economic growth are maximised, this should also have a positive impact on employment. Regional policy is not primarily oriented to the business cycle. It must, above all, promote a long-term response to the problem of chronic regional unemployment.

Second, the European Council in Edinburgh decided that 'greater emphasis will be given to *ex ante* appraisal, monitoring and *ex post* evaluation'. Therefore, the legislation for the Structural Funds revised in 1993 provides for more thorough evaluation. It makes a much clearer distinction between the three stages of scrutiny and implementation of the Funds: appraisal, monitoring and *ex post* evaluation. The revised Regulation stipulates, in this context, that 'assistance will be allocated where appraisal shows medium-term economic and social benefits commensurate with the resources deployed'. The Framework Regulation specifies, moreover, that the Member States are to incorporate in their development plans and applications for assistance specific quantified objectives for the operations proposed.

Evaluation will be greatly facilitated by prior appraisal, to the extent that it involves subsequent verification that the objectives initially determined have been satisfactorily achieved and/or a judgement on any differences observed in relation to such objectives. However, it is important to ensure that the quantification of objectives does not undermine the principles of market economies. Evaluation activities are essential to ensure the efficiency and effectiveness of regional policy measures but they should not be confused with procedures characteristic of a planned economy. A decentralised market economy makes it impossible for the government to predict the precise outcome of their activities. Economic improvements are largely the result of individual decisions by participants in the economic process (private enterprises and consumers) as well as the wider economic and policy framework. Regional policy cannot dictate what will happen if certain policies are pursued. Consequently, the Commission's requirements for evaluation should not be too demanding, bearing in mind the limited influence that regional programmes have over economic events, particularly where the level of financial support is limited.

While systematic evaluation in European regional policy only started following the decisions taken in 1993, some practical experience is available in Germany of the effects of regional aid especially provided under the Joint Task. The results are shown in more detail in Chapter I.6 of the 24th GA-Framework Plan for 1995–1998 (Deutscher Bundestag 1995). They are limited to western Germany and have encountered the kinds of measurement problems already mentioned. Overall, the evaluators reached a favourable judgement on the investment incentives and stated that there is a need for this in Germany.

A third issue follows from another decision by the summit in Edinburgh where the European Council requested that the 'administrative procedures should be simplified'. The revised Regulations of 1993 subsequently allowed Member States to submit Single Programming Documents (SPDs) comprising the development plan and the applications for assistance relating to it and leading to a single decision by the Commission incorporating the details otherwise set out in Community Support Frameworks and Operational Programmes. The introduction of SPDs was the only major change in terms of administrative procedures made by the revised Regulations. In Germany there was no simplification compared with the previous period. The SPD procedure was not permitted by the Commission for Objective 1 programmes in Germany. The administrative burden became heavier in eastern Germany because a wider set of priorities had to be established and the Operational Programmes already submitted in the Regional Development Plan had to be rewritten.

Fourth, the European Council in Edinburgh confirmed the principle of concentration introduced in 1988. The Council decided that 70 per cent of the financial resources of the Structural Funds should be spent in Objective 1 regions. Therefore, some 96 becu will be available in regions representing 26.6 per cent of the total population of the EU. Concentration is much less significant in the remaining 30 per cent of resources. At the end of 1994 Objective 2 regions covered 16.8 per cent and Objective 5b areas 8.2 per cent of the EU population. Areas eligible under Objectives 1, 2 or 5b include, in total, more than half of the EU population. In addition, Community Initiatives where Structural Funds resources are also spent go considerably beyond these areas. The questions should be asked whether this geographical scope is consistent with the concentration principle and whether the reduction of disparities in the Community could be achieved more efficiently with less-extensive eligibility rules.

A similar question can be asked about the scope of assistance as laid down in Article 1 of the ERDF Regulation. German regional policy is concentrating financial assistance essentially on productive investment and business-related infrastructure, while the ERDF offers a wide catalogue of measures supplemented by ESF and EAGGF. EU policy tends to use the wide range of measures fully whereas, in Germany, the tasks of the Social and Agricultural Funds are part of labour and agriculture policies as well as other specific policies such as education and environment. There is nothing wrong with these measures and policies. However, the emphasis of regional policy should be on investment promotion, bearing in mind the basic objectives of growth and employment. If too many objectives are set, this distracts attention from the major goals.

One final observation: German experience suggests that greatest success has been achieved in regions that developed their own initiatives and mobilised available potential. Regional policy should, therefore, mainly focus on incentives and support for indigenous development. The key phrase is 'help for self-help' in accordance with the important subsidiarity principle. Actors in the regions know best what is needed.

Table 21.1 Overview of EU funding for German programmes under Objectives 1, 2 and 5b for the period 1994–1999 (1994–1996 for Objective 2) as well as Community Initiatives* (mecu, 1994 prices)

I. Objective 1 and Community Initiatives

Country	*Objective 1*			*Community Initiatives*	*Total*
	ERDF	*ESF*	*EAGGF/FIGF*	*(all funds)*	
Berlin (East)	516.0	221.1	8.2	43.6	788.9
Brandenburg	1075.0	496.3	601.1	254.9	2427.3
Mecklenburg-Vorpommern	824.0	383.4	690.2	127.8	2025.3
Sachsen	2014.0	874.9	481.5	359.4	3729.8
Sachsen-Anhalt	1264.0	550.0	556.0	121.0	2491.0
Thüringen	1127.0	489.6	391.0	113.5	2121.1
Total		**13640.0**†		**1043.8**†	**14683.8**† ‡

II. Objectives 2 and 5b and Community Initiatives

Country	*Objective 1*		*Objective 5b*			*Community Initiatives*	*Total*
	ERDF	*ESF*	*ERDF*	*ESF*	*EAGGF/FIGF*	*(all Funds)*	
Baden-Württemberg	–	–	27.000	5.000	41.840	52.308	126.148
Bayern	9.530	5.130	207.281	117.646	235.292	120.015	694.894
Berlin (West)	102.112	56.216	–	–	–	20.897	179.225
Bremen	30.490	16.420	–	–	–	30.144	77.054
Hamburg	–	–	–	–	–	11.866	11.866
Hessen	18.277	2.980	32.306	6.461	41.997	32.391	134.412
Niedersachsen	29.845	12.670	98.042	49.021	98.042	101.334	388.954
Nordrhein-Westfalen	263.800	97.570	23.407	4.645	18.078	299.094	706.594
Rheinland-Pfalz	15.246	8.210	44.511	22.256	44.515	45.899	180.637
Saarland	34.378	14.733	7.390	8.536	7.804	50.941	123.782
Schleswig-Holstein	10.000	5.393	34.375	17.185	34.366	39.389	140.708
Total	**733.0**		**1227.0**			**849.583**§	**2809.587**§

Rate for 30 November 1995 ***Total (I+II) 17493.38***

* The Guidelines of the European Commission for the individual Community Initiatives provide for the following time periods:
1994–1997 for the Initiatives RECHAR, RESIDER, RETEX, KONVER;
1994–1999 for the Initiatives INTERREG, LEADER, Employment, ADAPT, SME, URBAN, PESCA.

† Inclusive of 1076.1 MECU for ESF Federal Programme (not divided into *Länder*).

‡ Including amounts not divided into Länder for the evaluation and support structure as well as federal programmes in the Community Initiatives ADAPT and Employment totalling 23.6 mecu.

§ Including amounts not divided into *Länder* for the evaluation and support structure as well as federal programmes in the Community Initiatives ADAPT and Employment totalling 45.305 mecu.

Source: Federal Ministry of Economics, Bonn

CHAPTER 22

Conclusions

An Agenda for Reform

John Bachtler and Ivan Turok

Introduction

This book has brought together practical experience of EU structural policies in different European regions. It has provided different perspectives on the operation of the policies from people closely involved in studying, managing or advising on the process. We hope it offers a more comprehensive and detailed understanding of the Structural Funds than has been available before. This final chapter seeks to summarise the key issues emerging from the preceding chapters and, taking an EU-wide view, to lay out an agenda for reform in the light of past weaknesses and future challenges.

The Context for Reform

In considering how EU structural policies might evolve in the future, it is important to clarify the magnitude of the challenge confronting EU and Member State authorities. The first part of the book (Chapters 2 and 3) showed how social solidarity and regional cohesion have always featured on the agenda of European integration, often to balance the pursuit of global economic competitiveness and free trade. The task facing EU regional policy has mounted over the past decade with the enlargement of the Union and the development of the Single Market. The prospects are that the structural and cohesion policies will face even bigger challenges in future as a result of structural changes, the continued growth of unemployment right across Europe, intensified pressures of international competition and further enlargement of the Union to include poorer countries in central and eastern Europe (CEE).

Regional disparities in the EU

Regional policy has existed at a European level for almost 25 years, although it was very weak early on. Despite a massive increase in resources since the late 1980s, the policy is still marginal in relation to the size of the economy of the Union, the scale of regional disparities and its role as the principal means of promoting convergence. The relationship between economic integration and regional convergence is subject to different interpretations with evidence of both convergence and divergence in wealth levels over the post-war period (Chapter 3). Several studies have found a long-term narrowing of regional income differences (attributable to reduced inter-regional disparities within countries) over the past 30–40 years, but without a clear or consistent pattern of convergence between EU countries. Trends also vary according to the spatial scale of analysis and some regions have converged or diverged much more than others.

It is clear that convergence is a slow and difficult process. According to studies underlying the recent Cohesion Report published by the European Commission (1996d), the gap in income between the four weakest Member States (Greece, Spain, Ireland and Portugal) and the EU average diminished by about a quarter between 1983 and 1993, with marked differences between the four. However, disparities in income between regions remained virtually unchanged over the ten-year period and disparities in unemployment widened significantly – ranging (in 1993) from 4.6 per cent in the 25 regions with the lowest unemployment rates to 22.4 per cent in the 25 regions with the highest rates. Regional income and unemployment disparities within almost all countries widened over the same period. Measures of 'social cohesion' indicate an intensifying problem of youth and long-term unemployment and a rising incidence of people living below the poverty line (Commission of the European Communities 1996d).

Lagging regions, especially in the cohesion countries of Portugal, Spain, Greece and Ireland, face a formidable combination of obstacles to future development. Slower economic growth or stagnation in the richer countries is limiting the opportunities for spread effects from core regions and restricting the possibility of inter-regional transfer payments (evident in the current negative German attitude to increasing the EU budget). It has also limited the scope for compensating migration from poor to rich areas which has played some part in past EU regional convergence (Mas *et al.* 1995). Many lagging regions remain disadvantaged by their dependence on slow-growing or declining industries and some lack the kinds of institutions necessary to help them become 'learning economies', such as research centres, technical colleges and universities. The removal of European and global protectionist barriers will bring further pressures on regional competitiveness – in the textiles sector through the phasing out of the Multi-Fibre Agreement and progressive improvement of the access of CEE countries under accession agreements and in agriculture through removal of subsidies under World Trade Organization agreements and reform of the Common Agricultural Policy. European integration is also reducing the possibilities for lagging regions and nations to respond to economic, sectoral and technological changes by developing new sources of comparative advantage (Shepley and Wilmott 1995).

Economic and monetary union

Two major influences on the future of EU regional policy are bound to be economic and monetary union and EU enlargement. The regional implications of EMU are highly uncertain. Its form and scope have still to be decided; it is not clear when it will begin, which countries will participate and, crucially, what the different political and economic implications are for member and non-member countries and regions. Proponents hope that the economic stringency required by EMU convergence conditions will promote effective structural change in less-developed regions through improved labour market efficiency and increased productivity. However, research suggests that, at least during a transitional period, peripheral regions are likely to be disadvantaged because of their inferior ability to compete and asymmetric regional adjustment.

The lagging regions begin the transition to EMU from an unfavourable starting point. They are likely to be heavily disadvantaged by the loss of exchange rate flexibility and national monetary sovereignty and it is questionable whether regional labour markets embody sufficient flexibility (notably in regional wage rates) to adjust to adverse shocks (Abraham and Van Rompuy 1995) or indeed whether this would be an appropriate and constructive response. During the transitional phase the efforts to reduce inflation (e.g. curbing public expenditure) may slow down economic growth and dampen down the prospects of regions with below-average GDP levels. In the absence of exchange rate flexibility, adjustment in the labour market may become a key mechanism for maintaining or improving competitiveness. The costs are likely to include higher unemployment, lower wages and inferior working conditions for workers in sectors exposed to international competition and related industries – especially in high-inflation and low-productivity countries and regions dependent on cost for their competitiveness. Adjustment mechanisms may be needed to help accommodate economic shocks; without adequate cohesion policies, EMU may destabilise development and economic integration within the EU (Begg and Mayes 1993). Yet in the lead up to EMU there is a danger that the convergence criteria will lead to cutbacks in regional support at national and EU levels. Payments under the Cohesion Fund are already conditional on progress being made to reduce budget deficits in the cohesion countries to under three per cent. During 1996 it was suggested that such a link could be extended to the Structural Funds, thereby suspending payments to states with an excessive budget deficit, although this is probably unrealistic.

EU enlargement

The future enlargement of the Union is also still subject to decisions about the scope and timetable for accession. Despite French and German political statements predicting enlargement by the year 2000, it seems likely that a 'first wave' of new Member States (potentially Poland, Hungary, the Czech Republic and Slovenia, as well as Cyprus) will join around 2003 at the earliest. The effect of enlargement depends on the rate of economic growth and structural change in both the EU and CEE over the intervening period, as well as the conditions under which the new Member States join the Union.

There is likely to be an uneven burden of adjustment within western Europe to free trade with CEE, as with EMU. Some have argued that a combination of successful economic and political reform in eastern Europe, plus a complete liberalisation of east-west trade, would yield considerable benefits in terms of increased manufacturing output and employment in the EU's peripheral regions. Given their mix of industries, the peripheral regions would benefit from the rise in intra-industry trade in the consumer goods sector (as opposed to the capital goods sector) (Hudson 1994; Commission of the European Communities 1993c). The liberalisation of trade and factor movements between CEE and western Europe could improve resource allocation and economic welfare in both parts of Europe – although this perhaps assumes that western Europe expands capital intensive production and eastern Europe labour intensive production. Whereas the beneficial effects in the East may be large and widespread, the advantages in the West may be small and there may be costs arising from the rundown of marginal sectors such as textiles and agriculture. So the political costs may outweigh any efficiency improvements (Jackman 1995; Baldwin 1993).

The CEE states represent major potential markets for capital goods required for the restructuring process, so the benefits might accrue mainly to the richer parts of the EU that produce products or services with a relatively high scientific or technological content. Conversely, opening up EU markets to imports of agricultural produce and low-tech, labour-intensive products (steel and other metal production, wood, textiles, clothing, footwear, etc) could undermine the poorest EU regions, especially areas in Portugal and Greece which specialise in these sectors (Hall and Van der Wee 1995). In terms of sectoral structure and productivity, the regions most at risk could be those with a large or above-average share of agriculture, an above-average share of manufacturing industry, low labour productivity and unfavourable locations. These include regions mainly on the periphery, such as Orense, La Corruna, Almeria and Burgos.

Accession of even a limited number of new Member States will place considerable strain on the EU budget. Unlike the most recent enlargement to include Sweden, Finland and Austria, the new Member States will not be net payers. The per capita income of Slovenia (the richest of the CEE countries) was $6490 in 1993, significantly below that of Greece ($7390). Comparable figures for Hungary ($3350), the Czech Republic ($2710) and Poland ($2260) show still greater disparities. The proportion of the economically active engaged in agriculture in the CEE countries is four or five times that of the EU. Such indicators suggest a major skewing of the EU's cohesion policies towards the new Member States if the objective of convergence is to be maintained. We return to this issue below.

Balance of Achievements

The agenda for reforming the Structural Funds has many levels and dimensions. It encompasses the strategic changes to the European integration process discussed above, the institutional and financial arrangements with which the EU decides to operate in the next decade and numerous technical and operational issues. Before spelling out an agenda for reform in more detail, it is useful to reflect briefly on the balance of achievements of EU regional policy.

The quantitative impact of the Structural Funds is hard to determine because of serious methodological and data obstacles to evaluation and the wide range of economic and social agencies involved in co-financing and delivering programmes. Commission documents such as the recent Cohesion Report provide a range of estimates for outputs and impacts, with a 'health warning' regarding the reliability of the figures (Commission of the European Communities 1996d). In the cohesion countries EU support is estimated to have increased growth by 0.5 per cent per year over the 1989–1993 period (with associated creation/maintenance of over 500,000 jobs) and by at least 0.5 per cent over the 1994–1999 period. In Objective 2 regions estimates suggest 530,000 net jobs created or maintained over the 1989–1993 programming period and in Objective 5 regions about 500,000 jobs over the period 1989–1999. Under Objective 3 the EU has financed between 2 and 15 per cent of Member States' active labour market policies focused on exclusion.

It is probably more productive to discuss the achievements of the EU policies in qualitative terms, concentrating on the *process* of regional development. As the Cohesion Report also notes, 'part of the added value of EU policies relates to the emphasis on innovation linked to the specific qualities of the delivery system itself' such as 'enhanced policy changes and the development of new structures' (Commission of the European Communities 1996d, p.10). These issues have provided the subject matter of much of this book.

The assessment began with Chapters 4–12 in Part II which focused on EU-funded regional programmes and procedures in the UK. Most chapters showed how important the Structural Funds have become to cash-strapped local authorities and development agencies. Central government has maintained a tight grip on the programmes and institutional arrangements, which is believed to have stifled local creativity and added value from the Funds. Commission procedures have also been criticised as slow and bureaucratic. Nevertheless, there have been signs of local innovation in policies and projects – such as the community economic development and environmental priorities in western Scotland (see Chapters 5 and 10) – and increased evidence of networking among local authorities and other partners (see Chapters 4 and 7). There has also been renewed interest in regionalism and strategic planning, although this is undermined by the competitive bidding mechanisms for resource allocation and, of course, by the lack of a regional tier of government in the UK.

Elsewhere in Europe similar arguments are made about arbitrary geographical boundaries and the proliferation of institutions and burdensome administrative procedures, as the chapters in the third part of the book showed. Yet it seems that issues of strategy and co-ordination may be dealt with more effectively and EU regional plans and budgets appear to be more closely aligned with existing national arrangements, partly, perhaps, because some governments have demonstrated more flexibility in negotiations with the Commission and willingness to learn from other countries. There remains some concern that the regional plans are designed above-all to draw down the Funds and are not rooted strongly enough in analysis of the local economy or reflect clearly the collective views and commitment of the various local partners.

The final part of the book reflected on some of the policy lessons and future challenges. The Commission has clearly found it difficult to design, negotiate and manage such a large and wide-ranging process with a relatively small professional staff. This may help to explain the lack of guidance, over-emphasis on procedures, delays and inconsistent decision making alluded to by many local and national authorities. An understandable concern that EU funds may simply get substituted for domestic resources could also have caused the Commission to get closely involved in scrutinising the internal policies and processes of Member States, prompting criticisms of excessive interference.

What, in the view of contributors to this volume, has been achieved through EU regional policy? First, it appears to have generated greater interest in strategic thinking and planning when this was on the decline or did not exist in some countries. The structural policies require a more integrated approach to planning and implementing projects than is typical in the field of economic development. Local and regional authorities are encouraged to make decisions in a more strategic manner, based on an understanding of local economic circumstances and paying regard to the policies of other agencies in their areas. The emphasis on overarching regional programmes rather than discrete projects may also lead to a more considered approach to resource prioritisation and more coherent investment decisions. This is clearly a learning process for all concerned and unlikely to be achieved overnight. Moreover, in a context of constrained public expenditure, the inevitable scramble for resources is bound to pose a constant threat to strategic planning.

Second, the structural policies have also encouraged more emphasis to be placed on the role of institutional co-operation in economic development. Several chapters demonstrate the novel arrangements and committees established as a result of EU requirements for collective participation in strategy making, implementation and monitoring. As long as these partnerships progress beyond a token or symbolic form, they are likely to have an important role to play in co-ordinating development policies and linking projects. New agencies and groups have also been encouraged to participate in economic development thinking and decision making, such as the voluntary sector and trade unions in some countries. In most places this could go even further. There remains a danger in some places that national governments dominate procedures to the detriment of the regional partnership and that decision-making committees serve an exclusive rather than inclusive purpose.

Third, the policies have had a useful focus on job creation and productive investment. Clarity of purpose is important for consistent and effective development programmes and regional unemployment and low incomes have undoubtedly been the prime reason for the progressive enhancement of the Structural Funds. The precise boundaries of what is deemed to be 'economic development' will always be a matter for interpretation and argument, but having a single broad objective is widely regarded as helpful in concentrating minds and efforts. The Commission has often been approached to widen the uses to which the Funds can be put (leisure facilities are popular in some regions while a stronger case has been made for housing in the poorest countries, given its impact on living standards). This has generally been resisted on the grounds of diluting economic development activity. Difficulties may arise when expenditure on national social programmes (such as housing) is reoriented towards certain economic activities simply because they are eligible for EU co-funding.

Fourth, the Commission has tried to encourage greater dynamism and innovation in economic development and to avoid policies becoming monotonous and routine. Recent examples of new ideas being introduced and disseminated through EU programmes include technology policies, community economic development and integrated environmental and economic measures. The emergence of new networks and alliances among local authorities across different regions may also promote greater sharing of experience. In addition, the three-year time-scale of many regional programmes is intended to be long enough to pursue a particular policy seriously and expect a tangible impact but short enough to allow periodic changes in emphasis and experimentation. Bearing in mind Commission-induced administrative and negotiation delays at the outset, as well as crucial lead-in time to plan and develop new projects on the ground, many local partners consider this to be too short for effective learning. Different types of policy also have different time-scales and the benefits of some may not be apparent within the three-year period.

Fifth, the EU policies have sought to introduce more systematic procedures into economic development decision making. These range from detailed scoring systems, when project applications are vetted by advisory groups and management committees, to thoroughgoing appraisal, monitoring and evaluation techniques for regional programmes. Naturally, there has been some resistance from partners and Member States used to more informal and flexible arrangements but, on balance, the need for more transparent and rigorous approaches seems to be recognised. Of course, there are limits to what can be achieved through purely quantitative measures and techniques and over-reliance on them creates its own problems of rigidity and distortion. Regions and countries with established systems already in place may also find the Commission's requirements an unnecessary extra administrative burden. An issue which has received an unexpected amount of criticism has been the Commission's approach to designating eligible areas, which is variously criticised as inflexible, inconsistent, arbitrary and unworkable.

Finally, the Commission has often tried to shape the content and policy priorities of regional programmes. In some cases it has pressed for a broader development programme with additional spending priorities to those desired by the Member State. In others it has demanded that support for certain activities be downgraded, such as roads and basic infrastructure. This must be one of the most controversial features of the structural policies, prompting accusations of interference in local and national affairs and ignorance of the principle of subsidiarity. There are various reasons for the Commission's involvement in setting programme priorities, including a belief that certain policies are more effective than others. Unfortunately, there is usually very little firm evidence to support this. There may, therefore, be a role for the Commission to encourage more systematic, cross-national, conceptual and empirical research on the impact and cost-effectiveness of different development policies and instruments encapsulated in the notion of 'thematic evaluation' (Turok 1997).

An Agenda for Reform: Internal Demands

Policy objectives

An agenda for reforming EU structural policies must start with their objectives. Article 130a of the Treaty on European Union refers to a 'cohesion' objective in terms of promoting equity: 'reducing disparities between the levels of development of the various regions and the backwardness of the various regions, including rural areas'. This is defined more closely in the Cohesion Report. Cohesion is considered to mean *economic* convergence of basic incomes, competitiveness and employment through higher GDP growth and *social* solidarity through reducing unequal access to employment opportunities, the marginalisation of sections of society and the incidence of poverty. These political goals are considered the 'irreducible ambitions which structure European society and help to determine its sense of identity' (Commission of the European Communities 1996d, p.14).

While not disputing the value of this vision and the need for greater economic and social cohesion within the EU, it is arguable that these objectives are not a practical set of principles for EU structural policies as currently constituted. First, it is unrealistic for the EU to meet the objectives of economic convergence or social solidarity. The form and scale of regional disparities across the EU are attributable to an enormous range of social, economic, political, geographical and cultural factors and forces, some of which have defied the efforts of national governments and are beyond the present resources or instruments of the EU. The narrowing of regional disparities is a long-term process, made more difficult by EU enlargement eastwards. Moreover, the equity objective of EU regional policies tends to be contradicted by the overwhelming efficiency goal of EU economic and RTD policies.

Second, there is a gap between the ambitions of cohesion and the priority, resources and scope for action accorded to EU policies by the Member States. Hitherto, the structure and coverage of EU regional policy has been primarily determined by political factors; the approach to funding and allocation has been driven by the desire of Member States to maximise their share of the available budget and the use of the Funds as compensation or 'side payments' for the results of other policies, rather than optimising their potential contribution to regional problems and disparities in the EU. In addition, from the perspective of Member State governments and individual citizens, it is arguable that economic convergence and social cohesion between EU regions are less important than regional and social disparities within Member States, implying that the objectives of EU regional policy should at least embody some reference to intra-country disparities. This is supported by the finding that inter-regional trajectories within countries appear to have a major bearing on EU-wide convergence or divergence.

It would be more convincing if the EU's goals of solidarity, mutual support and cohesion were expressed in more realistic terms and reflected more closely political and popular priorities at the current stage of the Union's development. The present mismatch between ambitions and resources makes it inevitable that the EU will fail to achieve its stated objectives. Reconciling these contradictions should be the starting point for reform.

Policy focus

The current geographical spread of EU regional policy needs to become more focused, especially with the anticipated increasing demand on EU resources. The current assisted areas designated under Objectives 1, 2, 5b and 6 contain almost 51 per cent of the EU's population. This contradicts the principle of concentration of resources on areas of greatest need. The 1993 reforms led to a significant dilution of this principle: 13 of the 15 EU Member States now have Objective 1 or 6 regions and there are far too many Objective 2 areas. Some of the latter are small and fragmented and several comprise non-contiguous sub-regions and are unrelated to their wider economic area. The spatial objectives have produced a 'map bureaucracy' with artificial divisions between activities supported in neighbouring areas. The lack of coherence with assisted areas designated under national regional policies has created further complexity. The outcome is a patchwork of areas subject to different regulations, measures and aid ceilings. This limits the potential for coherent regional strategic planning and promotes confusion among local partners.

The approach to area designation lies at the heart of the relationship between national and EU regional policies and is a key issue for the reform. The Directorate-General for Regional Policies (DG XVI) believes there should be coherence between these areas; the Cohesion Report advocates that eligibility under the Structural Funds should be one of the criteria for determining eligibility for national assistance. Yet the Directorate-General for Competition Policy (DG IV) has argued that the approaches to area designation can vary since national and EU regional policies have different objectives and instruments. The practical implication is that DG XVI and DG IV have used different approaches to designating areas for regional policy. Over the past decade Structural Fund areas have been designated on a relatively common basis throughout the EU, whereas for competition policy purposes DGIV has used both EU and national averages (thereby taking into account internal regional disparities within individual Member States) in determining whether the assisted areas designated by national governments should be approved. In recent years there appears to be have been some convergence in the two approaches; the 1993 redesignation of Objective 2 areas involved a greater use of national measures of disparity while DG IV has shown more flexibility in approving designated assisted areas (Wishlade 1997).

The key question for the next reform is how to reconcile the need for an objective, uniform EU-wide approach to assessing regional disparities and designating clear target regions, with the more comprehensive national-level or regional designation systems influenced by additional, practical considerations. While the EU-wide approach suffers from a lack of comparable data and the limited relevance to policy of indicators such as GDP per capita, the latter approach is open to manipulation by Member States, jeopardising the goal of concentration. There are additional question marks surrounding the basic building blocks of priority area designation in some countries, labour market or travel-to-work areas. They tend to be so large as to obscure serious concentrations of unemployment, include very prosperous localities and blunt spatial priorities for economic development.

Policy structure

Since the 1988 reform the basic principles underlying EU structural policy have become progressively institutionalised. The Commission services and majority of Member States now have eight years' experience of implementing the Structural Funds, in some cases through three complete programming cycles (1989–1991, 1992–1993, 1994–1996). For regions such as Strathclyde, Naples, Groningen-Drenthe and Auvergne, the experience of managing integrated development operations dates back to the mid-1980s. In the light of this experience there is widespread agreement that the current structure is over-complex and bureaucratic, with a long list of systemic and operational requirements for reform (Bachtler 1997a; 1997b).

For a start, there are too many Funds and objectives with different institutional arrangements. Structural policy resources are allocated via five main funding sources, administered by four different Directorates-General, to four geographic objectives (1, 2, 5b and 6) and three horizontal objectives (3, 4 and 5a), producing a complicated matrix of expenditure allocation.

Table 22.1 Structural Funds and Objectives

	ERDF	*ESF*	*EAGGF*	*FIFG*	*Com.Inits*
Objective 1	*	*	*		*
Objective 2	*	*			*
Objective 3		*			*
Objective 4		*			*
Objective 5a			*	*	*
Objective 5b	*	*	*		*
Objective 6	*	*	*	*	*

Activities relating to regional economic development (ERDF), employment and training (ESF) and agricultural aid, fisheries support and rural development (EAFFG and FIFG) are also generally administered by different government ministries at Member State level, so there is a formidable bureaucratic structure even before the Funds have reached local partnerships. Furthermore, each Fund has different regulations, award possibilities, aid ceilings and reporting requirements. There is also an expectation that regional programmes should exploit the funding possibilities of the European Investment Bank and European Coal and Steel Community lending instruments. Within this fragmented system regional programme offices or executives are required somehow to integrate these instruments at the local level. The practical implementation of this system is cumbersome and confusing, with widespread complaints about overlap and contradiction in the rules and procedures.

As noted in several of the 'policy perspective' chapters (19–21) the Community Initiatives have been a particular concern of Member State authorities, especially during the 1989–1993 programming period. Following the Green Paper consultation exercise in 1993–1994 the Commission attempted to respond to the criticisms and the Community Initiatives were rationalised and administrative requirements were simplified (although with increased expenditure). However, they are still subject to some serious criticisms:

- The CIs are perceived to duplicate existing regional and sectoral programmes undertaken by other parts of the Commission or national governments and many priorities (e.g. SME support) could be readily incorporated within the CSFs and SPDs.
- Implementation continues to be bureaucratic – Chapter 21 referred to more than 100 CI programmes in Germany – with administrative costs utilising a substantial portion of the resource allocations for some of the smaller initiatives.
- Consultation with national authorities is considered inadequate. The CIs provide a route for regional and sectoral interest groups to gain additional resources for specific problems but by-passing national governments can create difficulties. When new CIs are launched it is difficult for Member States to comment on or question Commission proposals without endangering their prospective funding allocations.

The scope of EU regional policy and its relationship with other areas of policy also needs to be reconsidered. In recent years it has widened progressively to embody diverse measures, including enterprise development, support for the business environment, human resource development, research and technological development, environmental change, community economic development, physical infrastructure and regeneration activity. Integrating these areas of activity has been very difficult, partly because some of the sectoral government ministries responsible are not centrally involved in programme development or implementation.

Two examples illustrate the point. First, in the area of RTD, the Commission has encouraged Member States to increase the importance of research, innovation and technology in their regional programmes. In practice, the experience of many regions has not been positive; despite a commitment to RTD in their CSFs/SPDs, it has been difficult to generate actual projects, absorb the funding and meet targets. It has become clear that programmes and implementation structures are not always appropriate for promoting RTD. Some regions have been fundamentally re-thinking their approach, turning to specific Regional Innovation Strategies (RIS) and Regional Innovation and Technology Transfer Strategies (RITTS) instead. This experience illustrates the need for regional policies to be designed with closer involvement of sectoral policy interests, especially where new themes are being introduced (Bachtler and Taylor 1997).

Second, under successive EU Environmental Action Programmes, environmental issues have been given a higher profile in many aspects of EU policy. Within the Structural Funds the regulations require Member State authorities to involve environmental policy makers in the preparation and implementation of programmes, undertake environmental impact assessments and include environmental indicators as part of project selection, monitoring and evaluation. Although partly successful (see Chapters 10 and 13), environmental issues continue to be seen as a restriction on economic development rather than as part of a commitment to sustainable development. Again, this illustrates the need for further work to link regional and environmental policies (Clement and Bachtler 1997).

Programming procedures

Another category of reform issues arises from the practical experience of programming procedures. The SPD/CSF approach is more widely accepted in some areas than in others. As several chapters have illustrated, the programming system can be helpful in identifying the real development needs of regions, formulating strategies and priorities and as a vehicle for pulling together a wide range of partners in a co-operative approach. This view is not universal; the process of strategy development is considered to be less useful in some countries, especially in decentralised systems (such as Germany) where regional authorities already have their own strategies and policies in place.

Negative perceptions have been exacerbated by tight timetables and delays. Every programming period since 1989 has begun late. This was understandable in 1989–1990 when a completely new structure was being established, but it is no longer acceptable. At the time of writing, none of the new Objective 2 programmes for the 1997–1999 period was expected to start before March 1997. The current three-year programming cycle for Objective 2 programmes is generally considered too short, bearing in mind the demands of strategy formulation, negotiation and approval. There is constant pressure to allocate and draw down the money, so concerns about effectiveness and learning from experience are subordinated. One of the most urgent requirements is for longer periods of stability.

There are several specific operational problems that also need to be addressed, relating to different stages in the programming process.

Programme preparation

The preparation of regional development programmes is a complex exercise. While national authorities generally play a leading role in co-ordinating and supervising the preparation of plans and negotiating with the Commission, a range of regional/local partners is also involved, including regional and local authorities, development agencies, environmental representatives and (to a varying extent) social partners. An important lesson from the past eight years is that a partnership approach is time-consuming and difficult, especially in the absence of a regional level of government. This needs to be recognised in the timetable for programme submission to avoid the 'concertina' approach of the past, whereby major planning tasks were compressed into short periods of time. The partners also need to be provided with early and consistent guidance by the Commission on strategic and financial issues. The Commission's requirements for development plans also need to recognise the methodological difficulties involved; a realistic 'prior appraisal of impact', for example, represents an almost impossible task in forecasting accurately the effects of structural actions.

Appraisal

Regional development plans and draft SPDs submitted to the Commission are usually subject to independent *ex ante* appraisal. The systematic way in which this has been conducted in recent years represents a significant step forward for the Commission. It provides baselines for future assessment of outputs and impacts and helps to enhance programmes with indicators of performance. However, the whole appraisal process needs to be more open and transparent. In preparing for the launch of programmes in 1994 some appraisals were conducted without any contact with the national authorities responsible for drafting the programming documents. They were rarely made available to the Member States and regions until after the negotiation of CSFs/SPDs. This inhibits the openness required for effective evaluation and prevents misunderstandings and errors within appraisal studies from being identified. A more interactive, consensual approach to appraisal, with informal discussions between Commission services and Member State authorities over the selection of experts and the conduct of appraisals, would be more efficient (Bachtler and Michie 1995).

Negotiation and approval of programmes

The time-scale of the approval process is one of the main reasons for the delays referred to above. Following the 1989 reform programme approval took between one and two years, despite an official six-month time limit. In 1993–1994 negotiation schedules still took up to eight months in some cases. In retrospect it appears that the process often contributed to better regional programmes in terms of strategic coherence, the balance of interventions and management structures. However, there are many examples of tedious and protracted negotiations (memorably described in one case as 'discussions between the deaf') where the Commission intervened in a manner and at a level of detail that was perceived to go well beyond the regulation requirements.

Member States cite three specific areas where the negotiation process could be improved. First, the ground rules for negotiation should be made clear in advance and be consistent across countries and regions; there is some evidence of different interpretations of project eligibility between countries. Second, the requirements for plan and SPD amendments should be limited to substantive issues; in some cases the changes requested by the Commission were minor and related more to the presentational form of plans. Third, there should be greater scope for respecting national policy priorities and institutional structures. In several instances Commission negotiators have clearly tried to insist on as many eligible measures as possible being included in the CSFs, regardless of their suitability to the national/regional approach. We recognise that negotiation is a two-way process and that there is also a case for some Member States to respect the requirement that plans/SPDs are more than vehicles for drawing down EU funding. The Commission also has a role in programme preparation and a responsibility to ensure the effective allocation of Community resources.

Programme management

There is clear evidence of improved institutional co-operation in economic development. In many regions the partnership arrangements have increased the level of communication and co-ordination between funding agencies and beneficiary organisations. However, the learning process has not been easy: most countries have experienced difficulties with different actors working at different levels within the implementation process, often with conflicting goals and agendas and variable relationships with Commission services. Lower levels of government have often perceived the Structural Funds as an opportunity to gain more autonomy with respect to their economic development responsibilities and resources. Local involvement in administration of the Funds may also lead to inefficiencies, with excessive numbers of people or bodies involved in the scrutiny and approval of project applications and few compensating gains.

Such programme management issues generally need to be resolved by individual Member States and regions, according to national systems and practice. There may be a role for the Commission to disseminate good practice and training in the organisation and management of programmes. The Commission also needs to consider the criticisms made of its role in relation to project management. First, there is a widespread belief that it is excessively involved in detailed operational matters, such as the use of indicators or project selection. Second, Commission guidance is often perceived to be abstract and imprecise, creating difficulties in determining the eligibility of projects. Rules may need to be clearer and simpler. Third, there are inconsistencies in the 'Commission approach' because of inter-departmental and inter-directorate differences (for instance between DG XVI and DG V). Desk officers are perceived to vary greatly in competence and knowledge. Some have insufficient appreciation of national conditions and systems, leading to inappropriate advice.

Financial management

Several difficulties in the financial management of regional programmes have been encountered. The co-financing of the Funds is a problem for many regions. Their ability to co-fund and absorb EU expenditure varies according to their economic situation as well as access to local funding sources. The problem has intensified with the growing complexity of programmes and shift away from straightforward infrastructure investment. Additionality may also be difficult to demonstrate. In some Member States (e.g. Austria) a small amount of money is spread thinly over numerous aid schemes and the Structural Funds may not coincide with national territorial units, causing methodological and organisational difficulties in demonstrating additionality. Finally, the ability of authorities to project spending levels is generally difficult, especially where experience and knowledge of the capacity for private sector involvement is lacking. Local authorities may be constrained by existing budgetary programming cycles in which it is difficult to make forecasts. Such problems demand much greater flexibility in the way programme finances are managed, with easier virement between years, Funds, priorities and measures. Some safeguards may still be necessary to prevent simple substitution of EU funds for domestic expenditure.

Monitoring and evaluation

The improvements made to the quality of monitoring and evaluation of regional development operations over the past eight years may be one of the more successful aspects of EU regional policy. The Commission has made considerable investment in evaluation resources, both in administrative competence (for example, the Evaluation Unit in DG XVI) and in research on evaluation techniques and the dissemination of good practice, for instance through the MEANS programme based at C3E in Lyon. Member States have also shown increased awareness of the value of monitoring and evaluation and invested in management information systems capable of tracking financial and physical outputs. The result has been an improvement in the data available for assessing the outputs of EU interventions and the intellectual rigour of evaluation. However, there is still a long way to go before the impact of the Structural Funds can be accurately assessed. In terms of procedural improvements there is a need to emphasise that evaluation should be conducted in partnership between the Commission, Member States and local authorities; it should be consistent with programme expenditure and the process should be open and transparent, with continued improvements in dissemination. Further methodological research is also needed, alongside thematic evaluative studies of particular policies and procedural issues in different countries and regions, to facilitate improved learning and transfer of experience.

This discussion of structures and procedures suggests major changes are required to the organisation of EU regional policy, including a rationalised structure of Funds and objectives, rationalisation of Community Initiatives, greater responsiveness to existing structures and systems within countries and regions and further development of procedures to rectify problems encountered in programme preparation, appraisal, management, monitoring and evaluation.

One of the most important motivations in weighing up the future direction of reform is the need to establish popular and political confidence in European institutions, notably the Commission. This goes well beyond EU regional policy but, from the perspective of European regional development, our experience suggests there has been an increase in frustration and disillusionment with EU regional policy among many of those involved at national, regional and local levels. The Commission is the principal target by virtue of its central role in programme development and management. The criticism often seems inconsistent and unfair; for some, the Commission has too many responsibilities while for others, it has insufficient. The Commission is frequently forced to interpret vague regulations approved by the Council of Ministers; its role and obligations are often misunderstood or misinterpreted, it lacks the resources to carry out many of its functions, it is an easy target for people seeking to attribute blame and yet it gets little credit for encouraging innovation or promoting effective regional development.

Nevertheless, given the wide scope and remit of EU regional policy, it is vital that the forthcoming reform resists the temptation to tinker at the margins and that the rationale for the policy is justified in a fundamental reappraisal of the institutional structure and relationships between the Commission and Member States.

The Agenda for Reform: External Requirements

Looking beyond the internal agenda, for reform it seems likely that the EU will expand eastwards in the first decade of the next century. Whether in 2000 or a few years later, EU regional policies will have to be revised (further) to accommodate the new Member States. What are the implications for the Structural Funds?

The starting point is the conflict of national interest with respect to the implications of enlargement. Accession under current arrangements would theoretically mean three options:

- The Structural Fund budget would need to expand. This is opposed by net contributors, such as Germany, which has indicated that it would actually prefer to reduce its payments to the EU budget.
- The current major recipients of EU regional aid would lose some or most of their allocations. This is opposed by net beneficiaries, such as Spain, which state they need to keep their allocation as protection against potential competitive disadvantages arising from enlargement.
- New Member States would be treated differently. This is opposed by them since they place considerable weight on parity of treatment with existing Members in view of their needs for support and their status within the Union.

Difficult political choices will have to be made. The cost implications for the EU budget are at the heart of the debate. Over the past five years they have been subject to several projections. In 1990 Commission calculations suggested that applying the same criteria to the underdeveloped parts of the EU and central European economies would require an increase of 22 billion ECU (becu) in the EU budget, increasing the proportion of its own resources from 1.2 per cent of Community GDP (1992 position) to 1.6 per cent. More recent research has produced estimates ranging from 12 to 26 billion ECU (becu) as the additional annual cost to the Structural Funds of admitting the four Visegrad countries – Poland, Hungary, Czech Republic and Slovakia. Together with agricultural support, and taking account of receipts from these Visegrad states, this would imply an increase in the EU budget of up to 68 per cent (equivalent to around two per cent of EU GDP). Similar estimates for the accession of the Balkan states (Bulgaria and Romania) and the three Baltic states suggest an additional annual increase in the Structural Funds of between 8 and 16 billion ECU (becu). (Bárta and Richter 1996; Begg, Gudgin and Morris 1995; Brenton and Gros 1993).

The very significant increase in the EU budget for regional policy implied by these figures may be offset by several factors (Bachtler, Downes and Raines 1997). First, it might be argued that such large-scale transfers are unwarranted. The relatively low national incomes of these countries mean that even small amounts of support by EU standards would have a major impact on investment and purchasing power there. Besides, it is unlikely that all CEE countries will join in the first instance.

Second, in assessing GDP per capita relationships between the EU and CEE, the leading candidates for accession are generally experiencing growth rates above the EU average (6–7% in 1996 in the case of Poland). If continued, this will reduce the disparities between the EU and new Member States. Furthermore, regional differences within the latter are growing; there is a widening divide between the 'locomotives' of transition (capital cities and major urban areas) and other regions. Some cities and regions, such as Prague, may exceed the current qualifying threshold for Objective 1 status by 2003, thereby reducing the physical extent of the highest-level assisted areas. In addition, per capita figures used in making some of the above estimates are not regarded as credible measures of GDP in some of the transition economies owing to substantial under-reporting and under-registration of GDP. It can be expected that some improvements in statistics collection and reduction of the black economies of the transition economies will take place over the next six or seven years, which again would reduce the GDP per capita differential with the EU.

Third, a crucial factor is the degree to which the CEE countries have the economic, financial or institutional capacities to absorb major transfers. The ability of countries or regions to absorb transfers depends on their economic policies, notably macro-economic conditions promoting increased competitiveness and productivity and the institutional capacities to select, manage and implement 'good' projects achieving an economic rate of return. The differing potential of transfers is shown by the contrasting development trends in recent years of Portugal and Greece, both of which have been receiving similar amounts of EU structural support (about 4% of national GDP by 1994); whereas Portugal has narrowed the development gap with the rest of the Union, the lagging position of Greece has changed little (Commission of the European Communities 1994b). Current estimates of the absorption capacity of the CEE countries range from two to five per cent of GDP. The potential size of transfers would be significantly reduced at the lower end of this range.

These factors would lower the costs of EU enlargement considerably, although existing recipients would still suffer major cutbacks unless the regional budget was expanded. Three additional issues need to be considered: the implications for area designation procedures, co-funding possibilities and the type of regional policy instruments in the potential new Member States (Bachtler, Downes and Raines 1997).

Inclusion of the transition economies in the current systems for area designation would probably over-stretch their usefulness. Certainly, continued use of the GDP per capita indicator would create difficulties because of the very low levels of the income in the new Member States. Thresholds for area designation would have to change and many existing priority regions would inevitably lose out.

The potential for co-financing of Structural Fund expenditure by CEE national governments may be limited. Although budget deficits have generally been low – about two to three per cent of GDP – or even in surplus (Czech Republic, Slovenia), the financial resources available to most CEE economies for economic development are small by EU standards. The EU may need to consider funding more than the current 75 per cent ceiling on development programmes or to employ alternative funding mechanisms, such as loans and credit instruments.

Regional policy is still very new in much of CEE. Most countries are beginning to establish concepts or ministries and some are beginning to use the PHARE programme as a kind of pre-accession Structural Fund. The institutional infrastructure for implementing regional policy is relatively good at national level but is poor or non-existent at regional level. For some, it may be more appropriate to establish a national industrial policy with a regional dimension rather than a regional structural policy in the first instance.

Future Scenarios

EU structural and cohesion policies are currently in the early stages of a three-year process of debate over future reform. Until mid-1997, this debate was relatively low profile. The Inter-Governmental Conference (IGC) revising the Treaty of European Union, gave EU regional policy little attention, the Conference being dominated by monetary union, the development of common policies in areas such as defence, foreign policy and internal affairs, as well as streamlining decision-making and the role of European institutions. Although Spain, Greece and Portugal had advocated strengthening the structural policies, with a discussion of the financial implications of enlargement in parallel with the IGC, such matters were postponed until a later date.

The parameters for future EU structural policies were established by the July 1997 'Santer budget' proposal from the Commission. The key decisions on the income side concern the scale of national contributions over the 2000–2006 period, the resource criteria by which they are calculated and the assignment to the EU of additional means of generating its own resources. Decisions on the expenditure side include the scale of planned spending – taking account of the time-scale and costs of enlargement, the introduction and impact of EMU and reforms to the CAP – and the allocation of the budget between priorities. The initial indication of the likely future orientation of the Structural Fund objectives in the Santer budget allows for a period of discussion and approval by the Council, European Parliament and other relevant institutions before the Commission prepares draft regulations for the reformed Structural Funds in early 1998. Theoretically, approval of these regulations during 1998 would leave a full year for the preparation, submission, appraisal, negotiation and approval of new programmes before the new programming cycle begins at the start of 2000.

Although some southern EU states initially proposed a greater budget for EU regional policy, notably the Spanish who advocated a new 'fifth resource', there is a general acceptance that the next funding period will not involve Structural/Cohesion Fund expenditure exceeding the 1999 level of 0.46 per cent of EU GDP – a level which may have to accommodate any allocations to new Member States from Central and Eastern Europe. In the short term, this may not be a major problem. It is unlikely that countries like Poland and Hungary will join the EU until near the middle of the next decade (ie. towards the end of the next EU budget period); it has also been argued that the newcomers should only enter the EU regional policy system gradually in order to allow them time to adapt. Consequently, there may be no immediate pressure – from a budgetary perspective – to eliminate large areas or funding objectives from the EU regional policy support system in the year 2000. This would seem to militate against radical change to the Structural Funds apart from a reshuffling of the objectives, simplified administration and limited cutback in the current designated areas. There would also appear to be scope for a lengthy transition phase to the more substantial changes required around 2005 or 2006 and generous transition provisions for de-designated areas.

The positions being adopted by Member States and regions signal a general consensus over the need to reform EU structural and cohesion policies. Most Member States agree that the Funds play an important role in promoting social solidarity and economic cohesion but recognise that current problems and future challenges from enlargement mean that reform is necessary. 'Simplification' and 'concentration' are the most commonly used terms but with little agreement on how they should be achieved. There are numerous contradictions between the proposals put forward for improved efficiency and parallel proposals for more complex ways of implementing the Funds such as conditionality or differentiation of award rates. Everyone agrees on the principle of geographic and thematic concentration but there are few signs of a willingness on the part of Member State authorities to give up assisted areas. Several different models for the future configuration of Funds, objectives and initiatives have been proposed.

Simplification of bureaucracy and procedures

The minimum requirement for reform is to rectify the bureaucratic and procedural problems associated with the current approach to programming. Technical and operational changes could simplify the process of preparing, negotiating, implementing and evaluating regional programmes – perhaps by eliminating much of the role of the Commission services in approving operational details. Using global grants could provide greater flexibility and efficiency. The Funds could be concentrated on specific themes such as SMEs, research, innovation and technology or community economic development. The use of Community Initiatives could be reduced and generally integrated within CSFs and SPDs.

Greater geographical concentration

The geographical coverage should be reduced to concentrate on areas in greatest need. A reduction from the current 50.6 per cent to 35–40 per cent of the EU's population appears likely. The status of the cohesion countries is unlikely to change prior to enlargement but there is considerable scope for greater regionalisation and focusing of aid within them. Policies in the Objective 2 regions could be targeted on development opportunities in, or close to, concentrations of unemployment, rather than the current large and generally arbitrary regions. National and local authorities would need to be more closely involved in area designation. Few areas are likely to lose assisted area status immediately. Transitional arrangements will be provided for de-designated areas to mitigate against a sudden loss of funding and to ensure that the valuable experiences of integrated strategic development are not lost.

Rationalisation of the Funds

Several proposals have been put forward for rationalising the complex matrix of Funds and objectives. They include the creation of separate Urban and Rural Funds to integrate approaches to the two types of area. A Bavarian proposal to merge ERDF, ESF, EAGGF, and, potentially, the Cohesion Fund into a single combined European Structural Fund is more radical. This would have a general geographic objective and a few priority sector-related objectives. It would operate through a general catalogue of eligible measures from which designated regions would select appropriate options without requiring prior approval. One of the main difficulties will be closer integration of mainstream ESF and EAGGF expenditure with spatially targeted policies, given the wider interest (especially within DGV and DGVI) in stronger policies to combat unemployment and social exclusion and to promote rural development. Reflecting the fact that radical change may not be possible in 2000, Commission and Member States proposals are focusing on a rationalised structure of three objectives: one for the least developed regions (currently Objective 1), with strictly observed designation criteria; a second objective promoting structural change, including both the current Objectives 2 and 5b; and a third 'horizontal' objective merging the current Objectives 3 and 4.

EU regional policy and subsidy discipline

Some proposals for the reform of the Structural Funds have advocated that lower receipts from EU regional policy should be compensated with greater flexibility in providing state aid. Germany's regional aid has been regularly subject to control by EU competition policy authorities, so it is particularly sensitive about EU subsidy discipline. The magnitude of structural change, especially in the new *Länder*, is also placing great pressure on German authorities to assist vulnerable firms. Greater flexibility in subsidy discipline is likely to be opposed by other Member States and the Commission, possibly apart from a further relaxation of the de minimis rules. On the contrary, DGIV has prepared proposals which would significantly reduce the coverage of many national regional aid areas – by half in the case of Austria and Ireland, by a quarter in Belgium, France, Portugal and the UK – although allowing some small increases in the Netherlands and Nordic countries.

Restructuring the relationships between the EU and Member States

Changing the balance of responsibilities between European institutions and Member States by invoking the principle of subsidiarity is clearly a sensitive issue, especially in the UK. Most disinterested observers believe that a general shift in powers 'downwards' towards national, regional and local authorities would be helpful. It would bring decision making and resource allocation closer to the people and places actually experiencing the problems. This could go furthest and quickest in countries with well-established institutional capacity and experience of promoting local and regional development. It would leave the EU with a more limited role in negotiating the broad policy framework, principles and ground-rules for regional programmes – for example decisions about area designation, programme priorities and broad expenditure allocations. Detailed operational matters such as project approval procedures and monitoring arrangements should be determined locally. The German 'Joint Task' approach provides one example of how such a system might work in practice. This approach would make EU regional policy more flexible and capable of accommodating an increasingly complex policy environment – especially in a 'multi-speed' Europe with some countries more integrated than others – and a more diverse geographical structure. It would mean that the Commission could not generally prescribe or prohibit particular policy measures. It would have to rely more on persuasion based on sound arguments and firm supporting evidence.

The Commission may have a role in overseeing arrangements within individual countries and helping to avoid abuses of power by particular authorities and 'gatekeepers' within the system. It would also have a vital catalytic role in promoting policy innovation, evaluation and good practice, funding pilot initiatives, enabling exchange of experience between countries and regions and supporting cross-border schemes and inter-regional networks. Overall, a more fully-developed matrix structure of horizontal and vertical decision making in EU regional policy would be novel and potentially highly effective in facilitating mutual learning, policy dynamism and programme responsiveness to variable circumstances.

This would impose greater obligations on the Member States. It would require more active involvement of the Council of Ministers in the implementation of EU structural and cohesion policies, formalising a committee structure for regional policy ministers, and a commitment by national governments (at least in some countries) to fund regional development more substantially than hitherto. It would also require some national authorities to facilitate positively a devolved structure of partnership-based economic development.

The principle of subsidiarity is sound but should not stop at national level. A partnership approach to regional development is emerging in several countries and has important advantages over other organisational structures and forms of decision making. However, it relies on the development of trust and long-term thinking among the partners. National and European authorities will have to concede certain powers and functions in order for regional partnerships to be taken seriously by their constituent organisations. In the absence of a regional level of government, the creation of independent secretariats within the regions to manage the programmes and facilitate networking and collaboration among the partners – as exists in parts of Scotland, Wales and Sweden – is a feature of successful partnerships that should be encouraged.

Accommodating EU enlargement

Extension of EU regional policies to the new Member States will probably require a distinctive approach. Unless the existing framework is restructured, it may be necessary to create an Objective 7 or Transition Fund that addresses the particular national and regional problems, funding resources and institutional capabilities of the CEE countries as discussed above. Preparations for accession should involve PHARE intensifying its support for institution-building, training and pilot regional development programmes according to the principles of EU structural policies. EU-CEE initiatives like INTERREG and ECOS-OUVERTURE should be exploited to build and disseminate experience in integrated strategic development and programming. Within the transition economies the current priority is to move from regional policy concepts to legislation and to assign regional development responsibilities to government departments and agencies. In virtually all countries an intermediate regional level needs to be created.

These options and suggestions are not mutually exclusive nor exhaustive. They do identify several possible scenarios and outcomes and may, therefore, assist debates about the way forwards. Whatever options are chosen, future EU regional policy should embody several basic principles: a realistic set of objectives in line with the resources committed, the flexibility and durability to accommodate challenges such as EMU and enlargement, added value in relation to Member States' own policies and efficiency in implementation. The time-scale and scope of the reform are important; it is likely that the EU will make relatively minor changes to regional policy for the period 2000–2006 and concentrate on the internal agenda for reform, such as securing a greater geographical and thematic focus. The enlargement issue might be addressed in a second reform nearer the middle of the next decade. The EU is not short of pressure or advice – national, regional and sectoral interests have begun lobbying in earnest – and there is bound to be more policy discussion and academic debate on EU regional policy than ever before. We hope this book contributes to make the discussion better informed than it might otherwise be.

The magnitude of the challenges confronting regional policy in the EU is unprecedented. At the heart of the agenda for reform lies the question of whether the Union can respond effectively to promote economic and social cohesion while instilling the confidence of ordinary people, communities and governments in European institutions and policies.

References

Aalbu, H., Sommerseth, K. and Pedersen, E. (1996) *EUs mål-6-programmes. Hva kan Norge laere?* NF-rapport nr 6/96. Bødø, Norway: Nordlandsforskning.

Abercrombie, P. and Matthew, R.H. (1949) *The Clyde Valley Regional Plan 1946: A Report Prepared for the Clyde Valley Regional Planning Committee.* Edinburgh: HMSO.

Abraham, F. and Van Rompuy, P. (1995) 'Regional convergence in the European monetary union.' *Papers in Regional Science: The Journal of the RSAI 74,* 2, 125–142.

Allen, J. (1992) *The Nature of a Growth Region: The Peculiarity of the South East.* Occasional Paper Series No.1, The South East Programme, Faculty of Social Sciences. Milton Keynes: The Open University.

Anderson, J.J. (1990) 'Sceptical reflections on a Europe of the regions.' *Public Policy 10,* 417–447.

Arms Conversion Project (1995) *Diversification '95.* Glasgow: Arms Conversion Project.

Armstrong, H.W. (1994) 'EC regional policy.' In A.M. El-Agraa (ed) *The Economics of the European Community.* New York, London: Harvester Wheatsheaf, 4th edition.

Armstrong, H.W. (1995a) 'An appraisal of the evidence from cross-sectional analysis of the regional growth process within the European Union.' In H.W. Armstrong and R.W. Vickerman (eds) *Convergence and Divergence Among European Regions.* London: Pion.

Armstrong, H.W. (1995b) 'Convergence among regions within the European Union, 1950–1990.' *Papers in Regional Science 74,* 2, 143–152.

Armstrong, H.W. (1995c) 'Trends and disparities in regional GDP per capita in the EU, USA and Australia.' Unpublished Report for the European Commission DGXVI, Brussels.

Armstrong, H.W. and Twomey, J. (1993) 'Industrial development initiatives of district councils in England and Wales.' In J. Harrison and M. Hart (eds) *Spatial Policy in a Divided Nation.* London: Jessica Kingsley Publishers.

Armstrong, H.W. and Vickerman, R.W. (1995) *Convergence and Divergence Among European Regions.* European Research in Regional Science Series No. 5. London: Pion.

Armstrong, H.W., Balasubramanyam, V.N. and Salisu, M. (1996) 'Domestic savings, intra-national and intra-EU capital flows, 1971–1991.' *European Economic Review 40,* 6, 1229–1235.

Association of County Councils (1992) *The Impact of Reduced Military Spending on Local Economic Activity: a Case for European Commission Assistance.* London: Association of County Councils.

Association of Metropolitan Authorities (1992) *The New Europe: Implications for Local Government.* London: HMSO.

Audit Commission (1989) *Urban Regeneration and Economic Development: The Local Government Dimension.* London: HMSO.

Audit Commission (1992) *A Rough Guide to Europe.* London: HMSO.

Bachtler, J. (1997a) *The Preparation of Regional Development Programmes: Member State Perspectives.* Regional and Industrial Policy Research Papers, European Policies Research Centre, University of Strathclyde, Glasgow.

Bachtler, J. (1997b) *Implementing Regional Development Programmes in the Member States.* Regional and Industrial Policy Research Papers, European Policies Research Centre, University of Strathclyde, Glasgow.

Bachtler, J. (ed) (1994) *Peripherality, Economic Development and EU Regional Policy: Ex-Ante Appraisal of the Regional Development Plan of the Highlands and Islands 1994–1999.* Glasgow: European Policies Research Centre, University of Strathclyde, Glasgow.

Bachtler, J. and Michie, R. (1993) 'The restructuring of regional policy in the European Community.' *Regional Studies 27,* 8, 719–725.

Bachtler, J. and Michie, R. (1994) 'Strengthening economic and social cohesion? The revision of the Structural Funds.' *Regional Studies 28,* 8, 789–796.

Bachtler, J. and Michie, R. (1995) 'A new era in regional policy evaluation? The appraisal of the structural funds.' *Regional Studies 29,* 8, 745–751.

Bachtler, J. and Taylor, S. (1996a) 'Extended synthesis of agreed Single Programming Documents in Objective 2 areas, 1994–96.' Unpublished Report to DG XVI, Commission of the European Communities, Brussels.

Bachtler, J. and Taylor, S. (1996b) 'Regional development policies in Objective 2 regions: a comparative assessment.' *Regional Studies 30,* 8.

Bachtler, J. and Taylor, S. (1997) 'Regional development strategies and RTD in Objective 2 regions.' Paper to the 6th European STRIDE Conference, Inter-regional co-operation and research and technological development, Bremen, 3–4 March 1997.

Bachtler, J., Downes, R. and Raines, P. (eds) (1997) 'The impact of EU enlargement on Cohesion.' Unpublished Report for the European Commission DGXVI, Brussels.

Bailey, N. (1995) *Partnership Agencies in British Urban Policy.* London: UCL Press.

Balchin, P.N. (1990) *Regional Policy in Britain: the North-South Divide.* London: Paul Chapman Publishing.

Baldock, D., Beaufoy, G., Haigh, N., Hewett, J., Wilkinson, D. and Wenning, M. (1992) *The Integration of Environmental Protection Requirements into the Definition and Implementation of Other EC Policies.* London: Institute for European Environmental Policy.

Baldock, D. and Corrie, H. (1989) *The EC Structural Funds: Environmental Briefing.* London: Institute for European Environmental Policy.

Baldock, D. and Wenning, M. (1990) *The EC Structural Funds: Environmental Briefing 2.* London: Institute for European Environmental Policy.

Baldwin, R.E. (1993) *Towards an Integrated Europe.* London: CEPR.

Ball, R.M. (1995) *Local Authorities and Regional Policy in the UK: Attitudes, Representations and the Local Economy.* London: Paul Chapman Publishing.

Barber, S. and Millns, T. (1993) *Building the New Europe.* London: Association of County Councils.

Barro, R. (1991) 'Economic growth in a cross-section of countries.' *Quarterly Journal of Economics 106,* 2, 407–443.

Barro, R. and Sala-i-Martin, X. (1991) 'Convergence across states and regions.' *Brookings Papers on Economic Activity 1*, 107–182.

Barro, R. and Sala-i-Martin, X. (1992) 'Convergence.' *Journal of Political Economy 100*, 223–251.

Bárta, V. and Richter, S. (1996) *Eastern Enlargement of the European Union from a Western and an Eastern Perspective.* Research Reports, No.227, March. Vienna: The Vienna Institute for Comparative Economic Studies (WIIW).

Bartels, C.P.A. and van Duijn, J.J. (1981) *Regionaal economisch beleid in Nederland.* Assen: van Gorcum.

Begg, I.G. and Mayes, D.G. (1993) 'Cohesion, convergence and economic and monetary union.' *Regional Studies 27*, 2, 149–165.

Begg, I.G., Gudgin, G. and Morris, D. (1995) 'The assessment: regional policy in the European Union.' *Oxford Review of Economic Policy 11*, 2, 1–17.

Benington, J. and Harvey, J. (1994) 'Spheres or tiers: the significance of trans-national local authority networks.' In P. Dunleavy and J. Stanyer (eds) *Contemporary Political Studies.* Belfast: Political Studies Association.

Bennett, R.J. and Krebs, G. (1994) 'Local economic development partnerships: an analysis of policy networks in EC-LEDA local employment development strategies.' *Regional Studies 28*, 119–140.

Bentley, G. and Mawson, J. (1984) *The Economic Decline of the West Midlands and the Role of Regional Planning – A Lost Opportunity.* Working Paper 17, ESRC Inner Cities in Context Research Programme. The West Midlands Study. INLOGOV. The University of Birmingham.

Bentley, G. and Shutt, J. (1995) 'European union regional policy and the English regions: contrasting case studies and lessons for the future.' Paper to the 9th AESOP Congress, University of Strathclyde, Glasgow, 16–19 August 1995.

Birmingham City Council (1994) *The City of Birmingham and Europe Report of the European and International Affairs Task Force.* Birmingham: Birmingham City Council.

Blakely, E.J. (1994) *Planning Local Economic Development.* London: Sage.

Boltho, A. (1990) 'European and United States regional differentials: a note.' *Oxford Review of Economic Policy 5*, 2, 105–115.

Boothroyd, P. and Davis, H.C. (1993) 'Community economic development: three approaches.' *Journal of Planning Education and Research 12*, 230–240.

Brenton, P. and Gros, D. (1993) *The Budgetary Implications of EC Enlargement.* CEPS Working Document No.78, May. Brussels: Centre for European Policy Studies.

Brownill, S. (1990) *Developing London's Docklands: Another Great Planning Disaster?* London: Paul Chapman Publishing.

Buck Consultants International and Nederlands Economisch Instituut (1994) *Vestigingslocaties in de Toekomst, een Confrontatie van Vraag en Aanbod (Business sites in the future, supply and demand).* Ministry of Economic Affairs: The Hague.

Bundesministerium für Verkehr (1993) *Ergänzende Information zum Bundesverkehrswegeplan 1992.* Bonn: Bundesministerium für Verkehr.

Button, K. and Pentecost, E. (1995) 'Regional economic convergence in Great Britain and Germany.' In H.W. Armstrong and R.W. Vickerman (eds) *Convergence and Divergence Among European Regions.* London: Pion.

Cardoso, A.R. (1993) 'Regional inequalities in Europe: have they really been decreasing?' *Applied Economics 25*, 1093–1100.

CEOPS and Commission of the European Communities (1993) *Methods to Give Meaning to the Evaluation Obligation*. Brussels: Commission of the European Communites.

Champion, A. and Green, A. (1992) 'Local economic performance in Britain during the late 1980s: the results of the third Booming Towns study.' *Environment and Planning A, 24,* 2, 243–272.

Cheshire, P. and Carbonaro, G. (1995) 'Convergence-divergence in regional growth rates: an empty black box?' In H.W. Armstrong and R.W. Vickerman (eds) *Convergence and Divergence Among European Regions*. London: Pion.

Chester-Kadwell,.B. and Martin, S.J. (1994) *The Local Authority and Economic Regeneration in the Mid 1990s: Co-Ordination, Community Involvement and Partnership*. Luton: Local Government Management Board.

Claridge, C. (1995) 'Economic and social development in the most peripheral part of the UK in the context of EU programmes.' Paper to the 9th AESOP Congress, University of Strathclyde, Glasgow, 16–19 August 1995.

Clement, C. (1991) 'Regional economic policy for the next five years.' *Journal of Economic and Social Geography 82,* 2, 227–231.

Clement, K. (1994) 'Cross-national comparative environmental assessment of North Sea Objective 2 Plans.' In J. Bachtler (ed) *External Appraisal of the Single Programming Documents for 2: North Sea Regions*. Unpublished Report for European Commission DGXVI, Brussels.

Clement, K. and Bachtler, J. (1997) 'Regional development and environmental gain: Strategic Assessment in the EU Structural Funds.' *European Environment 7,* 1.

Commission of the European Communities (1975) Council Regulation EEC No 724/75 of 18.03.75 in *Official Journal of the European Communities*, No L 73; 21.03.75. Brussels: Commission of the European Communities.

Commission of the European Communities (1985) 'Speech by European Commission President Jacques Delors and the European Parliament, March 1985.' Bulletin EC 3, 4, p.6.

Commission of the European Communities (1988a) Council Regulation EEC No 2052/88 of 24.03.88 in *Official Journal of the European Communities*, No L 185; 15.07.88. Brussels: Commission of the European Communities.

Commission of the European Communities (1988b) Council Regulation EEC No 4253/88 of 19.12.88 in *Official Journal of the European Communities*, No L 374; 31.12.88. Brussels: Commission of the European Communities.

Commission of the European Communities (1989) *Guide to the Reform of the Community's Structural Funds*. Luxembourg: Office for Official Publications of the European Communities.

Commission of the European Communities (1990) *Community Support Framework 1989–93 for the Development and Structural Adjustment of the Regions whose Development is Lagging Behind. Objective 1, United Kingdom (Northern Ireland)*. Luxembourg: Office for Official Publications of the European Communities.

Commission of the European Communities (1992a) *Memorandum on the Current Environmental Dimension of the Revised Structural Fund Arrangements: A Perspective with Proposals for the Future,* DG XI. Brussels: Commission of the European Communities.

Commission of the European Communities (1992b) *The Economic and Social Impact of Reductions in Defence Spending and Military Forces on the Regions of the Community. Regional Development Studies 5.* Luxembourg: Office for Official Publications of the European Communities.

Commission of the European Communities (1993a) COM (93) 282 Final, *The Future of the Community Initiatives under the Structural Funds,* 16.7.93. Brussels: Commission of the European Communities.

Commission of the European Communities (1993b) Council Regulation EEC No 2081/93 of 20.07.93 in *Official Journal of the European Communities* No L 193; 31.07.93. Brussels: Commission of the European Communities.

Commission of the European Communities (1993c) *Trade and Foreign Investment in the Community's Regions: The Impact of Economic Reform in Central and Eastern Europe.* Luxembourg: Official for Publications of the European Communities.

Commission of the European Communities (1993d) *Community Structural Funds, 1994–99, Regulations and Commentary.* Luxembourg: Office for Official Publications of the European Communities.

Commission of the European Communities (1993e) 'Towards sustainability – a European Community Programme of Action in relation to the environment and sustainable development.' *Official Journal No C138 and COM (92) 23 Final.*

Commission of the European Communities (1994a) *Fourth Annual Report on the Implementation of the Community Structural Funds.* Brussels: Commission of the European Communities.

Commission of the European Communities (1994b) 'Competitiveness and cohesion: trends in the regions.' *Fifth Periodic Report on the Social and Economic Situation and Development of the Regions.* Brussels: Commission of the European Communities.

Commission of the European Communities (1994c) *White Paper: Growth Competitiveness, Employment – The Challenges and the Ways forward into the 21st Century.* COM (93) 700. Brussels: Commission of the European Communities.

Commission of the European Communities (1994d) *Single Programming Document 1994–1996, the West Midlands.* Brussels: Commission of the European Communities.

Commission of the European Communities (1994e) *Interim Review of Implementation of the European Community Programme of Policy and Action in Relation to the Environment and Sustainable Development 'Towards Sustainability' COM (94) 453 Final.* Brussels: Commission of the European Communities.

Commission of the European Communities (1994f) *Guide to the Community Initiatives 1994–99.* Luxembourg: Office for Official Publications of the European Communities.

Commission of the European Communities (1994g) *Europe 2000+: Co-Operation for European Territorial Development.* Luxembourg: Office for Official Publications of the European Communities.

Commission of the European Communities (1995) *The Structural Funds and the Reconversion of Regions Affected by Industrial Decline in the UK, 1994–96.* Luxembourg: Office for Official Publications of the European Commission.

Commission of the European Communities (1995a) *A European Strategy for Encouraging Local Development and Employment Initiatives.* COM(95) 273. Brussels: Commission of the European Communities.

Commission of the European Communities (1995b) *Highlands and Islands Single Programming Document 1994–99.* Luxembourg: Office for Official Publications of the European Communities.

Commission of the European Communities (1995c) *Structural Funds: The United Kingdom within the European Context.* Brussels: Commission of the European Communities.

Commission of the European Communities (1995d) *The new regional programmes under Objectives 1 and 2 of Community Structural Policies: A Summary of the Results Expected and Obtained from their Establishment.* COM (95) 111 final. Brussels: Commission of the European Communities.

Commission of the European Communities (1995e) *The Structural Funds: Initial Assessment of the 1989–1993 Programming Period.* Brussels: Commission of the European Communities.

Commission of the European Communities (1996a) *Prospects for the Development of the Central and Capital Cities and Regions. Regional Development Studies.* Luxembourg: Office for Official Publications of the European Communities.

Commission of the European Communities (1996b) *Note for Guidance Concerning Operations in the Declining Industrial Areas (Objective 2) for the Second Programming Period 1997–99.* Brussels: Commission of the European Communities.

Commission of the European Communities (1996c) *Structural Funds and Cohesion Fund 1994–1996: Regulations and Commentary.* Brussels: Commission of the European Communities.

Commission of the European Communities (1996d) *First Report on Economic and Social Cohesion.* Luxembourg: Office for Official Publications of the European Communities.

Commission on Social Justice (1994) *Social Justice: Strategies for National Renewal.* London: Vintage.

Costello, D. (1993) 'The redistributive effects of interregional transfers: a comparison of the European Community and Germany.' In European Commission, Directorate General for Economic and Financial Affairs. *European Economy, The Economics of Community Public Finance,* No. 5.

Council Regulation 2082/93, Article 9.

Court of Auditors (1992) Special Report No.3/92 concerning the environment together with the Commission's replies. *Official Journal No. C 245, 23 September 1992.*

Crafts, N. (1992) 'Productivity growth reconsidered.' *Economic Policy 15,* 388–426.

Cuadrado-Roura, J.R. and Garcia-Greciano, B. (1995) *Regional Convergence: An Analysis Using the Fixed Effects Model.* Paper to the Forty-Second North American Congress of the Regional Science Association International, Cincinnati.

Dabinett, G. (1993) 'Markets and the state and the role of local regeneration strategies: a case study of the defence sector in the UK in the 1980s.' *Local Economy 8*, 338–351.

DATAR and Reclus (1989) 'Les villes Européennes.' Montpellier.

De Groene, H., Heijs, J. and Kleyn, W. (1995) 'Spatial economic policy until the year 2000.' *Journal of Economic and Social Geography 86*, 5, 481–487.

Department of Economic Development (1990a) *Industrial Development Operational Programme. Northern Ireland 1990–93.* Belfast: Department of Economic Development

Department of Economic Development (1990b) *Competing in the 1990s – The Key to Growth.* Belfast: Department of Economic Development for Northern Ireland.

Department of Environment (1994) *Regional Guidance for the South East, RPG 9.* London: HMSO.

Department of Environment (1995) *1991 Deprivation Index: A Review of Approaches and a Matrix of Results.* London: HMSO.

Department of Finance and Personnel (1989) *Regional Development Plan for Northern Ireland 1989–93.* Belfast: European Community Structural Funds.

Deutsche Bundespost Telekom (1994) *Telekom 2000 – Schrittmacher beim Aufbau Ost.* Deutsche Bundespost Telekom.

Deutscher Bundestag (1995) 'Vierundzwanzigster Rahmenplan der Gemeinschaftsaufgabe Verbesserung der regionalen Wirtchaftsstruktur' für den Zeitraum 1995 bis 1998 (1999), veröffentlicht als Drucksache des Deutschen Bundestages, 13. Wahlperiode, 13/1376 vom 16.06.1995 (Sachgebiet 707), Bonn.

Deutsches Institut für Wirtschaftsforschung, Institut für Weltwirtschaft an der Universität Kiel und Institut für Wirtschaftsforschung (1995) *Gesamtwirtschaftliche und unternehmerische Anpassungsfortschritte in Ostdeutschland.* Zwölfter Bericht, Institut für Wirtschaftsforschung: Halle.

Dewhurst, J.H.L. and Mutis-Gaitan, H. (1995) 'Varying speeds of regional GDP per capita convergence in the European Union 1981–91.' In H.W. Armstrong and R.W. Vickerman (eds) *Growth and Divergence Among European Regions.* London: Pion.

Dinan, D. (1994) *Ever Closer Union?* London: Macmillan.

Dixon, R.J. and Thirlwall, A.P. (1975) 'A model of regional growth rates along Kaldorian lines.' *Oxford Economic Papers 27*, 2, 207–214.

Downes, R. (1995) 'Regional policy in Austria.' In J. Bachtler (ed) *Regional Policies in EFTA and the EU: A Comparative Assessment.* Unpublished Report. Glasgow: University of Strathclyde.

Dunford, M. (1993) 'Regional disparities in the EC: evidence from the REGIO databank.' *Regional Studies 27*, 8, 727–744.

Dunford, M. (1994) 'Winners and losers: the new map of economic inequality in the European Union.' *European Urban and Regional Studies 1*, 2, 95–114.

Eckey, H.F., Horn, K. and Klemmer, P. (1990) *Abgrenzung von Regionalen Diagnoseeinheiten für die Zwecke der Regionalen Wirtschaftspolitik (Delimination of Regional Diagnostic Units for Regional Policy Purposes).* Bochum: Kassel.

Erhversministeriet (1995) *Regionalpolitisk Redegorelse 1995.* Copenhagen: Erhversministeriet.

European Defence Observatory (1994) 'Meeting the challenge of change'. *Outlook Issue 1*. Preston: Lancashire Enterprises plc.
European Parliament (1991) *A New Strategy for Economic and Social Cohesion After 1992*. Study by the National Institute for Economic and Social Research for the European Parliament, Brussels/Luxembourg.
Falleur, M. de. and Vandeville, V. (1995) 'Cross-border flows of workers in Europe: facts and determinants.' In H.W. Armstrong and R.W. Vickerman (eds) *Convergence and Divergence Among European Regions*. London: Pion.
Federal Chancellery (BKA) (1995) *Regional Policy and European Union*. Vienna: BKA.
Federal Chancellery (1995) *Regionalpolitik und Europäische Union (Regional Policy and European Union)*. Vienna: Federal Chancellery.
Foley, P. (1992) 'Local economic policy and job creation: a review of evaluation studies.' *Urban Studies 29*, 3/4, 557–598.
Fothergill, S. (1992) 'The new alliance of mining areas.' In M. Geddes and J. Benington (eds) *Restructuring the Local Economy*. London: Longman.
Fothergill, S. and Gudgin, G. (1979) 'Regional employment change: a subregional explanation.' *Progress in Planning 12*, 3.
Geddes, M. (1992) 'The sectoral approach to local economic policy'. In M. Geddes and J. Benington (eds) *Restructuring the Local Economy*. London: Longman.
Glasson, J. (1992) 'The fall and rise of regional planning in the economically advanced nations.' *Urban Studies 29*, 505–531.
Gore, T. (1995) 'A case of microscopic vision? The eligibility of small urban areas for EC Structural Fund Assistance.' Paper presented at the 9th AESOP Congress, University of Strathclyde, Glasgow, 16–19 August 1995.
Gorecki, P.K. (1993) 'The impact of the structural and cohesion fund on Northern Ireland.' *Business Outlook and Economic Review*, June, 8, 2, 25–38.
GOYH (1994) *Yorkshire and Humberside Objective 2 Programme 1994–1996*. Leeds: Government Office for Yorkshire and Humberside.
GOYH (1996) *Yorkshire and Humberside: A Compendium of Business Support Projects*. Leeds: Government Office for Yorkshire and Humberside.
Graham, D. and Spence, N. (1995) 'Contemporary deindustrialisation and tertiarisation in the London economy.' *Urban Studies 32*, 6, 885–911.
Grahl, T. and Teague, P. (1990) *1992 – the Big Market: The Future of the European Community*. London: Lawrence and Wishart.
Greenwood, J., Levy, R. and Stewart, R. (1995) 'The European union structural fund allocations: lobbying to win or recycling the budget?' *European Urban and Regional Studies 24*, 317–338.
Gudgin, G. (1995) 'Regional Problems and Policy in the UK.' *Oxford Review of Economic Policy 11*, 2, 18–63.
Hall, P. (1989) *London 2001*. London: Unwin Hyman.
Hall, R. and Van der Wee, M. (1995) 'The regions in an enlarged Europe.' In S. Hardy, M. Hart, L. Albrechts and A. Katos (eds) *An Enlarged Europe: Regions in Competition*. London: Jessica Kingsley Publishers.
Harrison, R. and Hart, M. (1987) 'Innovation and market development: the experience of small firms in a peripheral economy.' *Omega 15*, 200–211.

Harrison, R. and Hart, M. (1990) 'The nature and extent of innovative activity in a peripheral economy.' *Regional Studies 24*, 383–393.

Harrison, R.T. (1989) 'Industrial development in Northern Ireland, the industrial development board.' In M. Connolly and S. Loughlin (eds) *Public Policy in Northern Ireland: Adoption and Adaptation.* Belfast: Policy Research Institute.

Harrison, R.T. (1990a) 'Industrial development policy.' In R.I.D. Harris, C.W. Jefferson and J.E. Spencer (eds) *The Northern Ireland Economy: A Comparative Study in the Economic Development of a Peripheral Region.* Harlow: Longman.

Harrison, R.T. (1990b) 'Northern Ireland and the Republic of Ireland in the Single Market.' In A. Foley and M. Mulreany (eds) *The Single European Market and the Irish Economy.* Dublin: Institute of Public Administration.

Hart, D. (1992) 'US urban policy evaluation in the 1980s: lessons from practice.' *Regional Studies 25*, 3, 255–261.

Haughton, G. and Williams, C. (1995) *Corporate Cities.* Hampshire: Avebury.

Heijs, J., Kleyn, W. and de Groene, H. (1996) 'Ruimtelijke ordening en economie, samen op weg?' *Stedebouw en Ruimtelijke Ordening,* nr. 2, The Hague, NIROV.

Hewitt, V.N. (1990) 'The public sector.' In R.I.D. Harris *The Northern Ireland Economy: A Comparative Study in the Economic Development of a Peripheral Region.* Harlow: Longman.

Highlands and Islands Enterprise (1992) *A Strategy for Enterprise Development in the Highlands and Islands of Scotland.* Inverness: HIE.

Highlands and Islands Partnership Programme (1994) *The Selection Process and Geographical Targeting.* Inverness: HIPP.

Highlands and Islands Partnership Programme (1995) *Geographical Targeting: A Discussion Paper.* Inverness: HIPP.

Hildebrand, P. (1993) 'The European community's environmental policy, 1957 to 1992.' In D. Judge (ed) *A Green Dimension for the European Community: Political Issues and Processes.* London: Frank Cass.

Hills, J. (1995) *Inquiry into Income and Wealth, Volume 2.* York: Joseph Rowentree Foundation.

Hinde, K. (1994) 'Labour market experiences following plant closure: the case of Sunderland's shipyard workers.' *Regional Studies 28*, 7, 713–724.

Hirschman, A.O. (1958) *The Strategy of Economic Development.* Cambridge, Mass.: Yale University Press.

Hirst, P. and Zeitlin, J. (1989) *Reversing Industrial Decline. Industrial Structure and Policy in Britain and Her Competitors.* Oxford: Berg.

Hitchens, D.M. and Birnie, J.E. (1989) *Northern Ireland Manufacturing Productivity: A Comparison with Great Britain.* Belfast: NIERC.

Hitchens, D.M., Wagner, K. and Birnie, J.E. (1989) *Northern Ireland Manufacturing Productivity Compared with West Germany.* Belfast: NIERC.

Hogwood, B.W. and Gunn, L.A. (1984) *Policy Analysis for the Real World.* Oxford: Oxford University Press.

Hooge, L. and Keating, M. (1994) 'The politics of European Union regional policy.' *Journal of European Public Policy 1*, 3.

House of Commons (1989) *Third Report. The Employment Effects of Urban Development Corporations, Select Committee on Employment, HC 327 I and II.* London: HMSO.

House of Commons (1995) *Fourth Report: Regional Policy. Report together with the Proceedings of the Committee. Trade and Industry Committee.* London: HMSO.

Huber, W. (1995a) 'Subsidiarity or/and integration? Cooperative policies for complex problems.' In M. Steiner *Regionale Innovation.* Graz: Joanneum Research.

Huber, W. (1995b) 'Fünf fette Jahre für die Regionalpolitik?' (Five lucrative years for regional policy?). *Raum, Österreichische Zeitschrift für Raumplanung und Regionalpolitik, 17.*

Hudson, R. (1994) 'East meets West: the regional implications within the European union of political and economic change in eastern Europe.' *European Urban and Regional Studies 1*, 1, 79–83.

Industrial Development Board (1991) *Strategic Development Planning.* Belfast: IDB.

Industrial Development Board (1993) *Annual Reports and Accounts 1992/1993.* Belfast: IDB.

Jackman, R. (1995) 'Regional policy in an enlarged Europe.' *Oxford Review of Economic Policy 11*, 2, 113–125.

John, P. (1994) *The Europeanisation of British Local Government: New Management Strategies.* Luton: Local Government Management Board.

Johnson, S. and Corcelle, G. (1995) *The Environmental Policy of the European Communities*, Second Edition. The Hague: Kluwer Law International.

Jud, T. and Steiner, M. (1995) 'Regional development institutions – A descriptive analysis for Austria.' Paper presented at the Regional Studies Association Conference, Gothenburg, 'Regional Futures: Past and Present, East and West'. Sweden: May 1995.

Keating, M. (1993) 'The continental meso: regions in the European Community.' In J. Sharpe (ed) *The Rise of Meso-Government in Europe.* London: Sage Publications.

Keating, M. and Boyle, R. (1986) *Remaking Urban Scotland.* Edinburgh: Edinburgh University Press.

Kleyn, W.H. and de Vet, J.M.(1994) 'Omgaan met schaarse ruimte, tussen plan en markt.' *Economisch Statistische Berichten,* 1080–1085.

Kleyn, W.H. and Oosterwijk, J.W. (1992) 'Regional impact and policy responses to the Single European Market: the Dutch perspective.' *Regional Studies 26*, 4, 411–415.

Leonardi, R. (1992) 'The role of sub national institutions in European integration.' *Regional Politics and Policy 2*, 1 and 2.

Leonardi, R. and Nanetti, R.Y. (1990) *Regional Development in a Modern European Economy: The Case of Tuscany.* London: Pinter.

Liikanen, E. (1995) *Brysselin Päiväkirjat (1990–94) (My Brussels Diary (1990–94)).* Helsinki: Otava.

Lipietz, A. (1992) 'The regulation approach and capitalist crisis: an alternative compromise for the 1990s.' In M. Dunford and K. Kafkalas (eds) *Cities and Regions in the New Europe.* London: Belhaven.

Lloyd, P.E. (1995) 'Memorandum submitted to the House of Commons Trade and Industry Committee on Regional Policy'. *Trade and Industry Committee Fourth Report. Regional Policy, Vol II: Memorandum of Evidence.* London: HMSO.

Lloyd, P.E., Bentley, G., Hart, T., Haughton, G., Meegan, R., Peck, J. and Shutt, J. (1995a) 'Contested governance: European exposure in the English regions.' Paper presented to the Regional Studies Association Conference, Gothenburg, 'Regional Futures: Past and Present, East and West.' Sweden: May 1995.

Lloyd, P., Bentley, G., Hart, T., Haughton, G., Meegan, R., Peck, J. and Shutt, J. (1995b) *Evaluation of 5 Single Programming Documents for Objective 2 Funding.* CRED Research Unit, Department of Geography, Liverpool: University of Liverpool.

Lloyd, P., Meegan, R., Krajewska, S., Haughton, G. and Turok, I. (1996) *Social and Economic Inclusion Through Regional Development: The Community Economic Development Priority in European Structural Funds Programmes in Great Britain.* Brussels: Commission of the European Communities.

Local Authority Associations (1994) *Briefing by the Local Authority Associations in England and Wales on the Additionality of European Funding.* London: LAA.

Local Government International Bureau (1991) *Responding to the Challenge of EC Law, Paper No. 9.* London: LGIB.

Local Government International Bureau (1992) *International Local Authority Networks Linking to the United Kingdom.* London: LGIB.

Loftman, P. and Nevin, B. (1994) 'Prestige project developments: economic renaissance or economic myth? A case study of Birmingham.' *Local Economy 8*, 4, 307–325.

London Planning Advisory Committee (1993a) *Industrial Land Demand in London.* London: LPAC.

London Planning Advisory Committee (1993b) *The Regeneration Effect of a Channel Tunnel Rail Link Station at Stratford.* London: LPAC.

London Planning Advisory Committee (1994) *Advice on Strategic Planning Guidance for London.* London: LPAC.

Mackintosh, M. (1992) 'Partnership: issues of policy and negotiation.' *Local Economy 7*, 3, 210–224.

Malecki, E.J. (1995) 'Flexibility and industrial districts.' *Environment and Planning A, 27*, 11–14.

Mankiw, N.G. (1995) 'The growth of nations.' *Brookings Papers on Economic Activity: 25th Anniversary Issue 1*, 275–326.

Marin, B. (1990) *Governance and Generalised Exchange: Self Organising Policy Networks in Action.* Frankfurt: Campus/Westview Press.

Marks, G. (1993) 'Structural policy and multi level governance in the EC.' In A. Cafruny, and G. Rosenthal (eds) *The State of the European Community Vol. 2: The Maastricht Debates and Beyond.* Boulder: Lynne Rienner.

Martin, R. (1993) 'Remapping British regional policy: the end of the North–South divide?' *Regional Studies 27*, 8, 797–805.

Martin, S.J. (1993) 'The Europeanisation of local authorities: challenges for rural areas.' *Journal of Rural Studies 9*, 2, 153–161.

Martin, S.J. (1996) 'Economic convergence or crisis management? Subsidiarity and local economic strategies in the UK.' In P. Devine, Y. Katsoulacos and R. Sugden (eds) *Competitiveness, Subsidiarity and Objectives.* London: Routledge.

Martin, S.J. (1997a) 'Local government in Europe: keys to success.' *European Information Service 179,* 3–5.

Martin, S.J. (1997b) 'European Union Capital Funding and Local Authorities in England and Wales.' Report for the Audit Commission, London.

Martin, S.J. and Pearce, G. (1993) 'Regional economic development strategies: strengthening meso-government in the UK.' *Regional Studies 27,* 681–685.

Martin, S.J. and Pearce, G. (1994) 'The demise of the Lone Ranger: prospects for new unitary authorities in the new Europe.' *Local Government Policy Making 20,* 5, 4–20.

Mas, M., Maudos, J., Perez, F. and Uriel, E. (1995) 'Public capital and convergence in the Spanish regions.' *Entrepreneurship and Regional Development 7,* 309–327.

Mawson, J. (1995) *Is it Possible to Achieve a Greater Degree of Regional Accountability to Legislation? Policy Workshop on Regional Government in England for the Association of District Councils.* Birmingham: Centre for Urban and Regional Studies, University of Birmingham.

Mawson, J. (1996) 'The re-emergence of the regional agenda in the English regions: new patterns of urban and regional governance?' *Local Economy 10,* 300–326.

Mawson, J. and Spencer, K. (1995a) *Pillars of Strength? The Government Offices for the English Regions.* Dundee: University of Dundee, Mimeo.

Mawson, J. and Spencer, K. (1995b) 'The government offices for the English regions.' In S. Hardy, M. Hebbert and B. Malbon (eds) *Region-building.* London: Regional Studies Association.

McAleavey, P. (1993) 'The politics of European regional development policy: additionality in the Scottish coalfields.' *Regional Policy and Politics 3,* 88–107.

McEldowney, J.J. (1991) 'Evaluation and European regional policy.' *Regional Studies 25,* 261–266.

Ministry of Economic Affairs (1950) *Landelijke Spreiding der Industrialisatie Door Regionale Concentratie.* The Hague: Staatsuitgeverij.

Ministry of Economic Affairs (1988) [Herijkingsnota] 'White paper on the reassessment of regional policy.' The Hague: SDU.

Ministry of Economic Affairs (1990) *Regio's zonder Grenzen, het Regionaal-Economisch Beleid in de Periode 1990–1994.* The Hague: SDU.

Ministry of Economic Affairs (1994) [Ruimte voor Economische Activiteiten] 'Room for Economic Activities.' SDU: The Hague.

Ministry of Economic Affairs (1995) *Ruimte voor Regio's, het Ruimtelijk-Economisch Beleid tot 2000.* The Hague: SDU.

Minns, R. and Tomaney, J. (1995) 'Regional government and local economic development: the realities of economic power in the UK.' *Regional Studies 29,* 2, 202–207.

Molle, W. (1994) *The Economics of European Integration: Theory, Practice, Policy.* Aldershot: Dartmouth, 2nd edition.

Moore, C. (1992) 'Regional government in the UK: proposals and prospects.' *Regional Policy and Politics 2,* 223–241.

Morphet, J. (1993) 'Mandarins lay strategy to seize the regional ground.' *Planning 989.*

Myrdal, G. (1957) *Economic Theory and Underdeveloped Regions.* London: Duckworth.

Netherlands Economic Research Institute (1989) 'Economic and technological trends and changing requirements in the business environment.' Rotterdam.

Network Demilitarised (1994) *The Conversion of Military Sites.* Trowbridge: Wiltshire County Council.

Neven, D. and Gouyette, C. (1995) 'Regional convergence in the European Community.' *Journal of Common Market Studies 33,* 1, 47–66.

North, D.C. (1955) 'Location theory and regional economic growth.' *Journal of Political Economy LXIII,* 243–258.

Northern Ireland Audit Office (1990) *Industrial Development Board for Northern Ireland: Review of Performance. Report by the Controller and Auditor General for Northern Ireland.* London: HMSO.

Northern Ireland Audit Office (1993) *Industrial Development Board: Selective Financial Assistance Criteria. Report by the Comptroller and Auditor General for Northern Ireland.* London: HMSO.

Northern Ireland Economic Research Centre (1991) *Economic Forecasts for Northern Ireland 1991–2000.* Belfast: NIERC.

Northern Ireland Economic Council (1993) *R&D Activity in Northern Ireland. Report No 101.* Belfast: NIERC.

Northern Ireland Economic Research Centre (1993a) *Training, Skills and Company Competitiveness: A Comparison of Matched Plants in Northern Ireland and Germany.* Belfast: NIERC.

O'Neill, N. (1995) *Strategies and Policies: Economic Development in North Sea Regions.* Aberdeen: University of Hull and the North Sea Commission.

ÖIR (1992) *EG-Integration and Austria's Policy in Spacial Planning.* Vienna: ÖIR.

ÖIR (1996) *Regionale Industriepolitik für Österreich (Regional Industrial Policy for Austria).* Vienna: Österreichisches Institut für Raumplanning (Austrian Institute for Spatial Planning.).

ÖROK (1991) *Österreichisches Raumordnungskonzept (Austrian Regional Planning Concept). Vienna: Österreichisches Raum-ordnungskonferenz.(Austrian Conference on Regional Planning)*

ÖROK (1996) *Austrian Regional Panning Concept.* Vienna: ÖROK.

Padoa-Schioppa, T. (1987) *Efficiency, Stability and Equity.* Oxford: Oxford University Press.

Park, S.O. and Markusen, A. (1995) 'Generalising new industrial districts: a theoretical agenda and an application from a non-Western economy.' *Environment and Planning A, 27,* 81–104.

Pearce, G. and Martin, S.J. (1996) 'The measurement of additionality: grasping the slippery eel.' *Local Government Studies, 22,* 1, 78–92.

Peck, J. and Tickell, A. (1994) 'Too many partnerships – the future for regeneration partnerships.' *Local Economy 9,* 3, 251–265.

Perroux, F. (1970) 'A note on the concept of growth poles.' In D.L. McKee, R.D. Dean and W.H. Leahy (eds) *Regional Economics: Theory and Practice.* London: Macmillan.

Peterson, J. (1995) 'Decision making in the European Union: towards a framework for analysis.' *Journal of European Public Policy 2,* 1, 69–93.

PIEDA (1994a) 'An evaluation of the West Midlands CSF.' Report for the Department of the Environment. Manchester.

PIEDA (1994b) 'An evaluation of the Eastern England CSF.' Report for the Department of the Environment. Manchester.

Prud'homme, R. (1994) 'The potential role of the EC budget in the reduction of spatial disparities in a European economic and monetary union.' In European Commission, Directorate General for Economic and Financial Affairs. *European Economy, The Economics of Community Public Finance*, No. 5, Brussels/Luxembourg.

Pyke, K., Becattini, G. and Segenberger, W. (1990) (eds) *Industrial Districts and Inter-Firm Cooperation in Italy*. Geneva: International Institute for Labour Studies.

Quah, D. (1993) 'Empirical cross-section dynamics in economic growth.' *European Economic Review 37*, 426–434.

Ramsden, P. (1994) 'Regional strategies; building partnerships: the reform of the Structural Funds and the future of Community initiatives.' Paper to Conference 'Europe of the Regions: New EU Developments and Initiatives in Yorkshire and Humberside', Leeds Metropolitan University.

Regional Policy Commission (1996) 'Regional economic development strategies.' Report of the Committee of Inquiry chaired by Bruce Millan for John Prescott MP, Sheffield Hallam University.

Roberts, P. (1993) 'Managing the strategic planning and development of regions: lessons from a European perspective.' *Regional Studies 27*, 758–768.

Roberts, P. (1996) *Regional Planning: Update and Overview*. Town and Country Planning Association Annual Conference, London.

Roberts, P., Hart, T. and Thomas, K. (1993) *Europe: A Handbook for Local Authorities*. Manchester: CLES.

Robson, B. (1994) 'Urban policy at the crossroads.' *Local Economy 9*, 3, 216–223.

Romer, P.M. (1986) 'Increasing returns and long-run growth.' *Journal of Political Economy 94*, 1002–1037.

Roper, S. (1993) *Government Grants and Manufacturing Profitability in Northern Ireland*. Belfast: NIERC.

Russell, L. (1995) *The Strathclyde European Partnership*. Brussels: Scotland Europa Centre.

Ryan, P. (1991) 'The European Community's environment policy: meeting the challenge of the 1990s.' *European Environment 1*, 6.

Scottish Affairs Committee (1995) *First Report: The Operation of the Enterprise Agencies and the LECs, Volume 1*. London: HMSO.

Scottish Office (1993) *Progress in Partnership*. Edinburgh: HMSO.

SERPLAN (1990) *A New Stategy for the South East*. The London and South East Regional Planning Conference.

SERPLAN (1993) *A Regional Profile of the South East*. The London and South East Regional Planning Conference.

Sheehan, M. (1993) 'Government financial assistance and manufacturing investment in Northern Ireland.' *Regional Studies 27*, 527–540.

Sheehan, M. and Roper, S. (1993) 'Government grants and the investment decisions of Northern Ireland manufacturing companies.' Draft working paper, Northern Ireland Economic Research Centre, Belfast.

Sheffield Business School (1993) *Yorkshire and Humberside Steel Area: IDO and RESIDER Programmes Evaluation Study.* Sheffield: Sheffield Hallam University.

Shepley, S. and Wilmott, J. (1995) 'Core vs. Periphery.' In A. Amin and J. Tomaney (eds) *Behind the Myth of European Union: Prospects for Cohesion.* London: Routledge.

Shutt, J. (1995) *Regenerating Britain: Constructing a New Agenda for Regions and Cities in the 1990s.* Yorkshire and Humberside Regional Bulletin, August 1995. Leeds: ReRo, Leeds University.

Shutt, J. (1996) 'Appraising "Europe" in the regions 1994–1999: a case study of recent experiences in Yorkshire and Humberside.' In J. Alden and P. Boland (eds) *Regional Development Strategies in Europe.* London: Jessica Kingsley Publishers.

Shutt, J. and Robertson, M. and Sear, L. (1995) 'Strengthening ERDF Business Development Support in Yorkshire and Humberside.' A final report to GOYH following the Objective 2 Business Support Workshop. Leeds: Leeds Metropolitan University.

Strathclyde European Partnership (1995) *Western Scotland Single Programming Document.* Glasgow.

Strathclyde Regional Council (1992) *A Survey of New Industrial and Business Floorspace 1981–1991.* Glasgow: SRC.

Strathclyde Regional Council (1993) *Greening the Conurbation: A Shared Vision for the Clyde Valley.* Glasgow: SRC.

Strathclyde Regional Council (1994) *Vacant and Derelict Land in the Conurbation: Problems, Opportunities and Priorities.* Glasgow: SRC.

Strathclyde Regional Council (1996) *Strathclyde Structure Plan 1995.* Glasgow: SRC.

Sturn, D. (1994) *Decentralized Industrial Policies in Practice.* Glasgow: Scottish Enterprise.

Swann, D. (1992) *The Economic of the Common Market.* London: Penguin, 7th edition.

TERP/CBEA (1993) *Evaluation Framework for the programmes of the EU-Structural Funds.* Amersfoort: Leiden.

The Herald, (1995) 'Concern at EU Cash Share-Cut.' 8th February.

The Scotsman (1994) 'Government Blamed for £240m Euro Delay.' 20th January.

The Scotsman (1994) 'MP Attacks Euro-Fund Sell Out.' 20th September.

The Scottish Office (1993) *The Highlands and Islands Objective 1 Plan 1994–99.* Edinburgh: Scottish Office.

Thomas, I.C. (1992) 'Additionality in the distribution of European regional development fund grants to local authorities.' *Local Economy 6*, 4, 292–310.

Thöni, E. (1995) 'EU-structural fund transfers, industrial policy and subsidiarity.' In M. Steiner *Regionale Innovation.* Graz:

TNO-INRO (1994) *Ruimtelijk-economische ontwikkelingspatronen in Nederland.* The Hague: Ministry of Economic Affairs.

Totterdill, P. (1992) 'The textiles and clothing industry: a laboratory of industrial policy'. In M. Geddes and J. Benington (eds) *Restructuring the Local Economy.* London: Longman.

Townsend, A. (1993) 'The urban-rural cycle in the Thatcher growth years.' *Transactions of the Institute of British Geographers, New Series 18*, 2, 207–221.

Tsoukalis, L. (1991) *The New European Economy.* Oxford: Oxford University Press.

Tsoukalis, L. (1992) *The New European Economy.* Oxford: Oxford University Press, 2nd edition.

Turner, R. and Gregory, M. (1995) 'Life after the pit: the post-redundancy experiences of mineworkers.' *Local Economy 10,* 2, 149–162.

Turok, I. (1992) 'Property-led urban regeneration: panacea or placebo?' *Environment and Planning A, 24,* 631–679.

Turok, I. (1994) 'Targeting sectors to boost Highlands and Islands development.' *Town and Country Planning,* February, 54–55.

Turok, I. (1995) 'Structural funds and Economic Development Strategy: The case of SME Programmes in Scotland.' Paper presented to the Regional Studies Association Conference, Gothenburg, 'Regional Futures: Past and Present, East and West.' , Sweden. May 1995.

Turok, I. (1997) 'Evaluating European support for business development.' *Entrepreneurship and Regional Development.*

Van der Linden, J.A. and Dietzenbacher, E. (1995) 'The nature of changes in the EU cost structure of production 1965–85: an RAS approach.' In H.W. Armstrong and R.W. Vickerman (eds) *Convergence and Divergence Among European Regions.* London: Pion.

Vickerman, R. (1992) *The Single European Market.* Hemel Hempstead: Harvester Wheatsheaf.

Von Moltke, K. (1987) *The Vorsorgeprinzip in West German Environmental Policy.* London: Institute for European Environmental Policy.

Wagner, J. (1995) 'Firm, size and job creation in Germany.' *Small Business Economics 7,* 6, 469–474.

Wannop, U. (1995) *The Regional Imperative.* London: Jessica Kingsley Publishers.

West Highlands Free Press (1994) 'Objective 1 could hit big road improvements.' 30 December.

West Midlands Regional Forum of Local Authorities (1993) *The Regional Strategy: the West Midlands European Regional Development Strategy.* Stafford: WMRFLA.

Whyte, J. and Witcher, B. (1992) *The Adoption of Total Quality Management in Northern England. An Interim Report.* Durham University Business School Occasional Paper 9236, Durham.

Wiehler, F. and Stumm, T. (1995) 'The powers of local and regional authorities and their role in the European Union.' *European Planning Studies 3,* 227–250.

Wilkinson, D. (1992) *Maastricht and the Environment.* London: Institute for European Environmental Policy.

Williamson, J. (1965) 'Regional inequality and the process of national development: a description of the patterns.' *Economic Development and Cultural Change 13,* 2, 3–45.

Wishlade, F. (1994) 'Achieving coherence in European Community approaches to area designation.' *Regional Studies 28,* 1, 79–97.

Wishlade, F. (1997) *Issues and Options in Area Designation.* Regional and Industrial Policy Research Papers, European Policies Research Centre, University of Strathclyde, Glasgow.

Woodford, J. (1991) *Conflict or Convergence? Environmental Priorities and the Structural Funds.* Environmental Policy Discussion Paper No.1, European Policies Research Centre, University of Strathclyde, Glasgow.

Wulf-Mathies, Dr M. (1995) A speech by Commissioner at the meeting organised by the Centre for European Policy Studies, October 1995, Brussels.

Wulf-Mathies, M. (1996) *Effectiveness, Control and Simplification: Striking the Right Balance.* Presentation to an informal meeting of Ministers responsible for regional policies and spatial planning, Commission of the European Communities, Brussels.

Yorkshire and Humberside Partnership (1993) *Yorkshire and Humberside Regional Strategy: A Partnership for Europe.* Barnsley: Yorkshire and Humberside Partnership, c/o YHRA.

Yuill, D., Allen, K., Bachtler, J., Clement, K. and Wishlade , F. (1991) *European Regional Initiatives.* 11th Edition. London: Bowker-Saur.

The Contributors

Harvey Armstrong is Professor of Economic Geography at Sheffield University. He has published extensively in the areas of regional policy, local labour market analysis, the economic analysis of small states and European Union regional disparities. He has previously worked at Loughborough University, Lancaster University and the University of British Columbia as a visiting professor. His books include *Regional Economics* (Heinemann) and *Convergence and Divergence Among European Regions* (Pion).

John Bachtler is Professor of the European Policies and joint Director in the European Policies Research Centre, University of Strathclyde, Glasgow, UK. His research interests include comparative study of regional policies in Western Europe, the structural and cohesion policies of the European Union and the development of regional policy in the transition economies of Central and Eastern Europe and the former Soviet Union. He has published extensively in these fields and worked for numerous government departments throughout Europe as well as services of the European Commission.

Martin Bekker has worked for private research and consultancy firms since 1990. Two years ago he joined the B&A Group in the Hague where he has been involved in drawing up and evaluating several regional development programmes. He has also published work on the Dutch evaluation methodology and the impact of EU programmes in the Netherlands.

Gill Bentley is a lecturer at the Centre for Urban and Regional Studies at the University of Birmingham. Her intrerests are teaching and research in local and European regional economic development and policy, and include having been part of the team to evaluate five of the 1994–96 English Single Programming Documents for the European Commission. Formerly a lecturer in local economic development at Coventry University, she previously worked for six years for Sheffield City Council, in the Department of Employment and Economic Development.

John Bryden is Professor of Human Geography and joint Director of the Arkleton Centre for Rural Development Research at the University of Aberdeen. He is also programme director of the Arkleton Trust. His main interests lie in rural economic and social change, on which he has undertaken and co-ordinated extensive research in Europe and elsewhere since the 1970s. He has acted as consultant for many organisations including the

European Commission, Council of Europe, OECD, World Bank, and Economic and Social Research Council.

Keith Clement is a Lecturer in the Graduate School of Environmental Studies and a Senior Research Associate in the European Policies Research Centre, both departments within the University of Strathclyde, Glasgow, UK. He holds a number of editorial board and refereeing appointments, and he acts as an Expert Adviser for a range of public sector organisations, including the OECD Environmental Directorate. His principle research interests are strategic environmental assessment of economic programmes and instruments for improving environmental performance within industry.

Gordon Dabinett is a Senior Lecturer in Urban and Regional Studies at Sheffield Hallam University. He contributes to a variety of research and consultancy activities in CRESR, a designated research institute within the University which undertakes social and economic studies and policy assessments. His particular interests are policy evaluation, telematics, defence conversion, urban policy and regional development.

Dieter Drerup is Head of European Affairs Section in the Regional Policy Department, Federal Ministry of Economics, Bonn, Germany.

Rona Fitzgerald is a Research Fellow at the European Policies Research Centre, University of Strathclyde, Glasgow, UK. Her research interests include regional policy in the EU Member States, the Structural Funds and European Integration.

Vincent Goodstadt is Director of the Glasgow and Clyde Valley Structure Plan Joint Committee, Glasgow, UK.

Markus Gruber is Researcher in the Institute for Technology and Regional Policy, Joanneum Research, Graz, Austria.

Trevor Hart is Senior Lecturer at the School of the Built Environment, Leeds Metropolitan University, UK.

Mårten Johansson is Director at the Nordic Group for Regional Analysis (NOGRAN), Nordic Council of Ministers, Helsinki, Finland.

Conor Kearney works as an independent consultant in Brussels. He is a Visiting Senior Research Fellow at the European Policy Centre of the University of Strathclyde and a Senior Project Manager for the Centre Européen d'Expertise en Evaluation in Lyon. Between 1991 and 1994 he worked in the European Commission's Directorate General for Regional Policies, evaluating programmes assisted by the Structural Funds. Prior to that he had been Principal Research Officer for the Northern Ireland Economic Council.

Ronan de Kervenoael is currentaly undertaking research at the University of Sheffield and was formerly a research assistant at the University of Lancaster. His research interests and publications include regional policy and the role of regional level institutions in economic regeneration policy in Britain and in France.

Willem H. Kleyn works for the Ministry of Economic Affairs, The Hague, Netherlands.

Richard Lagrange currently works in the area of regional policy and the distribution Structural Funds at the Délégation à l'Aménagement du Territoire et à l'Action Régionale (DATAR), Paris, France.

Steve Martin is Principal Research Fellow at Warwick Business School, University of Warwick. His research interests are in the evaluation of public policy. He has published widely on issues relating to local and regional regeneration strategies and has recently completed a major study of the responses of British local authorities to closer European integration and research for the Audit Commission on the management of EU-funded programmes in England and Wales.

James McEldowney is employed by the European Commission on secondment from the Northern Ireland Civil Service. Formerly a Senior Research Officer with the Northern Ireland Economic Research Centre, he has worked as a researcher at the University of Glasgow and at the Glasgow based Planning Exchange. His research interests are the area of regional and rural development and human resource management. He has studied at the Strathclyde Business School, University of Glasgow and Birkbeck College, University of London.

Rona Michie is Research Fellow at the European Policies Research Centre, University of Strathclyde, Glasgow, UK. She specialises in rsearch in the implementation of the Structural Funds in the Member States of the EU.

David North is Reader in Local Economy and a member of the Centre for Enterprise and Economic Development Research at Middlesex Univeristy. A graduate of Sheffield and London Universities, he has 25 years of research and publication experience in the field of regional and local economic development including recent work on the contribution of small businesses to local economic regeneration. His contribution to this book is based on current research which monitors urban regeneration policy in London.

Peter Roberts is Professor of European Strategic Planning at the University of Dundee. His research interests include the evolution and operation fo regional planning, Europeam regional and spatial policy, the interface between environment and economic development, and urban regeneration. He has undertaken studies of regional planning, management and development in the UK and elsewhere in Europe.

Heinz Schrumpf is Head of the Regional Research Group at the Rhine-Westphalia Institute for Economic Research, Essen, Germany.

Ronnie Scott who sadly died earlier this year, was a Senior Research Officer in the Northern Ireland Economic Research Centre. One of Northern Ireland's leading economists, he had previously worked as an economic advisor in the Department of Economic Development, Northern Ireland Civil Service.

John Shutt is currently Eversheds Professor of Regional Business Development at Leeds Business School, Leeds Metropolitan University and is Director of the European Economic Development Unit (ERBEDU) established in 1995. He was previously Deputy Director of the Centre for Local Business Strategies, Manchester and has worked for Sheffield and Birmingham City Councils and Central LancashireDevelopment Corporation He has extensive overseas and UK experience in local economic development policy.

Sandra Taylor is Research Fellow in the European Policies Research Centre at the University of Strathclyde, Glasgow, UK. She has also undertaken range of research studies examining the design and operation of regional development studies in the EU Member States as well as transiton economies.

Ivan Turok is Professor of Urban Economic Development at the University of Glasgow. He was previously Professor of Urban and Regional Planning at the University of Strathclyde. His research interests include urban unemployment and urban regeneration, local and regional development, and the theory and practice of policy evaluation. He has undertaken several studies of the structural funds in the context of business development, community economic development and European regional partnerships. He is currently engaged in a major study of economic competitiveness and social cohesion in Britain's cities.

Richard Wells served the European Commission in Brussels from 1973-1978 and became deputy chef de cabinet in 1976. In 1987 he returned to London where he was responsible for UK policy on the EU Structural and Cohesion Funds and latterly became Director for European Cohesion in the Department for Trade and Industry. He is currently on secondment as Adviser to the Government of Gibraltar.

Subject Index

Author Index